The Making of
Chicana/o Studies

LATINIDAD

Transnational Cultures in the United States

This series publishes books that deepen and expand our knowledge and understanding of the various Latina/o populations in the United States in the context of their transnational relationships with cultures of the broader Americas. The focus is on the history and analysis of Latino cultural systems and practices in national and transnational spheres of influence from the nineteenth century to the present. The series is open to scholarship in political science, economics, anthropology, linguistics, history, cinema and television, literary and cultural studies, and popular culture and encourages interdisciplinary approaches, methods, and theories. The Series Advisory Board consists of faculty of the School of Transborder Studies at Arizona State University, where an interdisciplinary emphasis is being placed on transborder and transnational dynamics.

Marta E. Sánchez, Series Editor, School of Transborder Studies

Rodolfo F. Acuña, *The Making of Chicana/o Studies: In the Trenches of Academe*

Marivel T. Danielson, *Homecoming Queers: Desire and Difference in Chicana Latina Cultural Production*

Regina M. Marchi, *Day of the Dead in the USA: The Migration and Transformation of a Cultural Phenomenon*

Priscilla Peña Ovalle, *Dance and the Hollywood Latina: Race, Sex, and Stardom*

The Making of Chicana/o Studies

In the Trenches of Academe

RODOLFO F. ACUÑA

RUTGERS UNIVERSITY PRESS

NEW BRUNSWICK, NEW JERSEY, AND LONDON

Library of Congress Cataloging-in-Publication Data

Acuña, Rodolfo.
    The making of Chicana/o studies : in the trenches of academe / Rodolfo F. Acuña.
        p. cm. — (Latinidad : transnational cultures in the United States)
    Includes bibliographical references and index.
    ISBN 978-0-8135-5001-5 (hardcover : alk. paper) — ISBN 978-0-8135-5002-2
(pbk. : alk. paper)
    1. Mexican Americans—Study and teaching (Higher)—History. I. Title.
II. Title: Making of Chicana studies.   III. Title: Making of Chicano studies.
    E184.M5A625   2010
    973′.046872—dc22

                                                                    2010041967

A British Cataloging-in-Publication record for this book is available from the British Library.

Copyright © 2011 by Rodolfo F. Acuña

Visit our Web site: http://rutgerspress.rutgers.edu

Manufactured in the United States of America

Contents

Preface

For over forty years I have been part of the building of Chicana/o Studies. Aside from the fact that Chicana/o Studies did not evolve from a traditional field of study and had no precedent, the major stumbling block has been the ethnocentrism of the institution that looks at the area of Chicana/o Studies through biases and even antipathy toward the study of minorities in general. The result is a distortion of what Chicana/o Studies are. A lack of literacy on the subject exists, with politicos and public alike attempting to impose their definitions on the developing programs and courses.[1]

As I write this, a battle is raging in the state of Arizona that will make all Mexican-looking people suspects of being undocumented workers and will ban La Raza Studies at the K–12 levels. The end is the censoring of books and screening teachers. Amidst this hysteria, a constructive dialogue is impossible, which is tragic, since it runs against the purpose of education. Chicana/o Studies, like other courses of study, has as its mission the production of knowledge that fosters the appreciation of other people and cultures, as well as knowledge that helps members of society solve and correct systemic problems and conflicts. Chicana/o Studies promotes what should be the goal of every modern and progressive state, which is to work toward the equality of its citizens, a goal that can only be accomplished by making corrections.

Data is produced and tested in order to learn the truth. For instance, recent Federal Bureau of Investigation statistics show the border is relatively safe and that crime has actually declined. However, driven by opportunistic Arizona politicos and a gaggle of extremists, the media is being pressured to send the message that Arizona is losing control of the border. Groups such as the Tea Partiers are pressuring state and federal authorities to get tough on "illegals." The loser is rational discourse, with many nativists accusing the FBI of lying. If the objective is to learn, should not the question be who is telling the truth? Is the FBI data flawed? Or, are politicians distorting the facts? The truth should matter, and it is the objective of Chicana/o Studies to learn the truth.

When I arrived at San Fernando Valley State College in 1969, some fifty Mexican American students were enrolled in the 18,000-student campus. Very few faculty members or administrators found this to be unusual, and most accepted this paradigm. After forty years of struggle, the Chicana/o Studies Department has expanded to some twenty-six tenure track professors and over forty part-time instructors. It offers about 166 sections per semester. It is a success story, with thousands of Chicana/o students graduating and contributing to society. However, this should be the rule, since 36.6 percent of Californians are Latinas/os.

Arizona is not an anomaly, and in traveling throughout the country I am asked inane questions about Chicana/o Studies. Some have accused Chicana/o Studies of breeding separatism and ethnic chauvinism. Many applaud Arizona's success in profiling immigrants, banning Chicana/o Studies, and censoring books, and copycat measures are in the making elsewhere. This nativist movement can only be combated through people standing up for their rights. The double standard of the media in applauding the excesses of the so-called Tea Party and Minute Men while condemning students and community for protesting injustice must be confronted. As Bill Straus of the Anti-Defamation League has said, "Exploring one's culture and roots is important to the overall identity that we all carry. We found there were baseless charges made about the program [La Raza Studies] and that it's not anti-American." Strauss added, "We also found that it [Tucson's La Raza Studies] turned dropouts into students and then into high school graduates. Committee members also found the ethnic studies program promoted pride and a sense of belonging, impelling Latino youth and attracting them to the classroom."[2]

As will be explored, identity has been an important component of Chicana/o Studies. The subject matter and the production of knowledge are critical to the courses that form Chicana/o Studies. But in my opinion, the soul of Chicana/o Studies is its pedagogy. I came into Chicana/o Studies because I wanted to teach students to love learning. I wanted to complete their literacy. I wanted to give them an alternative to gangs and the underground economy. As much as Chicana/o Studies is a content field, it is a pedagogical tool. Pedagogy is still very important to a community where over 60 percent of its students drop out of school.

A lot of the material and interpretation will be based on my involvement with Chicana/o Studies, which began before its inception in the spring of 1969. I was fortunate to have a ringside seat. I was the first chair of the San Fernando Valley State Chicano Studies Department, and at the age of thirty-five I was a full professor. Although a lot of material draws from my experience with Valley State and then California State University, Northridge, an attempt has been made to broaden the narrative with analyses of departments, centers, and programs throughout the Southwest, Northwest, and Midwest. To that end, I supplemented my personal experiences with newspaper and journal articles. Oral interviews were often difficult to obtain, since most of the early actors had moved on to other programs or reverted to their disciplines.

The journey begins with an introduction that establishes the importance of numbers and the growing need for Chicana/o Studies. At no other time has knowledge about a group of people been so vital. Latinas/os make up more than a third of the population in California and other southwestern states. They are about a third of Arizona, where xenophobes want to outlaw the study of Mexican Americans. However, Chicana/o Studies are entrenched; they came about just over forty years ago, spearheaded by a small group of students. The demographics grew them, and they are here to stay.

Chapter 1, "Becoming Chicana/o Studies," deals with the beginnings of this field of study. Chicana/o scholars are all over the map as to who established the field. In this book, I take the position that it was a long process, and one that distinguished between the corpus of knowledge and the courses of study that analyze the knowledge. Identity is a long process of becoming. What separates Mexican Americans from Mexicans is what the great Cuban José Martí called "*vida en las entrañas del monstruo*" (life in the innards of the monster).[3] Life in the United States after the conquest played an important role in the act of becoming.

Chapter 2, "The Sixties and the Bean Count," reconstructs the 1960s, a decade where the Mexican American community developed a common sense that bound the emerging middle class and took notice of their numbers and political potential. They became more sensitive to their inequality. They searched for ways to stem the school dropout problem and became outraged by racism toward Mexicans, forming proactive organizations in which youth played a significant role. Activism politicized youth whose identity was enhanced by numbers and the government funding of youth programs. Bilingual education and the continued activism of Dr. George I. Sánchez were critical in the becoming of Chicana/o Studies. The notion of Chicana/o Studies was not limited to California, but it was converging everywhere that a community had formed.

Chapter 3, "From Student Power to Chicano Studies," highlights the rise of student organizations and movements nationwide. The Mexican American Youth Organization in Texas and the United Mexican American Students in California are indicative of the times. They, along with the school walkouts of 1968, led to the transformation of the ideas of previous generations as youth called for courses that were relevant to their experiences and demanded the entrance of more Mexican Americans and other Latinos to colleges. The chapter attempts to reconstruct the disparate walkouts and community actions to gain access to higher education, and draw links between this and the Chicana/o movement. Finally, the story of the movements to establish Chicano Studies on the college campuses are recounted. The Valley State story is a major part of the narrative, as are the students' warfare inside the campuses that made it all possible.

Chapter 4, "In the Trenches of Academe," deals with Plan de Santa Bárbara and its aftermath. Juan Gómez-Quiñones was the driving force behind the conference, which has become legendary—more as a piece of literature than as an actual plan for the establishment of Chicano Studies. The rest of the chapter reconstructs the difficulty in establishing programs, since there was a disconnect between what students wanted and what higher education would permit. The academy is anything but democratic, and it is as Eurocentric as society is as a whole. Considerable space is given to outreach programs such as the Educational Opportunity Program that brought the numbers into the institution, giving students the space to lead the movement for Chicano Studies. An important part of the narrative is how and why Chicano Studies are constructed.

Chapter 5, "The Building of Chicano Studies" is about collecting knowledge and involving multiple disciplines to study, analyze, and teach this corpus through a prism of disciplines. The Educational Opportunity Programs are revisited, and the importance of them to building the trenches in academe is discussed. Statistics are an important part of this building process since the building of Chicana/o Studies is a science. Nothing happens by accident. In this analysis the establishment of other programs is recounted, and I give my view as to why many did not reach their full potential. The book posits that part of the success of the San Fernando program was the resistance of the institution that forced students to rebel and to forge a sense of place. Moreover, a common thread was that programs such as Long Beach State believed that they could buy their way into the structure rather than force the institution to pay for their costs. The adversity and sense of struggle at San Fernando, now California State University, Northridge, created the program.

Chapter 6, "Growing a Program," profiles the California State University System, as it is essential to know the environment in which technicians have grown Chicano Studies programs (which through struggle has become Chicana/o Studies). Moreover, although state universities and community colleges educate the majority of Chicana/o Latino students, very little has been written about teaching colleges that educate over 80 percent of Latinas/os. This constituency generally commutes to school and is affected by current events in the sending barrios. It also covers some of the forces that disrupted the formation of Chicano Studies, such as police provocateurs. The essential force in stabilizing and encouraging growth was the Movimiento Estudiantil Chicanos de Aztlán (MEChA), and its survival is dependent on its stability. The failure of the program managers to control outside groups (especially government agencies) have negatively affected the process of growing the numbers of the programs. Admittedly, left wing groups were often annoying; however, they were also indispensable to the fertilizing of ideas and the growing vitality of Chicana/o Studies.

Chapter 7, "The Mainstreaming of Chicano Studies," examines efforts to mainstream Chicano Studies, which is a very complex dilemma. The faculty must leverage the program in order to protect it and students. In the case of research institutions, soft money is almost a given, but a danger exists that private foundations will control the selection of chairs, scholars, and the ideological bent of the program. This form of social engineering has been common in academe and the formation of Chicana/o community organizations. In the academy they are favored because grants relieve the institutions of the cost for development, and they bring money to the institution, which takes a 20–40 percent service fee off the top. The foundations more often than not have a peer review process to screen programs and research grants—often choosing more mainstream careerists as reviewers. The book explores the grant to California State University, Northridge,

Operation Chicano Teacher (OCT), which short-circuited the process. However, the failure to cooperate in institutionalizing OCT eventually cost the university. The teacher training program graduated more Chicana/o teachers than any other institution at a fraction of the price. It also made Chicana/o Studies a player in the disparate committees on campus, which is exactly what many white faculty members did not want.

Chapter 8, "Getting It Right" explores the evolution of sexism and homophobia within Chicana/o Studies that took too long to get right—if then. Again, there was a difference between research and teaching institutions. Even today it is difficult to recruit Chicanas from tier-one universities. The chapter touches on a limited exchange between Chicana/o Studies and Mexican institutions, although contact is increasing with Women Studies programs. The participation of Chicanas has been vital among students. In the first years they balanced the lumpen tendencies of their male counterparts. The Chicanas' participation in Chicano Studies professional organizations has changed the trajectory of these associations, and their numbers have kept them alive. The chapter also briefly touches on the demographic shift in the proportion of Chicana doctorates, which almost ensures a gender transfer of power. Unfortunately, we have failed to maintain data and documentation on individual programs, which will make the task of growing programs much more difficult for women leadership. Indeed, the lack of Latinas at teaching institutions can only be remedied by understanding the epistemological underpinnings of the field and mapping out a course of action.

Chapter 9, "Resisting Mainstreaming," describes historical changes and how they have affected Chicana/o Studies, which have been eliminated or consolidated into Ethnic Studies units. A professionalization has transpired that in many instances has diminished the pedagogical thrust of the area of study. In the 1980s very few Chicanas/os were appointed presidents of institutions of higher learning. In the name of fiscal responsibility, institutions of higher learning moved to limit the number of minorities in the colleges and universities. The constant theme of the book is that students are the lifeline of the growth of Chicana/o Studies. The colleges brought in larger numbers of students, a smaller proportion of whom were as idealistic as in years past. Just as the student movement was regaining speed in the 1990s, it was overwhelmed by the anti-immigrant fervor of the time, and many students prioritized this fight back. Still, waves of hunger strikes were organized to regain control over their Chicana/o Studies programs and to break new ground. The University of California, Los Angeles, Hunger Strike was a milestone in this history and the founding of a Chicana/o Studies–like program that achieved department status in the next decade.

The epilogue concludes with the notion that despite efforts to malign Chicana/o student organizations, these activist groups remain at the forefront of the movement. Examples of their activism summarize the issues of the twenty-first century that continue to center around the protection of the foreign-born and to maintain access to higher education for Latinas/os, who still have the highest dropout rate in the country. Much of the struggle centers on the Development, Relief and

Education for Alien Minors (DREAM) Act. The epilogue also examines different theories on how Chicana/o and Latina/o Studies developed; however, in my view, not enough is known about Chicana/o Studies to construct a coherent theory.

Lastly, the appendix lists some of the Chicana/o and Latina/o Studies programs. Much more research is needed, however, to catalog the disparate programs.

Acknowledgments

I am indebted to many people, including the Chicana/o students at San Fernando Valley State College who dragged me into the fray. At the age of thirty-five I was a full professor. The students who founded the department include Miguel Verdúgo, Hank López, the late Raúl Aragón, Rebecca Villegas, Evelina Alarcón, Dianne Borrego, Everto Ruiz, Frank Lechuga, Ismael Campuzano, and José Luis Vargas, among others. As a group I include the incoming waves of students whose numbers and vitality grew the program.

I am always grateful to the Chicana/o Studies Department at California State University, Northridge. The faculty, staff, and students, especially MEChA, have made academe bearable. I especially take notice of the last wave of young faculty members, who are excellent teachers. I thank my office mate, Gabriel Gutiérrez, as well as Jorge García and Mary Pardo, with whom I have discussed this book. Thanks to Gerald Reséndez, a master teacher and one of my oldest colleagues. I am indebted to Adelaida R. del Castillo and Richard Griswold del Castillo of San Diego State. They generously shared documents from their department, as well as a list of Chicana/o Studies programs. I also thank the few people who responded to my survey of programs. I hope other scholars can build on this list. Accountability is important if we are to maintain communication.

I thank the reviewers: Carlos Vélez-Ibañez and Marta Sánchez of Arizona State University, who turned me on to Rutgers University Press. My editor, Leslie Mitchner, is a caring scholar who has pushed me. I greatly appreciate the artwork of Malaquias Montoya; my books are always seen in a better light when his art introduces them.

I am forever grateful to my deceased parents, Francisco Acuña and Alicía Elías. My mother was legally blind and did not complete the first grade, but she always cautioned me not to confuse schooling with education. I felt her presence every time I went to Tucson in the summer of 2010. The Mexican people there are so noble and have to put up with so much stupidity. My sons, Frank and Walter, and my five grandchildren, I love them. My daughter, Angela, continues to amaze me;

she is burdened with my expectations. It is not easy to have me as a father. When I was a child during the Depression, I always savored the last scrap of meat in the soup and the last bite of dessert. I held them in my mouth to drain every bit of flavor from them. I feel the same way about my wife, Lupita Compeán. She is that special ingredient that makes life worth living.

Abbreviations

ABDC	Anti-Bakke Decision Coalition
ACLU	American Civil Liberties Union
ACSSP	American Council of Spanish-Speaking People
AMAE	Association of Mexican American Educators
ASAA	Association Serving All Americans
ATM	August 29th Movement
BSU	Black Student Union
CASA	Centro de Acción Social Autónoma
CAUSA	Central American United Student Association ()
CCHE	Chicano Coordinating Council on Higher Education
CMAS	Center for Mexican American Studies
CORE	Congress of Racial Equality
CPUSA	Communist Party USA
CSCLB	California State College at Long Beach
CSULA	California State University, Los Angeles
CSUN	California State University, Northridge
CWP	Communist Workers' Party
EEOC	Equal Employment Opportunity Commission
EOP	Educational Opportunity Program
ESL	English as a second language
FEPC	Fair Employment Practices Commission
FLOC	Farm Labor Organizing Committee
HSIs	Hispanic-serving institutions
LACA	Latin American Civic Association
LACC	Los Angeles Community College
LAPD	Los Angeles Police Department
LEAA	Law Enforcement Assistance Administration
LLF	Latin Liberation Front
LRS	League of Revolutionary Struggle

LULAC	League of United Latin American Citizens
MACC	Mexican American Cultural Center
MACHOS	Mexican American Committee on Honor, Organization, and Service
MALC	Mexican American Liberation Committee
MALCS	Mujeres Activas en Letras y Cambio Social
MALDEF	Mexican American Legal Defense and Education Fund
MAPA	Mexican American Political Association
MASA	Mexican American Student Association
MASO	Mexican American Student Organization
MAUC	Mexican American Unity Council
MAYO	Mexican American Youth Organization
MDTA	Manpower Development and Training Act
MEChA	Movimiento Estudiantil Chicanos de Aztlán
NAACP	National Association for the Advancement of Colored People
NACCS	National Association for Chicana and Chicano Studies
NCOBD	National Committee to Overturn the Bakke Decision
NDEA	National Defense and Education Act
NEA	National Education Association
OCT	Operation Chicana/o Teacher
OEO	Office of Economic Opportunity
PASO	Political Association of Spanish-Speaking Organizations
PDID	Public Disorder Intelligence Department
ROTC	Reserve Officers Training Corp
RUP	Raza Unida Party
SASO	Spanish American Students Association
SFSC	San Francisco State College
SFVSC	San Fernando Valley State College
SQUISH	Strong Queers United in Stopping Heterosexism
SDS	Students for a Democratic Society
UC	University of California
UCLA	University of California, Los Angeles
UCSB	University of California, Santa Barbara
UFWOC	United Farm Workers Organizing Committee
UMAS	United Mexican American Students
UTEP	University of Texas at El Paso
VISTA	Volunteers in Service to America

The Making of
Chicana/o Studies

Introduction

Why study it if it is not American? This question is often asked by those who expect everyone to speak English. After all, why should anyone want to speak another language? The argument goes like this: English is the universal language of finance and diplomacy. Consciously or subconsciously, the American Firsters believe in the superiority of Western European culture. This view is a form of intellectual imperialism that creates polarity and spawns prejudice. Ethnocentrism is not confined to foreign relations but is virulent within the United States. Throughout a nation where many nationalities and cultures coexist and struggle for civic space, antipathy and even violence have been directed at immigrants. Part of the mission of Chicana/o Studies is to break down this ethnocentrism through the introduction of knowledge of Mexican people in the United States.

Rational thinking begins with the premise that no one appropriate way to behave, think, or look is rational. Rational thinking recognizes and respects the value of diversity of languages and beliefs. Diversity brings a variety of ideas and viewpoints to problem solving. As will be shown, the American-only mind-set has created divisions within the country where the belief in American exceptionalism is rampant; it is based on a faith that what Americans believe is true, discounting out of hand the views and experiences of others. For instance, a 2010 Public Policy Polling survey found that "49% of Americans say they trust Fox News to 37% who disagree." This belief follows party lines, with 74 percent of Republicans agreeing that they trust Fox News and "only 30% of Democrats saying they trust the right leaning network."[1] This distortion of reality often leads to people acting and voting against their own self-interests—blaming others for their perceived misfortunes and phobias. For instance, in April 2010 the governor of Arizona signed into law SB1070, which, among other things, requires all law enforcement officers in the state of Arizona to act on a "reasonable" suspicion that an individual is in the country "illegally," which is problematic since one-third of the state's population is Latino. This law has provoked moral outrage, and many people are supporting an economic boycott of Arizona, charging that the law encourages racial profiling and discrimination.

Underlying this hysteria are myths promulgated by news sources such as Fox that portray undocumented people as lawbreakers—often equating them with terrorists who want to take "their America" away from them. The assumption of SB1070 is that a suspect is guilty of a crime until proven innocent. This injustice is exacerbated by political opportunists such as Rep. Brian Bilbray (R-California), who denies that the Arizona law encourages racial profiling because "'trained professionals' can identify undocumented workers just by looking at their clothes."[2] Adding insult to injury, two days after the passage of SB1070 the Arizona governor signed HB2281 into law—holding that "any course, class, instruction, or material may not be primarily designed for pupils of a particular ethnic group as determined by the State Superintendent of Instruction. State aid will be withheld from any school district or charter school that does not comply." HB2281 has been eclipsed by SB1070; it comes at the end of almost a decade of controversy over La Raza Studies at Tucson High School, one of the most successful Chicana/o Studies programs in the United States. The curriculum discourages student dropouts and raises the students' civic awareness and encourages learning.

According to studies conducted by the Tucson Unified School District:

Graduation rates for TUSD Ethnic Studies seniors have ranged from 94% to 100% since 2004 in comparison to senior graduation rates at the same schools ranging from 68% to 92%.... Although 56% of students being served in the school district are Latina/o, with the vast majority being of Mexican descent, K–12 classes are designed for ALL students regardless of their racial, ethnic, linguistic, religious, sexual orientation. 763 high school students from diverse backgrounds were served in Tucson Mexican American Studies courses in 2009–2010. Projected enrollment for the 2010–2011 school year is about 2000 students.... Ethnic Studies high school students are: 3 times more likely to pass the AIMS Reading section, 4 times more likely to pass the AIMS Writing section, & 2 1/2 times more likely to pass the AIMS Math section.[3]

The passage of HB2281 is replete with debates not only about the content of Chicana/o Studies but also about what books the inquisitors should censor, outlawing several popular books on Chicana/o history. The case for censorship is based on exaggeration and factual distortions, such as that La Raza Studies is un-American.[4] This discussion is framed in an emotional context, with nativists targeting immigrants and claiming that they do not pay taxes and are freeloaders and a drain on the U.S. economy. Furthermore, they claim most Mexicans cross the border illegally, with almost all of them smuggling drugs into the country. They intentionally confuse undocumented immigration with the war on terror, which according to them can be won only through punitive immigration policies.[5] The fact is that in the 1990s undocumented immigrants paid between $90 and $140 billion a year in federal, state, and local taxes. Immigrant workers made up 12.4 percent of the U.S. labor force while composing 11.5 percent of the population; they earn about $240 billion a year and pay at least $90 billion a year in taxes. Studies show that they used about $5 billion in public benefits. Immigrants were projected to contribute $500 billion toward the Social Security system over twenty years—most of which they would not recover. According to the Department of Homeland Security and local police agencies, undocumented immigrants do not pose a security risk.

Stereotypes and myths thrive because of ignorance and fear. Without the structure to study Mexican Americans and other Latinos, they remain marginalized. The role of Chicana/o Studies is to organize and systemize the knowledge of people of Mexican descent, as well as to serve as a pedagogical tool to educate and motivate the massive numbers of Mexican Americans and Latinas/os in the United States. Unfounded and uninformed myths encourage and justify discrimination toward this population. Far from being freeloaders, Mexican Americans have carried their weight as workers, productive members of society, and soldiers in the nation's armed forces.

Too Big to Fail

A growing polarization would be disastrous. If allowed to fester, misinformation about Mexican Americans and Latinas/os can lead to hysteria, which is something that society cannot afford. By 2050 the total U.S. population is projected to soar to 438 million; the Latina/o population will triple to approximately one-third of the country (two-thirds of Latinas/os will be Mexican Americans). The projections are based on the assumption that immigration will slow during this period, and the increase will largely result from the fertility of Mexican American and Latina women whose median age is twenty-five or younger, as well as a lower birthrate and an aging white population.[6] This makes the size of the Latina/o population too large to ignore.

The size of the Chicana/o and Latina/o community can be appreciated in the context of nation-states. As of July 2007 Latinas/os were an estimated 45.5 million, or 15.1 percent of the national population of 301.6 million.[7] California alone had 13.2 million Latinas/os, followed by Texas with 8.6 million and Florida with 3.8 million. An estimated two-thirds to 70 percent of these totals are of Mexican origin. The power of numbers is highlighted by the 2008 election, when the Latina/o vote was concentrated in three states with large electoral college states: California (55), Texas (34), and Florida (27). In the first two states the Mexican population had reached a plurality.

If Latinas/os were an autonomous nation, they would form the third largest country in Latin America and the second largest Spanish-speaking nation in the world. That hypothetical country would be larger than Spain and Argentina. Mexican Americans alone would rank as the sixth largest Latin American nation and the fifth largest Spanish-speaking nation in the world. This phenomenon is recognized by the media and receives some attention from politicians. Higher education uses the numbers as a hook for attracting outside funding.[8] Latinas/os in Arizona, California, Nevada, New Mexico, and Texas are over 25 percent of the states' population.[9]

The population growth of Latinas/os in Idaho, Nevada, Oregon, Washington, and Wyoming has also been dramatic. By 2000, an estimated 2.2 million Latinas/os lived in New York—about a million Mexican origin people lived in the New York, New Jersey, and Connecticut region. By 2007 the Latina/o population in Alabama grew to 124,741; in Arkansas, 150,270; in Georgia, 740,843; in North Carolina, 638,444; in South Carolina, 168,920; and in Tennessee, 215,439.[10] Mexican Americans and other Latinas/os are no longer regional minorities. They are 22 percent of all children under the age of eighteen—up from 9 percent in 1980. One in five students in the United States is Latina/o, and there are 10 million Latina/o students in U.S. public kindergartens, elementary, and high schools. Latina/o students comprised 54 percent of the students in New Mexico, 47 percent in California, 44 percent in Texas, and 40 percent in Arizona. In 2007, 11 percent of Latina/o children under eighteen were first generation, 52 percent were second generation, and the rest were third generation or more.[11]

CATCHING UP: THE ROLE OF CHICANA/O STUDIES

Chicana/o Studies often shares space and experiences with other Latina/o groups, and the field is sometimes referred to as Latina/o Studies, which results in an epistemological distortion. Latina/o Studies generally includes more emphasis on the study of Latin American countries, whereas Chicana/o Studies examines the experiences of Mexicans in the United States.[12] The primary purpose of the area of Chicana/o Studies is to teach students and advocate for the interests of the Chicana/o community. When Chicana/o Studies was implemented some forty years ago, few students of Mexican extraction were in the nation's colleges, and even fewer classes were offered on the Chicano experience. Since that time, qualitative and quantitative increases have occurred in attention to research on the group, as well as the number of Mexican American students attending the academy.

Changes in the curriculum were forced by the dramatic growth in the Chicana/o student population, a growth that organizers used as leverage to make a case for reforms in how to teach Mexican Americans.[13] For instance, Los Angeles city schools' Mexican school population zoomed from 10 percent in 1960 to 22 percent in 1970. According to Amy Stuart Wells, "In 1968, there were about two million Hispanic school-age children in this country; by 1986, that number more than doubled to 4,064,000. While Hispanic students made up 4.6 percent of the school-age population in 1968, by 1988 they comprised 10.5 percent of that population."[14] Because of the growth of the general Mexican American population, there was more political attention paid to the group. In 1970 the census estimated that 9.07 million Spanish-surnamed persons lived in the United States; at least 4.53 million were of Mexican origin, living mostly along the 2,000-mile border separating Mexico and the United States, with pockets in the Midwest and Pacific Northwest. In 2010 the *Los Angeles Times* reported that for the first time since the nineteenth century California-born residents made up the majority statewide and in most counties. Even Los Angeles, which had "long [been] a mecca for new immigrants—will become majority California-born by the time the 2010 census is completed."[15] The majority of this native Californian segment was Latino.

The population explosion of Mexican people in the United States is accompanied by a growth in Mexican popular culture and scholarship. Throughout the Southwest, to show how ethnically sensitive they are, schools practically close instruction days prior to Cinco de Mayo and September 16 while children learn to dance the *jarabe tapatio*. Before 1970 few white or black people knew what a piñata was. Now, forty years after this cultural revolution, salsa has become the number-one condiment in the United States. The Latinization of America has impacted religious services, and mariachi masses are common in Seattle, Chicago, Los Angeles, Tucson, San Antonio, and elsewhere. With the growth of the Mexican American population, more attention has been paid to Mexican folklore, music, Cinco de Mayo, the Day of the Dead, and foods, to the point that they have become part of American culture.

Chicana/o Studies have played a role in the dramatic transformation of the study of Mexican Americans in the United States and even Mexicans in Mexico. Before December 31, 1970, not a single dissertation was written under the category of "Chicano." To date, 870 dissertations have been recorded under this heading. Under "Mexican American," a search reveals 82 dissertations were written before 1971, and 2,824 from 1971 to 2010. The search for "Latinos" shows 6 were written before 1971, and 2,887 from 1971 to 2010. This is also the pattern in dissertations on Mexico. Before 1971, 660 were found in the Proquest data bank; from 1971 to 2010 there were 9,078.[16] The number of books and journal articles on Chicanos and Latinas/os has also zoomed.[17]

Moreover, the growth of Chicano Studies was accelerated by the presence of Mexican American students on college campuses. In 1967 an estimated seventy students of Mexican origin attended the University of California, Los Angeles—and even fewer at many state colleges. From 1968 through 1973, undergraduate enrollment at the University of California system reportedly increased from 1.8 percent to 5.0 percent.[18] At the massive California State College system, the Chicana/o student population grew from 2.9 to 5.3 percent.[19] At the time, Mexican Americans were *reportedly* 10 percent of the state's population. Texas had a much longer tradition of Chicanas/os in higher education and a larger second- and third-generation Tejano student population; in 1974 approximately 1,900 Mexican American undergraduates attended the University of Texas at Austin, 4.85 percent of the university's total student population. At the time, almost 20 percent of the population of Texas was Mexican. The 1970 census suggests that barely over 20 percent of Mexican Americans, sixteen years old or older, graduated from high school.[20] The legacy of Chicano Studies during these early years was the establishment of beachheads that gave a home to student groups and knitted faculty, staff members, students, and community organizations into a common cause.

Even so, to this day a gap persists between the Mexican/general Latina/o population and white students in higher education. According to the American

Council on Education, in 2002–2004, 47.3 percent of white high school graduates, ages eighteen to twenty-four, attended institutions of higher education, compared to 41.1 percent of African Americans and 35.2 percent of Latinas/os. By 2003 the Latina/o student population grew to 1.6 million students (in 1972 there were 138,840 Latina/o students nationwide). Latina/o students trail Asian and white students in the number completing bachelor of arts degrees within six years, with Asians graduating at 62.3 percent; white students, 58.0 percent; Latinas/os, 42.0 percent; and African Americans, 36.4 percent. Among Latina/o college students, ages eighteen to twenty-four, 44.0 percent attended a two-year school, compared to about 30.0 percent of white and black undergraduates; in California in 2004, three-quarters of Latinas/os enrolled in public colleges were attending a community college, a number that is growing in response to escalating tuition costs at four-year universities.[21]

Despite the continuing gap between Latinas/os and whites in the professorial ranks, the struggle has produced changes. A 2007 survey showed that Latina/o doctoral candidates in all fields had increased by 140 percent since 1987. They earned a total of 1,489 research doctorates from July 1, 2006, to June 30, 2007; 22 percent of these were earned in the social sciences. However, in 2008 the number of Puerto Rican, Mexican, and other Hispanic students earning PhDs in history was approaching fewer than six, meaning Latinas/os will no longer be counted if the number decreases.[22] (Caution: these numbers must be further broken down because statistics lump all Spanish-surname recipients into a single category.)

AT RISK

The budget crisis and rising tuition costs are driving students to the brink. The University of California system in 2009 raised tuition 32 percent, putting the cost of education beyond the reach of most middle-class Latinas/os. In the past, the safety net was the Pell and Cal grants, which have been dramatically reduced. The California State University system is following a more dangerous route by reducing enrollment by 10,000 students in 2009–2010, and, in all probability, 20,000 the following year. The result is that those students are being pushed out: students who do not have the resources are stepping down in search of lower tuition. The community colleges have been flooded to the point that it is impossible to register for required classes. With this comes a cutting back of what administrators and faculty committees deem as nonessential courses, which generally means Ethnic Studies classes.[23]

The crisis not only impacts noncitizen immigrants; it also alienates a whole generation of Latina/o voters. In 2002 the Pew Hispanic Center found that approximately a third of the Latina/o electorate were naturalized U.S. citizens. They were young voters: 23 percent were between eighteen and twenty-nine years old, compared to 15 percent of their white counterparts.[24] With the shrinking opportunities for Latina/o students due to increased tuition costs, this sector is likely to become more discontented and proactive.[25]

These events are threatening to wipe out the gains of the past forty years. In 1968 Mexican Americans had no colleges of their own and did not have a critical mass of students in most public and private colleges. As a result of student activism, the number of Mexican American, Puerto Rican, and Cuban students increased to 98,453 (2.0 percent) in 1970 and 130,840 (2.4 percent) two years later. Whether institutions of higher learning admit it or not, the Latina/o population was a boon to higher education's growth during this period of declining white enrollment. During this period, Chicano Studies grew against all odds—in the spring of 1969, there were no more than 500 Mexican American students at the California state colleges, the largest public college system in the Southwest. According the Office of Civil Rights, only 7.1 percent of the students enrolled in institutions of higher learning were Latinos—California, 6.2 percent; Colorado, 5.3 percent; Illinois, 0.8 percent; New Mexico, 19.1 percent; Texas, 7.8 percent; and Washington, 0.9 percent.[26]

These totals do not separate community colleges from four-year institutions, and they include vocational schools such as DeVry Institute (now known as DeVry University), which in Illinois had only seventy-three Spanish-surname students.[27] While numbers are one measure of the of the Chicana/o drive for Chicano Studies, activity cannot solely be measured by the number of Chicana/o students in college. In most cases, the battle for Chicano Studies was led by less than a dozen Mexican American students, who, like the three hundred Spartans at the Battle of Thermopylae, fought against insurmountable odds.

The demand for more Chicana/o students and Chicano Studies was not isolated to the Southwest. It was fought for in Washington, Illinois, Michigan, Wisconsin, Minnesota, and in small pockets throughout the Midwest. The Mexican American students to a large degree followed the migrant worker corridors that flowed from Texas through the Pacific Northwest and the Midwest when they came to the United States with their families. They brought with them a sense of identity and knowledge of the struggle of César Chávez, the bracero program of an earlier period, and activist organizations such as the Mexican American Youth Organization (MAYO).[28]

Without a doubt there has been progress. For instance, today there are 223 Hispanic-serving institutions (HSIs)—that is to say, "colleges, universities, or systems/districts where total Hispanic enrollment constitutes a minimum of 25% of the total enrollment."[29] Even so, there is a long way to go: "Just over 10 percent of Hispanics in the country now have a college education—less than the national average for adults, which is over 25 percent, but a large increase from their educational attainment even ten years ago, according to the 2000 Census. Higher education's success in ensuring Latina/o educational achievement will become an increasingly important benchmark for assessing its contributions to the economic and civic health of this country."[30] Nonattendance of Mexican Americans and Latinas/os in higher education reinforces spatial and school segregation. While studies show Latinas/os learn more and do better in integrated schools, as a result of attending better funded schools, they continue to attend segregated schools with fewer certified teachers than in predominately white schools and generally have decaying infrastructures. Despite *Brown v. Board of Education* (1954), school segregation among Mexican Americans has increased during the past fifty years.[31] In response to efforts to integrate schools, white parents moved to all-white neighborhoods or sent their kids to private schools. By 2007 the average Latina/o student attended a school that was just below 60 percent of being an all-Latina/o school. Forty percent of Latina/o students attended schools that were intensely segregated. Some 46 percent of Latina/o students were from families earning below $25,000; only 9.2 percent were from high income families (more than $75,000).[32] Los Angeles Roosevelt and Garfield High Schools were entirely Latino, as were many schools throughout the Southwest. In California, 87 percent of the nonwhite students currently attend schools that are majority minority—in New York, 86 percent.[33] Often it is not until college that Latina/o and white students get to know each other as human beings. This tiny wedge is now at risk, and the consequences if there is no change will be disastrous.

AWAY WE GO!

The paranoid mentality of Arizona legislators, enforcement, and the public should not be considered exceptional. California has had a history of passing racist laws that exclude noncitizens from social services. These laws have targeted immigrants, affirmative action, and bilingual education. The difference is that in California such a law could never have gotten through the legislature because there are sixteen Latinos in the Latino Caucus in the California assembly, which would have blocked this sort of draconian legislation. Moreover, Republicans aspiring to statewide office learned from the backlash of Proposition 187 (1994), the anti-immigrant initiative, that Republicans cannot win statewide offices without the Latina/o vote. This reality has checked the opportunistic tendencies of most elected California officials.[34]

The California state constitution confers on the voters in state and local subdivisions the power to veto a law that is already operative through referendum. In California, the initiative process allows voters to bypass the legislature and, through a petition process, put the issue on the ballot for voter approval or rejection. The same constitution gives the electors the power to approve or reject any statute enacted by the legislature: Referendum. The latter is rarely used. However, the initiative process is widely abused, and many critics feel that this government by petition has paralyzed the state. Not all states provide for the initiative and referendum processes, however. Over 60 percent of initiative activity has occurred in Arizona, California, Colorado, North Dakota, Oregon, and Washington, with California and Arizona leading the way.

States such as Texas that may also have unhealthy histories of race discrimination and violence toward Mexicans do not, however, give citizens the power to initiate legislation by petition and consequently do not share this type of immigrant bashing. In other words, xenophobia is checked by political reality since the legislature has exclusive powers to legislate. The size of the Chicana/o and Latina/o electorate makes it too big to mess with.

The following chapters piece together the story of Chicana/o Studies. They show Mexican Americans, Latinos, and all Americans how far they have come and what is currently at risk in spite of that progress. What has been achieved is a tribute to the handful of students who believed that their community is important enough to be researched and served; they rebelled against the institutions that perpetuated the inequality of Mexican Americans. Tragically, this struggle is being forgotten by many of the Mexican Americans and Latinas/os who are its direct beneficiaries.

This particular story is told by a participant in the establishment of Chicano Studies during all forty years of its existence. The book makes an effort to include the struggle of other regions of the country. However, much of the narrative takes place in California because it is a bellwether for other states. California has the largest concentration of Mexican American students and Chicana/o Studies courses. Moreover, because of the number of Latinas/os there, they have access to national media.

The hysteria and success of the nativist movement is gripping the nation. It has spread to Arizona from California. An example is the anti-bilingual education laws that passed through the initiative process in California. Proposition 227 was passed in California in 1998 and in Arizona Proposition 203 was approved in 2000. This has encouraged nativist politicos who use the illusion of democracy to whip up nativist voters. The response of many Latinas/os to this xenophobia is to fight back; it is not even a matter of maintaining the status quo. Hate crimes against Latina/o immigrants have escalated from 426 in 2003 to 595 in 2007.[35] For example, in 2003 in Dateland, Arizona, "Pedro Corzo, a Cuban-born regional manager for Del Monte Fresh Produce, is gunned down by two Missouri residents—16-year-old Joshua Aston and his 24-year-old cousin Justin Harrison—who traveled with Aston's younger brother, 15-year-old Nicholas Aston, to a remote section of southern Arizona with the specific intent of randomly killing Mexicans." In April 2006 in Tucson, Arizona, a founder of the Minuteman movement, "Laine Lawless exhorts the leadership of the neo-Nazi National Socialist Movement (NSM) to launch a campaign of violence and intimidation against Latino immigrants." On May 7, 2007, in Maryville, Tennessee, "a Mexican grocery store is vandalized by five white men who shatter windows, damage a refrigerator and spray-paint neo-Nazi symbols." In January 2007 in Naco, Arizona, "Javier Dominguez-Rivera, a construction worker from Mexico, is shot dead at close range while on his knees by Border Patrol agent Nicholas Corbett." In October 2007 in Omaha, Nebraska, "Eduardo Garcia wakes up to find his truck and his wife's car set ablaze. Two other cars are also vandalized and have the words "white power" and a swastika spray-painted on them. No one is immediately arrested."[36] In 2008, Luis Ramírez, twenty-five, an undocumented worker for six years, picking crops and working in factories, died July 14 from head injuries in Shenandoah, Pennsylvania. A group from the town's high school beat him up. A representative for the Mexican

American Legal Defense and Education Fund said, "I do believe that the inflammatory rhetoric in the immigration debate does have a correlation with increased violence against Latinos."[37]

Nativists deny that they are racist or xenophobes. They claim that they base their attitudes on the growing violence in Mexico and along the border. According to them, they threaten American security. They insist that drastic measures must be taken to secure the border, win the war on drugs that President Ronald Reagan declared in 1982, and stop terrorists from attacking the United States.

Latinas/os respond that drugs are not a Mexican problem but the product of the U.S. marketplace. American policy forged the supply route through Mexico when it closed the sea lanes from South America to the United States. This opened routes through Mexico and created the Mexican drug cartels and the violence at the border. Contrary to popular belief, the traffic is not in marijuana—as it is too bulky and the finest grade is grown in the United States anyway—but in cocaine, heroine, crack, and methamphetamines, which can be smuggled more easily and is much more profitable.

As was the case with Prohibition in 1920–1933, which produced crime, the American market has created an irrational policy that has led to a prison industry. The United States has the highest incarceration rate in the world. The cost for drug enforcement for marijuana offenses has reached over $7 billion annually. The costs of building and maintaining prisons are bankrupting many states. Further, it is creating gangs trained as distributors and consumers. The United States also funds the war on drugs abroad, giving $8 billion annually to enrich the Latin American military. Contrary to popular belief, the United States has not given foreign aid to Mexico to build its infrastructure, to create jobs, or to stem undocumented immigration.[38] It is a matter of justice, but it is also a matter of self-interest for everyone to know more about Mexican Americans and Latinos. They will be one out of three Americans in four decades.[39]

CHAPTER 1

Becoming Chicana/o Studies

Becoming Mexican has been a long process marked by two phenomenons—three hundred years of Spanish colonialism and the creation of a 2,000-mile border—the result of which has been an identity crisis. At the time of the Spanish conquest a population of 25 million indigenous people lived in what is today Mexico—within eighty years it was reduced to about a million Indians. The imprint of European colonialism and imperialism produced a genetic makeup unique to those who would become Mexicans.[1] The Spanish constructed social categories based on race in order to control its subjects. At the top of the hierarchy were those of Spanish ancestry, or those who at least appeared to be; at the bottom were the Indians and Africans. On the eve of the Mexican War of Independence in 1810, Mexico was home to just over 6.0 million people: 1.1 million claimed to be Spaniards; 3.7 million, Indians; and 1.3 million, *castas* or mixed races. Since race was based on self-designation, many demographers today question the number of Spaniards, putting their number closer to 15,000.[2]

According to Ellen Yvonne Simms, "although not exclusive in colonial New Spain, one's skin color governed what one's status would be in society, and served as the basis of society in colonial New Spain."[3] At the bottom were the full-blooded Indians and Africans. In the nineteenth century, Mexican officials sought to establish a new Mexican identity, which resulted in civil wars.[4] The indigenous natives' share of the nation's population fell dramatically, from 60 percent in 1810 to 29 percent in 1920, while mestizos climbed from 29 to 60 percent. Meanwhile, the American filibuster of 1836 and invasion of 1846 took over half of Mexico's territory, further impacting Mexican identity.[5]

Becoming a Mexican changed in 1848. The American invasion of Mexico produced another identity crisis. Most Mexicans lived in separate communities along the 2,000-mile border separating the United States and Mexico. Regional differences affected how they identified themselves. They were not Americans because of the color of their skin and their accents. They were not yet Mexicans, because the

Mexican nationality took time to become. Mostly they identified with place and the community they lived in.[6] They were a minority within a majority.

Historian Trinidad Gonzales describes the process of identity building in the United States through the collective use of the labels "México Texano," "Mexicano," and "México Americano" that occurred from 1900 through the 1920s. According to Gonzales, "A Mexicano identity relates to an immigrant transnational identity as temporary residents living on what they perceived as occupied Mexican land during the early 1900s and by the 1920s as American territory." A México Americano was a México Texano who constructed his identity to call attention to his U.S. citizenship. Over time, identity was further changed by how people constructed space and meaningful locations.[7]

The Mexican border differs from the Canadian-U.S. border. Mexico has always had a larger and more racially diverse population than Canada. As of 2009, 111.2 million people live in Mexico, while 33.5 million people live in Canada. Racially, Mexico is 60 percent mestizo, 30 percent Indian, and 10 percent white and other. Pure Europeans form two-thirds of Canada, with Native Americans making up 2 percent of that nation. In 2008, in GDP per capita and in purchasing power parity (PPP) income, the United States ranked tenth in the world at $47,000 annually; Canada ranked twentieth, earning $39,300; and Mexico ranked eighty-second, earning $14,200. Canadians, like Americans, speak English (with some speaking French), while Mexicans speak Spanish and dozens of indigenous languages.[8] Mexico is where the Third World begins.[9] The long border and location distinguish Mexicans from other Latin Americans, who are often poorer than Mexicans but have more difficulty migrating to the United States because of distance. Further, most Latin American countries in North America are much smaller than Mexico, and this has affected the number and class of people migrating north.[10]

Newspapers are an excellent source of mapping the changing Mexican American identity. According to Edward Lee Walraven, 165 Spanish-language newspapers were published in the Mexican-Texas borderlands between 1830 and 1910, which promoted "cultural identity and education, morality and political involvement."[11] Four hundred and fifty predominately Mexican newspapers were published in the Southwest alone from 1910 to 1921. Some were supplements to English-language editions. The separation interests between the Mexican and Mexican American identity appears with the publication of Ignacio Lozano's *La Prensa* in 1913, which served the incoming wave of Middle-class Mexican political refugees of that year.[12] By the 1930s Spanish-language newspapers followed the Mexican migration into the Midwest, especially into Chicago, where newspapers were often published by Mexican organizations.[13] In time, they also began to differ according to the citizenship of readers or whether they spoke Spanish or English.[14] Proximity to Mexico and the fact that they settled what was once Mexico also distinguished them from other immigrants.

Today, other Latino groups are undergoing a similar process of identity formation. Becoming Latino differs today, however, since these Latino groups share Spanish-language television, radio, and newspapers with other Spanish-speaking groups.

Even their intonation is influenced by this contact. These differences affect the filtering process that they pass through, including variables such as legal status and time of arrival. Today only 24 percent of Central Americans are native-born U.S. citizens—16.7 percent of Guatemalans; 18 percent of Hondurans; and 18.3 percent of Salvadorans.[15] Nativity is important because of the maintenance of ties to the mother country.

BECOMING CHICANA/O STUDIES

Chicana/o Studies as an academic area of study differs from the corpus of knowledge produced by the individual writers who have contributed to this fund of knowledge. George I. Sánchez stands out in introducing Chicano Studies to higher education as an area of investigation and course of study. His efforts in bilingual education made him a precursor to the formation of Chicano Studies in the late 1960s. Putting this into context, the initiative that began the thrust toward Chicano Studies was the movement for compulsory education, which occurred in response to European immigration. In 1872 the *New York Times* wrote that the principle of universal education that had been popularized "in New England and other portions of the country" was changing. Owing "to foreign immigration and to unequal distribution of wealth, large numbers of people have grown up without the rudiments even of common-school education."[16] Over 5.6 million people in the United States did not know how to read or write. Only four states had passed compulsory education laws. By the turn of the century, California was one of the few southwestern states that required children to go to school, but it only enforced the law occasionally.[17]

In 1913 the *Los Angeles Times* reported that Texas had enacted a compulsory education bill; it was part of a strategy to prevent assistance at the polls to voters who could not read or write. Lawmakers aimed the bill "at the Mexicans of the western and Lower Rio Grande counties."[18] A Russell Sage Foundation study found that funding for schools decreased as larger numbers of immigrants entered the schools. The quality of education was "almost wholly a question of the dollar versus the child." Hence, the states that "oppose child labor, have compulsory education laws and enforce them, pay teachers well . . . have good buildings." The foundation also concluded that only nine states kept their schools open nine months or more; South Carolina and New Mexico opened schools 100 or 101 days. The United States ranked last among the "civilized" nations of the world in the length of school day and year. Texas ranked thirty-eighth in the number of children enrolled in school, and New Mexico ranked fortieth.[19]

The compulsory education laws impacted Mexicans within the United States as their numbers grew, as they moved to the cities, and as the second and third generations formed. Population growth and the shift to urban areas made them objects of study for church groups, educators, and sociologists. During the Spanish colonial period, many Spanish subjects were home schooled, where they were taught to read and write either by their parents or someone locally. Some students, such as Francisco Ramírez, the eighteen-year-old publisher of the Los Angeles newspaper *El Clamor Público* (1855–1859), achieved a high degree of literacy through home schooling.

Historian Guadalupe San Miguel writes that the available data on Mexican American education is speculative, and much depends on whether students lived in rural or urban areas—and on whether they were longtime residents or immigrants. According to San Miguel, "Chicanos encountered tremendous institutional and personal obstacles in their efforts to enroll in the public schools. Racial antipathy, lack of school facilities, poverty, and discriminatory school policies such as English-only laws were some of the more obvious obstacles. Despite these barriers a significant number of Chicanos, anywhere from 16 percent to 50 percent, matriculated in public schools from 1850 to 1940."[20] For example, in Los Angeles 38 percent of Mexican children attended schools, whereas in Texas "approximately 16.7 percent of Mexican school age children were enrolled in the public schools in 1850." Little progress was reported in Texas, and by 1900 only 17.3 percent attended school that year. The Mexican enrollment in San Antonio was 30.7 percent. It fell to 17.8 percent in El Paso.[21]

California passed a compulsory education law in 1874, but "working-class children of all backgrounds often skipped school and entered the work force directly." From 1908 to 1916 the total number of pupils in Los Angeles jumped from 33,422 to 54,796.[22] Lincoln Heights elementary school saw its percentage of "American" students drop from 85 percent in 1913 to 53 percent by 1921, while the percentage of Italian and Mexican students jumped from 8 percent to 22 percent, and from 4 percent to 20 percent, respectively. A 1924 census listed twenty-two elementary schools in mixed racial districts, with 52.3 percent "white" students (including European immigrants), 35 percent ethnic Mexican, 6.9 percent African American, 5.3 percent Asian, and 0.6 percent "other."[23]

When the races lived in close proximity, white parents sought to segregate Mexican children. The diversity in Los Angeles brought about curricular changes that "emphasized what administrators termed 'internationalism' studies," which anticipated the Ethnic Studies movement. Any positive effects were muted, with two-thirds of Mexican children testing "retarded" under school administered intelligence exams in 1908. Consequently, the children were tracked, put into remedial classes, and discriminated against along ethnoracial lines.[24] In the Belvedere District of East Los Angeles in 1918, the question of immigration became moot by the dramatic growth of the Mexicans in the area.

New Mexico had one of the highest concentrations of Mexican Americans. The Territory of New Mexico was a battleground. White Protestants wanted to secularize education and establish "a nonsectarian, tax-supported educational system which would teach 'American' social and political doctrines to both Protestant and Catholic children." Native New Mexican Catholics sided with the clergy and fought to retain control of the few public schools in the territory.[25] The first bishop of the Diocese of Santa Fe, John B. Lamy, arrived in New Mexico in 1850. Lamy, a priest in the Diocese of Cincinnati, Ohio, from 1839 to 1850, had witnessed the rise of anti-Catholicism and was determined to preserve Catholic hegemony. Lamy opened Spanish-language parochial schools in Albuquerque and Santa Fe, and in 1856 the church overwhelmingly defeated a referendum for the territory's first public school bill. Lamy imported orders of nuns and priests, led by the Jesuits, who conducted a crusade to control the schools, achieving public financing for parochial schools. Through the work of Father Donato María Gasparri, superior of the Society of Jesus in New Mexico, the Catholic Church maintained control of education in New Mexico during the 1860s and into the 1870s.[26]

Meanwhile, the state of education in New Mexico was dismal. In 1850, 25,085 adults could not read; a decade later that number increased to 32,785. Only seventeen public schools with thirty-three teachers functioned in the territory. In 1867 the legislature decreed that all children between the ages of seven and eighteen must attend school, but the law was never enforced. According to Dianna Everett, "Native New Mexican children went unschooled, while Anglo-American children received an education only if their parents could afford to pay the per capita fee."[27] Most schools were linguistically and racially segregated.[28] By 1913 only seven of eighty-seven students graduating from New Mexico's public high schools were of Mexican origin.

In 1863 the first Arizona Territorial Legislature allocated about $1,500 for public and mission schools, and most students were Mexican and Native Americans. The Tucson schools received one-third of the funds, with the stipulation that English would be taught. According to the 1860 Census, Tucson was 70.6 percent Mexican. The children were almost entirely Spanish-speaking.[29] In 1866 a Catholic school for boys opened in Tucson, and in 1870 the Sisters of St. Joseph opened a school for girls. The Mexican population preferred parochial schools because they had the freedom to teach the Spanish language and religion. Many Mexican families opposed coeducation, which was the norm at the public schools. In 1870 the sisters of St. Joseph established a school for girls; St. Augustine remained the school for boys. Rosa Ortiz ran a Mexican private school where Spanish was the principal language. The teaching of Spanish continued to be a source of friction, and in 1879 *La Sonora* complained, "The policy of our schools in excluding the study of the Spanish language from its curriculum is somewhat to be wondered at, especially in those places where a large percentage of the population is Spanish and the necessity for a knowledge of that tongue is so apparent."[30]

By the 1880s the size of the Mexican population in the territory's mining camps overshadowed that of Tucson. The mining centers of Clifton, Morenci, and Metcalf were Mexican camps. For the first two decades the mine owners had little incentive to build and maintain schools—most of the children were Mexican. The Shannon Company's mines built the first school in 1895. In 1899 the Arizona Copper Company started to take more interest in education and built a new school. About thirty students, mostly Mexican, attended. They were the children of smelter workers. As more white workers were employed at the turn of the century, the mine owners built segregated schools, spending less on education in Mexican areas. The Clifton mine owners spent $9.45 per student, whereas the Morenci camp, with more

Mexicans, spent $5.37 per student. At this point, no high schools existed in the
three towns. Clifton had four elementary schools. In North Clifton, mixed races were
placed in separate classes. In South Clifton, the school was all white. Chase Creek
had a Mexican and a white school. In 1905 even Mexicans voted against consolidating
the schools, no doubt because of company influence.[31]

THE SECULARIZATION OF EDUCATION

Protestant missionaries have an impressive history of evangelization among
Mexicans. Their efforts, including literacy courses, have been marred by their
advocacy of Americanization programs in the United States. Protestant missionaries
broke the monopoly of the Catholic Church and offered needed competition. In
Mexico and Europe, Protestants supported movements to secularize education.
Bloody confrontations in France, Italy, and Spain saw the pope intervene in the
affairs of the states.[32] Mexico's War of Reform (1858–1861) was part of this world-
wide struggle, and as late as the 1920s the bloody Cristero Revolt in Jalisco attempted
to restore church privileges.[33] These events hardened the worldview of many Mexican
and European clergy working with Mexican Americans.[34]

Hostilities over the separation of church and state in Spain affected Mexican
Americans because many of the priests and nuns that worked with them were from
that country.[35] The fight between parliament and the Crown over secularization
began in the early nineteenth century, and bloody street battles raged into the 1930s.
At the turn of the century in Catalonia, the Basque Province, Bilboa, Navarre, and
Aragon, violent mobs were led by religious orders.[36] The control of public education
was the central issue. In Spain more Catholic schools existed than public schools,
which many said prevented the development of a republic.[37] For a time, church
partisans won out, but in 1931 the Second Spanish Republic came to power, which
again attempted to separate church and state. This led to a renewal of hostilities
between those favoring the church and the secularists that included multiple factions.
Conservatives won when a military coup led by General Francisco Franco and the
Nationalists ended in the Spanish Civil War (1936–1939) and imposed the fascist
dictatorship of Franco that lasted until 1975.

SECULARIZATION IN MEXICO

Again, the struggle to secularize and modernize Mexican society is important:
many priests and adherents brought with them biases toward unions and progressive causes.[38] The effort to modernize Mexico was no less intense and bloody than
it was in Europe, lasting for most of the nineteenth century and into the 1920s. The
separation of church and state was a major cause of the wars between liberals and
conservatives, which began at the time of Mexican Independence in 1821 and came
to a head with the War of Reform (1858–1861), the rise of Mexican President Benito
Juárez, the church party's attempt to impose the Hapsburg Emperor on Mexico,
and the French Intervention of 1862–1867.

In the context of this struggle, Methodist, Presbyterians, Episcopalians, and other Protestant denominations acquired space to work in Mexico. They were held in check during the first years of the Mexican republic because Catholicism was the official religion of Mexico. The military and the church were not accountable to civil law and could be tried only by military and church tribunals. The Laws of Reform and Benito Juárez ended the church's franchise, and by 1873 laws of religious tolerance became part of the Mexican constitution and legalized Protestantism. Juárez and Melchor Ocampo (the minister of interior who drafted the laws) encouraged Protestant missionaries and also promoted a Mexican Catholic schismatic movement. Many schismatics merged with Protestant missionary societies that established seminaries and schools throughout northern Mexico.[39]

By 1892, 469 Protestant congregations ministered to about 100,000 converts in Mexico as they established a "network of private primary and secondary schools, teacher training schools, colleges for men and women." The Porfirio Díaz dictatorship had reversed many religious reforms. This reversal alienated Protestant clergy who actively opposed the dictatorship, publishing dissident newspapers and joining forces with anarcho-syndicalists. Many Mexican Protestants later joined the ranks of the Mexican Revolution in 1910.[40]

Aside from training Mexican ministers, Protestant schools developed courses of study. Mexican ministers were sent to the United States to minister to the Mexican immigrant population and continue their educational work.[41] By the early 1900s other sectors of the Mexican American community were asking for teacher training programs to meet the needs of Spanish-speaking students. By the late 1800s, Mexican Americans opened their own schools in the United States. In the early 1900s in New Mexico, Mexicans pressured authorities to establish a normal school to train teachers to educate Mexican students.[42]

World War I intensified movements directed at Americanizing the Mexican family's cultural patterns. Public school authorities established English-only schools that isolated students in Mexican schools in an effort, according to them, to meet their "special needs." They openly derogated Mexicans as being "dirty, shiftless, lazy, irresponsible, unambitious, thriftless, fatalistic, selfish, promiscuous, and prone to drinking, violence, and criminal behavior." Accordingly, they reasoned Mexicans lacked intelligence. IQ testing played a major role in justifying remedial programs that trained Mexicans for subordinate roles in American society. During the 1920s about half of Mexican students attended segregated Mexican schools. However, not all Protestants supported the jingoist strategy of cultural annihilation. Many reformers wanted programs stressing the cultural needs of Mexican children.[43] Reformers advocated for compassionate Americanization programs based on emphasizing the positive assets of Mexican culture, and they sponsored cultural and teacher exchanges with Mexico.[44]

Protestant ministers such as the Reverend Robert N. McLean, an associate director of the Presbyterian Board of Missions in the United States, were active in the Mexican and Puerto Rican communities, writing studies and establishing schools. They played an important advocacy role.[45] Mexicans also reacted negatively to the

English-only teaching requirements enforced in Texas and other states during World War I, which intensified segregation.

During this decade Mexican organizations established *escuelitas* (little schools) that offered reading and writing instruction in Spanish for preschoolers. California housed 30 percent of the Mexican origin population. Mexican organizations there established libraries and *escuelitas* whose course of study provided "training in Mexican culture, Spanish, and basic school subjects to supplement the inferior education many Chicanos felt their children received in the public schools."[46]

EARLY CONTRIBUTORS OF A CORPUS OF KNOWLEDGE

Among the early scholars contributing to the written fund of knowledge was University of Southern California sociologist Emory Bogardus.[47] By the 1920s agricultural economist Paul S. Taylor was writing about farm laborers, and Mexican anthropologist Manuel Gamio was researching Mexican immigrants.[48] O. Douglas Weeks's work on Texas politics and the founding of the League of United Latin American Citizens is essential literature for understanding the basis of Chicano Studies.[49] Equally important is folklorist, historian, writer, and teacher Jovita González de Mireles, from Roma, Texas, who collected Mexican folklore in the Rio Grande valley. And, University of Texas historian Carlos Eduardo Castañeda wrote the seven-volume *Our Catholic Heritage in Texas, 1519–1936*. During World War II, Castañeda served as regional director of the President's Committee on Fair Employment Practice.[50]

A bridge between these early scholars and Chicana/o Studies is University of Texas Professor George I. Sánchez. Born in New Mexico and educated in Jerome, Arizona, Sánchez taught in public schools and earned an EdD from the University of California at Berkeley. Sánchez later taught at the Universities of New Mexico and Texas and was a crusader for equal education for Mexican Americans. His politics were gradualist, in line with the labor-oriented progressives of *his* time. What makes Sánchez particularly relevant to Chicana/o Studies is his work with the Julius Rosenwald Fund's teacher-training program at the Louisiana Negro Normal and Industrial Institute at Grambling State College in Louisiana. He applied strategies learned there to Mexican American students.[51] In 1936 he left for Venezuela and then returned to New Mexico, where he helped form the Institute of the Southwest. Leaving for Texas in the fall of 1940, Sánchez sought to continue blending African American and Mexican American educational strategies. Along with his colleague, University of Texas history professor Herschel T. Manuel, he conducted research on pedagogy for Mexican children; both were strong advocates of bilingual education, which was important to the development of Chicana/o Studies.

Manuel began his study of Mexicans in 1929. Outraged by the lengths to which many Texan educators went to deny these children an education, he converted from objectivism, which described what *was*, to purposivism, which reached for what *should* and *could* be. In 1940 Manuel shifted his research to Puerto Rican children and their historic struggle against Americanization and English-only.[52] The Puerto

Rican connection is underscored by the work of Mexican missionaries with Puerto Ricans. For example, Pastor Alberto Báez, from Monterey, Mexico, was a Methodist minister who worked with Puerto Ricans in New York, advocating for their entitlements as citizens. Báez, the grandfather of singer Joan Baez, worked with Puerto Rican congregations for almost twenty years.[53]

Sánchez's work spanned four decades. The focus here is specifically on his contribution to the area of Chicano Studies—especially the early development of bibliographies, a tedious task that defined the known corpus of knowledge of the discipline. Starting in the 1920s several scholars attempted to compile basic reading lists. For example, Bogardus in 1929 compiled a bibliography of books he considered essential reading on Mexicans. However, the bibliography has little on Mexicans in the United States; most of the sources he lists are about Mexico.

In 1942 Ernesto Galarza's bibliography focused on Mexican Americans and included history, sociology, farm labor, and education. Two years later University of New Mexico professor Lyle Saunders compiled a bibliography that for the first time used the term "Mexican American." The bibliography has an excellent listing of educational materials, which was the preoccupation of many Mexican Americans in their quest for equality at the time.[54]

Sánchez and Howard Putnam in 1959 published a seventy-six-page annotated bibliography. It goes way beyond its predecessors. Without a doubt, the most relevant is the "Courses of Study" section. As expected, many listings deal with bilingual education and English as a second language, both of which are seen as keys to how to teach Mexican origin students. However, listings dealing with content of instruction and developing curriculum for Spanish-speaking students are also listed. Sánchez was well aware of the need for courses specializing in Mexican Americans, not only for teachers but also all students.[55]

Throughout the 1940s and into the 1970s, Sánchez was an activist-scholar. A conference on school attendance at Southwest State Teachers College at San Marcos in 1946 criticized school boards for not enforcing school attendance. The *Paris (Texas) News* reported, "Figures were quoted at the conference showing that in one county where school attendance and the school census are approximately the same, annual per capita apportionments amount to $25. In another, where attendance is not strictly enforced, those who do go to school benefit to the extent of $60 each per year. The state per capita apportionment is $30." Sánchez charged that that system was being rewarded for nonattendance. At this late stage, Mexican Americans were still struggling with the lack of enforcement of the compulsory education laws. "Of the 1,261,548 Anglo and Latin American children counted, there were 244,129 Latin Americans, but only 71,643 attended school . . . [of] the 228,511 Negroes, there was an enrollment of 197,961."[56]

LOST OPPORTUNITIES

World War II heightened Mexican Americans' awareness of their inequality. Important in this consciousness building were the Fair Employment Practices

Commission (FEPC) Hearings. During the war, 375,000–500,000 Mexican Americans served in the armed forces; this contribution to the war effort increased their feeling of entitlement as American citizens.[57] They became conscious that they were not sharing in the "equality of opportunity" that was supposedly part of the American patrimony. According to the liberal thought of the times, segregation and discrimination were individual abuses and should not be sanctioned but eliminated—education was a right, not a privilege.[58]

For the first time, Mexican American leaders were to a degree part of the national discourse on equality, and they felt a measure of power just to be able to appear before a national government regulatory agency. When civil rights attorney Manuel Ruiz testified before the FEPC, he found a lack of statistics proving discrimination toward Mexicans. The citing of data was critical to making a case for equal treatment, and without solid evidence the FEPC was enabled to avoid enforcing a presidential executive order to support fairer practices.[59] The hearing galvanized the Mexican American communities' pursuit of civil rights. The inequality of education was a benchmark in this discourse, and as the most provable grievance it helped define the issues.[60]

It did not escape Mexican American leaders that the end of the war brought new opportunities to white citizens that were being denied to African Americans and Latinos and Latinas. For instance, the GI Bill and the development of the California state college system gave millions of Americans the means to go to college. In California, white people had achieved a median education of the eleventh grade, qualifying just under half its population for higher education. Meanwhile, blacks achieved a median of 9.4 grades in 1960, and Latinos had a median of 7.7 in 1960.[61] Texas was even worse: the median number of years of education was 3.5 in 1950 for Mexican Americans—half that of California—compared with 10.3 for whites and 7.0 for nonwhites. In San Antonio, the median number of school years for Mexican Americans was 4.5, half that of the general population of the city. Cities like Tucson mirrored California. In 1950 the median number of school years that Mexican Americans completed in the city was 6.5. Many returning Mexican American veterans felt that their community simply did not have the educational human capital to take advantage of the new opportunities.[62]

The postwar period saw a proliferation of national education conferences led by Mexican American scholars. The First Regional Conference on Education of the Spanish-Speaking People in the Southwest took place at the University of Texas at Austin on December 13–15, 1945, focusing on school segregation and bilingual education. George I. Sánchez, Carlos E. Castañeda of the University of Texas at Austin, A. L. Campa of the University of New Mexico, and San Antonio attorney Alonso S. Perales took leading roles. Delegates from the five southwestern states were in attendance. The *Santa Fe New Mexican* reported that Sánchez chaired a New Mexico conference that dealt "specifically with fundamental problems in the education of Spanish-speaking people." Carey McWilliams keynoted the event.[63] Throughout the next two decades Sánchez helped define Mexican American education as well as civil rights issues.

In 1946 Judge Paul J. McCormick, in the U.S. District Court in southern California, heard the *Méndez v.Westminster School District* case and declared the segregation of Mexican children unconstitutional. Gonzalo, a Mexican American, and Felicitas Méndez, a Puerto Rican, spearheaded the suit. In April of the next year, the U.S. Court of Appeals for the Ninth Circuit affirmed the decision, stating that Mexicans and other children were entitled to "the equal protection of the laws," and that neither language nor race could be used as a reason to segregate them. In response to the *Méndez* case, the Associated Farmers of Orange County launched a bitter red-baiting campaign against the Mexican communities.[64] On June 15, 1948, in another segregation case, Judge Ben H. Rice Jr., U.S. District Court, Western District of Texas, found in *Delgado v. Bastrop Independent School District* that the school district had violated the Fourteenth Amendment rights of Mexican children. These two cases set precedents for the historic *Brown v. Board of Education* case in 1954.[65]

The postwar period also broadened organizational activity among Mexican Americans. Dr. Hector Pérez García founded the American GI Forum in Corpus Christi, Texas. The forum burst onto the national scene when a funeral home in Three Rivers, Texas, refused to hold services for Pvt. Felix Longoria, who had died in the Philippines during World War II. This incident brought a moral outrage over the issue of race.[66] Texas officials claimed that they never denied Longoria a proper burial and accused the forum of exploiting the issue. At hearings of the state Good Neighbor Commission, Dr. García and the forum's attorney, Gus García, did a brilliant job of proving the forum's case by presenting evidence of "Mexican" and "white" cemeteries and racist burial practices. However, the all-white commission found that there was no discrimination. The blatant bias of the commissioners further strained race relations, and from that point on the forum became more proactive. "Unlike LULAC [League of United Latin American Citizens], whose policy was not to involve itself directly in electoral politics, the forum openly advocated getting out the vote and endorsing candidates." The forum did not limit membership to the middle class and those fluent in English. It was less accommodating to the feelings of Euro-Americans. Like most of the other Mexican American organizations of the time, the forum stressed the importance of education. The GI Forum's motto was "Education is our freedom, and freedom should be everybody's business."[67]

A national Mexican American identity and consensus was being forged through conferences and the interaction of regional leaders. Racism toward Mexicans became a national topic with the epic film *Giant* (1956), director George Stevens's adaptation of the Edna Ferber novel about a great cattle ranch family in Texas, starring Rock Hudson, James Dean, and Elizabeth Taylor. Another book was Beatrice Griffith's *American Me*, published in 1948. The first true history of the Mexican American was Carey McWilliams's *North from Mexico* (1947).[68]

Identity was also forged by the Korean War, in which Mexican Americans served in the armed forces in disproportionate numbers. Six Mexican Americans won Medals of Honor during this conflict. The Mexican American GI generation was expanded by World War II and the Korean War.

Civil Rights: Numbers Count

In the first seven years of the 1950s, Mexican Americans filed fifteen school deseg-regation cases. Guadalupe San Miguel makes the point that the litigation strategy was implemented by an expanding Mexican American middle class that was conscious of its duty to protect the civil rights of the entire community. Education was foremost on their agenda as a strategy for this transformation. A priority was to end the policy of separate and unequal schools.[69]

The professor, along with Texas attorney Gustavo C. García, worked with pro-gressives such as Robert C. Eckhardt of Austin and A. L. Wirin of the Los Angeles Civil Liberties Union. García filed *Delgado v. Bastrop ISD* (1948), the decision of which made illegal the segregation of children of Mexican descent in Texas. García played a leading role in revising the 1949 LULAC constitution to permit non–Mexican Americans to become members. He was also active in the Felix Longoria case and advocated fair treatment for the *bracero*.

In April 1955 Chicanos sued the schools of Carrizo Springs and Kingsville, Texas. In Kingsville, Austin Elementary had been segregated since 1914; it was known as the "Mexican Ward School," with a 100 percent Chicano student popu-lation. The Texas GI Forum also fought police brutality cases. At the same time, Sánchez worked with "Robert Marshall Civil Liberties Trust of the American Civil Liberties Union (ACLU) . . . the Marshall Trust [was] designed for Spanish speak-ers of the Southwest, and in 1951 [it] appointed Sánchez, through the new organi-zation Sánchez founded—the American Council of Spanish-Speaking People (ACSSP)—to administer block grants for the funding of civil rights lawsuits." Sánchez used part of this money to defend the rights of Mexican immigrants.[70]

On May 3, 1954, the U.S. Supreme Court unanimously banned discrimination in jury selection. In Edna, Texas, an all-white jury found Peter Hernández guilty of the murder of Joe Espínosa and sentenced him to life imprisonment. The Court of Criminal Appeals turned down this case because, according to the court, Mexicans were white and therefore not a class apart from the white population. Hernández appealed, and the U.S. Supreme Court found that for twenty-five years the Court of Criminal Appeals had treated Mexicans as a class apart. As proof, it cited that out of 6,000 citizens considered for jury duty, the panel had never selected a Mexican juror. The lower court again tried Peter Hernández; this time he pled guilty and the court sentenced him to twenty years.[71]

The Hernández case is a landmark civil rights case. While black Americans were guaranteed the right to serve on juries by the Civil Rights Act of 1875, Mexican Americans had not won that right. Previous courts had held that Mexicans were not guaranteed this right by the Fourteenth Amendment since they were legally white. However, the Mexican American attorneys argued that Mexican Americans were "a class apart"; they did not fit into the black-white American paradigm. The Supreme Court upheld the argument and ruled that, as a "class apart" that had suf-fered historic discrimination, Mexican Americans were entitled to the protections of the Fourteenth Amendment. "In his 1957 address to the Race Relations Institute,

Sánchez got press attention with his claims that Mexican American discrimination had unique sources: the United States' colonial subjugation of the Southwest and its rapacious desire for cheap labor."[72]

By the 1960s, the strategy used by Mexican Americans since the nineteenth century to claim that they were protected by the Treaty of Guadalupe Hidalgo and that they had constitutional rights was coming apart. In the early sixties bilingual education was a cornerstone of the struggle for equal educational opportunity. Research on bilingual education had been conducted since the 1920s in response to race-based studies on intelligence. According to Carlos K. Blanton, "By the 1960s, leading psychologists, linguists and educators increasingly reasoned that bilingualism actually benefited intelligence."[73] Sánchez was a main actor in shifting the paradigm. His political activism cannot be separated from his pedagogical work.

On the Eve of Becoming Chicano Studies

Becoming involves developing a sense of community, which is not an easy task. A sense of the place and network where people live is essential. Becoming is a continual process of challenging the paradigms held to be true, which involves multiple small shifts, with communities sharing and developing a common heritage. Becoming Mexican American or a Chicano was not suddenly waking up and saying, "I am a Chicana/o." The same can be said of becoming a discipline—it takes time and involves numerous mutations. Chicano Studies mutated from Mexican Studies and developed a proper criterion for organizing its knowledge into disciplines. This framework took years, and the process of becoming Chicano Studies took a new form when Mexicans came to the United States. The community evolved from a rural-sectarian society where learning was not valued by those in charge. Becoming Chicano Studies involved forming a common identity and considering separate and distinct cultures, as well as the formation of a community of scholars and the collection of data and interpretation.

CHAPTER 2

The Sixties and the Bean Count

Los Angeles was a white city in 1960; within a decade it became Mexican once more. The Mexican American student population rose to 22 percent by the end of the decade, doubling from 1960. Similar shifts took place throughout the Southwest, Midwest, and Pacific Northwest. The inequality of education was on most people's mind, calling attention to the unequal status of Mexican Americans in income, labor, and opportunity. Mexican Americans, in order to draw attention to their needs, advertised their underclass status and demanded a correction. According to the 1960 Census, the median years of schooling of Spanish-surname persons in California was 8.6 years, 4.8 years in Texas, 7.0 years in Arizona, and 7.4 years in New Mexico. Quickly the poor quality of education and demands to improve it became the standard for progress in other areas.[1]

From 1946 to 1964 the nation grew as 76 million babies were born in the United States. This new youth population played an important role in the 1960s, and the U.S. Census took on new importance. Before the Census count even started, Mexican American leaders were infuriated when they lumped all Latinas/os under the category of "Spanish-speaking," making it difficult to derive accurate statistics. During the 1950s the growth rate among Latinas/os in the Southwest was 4.1 annually versus 3.1 for Euro-Americans; the 1960 Census dramatically undercounted 3,464,999 Spanish-surnamed persons in the Southwest who earned $968 per capita, compared with $2,047 for white Americans and $1,044 for nonwhites.

California showed the most dramatic growth, from 760,453 to 1,426,538, surpassing Texas at 1,417,810. Some 42 percent of Spanish-surnamed children were under the age of fifteen, and the median age for the group was twenty years, compared to thirty for white Americans. Social segregation still existed, and in places like Texas and eastern Oregon "No Mexicans Allowed" signs were common.[2] The organizational life of the Mexican American also expanded, and World War II and Korean veterans joined labor unions and political organizations. The careers of Edward R. Roybal (Los Angeles) and Henry B. González (San Antonio) were held up as examples of the existence of a "Sleeping Giant" and the untapped potential of the group.

The sixties generation was shaped by World War II and postwar participation in government agencies such as the U.S. Civil Rights Commission, which was formed in 1957 in response to the disruptions at Little Rock, Arkansas, resulting from efforts to integrate public schools. In a dramatic confrontation, President Dwight Eisenhower was forced to call out the National Guard. The Civil Rights Commission was composed of a fifteen-member committee representing groups from various walks of life, including racial and ethnic groups. This partial victory began a struggle to put teeth into the commission, with enforcement powers coming only after prolonged battles in the U.S. Senate, where Republicans and southern Democrats opposed the creation of the commission. The bill set up "a five member commission to enforce anti-discrimination orders, through the courts if need be. The operation would be run by a $12,000-a-year executive director; commission members would be paid $5,000 a year."[3]

The commission collected data and held hearings. Although painfully slow in coming, its findings laid the foundation for later civil rights legislation. While mostly focusing on African Americans, the expansion of the Latina/o communities in states such as California and Texas made them too large to ignore. Hearings in those states called attention to the plight of the Mexican American. The *Chicago Defender* reported in 1959: "The Commission said it expected the California hearings would yield much information in areas in which it has not previously had the opportunity to examine closely. It pointed to the existence in California of the Mexican-American and Oriental minorities and the continued large migration of Negroes to the State." These were the first hearings the commission held in the West.[4] California and Texas together numbered over three million Mexican Americans, and although they were gerrymandered, a number of legislators and Congress persons had critical numbers of Mexican Americans in their districts.

The hearings held in San Francisco and Los Angeles were explosive: Los Angeles Police Chief William Parker testified that "Negroes commit 11 times as many crimes as Caucasians, in proportion to their population. Persons of Latin-American origin commit five times as many and Orientals and other nationalities only one-third as many." Councilman Edward R. Roybal testified as to discrimination and the harassment of Spanish-speaking voters. During the hearings Parker responded to charges of police brutality by insulting the Mexican American and black communities: "Just to keep the record straight. I am not singling the Negro out. The Latin population that came here in great strength have presented a great problem because I have worked over on the East Side when men had to work in pairs. But that has evolved into an assimilation. And it is because some of those people were not too far removed from the wild tribes of the inner mountains of Mexico. I don't think that you can throw the genes out of the question when you discuss the behavior patterns of people."[5]

Parker later claimed that the attacks on him were led by ultraliberals. Mobilized, the Mexican American community expressed anger; among the first critics were Louis Díaz, mayor elect of Pico-Rivera; Raul Morín, chair of the American GI

Forum; Charles Samario, of the Council of Mexican-American Affairs; and Angelo
Basco, of the Eastside Young Democrats. The remarks reverberated throughout the
Southwest and energized the base. Parker's remarks proved racism at the highest
levels as the LA City Council and Board of Supervisors sided with Parker.[6]

COUNTING BEANS: THE NUMBERS

Fabio Rojas suggests that Black Studies is as much the product of student mobilization as it is bureaucratic decisions. The establishment of Black Studies, according to Rojas, was a sudden event that happened in 1968. He attributes much of the
drama and cohesiveness to Black cultural nationalism. The same can be said of
Mexican Americans. Attention and awareness grew with the size of the population
during the decade.[7] A difference was that Mexican Americans lacked an organizational infrastructure. Occidental College sociologist Paul Sheldon reported in 1961
that a Los Angeles Spanish-language newspaper recorded eighty-five Latino organizations while the Welfare Planning Council listed forty-seven. The Council of
Mexican American Affairs (CMAA) claimed forty-four member organizations.
Only two of the organizations had an office and a phone; none had a full-time staff.
Composed largely of veterans, the most prominent were the CMAA, the Community
Service Organization, the American GI Forum, and the Mexican American Political
Association (MAPA).[8]

Sheldon headed the college's Laboratory of Urban Culture, which sponsored
the Southwest Conference. Sheldon conducted valuable studies on the Mexican
American dropout problem. In 1957 he sponsored a conference on dropouts
chaired by attorney Henry López, the Democratic Party candidate for lieutenant
governor in 1958. The study showed that six of ten Mexican American students
dropped out in the tenth grade. Sheldon blamed the dropout problem on the lack
of counselors and the failure of the schools. The lack of relevant subject matter in
their course of study blunted the students' motivation to learn English. Sheldon
was active within the Mexican American community and among Mexican American
scholars—testifying on discrimination at the first hearing of the Commission on
Civil Rights in Los Angeles. The laboratory gave a voice to Mexican American
scholars such as University of Notre Dame sociologist Julian Samora and George I.
Sánchez.[9]

The 1960 Census study funded by the Ford Foundation and administered at the
University of California, Los Angeles, was a milestone because of its accumulation
of vast numbers of documents and studies. The Mexican American study was
controversial because Ford placed it under the direction of a UCLA economist Leo
Grebler, who knew almost nothing about Mexicans on either side of *la linea*. If an
"Anglo" was to be appointed, Mexican American activists preferred Paul Sheldon.
Some felt that the study should be based in Texas; in California, opposition to the
Ford study continued throughout its tenure. Grebler, to his credit, hired good
researchers and churned out studies that led to a mammoth book, which became
the prototype for studies on later censuses.[10]

Manuel H. Guerra, a University of Southern California Spanish professor and chair of the Mexican American Political Association's Education Committee, realized the implications of appointing a non–Mexican American scholar to head the $400,000 project. Guerra, along with renowned civil rights attorney Manuel R. Ruiz, charged at a press conference that Grebler did not have the qualifications. Grebler, a professor of Urban Land Economics, did not have the minimal knowledge of Mexican Americans, only recently having joined the UCLA faculty in 1958. Grebler hired Stella Leal Carrillo to tour him through Mexico because he was unfamiliar with the country.[11] Guerra charged that the preliminary reports were based on obsolete sources and that most of the staff did not speak Spanish.[12] The bottom line was that the critics knew that Ford was determining who was a legitimate scholar of Mexican American Studies.[13]

Identity, Language, History, and Cultural Conflict

The year 1963 was a transitional year for Mexican Americans who literally jammed a five-state conference sponsored by the President's Committee on Equal Opportunity, demanding more effective education for Mexican American youth. More than 2,000 attended, about 45 percent of whom were Mexican Americans. President Lyndon Johnson's secretary of Health, Education and Welfare insulted the delegates, telling them Mexican Americans were going through what the Italians did: "You are making a mistake when you say others should feel sorry for you." James Roosevelt intervened and told the secretary that Italians and Irish made it in society at a different time than the Mexicans. George I. Sánchez made a case for the need for industry to lead the way.[14]

In 1963 *Los Angeles Times* journalist Ruben Salazar wrote an important series on the Mexican American that introduced them on prime time. It was as if the columns validated the group. Salazar reminded Angelinos that Mexicans were here before them.

> Los Angeles has one of the largest Spanish-speaking urban populations in the Western Hemisphere. Most are "Mexicans." But historians tell us this does not accurately describe these people because in many respects they are "indigenous" to Southern California and the Southwest. Though they also help make up what generally is known as California's "Spanish heritage," Spain is not their "mother country." They are so highly heterogeneous that they can not be adequately understood by studying the cultures of Spain or Mexico. This is an attempt to trace where they came from, what they are and where they are going.[15]

Salazar reviewed the disparate labels describing Mexican Americans: la raza, pocho, Mexican American, cholo, American-born Mexican, Spanish American, and Latin American. Salazar retells the settlement of Los Angeles by mixed blood (Indian, African, and Spanish) immigrants from Mexico and reviews current scholarship—the research of Paul M. Sheldon, George I. Sánchez, and Van Nuys, California, high school teacher Marcos de León.

Mexican American educators criticized what Carey McWilliams called the "Fantasy Heritage" and the Anglos' preoccupation with nonwhite races, bringing into focus the question of identity that Marcos Del León said confused and heightened the insecurity of Mexican Americans.[16] The Mexican American had been made ashamed of his ethnic ancestry, despite the fact that "no man can find a true expression for living who is ashamed of himself or his people."[17]

The second article in the series opened with a photo of "Hoyo Mara" (Maravilla, or "marvelous hole"). Salazar interviewed Salvador (Macho) Chávez, a victim of the welfare system, for whom the state had done everything. Medical doctors and community leaders ticked off statistics on East LA from the 1950 Census, when three-quarters of Mexican Americans in Los Angeles had not finished high school. Dr. George Borrell asked, "Do you know that tuberculosis is a serious threat in Mexican-American ghettos? Yes, in our space age, tuberculosis is a serious problem among Mexican-Americans."[18] Borrell attacked the saying "When in Rome do as the Romans do." "Hell, Mexican-Americans aren't interlopers. They were in the Southwest and borderlands hundreds of years before the descendants of the people who now tell Mexican-Americans to 'Americanize.'"

In the third article, Salazar described the "Serape Belt"—the heart of Los Angeles where Mexican Americans live: "Handmade tortillas are bought here by people who don't think of them as exotic food. And at night you can go to a cantina to drink tequila con limon and listen to a mariachi band, relatively certain that no tourists will gape at you."[19] Salazar wrote about Sarita, who had tuberculosis, and Sarita's father and grandfather, hardworking people who never earned above average wages. Salazar took his readers on a tour of the Mexican barrios of San Fernando–Pacoima, Pico Rivera, Pasadena, Covina, and Glendora, using quotations from experts such as Sheldon to interpret and intertwine history, including the Zoot Suit Riots.

The fourth article in the series is titled "Mexican-Americans Lack Political Power." Again, the *Times*'s columnist takes the reader on a tour of Mexican American political history—Senator Dennis Chávez of New Mexico, Congressman Henry B. González of San Antonio, Mayor Raymond Telles of El Paso, Congressman Edward R. Roybal, John Moreno, and Phil Soto of the California Assembly. However, Salazar criticized the piñata politics of Mexican Americans, pointing to the recent splitting of the Mexican American vote in the Ninth Council District when Mexican Americans supported Gilbert Lindsay, a black, over a Mexican American candidate. Salazar also mentioned the failure to incorporate East Los Angeles in 1961.[20]

In the next article, Salazar identified the leaders in the Mexican American community. Relying on Sheldon's data, Salazar shows the diversity of opinion within the Mexican American community, clearly siding with those who wanted to retain their identity and defending ethnic politics. According to attorney Carlos Borja, "History demonstrates that Americans bring to the polls their special backgrounds and pull down the levers congenial to their national origins and religious ties."[21] Salazar completed his series with the theme of a lost identity and zeroed in on the

Treaty of Guadalupe Hidalgo. According to Salazar, white Americans looked at poor Mexicans as a people without a culture, but what they did not seem to realize was that they were protected by the Treaty of Guadalupe Hidalgo. Jesús Hernández, a social worker, told how he was reclaiming the loss of language and identity: "So one day I said to myself: So I'm a Mexican—so what? What's wrong with that? Nothing, I discovered." Hernández and others talked about the unjust Mexican American War and called on Mexican Americans to stop apologizing. Paul Bullock, of UCLA's Institution of Industrial Relations, interjects that three-quarters of the Los Angeles schools did not have Mexican or black students accentuating Mexican American student isolation.[22]

Salazar captured the mood of the community. His columns were based on conversations with community leaders and Mexican American and Euro-American scholars doing research on Mexican Americans. Notre Dame sociologist Julian Samora and George I. Sánchez were important sources. The lack of Mexican Americans was repeated over and over.[23] Before 500 community activists, Sánchez was quoted as bellowing, "Anglos should become Mexicanized gringos so that the advantages of the two dominant cultures in the Southwest can be exploited."[24] Sánchez urged the delegates to apply political pressure. The angry tone of the attendees led Grace Gil-Olivarez, a seminar chair, to say that the conference was "not called for the purpose of discussing discrimination, civil rights and liberties or moral wrongs but instead to take a more positive attitude toward our problems and accomplishments."

A new awareness among Chicana/o youth was emerging. A conference was held by the County Human Relations Commission and industrialist Tobias Kotzin at Camp Hess Kramer in Malibu, California, titled "Spanish-Speaking Youth at the Crossroads." The 100 high school and college students tackled questions such as "Are Mexican-Americans timid and hesitant in aspiring to advance?" "Should agencies other than those existing be set up to help these people?" Roosevelt High student Sally Alonzo, sixteen, reported that her workshop found that "many times we're embarrassed being Mexican-Americans when we should be proud. . . . Actually, we are very fortunate in being bilingual and bicultural. . . . Let's take advantage of these instead of worrying about it." These conferences included junior and senior high students the next years, and many of the participants became leaders in the 1968 East Los Angeles School Walkouts.[25]

As African Americans pushed the civil rights bill, Barry Goldwater's strategy was to feed on the discontent of many white Americans.[26] The Mexican American militancy caused friction between Mexican Americans and African Americans who often looked at civil rights as their exclusive domain. Euro-Americans often fanned the tensions by asking questions such as "How about the Mexicans?" "How about the blacks?" "How about the Asians?" Or "How about the Indians?" It was a way of deflecting questions about injustice toward a particular group.

Fighting over poverty funds increased tensions between black and brown. When a $2 million grant came down for gang prevention and it was earmarked almost exclusively for African Americans, Frank Biamonte of the East Central Area

Welfare Planning Council said that the feds did not understand Mexican Americans, adding that, although the "Negro" problems were legitimate, Mexican Americans had more complex problems, and that the Youth Opportunities Board was missing an opportunity to work with Mexican Americans. Dr. Francisco Bravo complained that the East Side had worked hard to get the funds.[27] The *Chicago Defender* alluded to the tensions between Mexican Americans and blacks, reporting that representatives of the Mexican American community met in a closed session with representatives of the Los Angeles County Human Relations Commission—saying they were not against civil rights but that agency's employees were afraid to anger blacks by giving to Mexicans—often laying off Mexican American workers.[28]

Rumblings in Academe: Not Just a Black Thing

In 1963 Guerra, speaking for MAPA, issued a report charging the California state college system with "*serious discriminatory policies and practices.*" Less than 1 percent of its administrators and faculties were Mexican American. Guerra accused the thirteen state colleges of using arbitrary hiring practices, citing the fact that there was only one department chair of Mexican origin in the system. Three campuses did not have a single Mexican American professor.[29] In September, Salazar reported on the formation of the ad-hoc Los Angeles County Mexican-American Education Committee. It sounded the clarion: "We recognize that an educational philosophy based primarily on the principle of assimilation has proven historically inadequate.... Accordingly, in order that schools may meet the needs of the Mexican-American community, we hold that school boards should establish a strong positive policy towards the acculturation of the Mexican-American child."[30]

The committee called for a curriculum that showed teachers how to teach Mexican American students. This committee was very active, reporting back to their disparate parties cosponsoring conferences with San Fernando Valley State College.[31] In February, Ruben Salazar wrote "What Causes José's Trouble in School?," an article about José Méndez, a sixteen-year-old dropout. Salazar wrote, "He is a 'Mexican' but doesn't have any real affinity for that culture because, after all, he's supposed to be an 'American.'" Educational policy and curriculum are oriented toward the education of the middle-class, monolingual, monocultural, English-speaking student, they contend. This put José at a great disadvantage. At the time, almost a quarter of Mexican Americans in California had less than a fourth grade education.[32]

The Education Committee supported high school teacher Sal Castro in 1964 when he was transferred from Belmont to Lincoln High School. Castro had spoken to Mexican American kids about running for the student council. The majority of the students were Mexican American, but the student government was white and Asian. As a result, he helped them form a political party in 1963. Castro had been involved in the Governor Pat Brown campaign in 1958 and the John F. Kennedy presidential campaign in 1960, so he applied those tactics to the student council race. Castro had them appeal to the "F.S."—foreign students who were mostly

Spanish-speaking—telling them, "You know what? I want you to imitate John Kennedy" and say a couple of words in Spanish. When the administration found out about Castro's involvement, they transferred him to Lincoln High School. The case mobilized the activist community.[33]

The next year the Association of Mexican American Educators (AMAE) formed in Los Angeles, with initial chapters in Los Angeles, Fresno, Sacramento, Madera, and San Diego.[34] A small but important network of concerned educators organized that was also involved in local organizations, such as MAPA and the Latin American Civic Association.

These studies generated discussion among the activists, and there were the inevitable divisions as to what was to be done. On one pole there were those who believed that Mexican Americans should take the example of black Americans and become more militant. The other pole said that Mexican Americans should form alliances with the white community and work through the system. Opportunists such as ultraconservative California superintendent of schools Max Rafferty capitalized on the divisions between Mexican Americans and blacks that competition for War on Poverty funding had widened. Rafferty wrote an article titled "The Forgotten Minority Is Rising" that was a crude attempt to draw a wedge between Mexicans and blacks. "The Negro has been monopolizing the civil rights news of late, to the point that he has come to be identified automatically in the public mind with that worthy cause. But there is another racial minority, confined originally to the Southwest but currently spreading into other states, which has an equal claim to consideration and redress. I'm speaking, of course, of the Mexican-American," said Rafferty.[35]

According to Rafferty, Mexicans were okay because they were not demanding and were pulling themselves up by their own "bootstraps." These divisions came to a head in the 1965 Los Angeles School Board race. MAPA endorsed Manuel Guerra for seat Number 4, and a coalition of Mexican American educators endorsed Ralph Poblano. African American minister Rev. James Edward Jones was endorsed by the black and the Jewish community for open seat number 2. Surprisingly, MAPA endorsed Jones for seat 2 and Poblano lost.[36]

Two years later Julian Nava was elected to the Los Angeles Board of Education. At the time, school board races were run districtwide, and less than 10 percent of the electorate was of Mexican extraction. His campaign manager, Richard Calderón, had mobilized youth and much of the activist sector.[37] Nava's election raised hopes; however, Julian was not a populist, and his style was to work within the system. His goals were curricular changes and hiring more Mexican American educators and administrators. Less than nine months after he was elected, the East Los Angeles walkouts occurred.

Various teachers specialized in Mexican American children. For example, on various campuses Philip Móntez taught classes on the Mexican child, and he sought government funds under the Foundation for Mexican-American Studies. Leonard Olguín and Uvaldo Palomares and his Magic Circle also popularized approaches in Mexican American education by making presentations before white elementary schoolteacher groups. By 1966 separate courses on Mexican Americans were being offered at a handful of institutions. For instance, I taught a course on Mexican Americans at the downtown campus of Mount St. Mary's College. The next summer San Fernando Valley State sponsored an NDEA (National Defense Education Act) institute for teachers on minority history. Nava was codirector and he headed the section of the Mexican American child. The institute was funded for two summers.[38] (Julian was the first Mexican American to earn a PhD in history from Harvard, and in 1968 there were only about a hundred Mexican Americans with doctorates. This was before affirmative action, and most of us relied on the GI Bill, worked full time, and were former high school teachers.)

THUNDER CLOUDS OVER THE LONE STAR

According to the *Brownsville Herald*, "On April 2, [1963,] Anglo-American city councilmen were defeated by a slate of candidates all of Mexican descent. 'Anglo' in terms along the Mexican border means all white persons other than those of Mexican extraction. . . . No people of this spinach-growing center are suffering the pains of a political war. . . . It's Anglo-American vs. Latin-American. 'Gringo' vs. 'Latino.'" The article went on to say, "The Mexican-descended residents are called Latins or Latinos. . . . 14.5 per cent of the population is Caucasian and is referred to as 'The Anglos,' words common to South Texas. There is a small Negro population— .5 per cent."[39] The Mexican American takeover of Crystal City caused a stir among the Euro-Americans, who cast it as another Battle of the Alamo. The Texas Rangers were present throughout the campaign "to serve and to harass" and after the election moved in anticipation of violence. District Attorney Curtis Jackson agitated passions by announcing that he was investigating possible election fraud. Newly elected council member Juan Cornejo responded that his people did not have to buy votes. The victory came after a hard-fought drive led by the International Brotherhood of Teamsters and the newly formed Political Association of Spanish-Speaking Organizations (PASO) to register Mexican Americans. What made it difficult was the poll tax that kept Mexicans from voting. Race discrimination bonded the Mexican American community. Throughout the campaign, the Texas Rangers harassed Los Cinco, as the Mexican American candidates were called. After their victory, a half dozen Rangers moved in, allegedly to keep law and order. The infamous Ranger Captain A. Y. Allee beat Cornejo, which caused a national incident, with U.S. Senator Ralph Yarborough publicly criticizing their brutality.[40]

PASO was an outgrowth of the Viva Kennedy campaign of 1960. For Mexican Americans, it was a historic moment, and San Antonian Alberto Fuentes Jr., the executive secretary of PASO, glowed that it was just the beginning. PASO had plans to take over all of South Texas. The *Brownsville Herald* wrote, "Fuentes noted that the 1960 census showed 800,000 Texans over 21 with Spanish surnames. He thinks the voting strength of Latinos in Texas now must be around 900,000. There are approximately 2.5 million paid-poll-tax voters in the state." Fuentes predicted that PASO had awakened a sleeping giant. However, dissident councilman

Mario Hernández griped that Crystal City had been the work of PASO and the International Brotherhood of Teamsters, whom he called "outsiders." Meanwhile, the losers continued to harass the newly elected council—seizing on every opportunity to charge the newly appointed Mexican American police of malfeasance.

Cornejo was having other problems: LULAC moved into Crystal City after the election and sought to organize a council. A by-invitation-only meeting was held that included out-of-town members as well as "members of the Crystal City Mexican Chamber of Commerce, Crystal City Councilman Mario Hernández and Zavala County Attorney Curtis Jackson." LULAC State Chairman Willie Bonilla, an attorney from Corpus Christi, introduced Richard Villarreal from Corpus Christi, a state executive director for LULAC, and Bill Edwards, state director of LULAC publicity. According to Martin García, the district director of PASO and a law student at St. Mary's in San Antonio, no PASO member had been invited to LULAC's meetings.[41]

According to Tom Henshaw of the *Corpus Christi Caller-Times*, "The little world of Crystal City was content, predictable and mildly prosperous." He described "Juan Conejo, 33, a Teamsters Union business agent who sometimes has to grope for the proper word in English since his formal education ended in 'an average of the eighth grade.'" Henshaw admitted that voting was a difficult pursuit for Mexicans. The poll tax of a $1.75 was hard to come by for Mexican Americans with large families who earned $0.70 a day for fieldwork. The reporter wrote that "the poll tax drive was successful is a measure of Latin resentment and restlessness not fully understood by Crystal City's Anglos who seem to have lost contact with their Latin community." By the registration deadline 1,129 "Latins" had "bought" poll taxes versus 512 whites. The Teamsters helped but contributed no more than $500; their strength was the 300 workers at the California Packing Company in Crystal City that could not be fired and did not fear reprisals.[42]

The splits within the Mexican American Crystal City community were systemic. As mentioned, PASO was born out of the Viva Kennedy campaign of 1960. Kennedy won Texas by a 46,233-vote margin—taking all of South Texas. Mexicans felt that their vote had delivered the Lone Star State to Kennedy. Accommodations were made between established organizations such as LULAC and the GI Forum and the Democratic Party. Meanwhile, PASO leaders had met with Californians and New Mexicans about starting a national political association, but the merger fell through when Texans compromised with the hope of attracting LULAC and the GI Forum members. According to Peña, "I don't know how we came to a Spanish Speaking Organization, but the idea was to, you know, you had the G.I. Forum, you had all these groups and they were all non-political, so we wanted a group where they could all become part of a political group."

A split developed soon afterward. Governor John Connally persuaded Willie Bonilla to run against Peña. The Corpus Christi crowd made Crystal City and the Teamsters an issue. According to the Bonilla supporters, "PASO didn't have no business in Crystal City. They had no business interfering with the city over there." Peña received a standing ovation when he said: "I do not apologize for Crystal

City... And we need more Crystal Cities. This is what PASO is all about. If it isn't, then we don't deserve to be here!"[43] PASO's activist sector, led by Peña, was a new breed. They were not mainly professionals, and, unlike LULAC or the forum, they did not have political contacts. Patronage flowed through Vice President Lyndon B. Johnson, who funneled it through the forum and LULAC. Crystal City unsettled this arrangement. PASO was attractive because it had a bigger tent and was more open to youth. The *New York Times* said of the Crystal City victory: "so far, Crystal City seems to be doing admirably just what those who organized wanted it to do: serve as an example, for the rest of Texas and some other sections of the country, of the power of the ballot box for politically underprivileged groups."[44]

The *Times* article admitted that segregation was unconstitutional but that "social and civic separation remained." The city kept separate tax books, and the Euro-American streets were paved while the Mexican ones were not. Mexican Americans should have won by a landslide. "Registrations now total 1,139 Mexican-Americans and 542 Anglos, and in last April's election the Mexican-American candidates won by an average of 818 to 709." Unlike the LULAC leadership, none of Los Cinco claimed to have more than a tenth grade education. None were from the middle class known to Euro-Americans. Cornejo was a Teamster business agent; Manuel Maldonado, a clerk at an Economart store; Antonio Cárdenas, a truck driver; Reynaldo Méndoza, an operator of a small photography shop; Mario Hernández, a real estate salesman. Cornejo remembered, "Mainly we didn't know each other at all. I knew only one or two of them briefly, but we were not friends at all. All five of us were persons of different walks of life. We had no familiarities whatsoever with one another."[45]

In the spring of 1960 E. C. Muñoz, an insurance salesman, ran for the school board. Muñoz wanted to find out what the board did, as it rarely published its agenda. School board elections were infrequently opposed, so few bothered to vote. Muñoz thought he had a good chance of winning if he turned out the Mexican vote. In a normal election only three hundred votes would be needed. However, when the whites found out that a Mexican was running, they turned out in mass, and Muñoz ran fifth.[46] It was clear that "no Mexicans need apply."

By 1964 the Crystal City Five was imploding. The Association Serving All Americans (CASAA) was formed, which comprised the Crystal City Chamber of Commerce and the Mexican Chamber of Commerce, along with Mexican American middle-class and business people. Cornejo predicted, "They will have the money, but we will have hard work. We'll walk the streets and go door-to door." Jesús (Jesse) Rodríguez, cochairman of CASAA, who owned two of the largest grocery stores in Crystal City, was active for the other side. By September of 1964, personal problems had beset several of the Mexican American council members, including bad checks and unpaid utility bills.[47] In 1965 CASAA swept the city council races. Even with this setback, the symbolic importance of the 1963 takeover cannot be overstated. It inspired youth throughout Texas and up the accordion trail into the Midwest.

Another factor contributing to the disintegration of the coalition was the financial vulnerability of its members. Maldonado, who led the ticket, was fired from

Economart. He had five children, and the council did not pay salaries. Antonio Cárdenas's trucking service cut his salary from $77.44 a week to $35.00. As the *Texas Observer* had predicted on May 16, 1963, "There is going to be a brutal tightening down on Mexicans in every town of South Texas because of what PASO and the Teamsters union so arrogantly pulled off at Crystal City. Race hatred and discrimination will build back up. Whereas if PASO and the Teamsters had been content with a mere majority of three and had not completely shut down the Anglos, the situation would have been entirely different." The *Observer* was the most liberal publication in the Lone Star State. The message was that in Texas it was acceptable to have an all-white body, but not all Mexican.[48]

The *New York Times* in August 1963 ran a lengthy article on the plight of the Mexican American. The theme was that Mexican Americans had a problem that white Americans did not have—language. According to the article, they were encumbered by an educational system that was monolingual and monocultural.[49] Aside from education, Mexican American leaders fought for equal employment rights. Newly elected Texas Congressman Henry B. González pushed the theme of Mexican American job inequality before the Senate labor subcommittee on manpower, asking for the end of the bracero program.[50]

The Invisible Minority

At the time, studies such as the National Education Association (NEA) report, *The Invisible Minority,* motivated Mexican American educators. The theme was how to teach Mexican American students. A powerful condemnation of the state of the education of Mexican American children, the report condemned the schools that taught 1.75 million Spanish surnamed children in the Southwest. It reported that Mexican American children "experience academic failure in school" and that little "headway" was being made. The NEA report praised to Tucson's program for building bilingual bridges. It starts out with a quote from a 13 year old Mexican girl:

ME

To begin with, I am a Mexican. That sentence has a scent of bitterness as it is written. I feel that if it weren't for my nationality I would accomplish more. My being a Mexican has brought about my lack of initiative. No matter what I attempt to do, my dark skin always makes me feel that I will fail.[51]

The report recalled a "Legacy of Hate" toward Mexicans, with the schools treating them as Anglos and wanting them to talk "*American.*"[52] It highlights programs with the strong bilingual education, calling on the schools to conduct research. The New Mexico Department of Education had received a pilot grant for English as a second language.[53] The report singled out a few exceptional programs that studied Spanish masterpieces and used materials from Latin American countries. It proposed specific alternative courses that should be taught in literature, theater, and history, as well as university courses to prepare teachers to teach the Mexican child. It specifically used the term "Cultural Studies."[54]

The NEA report helped form a consensus around bilingual education. Instead of small fragments throughout the country, it bound communities together as well as disparate racial and ethnic groups. Again the inequality of achievement was disturbing. In total, 75 percent of females and 72 percent of males had one or more years of high school—52 percent of Latinas and 48 percent of Latinos had as much education. As John D. Skrentny later put it, these statistics raised the question, "Is this a problem that requires government action?" According to Skrentny, the traditional approach ignored "the unique circumstances of children from Spanish-speaking homes . . . assume[d] that even with little or no experience in speaking English they would somehow learn as easily as their English-speaking classmates. Obviously, this did not happen." The NEA report talked about the "legacy of poverty" and linked it to the dropout problem. Skrentny added, "There is something paradoxical about the schools' well meaning effort to make the Mexican-American child 'talk American'—to eradicate his Spanish." Based on the NEA report, Skrentny concluded that these policies bred withdrawal, damaged self-images, enhanced inferiority complexes, and so on. (Bilingual education became the law of the land for a short time, and the systems went back to Americanizing students. Today the dropout problem is as bad as, if not worse than, fifty years ago.)[55] Language and identity were important weapons in this struggle toward literacy. *The Invisible Minority* report was a prelude to the Bilingual American Education Act of 1967.

NUMBERS, FUNDING, AND YOUTH

John Kennedy appealed to liberals and minorities by announcing his "New Frontier" initiative. A coalition of Republicans and southern Democrats readied to derail his civil rights agenda before he was assassinated in November 1963. Johnson, pushed by black militants, skillfully pushed major civil rights legislation through Congress and launched his Great Society (the so-called War on Poverty).[56] Johnson immediately established a Viva Johnson network headed by Dr. Hector García in Texas and Bert Corona in California. Vicente Ximenes, the ambassador to Ecuador, led the national effort. Ximenes brought in many Mexican American women as volunteers and staff, calling them the "best source of grassroots campaign work." Much of the patronage went through LULAC and the GI Forum. César Chávez and the farmworkers worked independently to support Johnson.[57]

LBJ proposed the Economic Opportunity Act of 1964 to coordinate the War on Poverty through the Office of Economic Opportunity (OEO),[58] which dramatically escalated the Manpower Development and Training Act (MDTA) of 1962. New programs such as the Job Corps, Head Start, Upward Bound, and Volunteers in Service to America (VISTA) fell under the OEO. Congress allocated $1.6 billion annually to eliminate poverty—an amount that, considering the 30–40 million poor living in the United States, did not go very far.[59] Mexican Americans were plugged into the system based on their numbers. Graciela Olivares of Arizona worked her way up the OEO bureaucracy to become Arizona's acting OEO director, but she was bypassed for the permanent position. Olivares was the first Chicana to organize on a national scale when Johnson appointed her to the Equal Employment Opportunity Commission (EEOC).[60]

Throughout this process, tensions increased between local elected officials and the new poverty programs. The politicos did not want minorities to form independent bases. Minorities in turn wanted what they perceived as their part of the pie. Meanwhile, the Vietnam War increasingly siphoned funds from programs. Mexican Americans and other Latinas/os grew frustrated with what they considered *atole con el dedo* (or being strung along). On March 28, 1966, the EEOC held a meeting in Albuquerque, New Mexico, to investigate Chicana/o employment problems. Fifty Chicanas/os, including Graciela Olivares, walked out because, although the commission advocated equal employment, Mexicans were vastly underrepresented on the EEOC staff itself. When asked for a reason, EEOC Executive Director Herman Edelman blamed Mexican American organizations, stating that only 12 of the 300 complaints filed since 1965 had come from Mexican Americans. The dissidents formed the Mexican American Ad Hoc Committee in Equal Employment Opportunity. President Johnson met with selected MAPA, GI Forum, and LULAC leaders at the White House on May 26, 1966, promising them a White House conference. LBJ did not keep his promise, fearing that Mexican American leaders would walk out and embarrass him politically.

In October 1967 Johnson held cabinet committee hearings in El Paso, Texas. He did not invite the leading Chicano activists—César Chávez, Reies López Tijerina, or Rodolfo "Corky" Gonzales. The conference coincided with the celebration of the signing of the Chamizal Treaty—regarding a disputed section of land on the Mexico-Texas border. LULAC and the GI Forum were the largest groups represented at the cabinet committee hearings. A group called La Raza Unida (the United People)—represented by Ernesto Galarza of San José, Corky Gonzales, and Reies López Tijerina—led a picketing of the conference. Representatives of fifty Chicano organizations met at San Antonio and pledged support to the idea of La Raza Unida; about 1,200 people attended.[61]

GENERATIONAL LITERATURE: WHAT WE REMEMBER

By the mid-sixties new studies were shared and debated, often mimeographed and passed around. One such study was Theodore William Parsons's 1965 dissertation, "Ethnic Cleavage in a California School," which underscored the cultural conflict in American society. It spoke of Mexican American eighth graders in Castroville, California, the artichoke capital of the world.[62] Parsons called his town Guadalupe, a town divided into Mexicans and whites following a controversy surrounding the town's church that was run by an Irish American priest who was loved by the whites and who Mexicans were tentative about. The priest called Mexicans sinful and told them that they had to pray more. Whites and Mexicans went to different masses; when Mexicans chose to attend the white mass they sat in the pews in back of the church.[63]

A controversy began when the priest started a fundraising drive for a mosaic of Mary. Donors would have their names put on a plaque as patrons. Among the first donors were two Mexican shopkeepers. Others followed. Not wanting to lose control, ten white farmers (who were in reality Italians) donated $2,000 each, on condition that the Mexican money be used elsewhere and the priest not use it for the mosaic. The church commissioned the mosaic from Italy. When it arrived, Mary was wearing a long red robe. The Mexicans called the figure the Virgén de Guadalupe, since she wore only a red robe. The new Virgin made the Mexicans feel good—it was their church. The Italian farmers were furious. To them, the image represented Mary, La Madonna.[64]

The racial and class division was well defined by the time the children reached kindergarten and they had a clear sense of racial identity. The ethnic cleavage was reinforced in grades K–8. Parsons traces the disparate treatment of Mexican and white students by teachers. In an interview with a teacher Parsons asks, "Do you often choose American children to show the Mexicans what you want them to do?" "I usually do. They need help, like I said, and it is good for the American children to take these responsibilities."[65] Another teacher said, "Most of my girls are fairly well dressed and they all smell good. The boys are the ones that smell like Mexicans."[66] Most whites believed that Mexicans were inferior. Parsons described how the town's social structure reinforced this racial belief. "Village Anglos define as 'high type' those Mexicans who demonstrate idea and behavior patterns most like those of the Anglos themselves."[67] In turn, Mexicans felt that white people only cared about themselves and ran things.

The Guadalupe school was 43 percent Anglo and 57 percent Mexican.[68] Parsons documented how assessments and tracking reinforced the attitude that Mexicans were inferior, which was ingrained by the daily posting of grades. Hence, to Anglos the Mexicans were "stupid; slow witted; unintelligent."[69] A survey showed that 94 percent of white students and 80 percent of Mexicans chose white students as being "smart," and 88 percent of white respondents and 70 percent of Mexicans chose Mexicans as being "dumb."[70]

BILINGUAL-BICULTURAL EDUCATION

During the decade, George I. Sánchez's dicta that American education, not language, was the problem gained currency. A bilingual education included a bilingual-bicultural experience.[71] It was a pedagogy where students were taught in Spanish and transitioned into English. Identity was an important part of the method, which was designed to build students' self-image and motivate them.[72] Lupe Anguiano joined the Department of Health, Education and Welfare and worked tirelessly for a comprehensive program.[73] However, Armando Rodríguez, who became the highest ranking Mexican American in the Office of Education by practicing what some would call the art of the possible, compromised and accepted the principle that bilingual education should be transitional, leading Anguiano to quit and join César Chávez.[74]

In November 1966 the *San Antonio Express* wrote, "First graders at Laredo's United Consolidated school district give the pledge of allegiance to the U.S. flag in Spanish and in English, one language at a time. The pledge begins each day of a highly unusual school program in which mixed classes of Latin and Anglo American children are taught in Spanish and English by bilingual teachers." It continued, "Bilingualism, in several different versions, is one of the most promising ideas brought forward in recent years to overcome Latin language difficulties." The Arizona Education Association asked, "Is bilingual education the answer to the problem of educating 1.75 million Mexican-American children in the five Southwestern states and reducing their very high dropout rate?" The association objected to the NEA's *Invisible Minority* report, calling English an "alien tongue." According to the article, "Critics of the NEA plan say it would tend to segregate Mexican-American children. What they need is not more segregation but less, say the critics."[75] This equivocation unsettled the Mexican American community that was responding to years of "No Spanish" rules in the public schools.[76]

However, the growth of the Mexican American electorate pushed the bill forward. The 1968 elections were on the horizon. On May 24, 1967, California Governor Ronald Reagan signed a bill into law that allowed bilingual education when "educationally advantageous to pupils." Even ultra-conservative U.S. Senator George Murphy, another actor turned politico, lamented that 50 percent of Mexican American pupils were dropping out of school: "This is a shocking statistic and I have reason to believe that the language problem contributes to this unfortunate situation." Republican Senator Thomas Kuchel of California also said that we should treat the ability to speak Spanish and other foreign languages as an asset.[77] In 1967 there appeared to be consensus that bilingual education was effective. Even Sen. Paul Fannin (R-Arizona) said, "children from different cultural backgrounds, especially those in which English is not the native language, have special needs requiring a special education. . . . It is a difficult task for any child to overcome the effects of a disadvantaged childhood, but it's an educational impracticability for a child to rise above the combined effects of a disadvantaged youth and a language barrier."[78] The mood would change within two decades as the nativists without evidence attacked bilingual education as un-American.

RAIN CLOUDS SPREAD OVER AZTLÁN

Government agencies funded conferences on the best way to implement programs such as Head Start.[79] Not all functionaries working for antipoverty agencies were poverty pimps—the vast majority were committed. Funding for teacher training programs often paid institutions of higher learning to do the right thing and sponsor teacher institutes and implement programs. For example, a public information officer for the Office of Economic Opportunity (OEO) told a local Lubbock, Texas, newspaper, "We are not saying that Lubbock's Head Start funds (approximately $202,000) will be cut off if Lubbock school authorities do not hire Mexican-American teachers. . . . We do say that if Lubbock does not hire some Mexican-American teachers, we will consider this when we allocate funds." The OEO had asked the Lubbock schools to hire eight Mexican American teachers, as 70 percent of the students were Mexican American. Lubbock, however, continued to resist integration.[80]

Mexican migrants fanned throughout the Pacific Northwest and Midwest, where they organized for better wages, housing, and education. During the peak of the harvesting season, as many as 25,000 migrant Mexicans resided in the state of Washington. Migrant children attended only twenty-one weeks of the school year. The Washington Citizens for Migrant Affairs pointed out that the migrant family had a median education of five years. The heart of the migrant community was in the agriculturally rich Yakima Valley, where in 1965 the Yakima Valley Council for Community Action organized to coordinate War on Poverty programs. The next year, Tomás Villanueva and Guadalupe Gamboa from Yakima Valley College traveled to California, where they met with César Chávez. In 1967 Villanueva helped organize the first Chicano activist organization in Washington. The Mexican American Federation was organized that year in Yakima to advocate for community development and political empowerment in the Yakima Valley. In May of that year, Big Bend Community College raised expectations by receiving a $500,000 grant for basic education of 200 migrants.[81]

Led by Lansing, Michigan, barber Ruben Alfaro, migrants, laborers, and students from Michigan State marched on the state capitol hoping to get a commitment from Gov. George Romney, to veto any legislation that would "take away the human dignity of the migrant workers." Michigan had more than 100,000 migrants. Romney refused to take a stand. The migrants were supported by the AFL-CIO "in their crusade for better pay, housing, medical care and education for the migrants' children." Alfaro received the support of César Chávez and the United Farm Workers and Sen. Robert F. Kennedy, who sent a telegram ending with "*Viva La Causa!*" They marched from Saginaw to Lansing, announcing, "Governor, our feet are sore. . . . Some of us have walked more than 70 miles to tell you about our problems." They handed the lieutenant governor their petition. The news reporter described the scene: "They held American and Mexican flags, and banners depicting the Virgin of Guadalupe— revered saint of Mexico. Hand-lettered signs carried such slogans as 'Viva La Causa,' 'Human Dignity for Migrant Workers' and 'Chicken Coops are for the Bird.'"[82] Mexican Americans did not get immediate relief, but Michigan eventually developed one of the best-endowed college programs for the children of migrant workers.

Wisconsin had about 11,000 migrants that trekked into the state during the harvest season from the sugar beet factory farms of Colorado, the strawberry fields of neighboring Illinois, and the year-round citrus orchards of Texas, where accounts said 5,000 pickers would pile on to trucks for towns such as Wautoma to pick cucumbers and other crops. At Wautoma, Manuel Salas, a labor contractor for Libby, McNeil and Libby, owned the town's only Mexican restaurant. His son Jesús Salas broke with his father and organized Obreros Unidos. Twenty-two in 1966, he led a sixty-mile march on Madison for better housing and treatment of migrants. His goal was a contract with Libby. A student at Stevens Point University, Salas delayed his college education to organize farmworkers; his family was from Crystal City and was motivated by PASO's 1963 takeover, where he was in contact with MAYO leaders.[83] He matriculated at the University of Wisconsin, Milwaukee, fighting for the admission of Chicanas/os into higher education. In 2003 he was appointed to the Board of Regents of the University of Wisconsin but resigned four years later when the governor betrayed his trust and supported punitive measures against undocumented immigrants.[84]

Arizona and New Mexico also had rich histories of struggle for education reform. In the 1910s La Alianza Hispano Americana and La Liga Protectora called for education reform, including adult and bilingual education. In 1925 the first desegregation case was filed against the Tempe School District.[85] In the 1930s many Mexican American youth were involved in the Mexican American Movement (MAM) that held conferences and advocated education for the community. It had strong ties with the Protestant community. A contingent attended Arizona State Teachers' College, where in 1937 Josephine and Rebecca Muñoz were among those who formed Los Conquistadores, the first Mexican American club at Arizona State University (then a teachers' college).

Throughout the 1960s César Chávez and the United Farm Workers were the leading Mexican American civil rights organization fighting for the rights of the most exploited sector of the community. Struggling against all odds, he was embroiled in a fight with the Delano, California grape growers. In 1965, Chávez called a secondary boycott against Delano grape growers to force them to come to the bargaining table. The boycott became part of the Mexican rights movement's civil rights agenda and was supported by all sectors of the Mexican American community as well as progressives.

In 1968 Alfredo Gutiérrez, who had been with the grape boycott since 1965, was a student at Arizona State University. He, along with graduate student Miguel Montiel, took over Liga Pan Americana, which had descended from MAM. They changed the name of the organization to the Mexican American Student Organization (MASO). Among the early activists were María Rose Garrido and Christine Marín. MASO developed strong ties with Gustavo Gutiérrez and the Arizona Farm Workers, which had ties to the United Farm Workers. The group was community oriented, led sit-ins, and supported the grape boycott.

In Tucson, Salomón Baldenegro was radicalized by the racism around him. As a youth, he was sent to Arizona Industrial School for Wayward Boys and Girls at Fort Grant for rebelling against schools authorities. His stay there left Baldenegro with a strong sense of justice and identification with the civil rights, antiwar, and labor movements, which led to his involvement in the civil rights movement at the University of Arizona. He recruited Raúl Grijalva, Guadalupe Castillo, and later

Isabel García as high school students. At the University of Arizona in 1967 he formed the Mexican American Liberation Committee and advocated bilingual and Mexican culture classes. This organization evolved into the Mexican American Student Association (MASA).[86]

At this point, the enclaves in the Midwest and Northwest were calling for school reform and students that mirrored many of the demands in the Southwest. Indeed, many students were originally from Texas. As with other states, the mass and direct action campaigns of the National Farm Workers Association (United Farm Workers) impacted students beginning in 1965.

New Mexico did not lack local organizations. Mexican Americans composed some 40 percent of the state, and most were eligible to vote. They had local, state, and federal elected officials. At its height, LULAC had nineteen councils. The Asociación Nacional Mexicana-Americana (ANMA) was founded in New Mexico in 1949; the miners' union had an impact on many Mexican Americans.[87] The main focus of many of the organizations was education. U.S. Senator Joseph Montoya was from New Mexico, where politics were based on ethnicity. The state had a large farmworker population and was influenced by César Chávez. Additional motivation came from Reies López Tijerina and his La Alianza Federal de Pueblos Libres. Tijerina appealed to students and the public through the theme of retaking the lands stolen from Mexicans by Euro-American settlers. Tijerina was known in most northern New Mexico provinces by 1962; four years later, La Alianza claimed 20,000 members.

The front line of the struggle of Mexican Americans was schools. The University of New Mexico had an interest in how to teach Mexican children. According to New Mexico Highlands University Professor Maurilio Eutimio Vigil, four basic problems plagued New Mexico: the suppression of Spanish language, history classes that did not reflect the Mexican American experience, a lack of Mexican American teachers, and the failure of school counseling programs. The year 1968 crystallized the protests against the schools at Albuquerque, Las Vegas, Española, Portales, Roswell, and Santa Fe. That year the Brown Berets and the Black Berets began operating in Albuquerque. The latter wore black berets in honor of Che Guevara. That same year in the northern part of the state, *El Grito del Norte* began publication.[88] The Mexican American Youth Association (later the Chicano Youth Association) began to appear on campuses.

At New Mexico Highlands University in Las Vegas, New Mexico, where in 1946 World War II veterans formed Alpha Zeta Iota. One of the founders was Donald A. Martínez, later known as Tiny. Highlands was a home for activist Chicanas/os and displayed a strong ethnic identity. By 1969 the Spanish American Students Association (SASO) was formed. By 1970 it presented demands for Chicano Studies and a reorganization of the College of Education to meet the needs of Mexican children. Martínez, the political boss of the area, wanted a Mexican American president for Highlands. He alternately served as district attorney and member of the Las Vegas School Board. SASO was at the forefront of this campaign and changed its name to Chicano Student Association.[89]

THE NOTION OF CHICANO STUDIES

World War II and the Korean War had made it possible for a small number of Mexican Americans to complete college. Some were teachers aware of the plight of the Mexican American people. The notion of classes teaching about Mexicans in the motherland and in the United States was current by the mid-1960s. Los Angeles State College was a natural receptor of this population, charging under ten dollars in fees as late as the 1950s. The state of California paid the entire tab, unlike today when student fees pay for a third of the cost of the California State University system's $5 billion budget. Many joined local organizations, and others vied for War on Poverty jobs, which subsidized training classes at the junior and four-year colleges. They received further exposure to programs through teacher institutes funded by the federal government.[90]

As such, many of us were introduced to the work of Edwin Fenton and other progressive educators.[91] Fenton's work predated Paulo Freire's *Pedagogy of the Oppressed*, written in 1968 and published in Spanish and English in 1970.[92] I used Fenton's methodology in two children's books and a high school/junior college text.[93] Most of us were also active in the Southern California chapter of National Council for the Social Studies, which at the time was under the sway of Fenton, who argued for a return to a Socratic method that involved the student in finding answers as an alternative to learning through a reductive process. The council took control of the state Textbook Adoption Committee, leading to an all-out fight with ultraconservative California State Superintendent of Schools Max Rafferty, who led the fight against the U.S. history text *Land of the Free*.[94] The disagreement became so heated that Rafferty labeled the inductive method subversive because it taught students to question.[95]

My dissertation on the "Age of Reform in Sonora, Mexico," was defended in 1968. My terminal degree was in Latin American Studies. In 1966 I became the chair of the advisory committee of the Latin American Civic Association's Head Start program, where I participated in the inevitable fights with other communities for funds and control of the program.[96] I accepted a position at Dominguez Hills College, where I developed courses on Mexican American and Latin American histories.[97] It was at Dominguez Hills that I learned the mechanics of area studies. At Dominguez Hills, every student had to have two majors, an area and a discipline. The areas were American, Asian, African, European, or Latin American studies. Since I was an early hire, I learned to write course proposals within this system, which complemented my high school and junior college experiences.[98]

A COMMON VOCABULARY: RACISM, DISCRIMINATION, AND INEQUALITY

The categories of "race" and "Mexican American" were not found in the *Los Angeles Times* until 1963, the year before the Los Angeles paper introduced "disadvantaged Americans." Otto Santa Ana's cognitive metaphor theory suggested that the euphemism "disadvantaged Americans" was applied to veer attention away from the notion of race and minimize paradoxes such as segregation and discrimination. The term automatically applied to blacks, and as a group it became more obvious to Mexicans. "The entailment disassociates institutional strictures from the disadvantaged student, as well as from the privileged student, as if each walks along unfettered on identical educational paths. This dissolves or atomizes the student's structural relationship to the school." The assumption is that if you remove the disadvantage everything will be equal, regardless of the color of the person's skin. It says nothing about racial oppression.[99]

The term was raised at the 100th annual convention of the NEA to deflect criticisms of the John Birch Society and "the thunder on the right." According to columnist Joe Rust of San Antonio, the term "disadvantaged Americans" was dubbed by the Educational Policies Commission, a joint agency of the NEA and the American Association of School Administrators, which predicted that the "disadvantaged would make up half the nation's population by 1970," and that if educators failed to face up "to special problems—their migration generates," American values would be endangered, and minorities would become "ignorant, incompetent, maladjusted charges on the community. The NEA's Educational Policies Commission went on to say that these new city dwellers are "culturally deprived persons whose habits and customs place them at a severe disadvantage when they come in contact with modern urban life." The "new city dwellers" were blacks from the South, Appalachian whites, Puerto Ricans, reservation Indians, and Mexican Americans. Rust specified the urban dwellers in San Antonio. Their schooling presented special problems to the average middle-class child. According to the EPC, "cherished American values are at stake, and the economic well-being, the stability and the security of the nation is undermined by the present waste of human potential."[100]

Vice President Lyndon Johnson politically charged the term "equality." At an Equal Employment Opportunities conference on November 14, 1963, at the Ambassador Hotel in Los Angeles, he said, "What we really seek, and I believe what really lies in our hearts—is a system where all of us from the standpoint of opportunity are the majority and there is no doubt in my mind when artificial barriers are removed, we will find that all of us are in the majority after all."[101] The sincerity of the statement was challenged by Dr. George I. Sánchez, who said that Johnson had manipulated the conference. Ramón Castro, a spokesman for the group, said that Mexican Americans had been "taken." The group told Celebrezze that he was not prepared to listen to the problems of Mexican Americans. He thought that their problem was integration. It is obvious that the group was seeking a separate identification from blacks. In another world, the dissidents could have been silenced, but numbers were getting to mean something.

More attention was paid by the press in 1964 to middle-class Mexican Americans. "Twenty-five years ago, who would have thought a Mexican-American could ever become postmaster of Santa Ana? Certainly not Hector Godínez, the present postal chief. Godínez was just another 'dirty Mexican' then 'lazy, mentally retarded, unworthy of this country.' That's how many people regarded Mexican-Americans in those days."[102] The theme of most articles at the time was that for Mexican American to make it they had to get "out of the Barrio" to find the American Dream. The dream could be found in places such as Orange County, where Mexican Americans were better off than in the Serape Belt.

This theme was countered, and some questioned the definition of "equality." "We who have heard the cries of hungry migrant children and seen the poverty of so many, who have seen indignity heaped upon indignity know that the promise of America is not complete," said Representative Henry B. González at a GI Forum convention.[103] Movements led by César Chávez and the farmworkers reminded Mexican Americans and others of inequality. Disadvantage was more complex than residence or making more money. In San Antonio, Father Sherrill Smith said, "I don't see how the church can be silent and be witness to injustice. Necessarily, it must speak through persons . . . bishops . . . priests." Father Smith began Project Equality, which told businesses supplying goods or services to the archdiocese "to take affirmative steps to hire and promote Mexican-Americans, Negroes and other minority persons," in addition to providing the archdiocese with a breakdown of the company's total labor force by ethnic group, race, and job category.[104] Meanwhile, the Black Power movement was taking the definition of "equality" to another level.[105]

CHAPTER 3

From Student Power
to Chicano Studies

By the end of the 1960s, 85 percent of Mexican Americans lived in urban spaces, 50 percent lived in California, 34 percent in Texas, and over a million in Los Angeles, making it the second largest Mexican city after Mexico City. The median age was 20.2, suggesting that most Mexican Americans were youth, a population that had doubled during the decade. Eighty-four percent were born in the United States, and only a fourth of Spanish-surname people held white-collar jobs. The decade gave Mexican American youth greater access to information—television, radio, and newspapers—they had more mobility than at any other time in history. However, none of this really explains fully how and why the perfect storm came together in the late 1960s.[1]

THE RISE OF THE MEXICAN AMERICAN YOUTH ORGANIZATION

Most of the Mexican American civil rights cases up to World War II originated in Texas, which had the largest repository of Mexicans in the United States. As early as 1910, parents in San Angelo, Texas, boycotted the schools because of segregated facilities. In September 1911, Tejanos convened El Primer Congreso Mexicanista, a conference that addressed educational reform. After World War I, an awareness of educational reform increased, and with the formation of the League of United Latin American Citizens (LULAC) the Mexican origin community sued local school districts. This activity continued into the 1950s. Led by Chicano attorney Gus García, they appeared before the U.S. Supreme Court. This fervor for education reform exploded in the sixties and was marked by the growth of the Mexican American Youth Organization (MAYO), which developed a strategy to take over school boards. At the forefront of educational reform was how to teach Mexican children and how to develop a positive self-image.[2]

As mentioned, the PASO 1963 Crystal City takeover proved that it could be done— that there was another way besides going through the existing social structure. By 1965 more moderate members of PASO returned to traditional politics, leaving the organization in the hands of left-leaning activists and political officials. This opened space for further progressive elements. An example was the La Casita Farms Corporation strike of 1966 that Tejano sociologist David Montejano calls the catalyst for the Chicano movement in Texas. The strike was supported by clergy, white progressives, and Mexican American students from Texas A&I University and future MAYO leaders throughout the state.[3]

The brutality of the Texas Rangers during the La Casita strike politicized students and activists. A march on Austin to petition the governor drew the political line, with Governor John Connally refusing to meet with the marchers in Austin. Having left in June, the marchers arrived at the state capitol in time for a Labor Day rally. The Rio Grande Valley was a battle zone, with arrests continuing in Rio Grande City through 1966 into 1967.

The United Farm Workers Organizing Committee (UFWOC; aka NFWA) placed a picket line on the international bridge at Roma on October 24, 1966, trying to persuade green-carders to turn back. Mass arrests were made for obstructing a bridge. Violence increased as the spring melon crop ripened and time neared for the May harvest. In June, when beatings of two UFWOC supporters by Texas rangers surfaced, tempers flared.[4]

The strike collapsed when the union was unable to stop commuters from Mexico from crossing the picket line. However, the strike brought attention to conditions in the Lone Star State. The Civil Rights Committee of Texas, headed by Carlos Turán, exposed the Texas Rangers' outrageous behavior. A Congressional Committee on Migratory Labor, headed by Senator Ted Kennedy and Senator Yarborough of Texas, also exposed the sorrowful state of Mexicans in the Rio Grande Valley. Willie Velásquez, later a MAYO founder, served as a committee chair. María Elena Martínez, who later became a member of MAYO and was the first woman to chair the La Raza Unida Party, cut her teeth on the strike. Because of La Casita, Texas became a social movement with boycott committees set up throughout Texas.[5] As the *Big Spring Herald* put it, "The strike is confined to part of the Lower Rio Grande Valley, made up of Starr, Hidalgo, Cameron and Willacy counties. An estimated 40,000 migrant farm laborers live in the Valley and leave annually to follow harvests across the nation."[6] Through these migrant corridors farmworkers exported their memories.[7]

MAYO was established in San Antonio in the heat of the Casitas strike in the spring of 1967. The founding members were José Ángel Gutiérrez, Willie C. Velásquez, Mario Compeán, Ignacio Pérez, and Juan Patlán. MAYO recruited Mexican American youth and university students.[8] Some students, like Gutiérrez, had studied under political science professor Charles Cotrell at Texas A&I University and St Mary's College in San Antonio. They were well aware of the Student Non-violent Coordinating Committee, Stokely Carmichael, the SDS (Students for a Democratic Society), the Port Huron statement, and the black civil rights movement. MAYO played an essential role in mobilizing students.[9]

The actions that brought MAYO to statewide and national attention were the high school walkouts. In the span of two years MAYO led at least thirty-nine walkouts, using them to recruit members and to advertise their numbers. MAYO empowered Mexican Americans and in turn seized control of school boards throughout the state. Inside a year, it established thirty chapters, with a total membership of 1,000. They debated school reform, which could only be affected by exerting power. During the major walkouts MAYO's mind-set was that of plans and takeovers. Each walkout was headed by a MAYO member from the high school or area. Willie Velásquez and Mario Compeán were in San Antonio, and Velásquez recruited priests, the Bishop's Committee, and the U.S. Commission on Civil Rights, contacts that he had made during the La Casita strike.[10]

The Making of a Movement

The first Texas walkouts occurred at Lanier High School in San Antonio on April 9, 1968. Teachers did not approve the students' nominees for student council and suspended student council member Elida Aguilar for insubordination. Seven hundred students walked out, demanding more academic courses, the right to speak Spanish, and more democracy. More to the point was the student demand for Mexican American history and culture classes. Students said the schools did not prepare them for college, and they turned to community leaders for support.

Willie Velásquez and MAYO organizers persuaded the students to form a coordinating committee and to incorporate larger concerns into their demands. This committee went after the school's revenue base, a favorite MAYO tactic. The importance of the strike was that, along with other walkouts, it would create momentum. Among early supporters were the Neighborhood Youth Corp, the Bishops Committee for Spanish Speaking, state senator Joe Bernal, Bexar County commissioner Alberto Peña, and San Antonio councilman Felix Treviño.[11]

The community meetings at the Guadalupe Church resembled rallies. The *San Antonio Light* reported Peña receiving a standing ovation as he told the gathering, "We're handicapped because we have an educational system that doesn't understand bilingual students."[12] Meetings continued throughout the week. The superintendent of the San Antonio District responded that the district was doing most of what the students were demanding and would have to get approval from the Texas Education Agency to offer a course on Mexican American history and culture. Peña said the youths deserved "broad support" and attacked the "old bugaboo that it's degrading or un-American to speak Spanish anywhere you please."[13]

A walkout was averted at South San Antonio High School less than a week after the Lanier walkout. Superintendent Max Fuentes Jr. charged that teachers were inciting students over the firing of a principal and teacher. The teachers threatened that 90 percent of their members would walk out and that the National Education Association would place sanctions on the district.[14] On May 16 students walked out, protesting racist policies and inadequate funding at Edgewood and Lanier and several south Texas high schools. "In the spring of 1968, 16-year-old Diana Briseno Herrera watched her Edgewood classmates spill out onto 34th Street. She was reluctant to join in. 'Because I believed in the system,' she says. 'I truly believed it would take care of its children, and the system did not.'"[15]

Among the supporters were parents, university students, clergy, and other activists. Janie Hilgen, a young Edgewood English teacher, stood with the students and told a newspaper reporter "their demands are not excessive." One demand was for the "extermination of mice, rats and roaches." Hilgen was one of two teachers suspended.[16] At Edgewood, Lanier, and several south Texas high schools, thousands of students protested against what they viewed as racist administrators, policies, and curriculum.

Velásquez, then a graduate student at St. Mary's University, exhorted the Edgewood students. "With the education you get at Edgewood, most of you are going to wind up either in Vietnam or as a ditch digger. . . . At Jefferson, Alamo Heights or Lee, there is a chance that you'll go to college. But 85 per cent of you will not go—$80 a week is the most you will earn the rest of your life. . . . Tell [Bennie F. Stemhauser] this is the problem."[17]

The walkout continued into the next day with signs reading "Better Education Now—Not Tomorrow," "We Want a CPA to Audit School Funds," "Texas Education Agency—Evaluate Edgewood," and "Let Teachers Teach What They Are Trained to Teach." An impasse continued, and on May 21, according to the *San Antonio Light*, "support from several quarters was promised to about 500 students and parents gathered at Holy Cross High School to discuss a campaign that includes a suit against the Edgewood School District for allegedly violating students' civil rights, investigation of the district's accounting books by the Department of Health, Education and Welfare (HEW), and a second walkout by students."[18]

The walkout students ended the boycott on Sunday, May 19, to show that they were not walking out on education.[19] The district was unable to attract qualified teachers. The all-Mexican Edgewood high spent $356 per student annually versus $594 at Alamo Heights, which was predominately white. On June 30, Demetro Rodríguez, Martin Cantú, Reynaldo Castañono, and Alberta Snid filed a suit against San Antonio in the federal district court citing the inequality in funding.[20] MAYO's objective was the political takeover of south Texas. Organization was based on the Texas experience: a study of Mexican history, family values, Tejano music, and the Spanish language.[21]

The first walkout in the Rio Grande Valley was at Edouch-Elsa High (and middle school) in Hidalgo County. Numerous incidents triggered the walkout. For example, Uvaldo Vásquez was publicly admonished for asking another student during a gym class, "*dame la pelota*" (give me the ball). In another instance, a counselor advised a Mexican girl to drop out because she was pregnant. Her friend confronted the counselor, and he was suspended for three days. Another student was told to cut his sideburns, although the rule was not applied to whites. By mid-October parents began informal meetings. Attending these meetings were a few MAYO, VISTA, and PASO members. The chair was Jesús Ramírez, a MAYO volunteer. A Mexican American teacher attempted to dissuade students from attending the meetings. State Senator Joe Bernal and Dr. Hector García, the founder of the GI Forum, were present. Bernal said, "these students are saying what we [the older generations of Mexican Americans] were saying when we were young or students . . . . they are asking for dignity and self-respect."[22] Nevertheless, the school board refused to meet with the students to discuss their grievances.

On November 13, the students rose from their desks and walked out "after the school board refused to call a special session to hear the demands." Upon the advice of MAYO organizers, they rallied around the flagpole and sang the "Star-Spangled Banner." The school officials bypassed the local police and reported the walkout to county sheriffs, who arrested Artemio Salinas (senior), Homer Treviño (senior), Xavier Ramírez (senior), Freddy Sáenz (sophomore), Raul Arispe (senior), and Mirtala Villarreal (junior). Villarreal was released, and the other five were held overnight. The complaint was signed by the school's principal, Melvin Pipkin, who issued the following statement: "We will not yield one iota as long as I am principal. . . . The students will not dictate the policy." He suspended 168 students for three days. This mobilized the community. Attorney Bob Sánchez, representing the students, said, "Some of the teachers here think they are teaching a bunch of animals. . . . Mexican Americans are not animals."[23]

The loathsome "No Spanish" rule was in force, although denied by the superintendent, A. W. Bell, who said, "We don't prohibit Spanish. We encourage English." Student Raul Arispe responded, "They gave you a choice. It was either bend over and take 5, 10, or 15 licks *con una tabla, un bate cortado por la mitad* [with a piece of wood, a bat cut in half], or get expelled." Another demand was to add courses on Mexican American history and culture. Attorney Sánchez urged the board to look for books on the Mexican American contributions to Texas history, and students demanded courses and counseling to prepare them for college and to put an end to discrimination against Mexican Americans.[24]

On November 18, 1968, at a pretrial hearing, federal court Judge Reynaldo Garza ruled that the school district could only legally expel a student after a hearing. On November 22 the Mexican American Legal Defense and Education Fund (MALDEF) filed a suit on behalf of the five expelled students, alleging that the district was denying the plaintiffs their constitutional rights to an education under the Fourteenth Amendment. Garza ordered the board to hold hearings for all 150 students before they expelled them. On November 26 all but thirty-one had school board hearings. On December 3 thirty-one of the expelled students sought to register in other districts, who refused to take them. On December 10, the La Joya Independent School District accepted them, and the parents bought a bus to transport the students to La Joya. Meanwhile, the court found the board policy unconstitutional, and the board agreed to readmit the students. The case was a major victory for the recently organized MALDEF.[25]

According to José Ángel Gutiérrez, MAYO participated in thirty-nine walkouts before the one in Crystal City in December 1969. Beachheads were established at struck schools, with local MAYO members leading walkouts in communities where they grew up. They hit a common nerve that many of the adults identified with: the right to speak Spanish, the right to learn about Mexican American history, the right

to get a quality education, and the right to schools free of discrimination. The walkouts started a movement, bringing to the surface the community's moral outrage.

THE EAST LOS ANGELES WALKOUTS

The first rumblings occurred in Los Angeles on March 1, 1968, at Wilson High
School over the cancellation of the play *Barefoot in the Park*. About 250 students
rallied at noon as students pelted teachers with food and eggs. Eight students were
suspended, and a walkout was averted. The principal alleged that student and community organizations were encouraging students to walk out.[26] On March 5, 2,700
of 3,750 Garfield High students walked out, and the sheriff arrested two students.
At Jefferson High, a predominately black school, 700 of the school's 1,900 students
boycotted the cafeteria and assembled on the athletic field. The next day walkouts
continued at Garfield and spread to Lincoln High.[27] According to the *Los Angeles
Times*, "They carried signs which said 'no more fences [around the school],'
'smaller classes,' 'strike now' and 'Chicano power.'" The *Times* named the Brown
Berets and the United Mexican American Students (UMAS) as instigators. Others
supporting the strike were high school students, college students, and the general
community. Coordinating the walkouts and, more important, keeping the disparate factions together was Lincoln High School teacher Sal Castro, who built on
a network that had been forged by students attending the County Human
Relations Commission's Mexican American youth conferences since 1963. The
Camp Hess Kramer alumni met with Castro several months before the walkout,
planning every phrase. Castro also met with members of the recently formed
UMAS, who acted as his cadre. Meanwhile, the Los Angeles police and sheriff
deputies harassed the student strikers and physically abused them.[28] The strike
spread to Wilson and Roosevelt. Nineteen juveniles and one adult were arrested.
The Los Angeles School Board agreed to a special meeting. Student Robert
Rodríguez said, "If we get the board here . . . we won't have to walk out. Once they
listen they will agree with what we want." There was unrest at other campuses, and
six young girls were arrested at Belmont High for congregating.[29]

On March 11, after a tumultuous meeting with over 500 students and parents
present, the Board of Education members agreed to most of the student demands.
The board voted to hold a special meeting at Lincoln High. Rumblings continued
at Jefferson and at Venice High School. The concessions satisfied only a few.
John Ortiz, representing the Garfield high student strike committee, said, "We will
not have a special session of the board until the police are removed from the
campuses."[30]

Boycotts continued at Venice High, where eight students were arrested. Among
them was a young female student who police roughed up for allegedly making
an obscene gesture. Fistfights broke out between students and police. Rumblings
occurred at junior high schools. Police and school authorities were determined to
hold the line with the Mexican American students. In contrast, they conceded
to the black student demands at Jefferson and announced the appointment of

a black principal, vice principal, and counselor.[31] Meanwhile, the faculty supported some of the demands but did not agree with the abolishment of IQ tests, and while they supported the upgrading of plant facilities, they said, "In general, the Mexican-American family does not emphasize education to the degree necessary in the total society. This apathy, in turn, leads to many problems inherent in the high school years of the student."[32]

A cornerstone demand was that the "textbooks and curriculum should be revised to show Mexican contributions to society and to show injustices they have suffered." The thirty-eight demands were simply that Mexican American schools should be made more accountable and equal to white schools.[33] Castro told board members that the students would walk out again, that the community was behind them, and that it was imperative to teach Mexican Americans and blacks about their heritage. Superintendent Jack Crowther continued to take a hard line, saying students would be treated as truants. Moreover, teachers were critical of the demands for more Mexican American teachers and criticized board member Julian Nava.[34] The conflict was strung out for over six months and was tainted by the indictment of Castro and twelve others on conspiracy charges.[35]

INTELLECTUAL CURRENTS

By 1968 a youth network had formed that was a conduit for ideas and information in the Mexican American community. Much of the information came by word of mouth. Even information from the farmworkers flowed through activist corridors. On May 13, 1967, an estimated 150–200 college and high school students from fourteen campuses met at Loyola University to discuss consolidating existing student organizations. The all-day conference was cosponsored by the Los Angeles County Human Relations Commission. Much of the conference leadership was involved in off-campus affairs, including the 1964 "No on 14" initiative that sought to make fair housing unconstitutional. The group sought to bring the various chapters together under UMAS and followed up with a December statewide conference.[36]

Influenced by the "Third Worldism" of northern California and the radical rhetoric of the Berkeley, San José, and Bay Area, the Chicana/o student leadership was evolving. They discussed New Mexico land issues, bilingual and bicultural education, the high drop-out rate, the inequality of educational opportunity, the draft, the disproportionate number of Chicanos dying in the Vietnam War, the farmworkers, political inequities, and discrimination. While nationalism remained a binding force, students were becoming more issues oriented.

That same year Berkeley professor Octavio Romano founded Quinto Sol Publications, which published *El Grito: A Journal of Contemporary Mexican-American Thought*, a self-supporting cultural magazine of Mexican American thought and cultural and artistic production. Romano cofounded the publication with Nick C. Vaca.[37] The first editorial began, "Contrary to the general pattern of ethnic minorities in the history of the United States, Mexican-Americans have retained their distinct identity and have refused to disappear into The Great American Melting Pot."

According to *El Grito*, in response to this resistance the United States has "produced an ideological rhetoric that serves to neatly explain away both the oppressive and exploitive factors maintaining Mexican-Americans in their economically impoverished conditions. . . . this rhetoric has been professional certified and institutionally sanctified to the point where today it holds wide public acceptance."[38] *El Grito*'s main foe was the stereotypical representation of the Mexican American. Romano proposed that "only Mexican-Americans themselves can accomplish the collapse of this and other such rhetorical structures by the exposure of their fallacious nature and the development of intellectual alternatives. . . . *El Grito* has been founded for just this purpose." It was a manifesto that merged with the student turmoil and fed the growing movement. *El Grito* expressed the temper of the times and the Chicano student movement. It included not only the social sciences but also Mexican American education, literature, and art.

The farmworkers' metaphors were a vital part of the nurturing of the Mexican American generation and Chicana/o youth. Although few worked in the fields, youth were only one generation away from this type of labor. In 1969 nearly 82 percent of Mexican Americans were native-born U.S. citizens, but 43 percent of the native-born had at least one parent born in Mexico.[39] In 1960, 16 percent of the male Spanish-surnamed population in the Southwest was farm laborers—not counting spouses and children who were involved in fieldwork—versus only 3.9 percent who were professionals. Mexican Americans supported the farmworkers. The NFWA flag, the black eagle, and the grape boycott were part of their consciousness building.[40]

Rodolfo "Corky" Gonzales and the Crusade for Justice nourished the movement. Colorado was not California. In 1970 Colorado had a total population of 2,210,000; New Mexico had 1,017,000; Arizona, 1,775,000; California, 19,971,000; and Texas, 11,199,000. Mexican Americans were 10 percent of Colorado, 30 percent of New Mexico, 15 percent of Arizona, 12 percent of California, and 16 percent of Texas.[41] Colorado was a relatively small state, with much of its Mexican population concentrated in the southern part of the state, more akin to northern New Mexico than Denver. Like Los Angeles, Corky and his followers were for the most part not native Spanish speakers. Corky grew up in a mean eastside barrio of Denver during the Depression. After a career in boxing, where he was a contender, Corky drifted into politics, where he became disillusioned after leading several demonstrations against police shootings before 1965. In 1966 he broke with conventional politics and founded the Crusade for Justice, which combined movement and cultural politics.[42]

Corky became one of the central figures of the Chicano movement and a strong proponent of Chicano nationalism. He reached out to the black power and Native American movements. His 1967 poem "I am Joaquin" best exemplifies the identity crisis of the times, and it had a great impact on later Chicano literature.[43] Throughout 1968 Corky visited Los Angeles and Tijerina. He also marched in Washington, D.C., issuing his Plan of the Barrio, which called for better housing, education, barrio-owned businesses, and restitution of pueblo lands.

In March 1969 the first Chicano Youth Conference in Denver produced "El Plan Espiritual de Aztlán" (The Spiritual Plan of Aztlán), a document written by Chicano poet Alurista (Alberto Baltazar Urista Heredia) that promoted the concept of ethnic nationalism and self-determination. Alurista best represents the idealism of the times.[44] The influence of Mexican history on Gonzales was clear. He named the Crusade for Justice's school after the massacre of Mexican students at Tlatelolco on October 2, 1968, in the Plaza de las Tres Culturas in Mexico City. The event bonded Chicana/o students with the student movement internationally.[45]

ON THE CAMPUSES

In California, the Educational Opportunity Program (EOP) expanded and unified the number of minorities entering colleges and universities. The program was established in 1965 at the Berkeley and Los Angeles campuses of the University of California with seed money provided by the University of California Board of Regents. Despite an enrollment of 80,000 students, a paucity of black and brown students were enrolled in proportion to their state numbers. The California plan was a response to the Watts rebellions of that year, as well as student activism on the University of California campuses. The fund was in the form of private gifts rather than a commitment of the California legislature. At the time, there was a 2 percent rule—that is, the percentage of students could be admitted to the University of California on a waiver of academic requirements such as grade point average and test scores. This exception was generally applied to athletes and students with special talents. In November 1967, it had been increased to 4 percent. At the University of California Los Angeles, 97 students were Native Americans; 303 were Mexican American; 514 were black; and 1,665 were Asian.[46]

In California EOP contributed to the development of the experimental colleges, which in turn gave students a sense of the failure of academe's course of study in meeting the needs of society. The first experimental college started at Berkeley as part of a reform movement, a revolt of sorts against the bad teaching of research institutions where "relevant" classes would be offered. These colleges spread to institutions such as Stanford and the University of California, Los Angeles (UCLA), where, as in the case of Berkeley, they met with opposition. The most successful was at San Francisco State College, where it served as a recruitment station for the Black Student Union. The San Fernando Valley State experimental college had begun in the fall of 1967. The SDS were heavily involved and made a similar push at nearby Valley Junior College in Van Nuys. At UCLA the founder of the experimental college was Rosalio Muñoz, a history major involved in student government. Their purpose was to reform the mainstream curriculum.[47] At Valley State, Mexican American students offered classes on the Mexican American experience through the experimental college to politicize the small number recruited. The experimental college also gave students the experience of organizing and teaching classes. These informal colleges were an important logical step for Mexican American students to develop their own curriculum, and in the spring of

1969 they allowed UMAS to develop and offer three courses for credit in English, political science, and Mexican American culture.[48]

The role of UMAS in the development of these courses was central to the movement toward Chicano Studies, spreading the notion of a need for curricular changes that would include Mexican Americans. The Valley State UMAS chapter was active at the various conferences and weekly meetings held by UMAS. Aside from improving communication, rivalry existed between the chapters. The draft and the dropout crises were discussed, as well the war and other issues. College courses, curriculum, the alienation on campus, and the dropout rate at the college level were also thrashed out.[49]

Meanwhile, a legislative mandate in 1968 established a state-funded version of EOP at the California state college system. Several campuses already operated outreach programs, which the individual colleges funded. EOPs focused on highly motivated low-income, first-generation college students. At California State College, Los Angeles (CSCLA), in June 1968 the Associated Students voted to give the Black Student Association and UMAS $40,000 for administrative costs and supplies. San Fernando Valley State College was close behind, and Stanley Charnofsky was the first chair of the EOP. UMAS and the Black Student Union (BSU) participated in the selection process, as some 200 students were recruited for the fall of 1968. The Economic Youth Opportunities Agency was an early funder of the summer projects. At SFVSC it was called Project Learn. They had classes and cultural activities. The majority of the students were black, but they also included Mexican American students.[50]

DIGGING THE TRENCHES

In 1967 Los Angeles State hired Ralph Guzmán, a respected political scientist and community activist who had been an assistant director of the Ford Foundation Mexican-American Study Project, to direct a Department of Commerce grant of $125,000 to study Mexicans in Los Angeles. The project would allow CSCLA to establish a national center.[51] From this point on, UMAS and BSU pressured the administration to offer courses on Mexican Americans and blacks. In July 1968 the student government agreed to fund courses with a grant of $39,000. BSU representative Robert Smith summed up the organization's disappointment: "It is regrettable that we had to go to this kind of effort to get the money. The time we spent pleading our cause could better have been spent drafting plans for the curriculum. The Afro-American and Mexican-American studies courses, after all, are part of our rights as students here. We represent the substantial majority of blacks and Mexican-Americans at the school."[52]

CSCLA had the highest percent of minority students, 20 percent, in California. Much of the Chicana/o student leadership had played an active role in the Los Angeles school walkouts in March of that spring. After the student government financed these classes, the dean of planning, Anthony Moye, said, "A substantial proportion of teachers who will work in Mexican-American areas of Los Angeles graduate from Cal State L.A. Now . . . they can be more effective teachers, because they will better understand the background of their students."⁵³ Moye did not speak to the irony of the institution not funding the classes. Unfortunately, an internecine struggle broke out at CSCLA, which led to the controversial resignation of Guzmán, which has left scars to this day, with Gilbert Cárdenas and Phil Castruita saying it was unfair and criticizing Carlos Muñoz, a graduate student, for leading the coup. CSCLA never recovered from the incident.

Up until January of 1969, five classes in Mexican American Studies were approved. The administration agreed to the creation of Mexican American and Afro-American Studies departments. The proposal included eleven courses to begin the next quarter. The administration conceded that the Mexican population was too large to ignore. Muñoz was appointed the coordinator of the proposed Mexican American Studies department. A coordinator was also named for the Afro-American Studies unit. The focus of both was community development.⁵⁴

The best-known student movement for the Ethnic Studies programs was at San Francisco State College (SFSC), influencing students of color statewide. However, SFSC was not the only campus experiencing student turmoil. During 1967–1968 eleven of the eighteen California state college campuses had encounters with black organizations. The Third World strike of 1968–1969 at SFSC, according to Rojas, "stands out as one of the most memorable moments in American educational history."⁵⁵ The Black Panthers within the BSU had created a prototype of Black Studies through the experimental college—African Americans numbered 800 out of 18,000 students. The civil rights movement and the assassinations of Martin Luther King and Malcolm X had given the movement its martyrs. A November 4 press conference opened with chants of about sixty black students of "power to the people" and an invitation to "John Brown whites" to join the struggle.⁵⁶

The governor and the college administration were senseless in ignoring the academic senate's recommended approval of a bachelor degree in Black Studies. The pretexts were that it was separatist, excluded Mexican Americans and Asians, and led to "reverse racism."⁵⁷ This resulted in months of guerilla warfare, with Governor Ronald Reagan appointing Samuel Ichiye Hayakawa president of the college and tightening the rules to prosecute protestors. The BSU in March 1969 got Black Studies, but at the cost of much of its leadership.

THE BREADBASKET OF POOR IN HIGHER EDUCATION

Higher education grew dramatically after World War II. Contributing to this growth was the National Defense Education Act of 1958, the Higher Education Facilities Act of 1963, and the Higher Education Act of 1965. By 1970 federal grants and loans totaled $4.42 billion, a fourfold growth during the decade. The recipient of much of the growth was in the junior colleges funded by local, state, and federal funds. At the time, they had open enrollment and no tuition. World War II had given them a tremendous boost, as many became training facilities for the military.

In California, as the tax burden was lifted from local governments, junior colleges expanded dramatically due to the baby boom generation and the rapidly growing Mexican American population. Nearly 300,000 Californians attended college part time or were enrolled in adult education studies. In 1960 the state's master plan for higher education created a three-tiered system of higher education and placed new restrictions on admissions to state colleges and universities, which in turn swelled junior college enrollment. The upper 41 percent of graduates could enter state colleges and universities. The remaining students were diverted to the state's junior colleges. In reality, this eliminated the poorest students from state universities and colleges. Their only alternative was the fifty-six districts (110 colleges) offering junior college courses.[58]

In most cases, the two year colleges were the only alternative for the masses of Mexican Americans. Statewide, only 50 percent of California students were eligible for admission. More than half did not have a "C" average.[59] These statistics were worse among Mexican Americans, most of whom only had the option of a junior college. In 1941 the Texas legislature granted direct state aid to the junior colleges in the amount of fifty dollars per full-time student. This was important because many local citizens saw students as a tax burden. These colleges were attractive because the fees were less than at four-year colleges, and students could live at home.

Necessarily, junior colleges were the frontline of the Chicano Studies movement. There was considerable agitation at East Los Angeles Junior College, where students were very active. The two main organizations were MASA and La Vida Nueva, who offered tutoring at the local elementary schools. These organizations also had a speaker's bureau and nurtured Chicana students such as Antonia Hernández, who became one of the nation's leading civil rights attorneys. At East Los Angeles College (ELAC) she was a tutor. MASA volunteers spoke to students about social issues such as drugs and created a support network for Chicana/o students. MASA bonded with its members through ethnic pride, closely participating in movement events.

In 1968 MASA demanded a Mexican-American Studies department. Carlos Montes charged that the ELAC president had reneged on a promise to support the grape boycott. In response, Mexican American students attempted to hoist the farmworker flag. Forty percent of the 6,200 day students were Mexican American. Blacks constituted 6–8 percent. La Vida Nueva and the SDS supported the BSU's demands for inclusion—more black students, more black courses, and more black staff. Mike Alonzo, a student body officer and president of La Vida Nueva, said that Mexican American students were "desirous of change at East Los Angeles . . . [and] were content to support the black students out of the feeling that concessions made to Negroes also would be made to them." A Mexican American Studies department was under development, yet there was a hardening of the administration's position.[60]

The events politicized student leaders. Montes became a member of Young Chicanos for Community Action and a leader in the Brown Berets. Meanwhile, on December 13, 1968, representatives of La Vida Nueva, along with UCLA UMAS undergraduate Reynaldo Macias, held a press conference to rally community and campus support for Mexican American Studies. After the press conference a small group once again hoisted the farmworker flag. By this time, La Vida Nueva had formed an alliance with the BSU, and its increasingly militant language was drawing criticism from established Mexican American leaders. In January 1969, 100 sheriff deputies arrived in riot gear to monitor demonstrations on campus, charging La Vida Nueva co-chair Willie Méndoza with inciting a riot, disturbing the peace, and assault and battery. The administration acceded to demands and hired Chicana/o professors. The events led to increased police and sheriff department infiltration. Meanwhile, Los Angeles City Junior College became more militant and had a core of about two dozen Mexican American students.

San Fernando Valley Chicano Studies

Today, California State University, Northridge (CSUN), is the largest Chicana/o Studies department in the United States, offering 166 sections per semester. In the spring of 1969 San Fernando Valley State was not the center of the largest Mexican American community, nor did it have a large Chicana/o student population on campus (some estimate fewer than fifty students).[61] Reluctantly, I accepted the chair of Mexican American Studies in the spring of 1969. My life experiences made me the right fit for the program. I had been a resident of the Valley for fourteen years, was active in community organizations throughout the 1960s, and I had a PhD and over twelve years' experience in developing curriculum in the secondary schools, junior and state colleges. At California State, Dominguez Hills, I developed Mexican American curriculum and worked with students. More important, I had a tenured position at Pierce College that served as a safety net in case the administration went after me.[62]

As mentioned, change had come to Valley State in 1967 as a critical mass of black students and a small number of Mexican American students enrolled on campus. The fact that the Mexican American student community was small helped forge their purpose and commitment. They refused to be swallowed up by the mainstream and/or the activist communities on campus. UMAS pressured the administration for a presence in the formation of EOP and recruitment of Mexican American students.[63]

A significant number of white radicals were active on campus. They belonged to every conceivable group—the Communist Party, the October League, Trotskyites, anarchists, and hippies. The antiwar movement was large, and hundreds of students gathered to hear speakers at the Free Speech Forum.[64] Chicana/o students participated in the anti–Vietnam War rallies and the civil rights movement, and they were supportive of the East Los Angeles walkouts. By the fall of 1968 they had been radicalized by their involvement; the only thing they lacked were the numbers.

Tensions exploded on November 4, 1968, two days before the better-known San Francisco State BSU strike, as twenty-six African American students occupied the fifth floor of the administration building, protesting the institution's treatment of minority students. The confrontation was touched off when an assistant football coach kicked a black player and called him the N-word during a game.[65] The BSU was led by Jerome Walker, president of San Fernando Valley State's BSU, and Archie Chatman (who later chose the name Adewole Umoja). The Los Angeles swat team invaded the campus, and arrests resulted in criminal penalties for the nineteen black students.[66] Although they were unarmed, the students were charged with—among other things—conspiracy, kidnapping, and false imprisonment. The courts sentenced some to twenty-five years in state prison, and many served more than six months jail time. In contrast, students during the same period who took over Columbia University—with guns and knives—received lighter sentences.[67] Walker and Chatman were decent young men, and Chatman mentored many of the Chicana/o students that had been recruited through EOP.

It was significant that the confrontation took place in the San Fernando Valley, where Mayor Sam Yorty waged his race war on challenger Tom Bradley, a councilman.[68] Yorty's theme in the Valley was, "I think that they're waking up in the city of Los Angeles and God bless you, with your help we're going to keep our city like we want it."[69] The Valley was uptight as its white paradise came tumbling down. The *Valley News* bannered on November 4, 1968, "Valley State Demonstrators Hold Building for 4 Hours." It went on to highlight "Herd Administrators, Workers into Room Students Seize Upper Floors, Show Knives Amid Threats of Violence." Mayor Sam Yorty red baited those wanting to help the black students.[70]

Academic campus life came to a standstill at Valley State. Students attended rallies daily, and on January 8, 400 students marched on the administration building to see acting president Delmar Oviatt and demand amnesty for black students indicted on November 4. Violence erupted as the crowd swelled to around a thousand students, and a riot broke out. Then, on January 9, police declared a peaceful rally at the Free Speech Area unlawful and arrested more than 286 students, faculty members, and community supporters. Among the Chicanas/os arrested were Miguel Verdúgo, Hank López, Everto Ruiz, Frank Lechuga, Raul Aragón, Diana Borrego, and Ismael Campuzano.[71] Also arrested was Warren Furumoto, a biologist and UMAS adviser, and Richard Abcarian, an English professor. "The police have stationed a temporary 'command post' in the custodial area of the school. Sgt. Daniel Cooke has told the Daily Sundial that 'fewer than 100 police officers' entered the campus at 7:30 A.M. and many will remain until the emergency state is no longer in effect." These acts of civil disobedience were no small potatoes in the context of the charges being brought against the San Fernando Valley State Nineteen. There was considerable pressure by the white establishment of the Valley to get tough on students. A state of emergency was declared on January 9, 1969.[72]

Moderate faculty on campus, led by Malcolm Sillars, members of the faculty senate, and faculty president Verne Bullough, called for a meeting with the student leaders. Abcarian deserves much of the credit for bringing the sides together. The African American students expanded this body to include UMAS, which had become increasingly militant. Black and brown students presented separate demands. Among the Chicana/o demands were "that a Chicano Studies Director be hired in February so he can prepare the implementation of the department in September 1969 . . . [that] the Chicano Advisory Board investigate the recruitment and firing practices of the Foreign Language Dept. . . . [and] the admission of 500 CHICANO students under the E.O.P. program in September 1969."[73]

With the students they hammered out what was to become known as the twelve-point agreement, which incorporated key elements of both black and brown demands. The BSU had made its demands on November 4, 1968.[74] The major concessions were agreements to implement Chicana/o Studies and Pan-African Studies departments and to bring in 350 black students and 350 Mexican American students per year until the campus enrollment equaled their proportion in the public schools.[75] The college established Pan-African and Mexican American Studies departments. Los Angeles State had a studies program, but it was not yet a department; rather, it was a research center that had not been certified by campus committees and generated only a few classes. A center is different than a department, which has much more power and autonomy.[76]

Most students came from the worse performing schools in Los Angeles and Ventura counties and had taken limited college prep courses, which counselors reserved for white and Asian students. Locally, San Fernando High School at the time had only about one-third Mexican American students, with few on a college track. SFVSC was attractive because fees ran about fifty dollars a semester. The mission of Chicano Studies was to protect students, give them the skills to succeed, and persuade them that it was to their long-range advantage to get an education—a socializing process that is normal in middle-class homes and schools.

I arrived at SFVSC in the spring semester of 1969. I was fortunate that the Mexican American students there differed from other campuses. They were a small close-knit group of no more than thirty active students. Valley State College had a small community mind-set without the intense factions present in Los Angeles proper. The students were ably led by Mike Verdúgo and Hank López, who knew the limitations of the group and steered away from quixotic ventures. Their first duty was to survive, and they participated but did not get sucked into the craziness of the times. They did not get bogged down with personal ambitions and did not carve out faculty positions for themselves. Verdúgo made recruitment a priority.

Verdúgo and López asked me to apply not so much because I stood out in a sea of candidates, but because they knew me and because I had a PhD. I also had experience in setting up Mexican American Studies courses. The members of the selection committee—faculty members and community activists—were my friends.[77] For example, I had worked with Louis García and Nellie Parra, who were community leaders in San Fernando/Pacoima for a decade. Julian Nava was a friend, and I knew Warren Furumoto from working in the Latin American Civic Association.

The committee members suggested the administration bring me in as a full professor. The reasoning was that this was at a lower pay level than my junior college pay. Nava pointed out that without a full professorship the chair would be vulnerable, and that the chair should negotiate from a position of power. I had to bargain this point with the administration, once threatening to resign.[78] The institution hedged on giving me tenure but assured me that it would do so at the end of the first academic year. Thus, thanks to the Chicano movement, I was a full professor at the age of thirty-five. The odds were that I would not last out the year, because there was a good chance I would be fired. My only insurance policy was the students.

The atmosphere at Valley State was strained. Many of the faculty and administration resented that, according to them, Chicano Studies and newly recruited students had come to the campus at the point of a gun. They did not grasp the contradictions of not studying Mexican Americans or blacks, as well as denying them access to higher education. They were bothered by the new program's relationship with students and could not fathom that they should be equal partners in the building process. The loss of control over portions of their curriculum bothered them, and they were frightened by what seemed to them the end of their orderly institution. Few recognized that student involvement made programs much more accountable, providing checks on the professional ambitions of the staff.

As mentioned, while most students do not know what they want, Valley State UMAS did. When asked what outcome the group expected, Miguel Verdúgo very concisely said that they would recruit 350 Mexican American students in fall of 1969, most of whom would not be academically prepared, and Mexican American Studies courses had to provide a safety net for them. The U.S. history requirement and English 150 were barriers for most the Mexican origin students in the fall of 1968. In the spring of 1969, students had recruited a young Mexican American woman, Martha Sánchez (now at Arizona State University), to teach the class through the English department, which she did with considerable success. The students said the school needed more classes such as the Mexican American English course that were controlled by Mexican Americans and taught by Mexican Americans. It was beautiful—there was no illusion that the program would become an intellectual powerhouse; it was there to serve the students. The roles played by Mike Verdúgo, Hank López, and other students made the program a success. My contribution was to draw up a curriculum that would get Mexican American students through college. Teaching them about Mexican Americans was not just about content but a vehicle for teaching them the skills to survive in other courses.

November 4, 1968, scared most professors who just wanted peace. Hence, there was little resistance to the massive proposal at the committee level. The main obstacles were limited resources, the Spanish department, which Chicana/o students had singled out in their twelve-point demands, and the racism of many faculty members. The institution provided limited clerical assistance, assigning the new department a small space on the fourth floor of the Towers next to Sierra Hall North. This was before computers, and most of the typewriters were manual. If it had not been for Julian Nava, who allowed his student assistant to help on occasions, I would have never completed the task at hand.[79]

Throughout the process, the administration played games, offering me three positions for fall 1969. I tied our demands to the Pan-African Studies allocation and agreed to an equal number faculty positions as Pan African Studies. However,

I learned through a white faculty member that the administration had promised black students seven positions, so I threatened to resign unless we received seven positions, which we would never have gotten if it had not been for a united student front. (The administration also brought in a St. Louis African American consulting firm to help Bill Burwell set up the Pan-African curriculum, which seemed fair at the time, considering the sacrifice of the group. The black movement generated a huge amount of energy that allowed Mexican American Studies the opportunity to take root.)

The Spanish department felt threatened by the new department. The truth is that Mexican Americans have always threatened Spanish and Latin American Studies programs. When EOP was formed, the Mexican American faculty members of the Spanish department placed an ad in the *Sundial* opposing the recruitment of "unqualified" students to the college. Spanish professors harassed the new department throughout the vetting process, saying that Mexican American Studies was reducing the quality of academic offerings and that the Spanish department had the right to flag the content of the new department's courses, and it did. Luckily, politically progressive professors neutralized the Spanish department. SFVSC had drawn a goodly number of radicals during the sixties from research institutions that had kicked them out because of their political activism. The number was small but committed, and invaluable in committees.

By March 1969 I had completed the proposed curriculum and took it to Santa Barbara, where participants formulated the famous El Plan de Santa Barbara.[80] The first draft of the major and minor was composed of forty-five classes, which the administration cautioned against. Administrators wanted a twelve-course package.

The Movement for Chicano Studies

UMAS at Valley State consisted of about thirty students, and a dozen or so were hard core. Rebecca Villegas, Evelyn Alarcón, and Dian Borrego were in the core group. Statewide, less than a thousand Chicana/o students attended the California State College and University of California systems. These students fought for Chicano Studies and the recruitment of Mexican Americans to the colleges and universities. Their sacrifices and accomplishments must be placed in context. Government and the establishment did not give them Chicano Studies, they took it. Less than 2 percent of Mexican origin students were in college, whereas the number of white students had increased by 58 percent in the first half of the decade. Financial help was limited, while the government fully subsidized the education of 4,200 Cuban refugee students. The ones who cared were this small band of Chicanas/os.

The acceptance of Chicano Studies programs did not end tensions. Almost immediately the Greek chorus forecast a lowering of academic standards.[81] Just as it seemed that tensions were lessening, federal and state governments began cutting back on support. The cutbacks did a lot to undercut the careful preparation of UCLA and CSCLA, both of which had been spared the violent and bitter confrontations of San Francisco State and San Fernando Valley State. The *Los Angeles Times* wrote, "At some—UCLA and California State College, Los Angeles are notable examples—careful preparatory work and cooperation among students, faculty and administration have resulted in well conceived plans for ethnic studies programs. At other schools turmoil and sometimes violence have surrounded the ethnic studies and minority recruitment questions."

Los Angeles State College UMAS staged a six-day camp in protest to cuts in EOP funds in June 1969. They supported the Unruh bill that augmented funds to disadvantaged students. Monte Pérez, the past chair of the organization, said that the educational complex "had failed Mexican-Americans and that EOP was one of the hopes for rectifying past social injustices against the group."[82] In November, the Committee on Education Development approved a Mexican American Studies degree for California State, Hayward, for the 1970–1971 academic year. It was an interdisciplinary program drawing from existing courses. According to the administration, "bring[ing] to bear the insight of the various disciplines," the degree was essentially a liberal arts degree.[83]

California State University, Fullerton, had one of the heaviest concentrations of students, with 247 Mexican Americans at the college. There were about seventy-three blacks, making it one of the few schools in southern California where Mexicans outnumbered African Americans. Fullerton appointed black professor James H. Fleming, the director of the New Horizon Educational program coordinator of Ethnic Studies. The Ethnic Studies model pulled together just over seventy existing courses. Not long afterward Chicanas/os demanded a separate department. Blacks were unaccustomed to being a minority within a minority and also pressed for their autonomy.[84] UMAS was active at the Claremont Colleges, hosting a conference in mid-April at which Corky Gonzales and Tijerina rallied the troops. In May, Claremont announced the creation of a Human Resources Institute to include centers for black and Mexican American Studies. At the time fifty Mexican American and eighty black students attended Claremont. They projected majors in black and Mexican American Studies.[85]

Aside from the state college and university campuses, Chicana/o students at the junior colleges dug trenches. An advantage of the junior colleges was that they were close to home. Many parents would not allow their daughters to leave their homes and go away to college before they got married. The Black Panther Party at Merritt Junior College (Oakland) initiated Black Studies courses in 1966. Bobby Seale and Huey Newton attended Merritt, where they began reading Frantz Fanon. Chicana/o students staged a weeklong protest from April 14 to April 21. They called for Froben Lozada of the Socialist Workers Party to head a new Mexican American Studies department. They also requested free textbooks, meals for needy students, and the hiring of Third World people. The students fenced in the white faculty in their meeting room. By April 23 the faculty approved the administration's recommendation that Lozada be appointed and that the student demands be accepted. By May the crisis subsided as the student demands were met.[86]

The Mexican American Club of Barstow College, in the Mojave Desert, visited high schools to recruit students. The Mexican American Club at Los Angeles Harbor College worked through high school counselors to contact high school dropouts. Bakersfield College had a theater skit about the problems of Chicana/o students. San Bernardino College sent teams into high schools to recruit, which led to a demand for Mexican American or Chicana/o Studies.

Moorpark College in Ventura County hired two full-time and two part-time Chicano instructors to teach 160 students in the fall of 1969 in response to student and community activism. In November, MEChA at Moorpark sponsored a one-day conference on Chicano Studies. Rightfully proud of their achievements, they went all out with a free lunch for the participants, who came from all over the state. However, a student from Merritt College found a grape in his fruit salad and ran through the dining hall hollering "Grapes!" (Chicana/o students supported the farmworker boycott of grapes). About 150 participants stomped out of the conference. Moorpark MEChA students were devastated but kept working, and Moorpark president John Collins issued an apology.[87]

A Los Angeles junior college dean saw Chicano Studies as a means to motivate Mexican American students to stay in college. Junior college growth depended on enrollment much more than the University of California and state colleges. Los Angeles Valley Junior College implemented a Mexican American Studies department in the fall of 1969, spearheaded by the students with the support of Professor Arturo Avila. Student demand was so dramatic that almost immediately faculties began to question the competence of the new hires. The same dean that expressed hope that it would motivate Chicanas/os when asked about their language problem responded, "many of their students have great trouble with Spanish and would be just as able to master English with real students as they would Spanish." Almost from the beginning a dichotomy existed: the institutions wanted more students, but white and then black faculty members felt challenged. They wanted students to enroll in their classes but resisted the large recruitment of Mexican American faculty members. This resistance grew as teacher unions increased in influence and seniority moderated the growth of Chicano Studies.[88]

Hey, Baby, Qué Paso?

In Texas the drive for Chicano Studies took another form. Led by MAYO, most activists moved their actions from the campuses to the community, and June 1969 marked the beginning of its Winter Garden Project. The organization based its growth on securing local elections, and although some of its members were caught up in the fervor of the National Chicano Youth Conference in Denver, it wanted a Tejano plan that was adapted to its needs, which, according to José Ángel Gutiérrez, would bring about the "building of Aztlan." MAYO was still in the business of walkouts, and it wanted to control city government and boards of education, using local organizers to build this vision. It joined boycotting students at University of Texas, Austin, for Mexican American Studies, but it had a statewide plan to transform education for Mexican Americans. Most university Tejano Chicano Studies programs targeted the research and development of Chicano knowledge but were not intended to build mass bases. If MAYO's priority had been the studies programs, the outcome would have been different, since most of its troops were needed for its ambitious community project. The surge was from below. This is not to say that MAYO was not interested in Chicano Studies. Indeed, they supported the formation of the Mexican-American Studies Institute for the State of Texas, directed by Américo Paredes.[89]

The University of Texas, Austin, campus attempted to defuse the initial thrust for Mexican American and Black Studies. "Dr. Henry Bullock [a black historian] is designing courses to bridge the gap between the ghetto and the middle class. His program isn't 'black studies,' a key word for the activists. . . . It is 'ethnic studies,' for ethnic situations are very much a part of the Mexican-Americans' life in Texas, too." The program began in the fall of 1970 and was attended by six hundred mostly white students. Approximately two hundred black students attended the campus. The Mexican American Student Organization and black students made proposals. University officials announced that three Negroes, including Bullock, were teaching Ethnic Studies—but it did not include any Mexican Americans. "We are not operating on the principle that only Mexican-Americans can teach Mexican-American studies and only blacks can teach black studies," said Bullock.[90] This did not satisfy Mexican American activists, and their protests led to the formation of CMAS in 1970.

The University of Texas, El Paso, due to its proximity to other southwestern states, was closer to Los Angeles than to Houston and was much more influenced by activities in New Mexico and even California. Students were attuned to César Chávez, Tijerina, and the Crusade for Justice. El Paso was more a part of Chihuahua than the Rio Grande Valley. In November 1969 the El Paso campus announced a plan of study that would lead to a minor in Mexican American Studies. It pulled together existing courses taught mostly by white professors. Chicana/o students called the plan paternalistic.[91]

Soy Chicano

Students were also active in Seattle, Washington, Arizona, New Mexico, and the Midwest. They met in Denver at the National Chicano Student Conference and simultaneously demanded greater access to higher education and special programs to make up for the years of neglect. In Tucson, a group of faculty in 1968 formed the Mexican American Studies program. By 1975 it became the Mexican American Studies Committee. In 1981 the Mexican American Studies and Research Center was formally organized. This did not satisfy many activists, who agitated for Mexican American Studies as well as the recruitment of more Mexican American students. The Mexican American Liberation Committee (MALC), led by Sal Baldenegro, co-chair of the University of Arizona Chicano student organization, protested the lack of Mexican American Studies in the high schools.[92]

The presence of Baldenegro was indispensable in keeping alive the notion of Mexican American Studies. In March 1969 MALC led walkouts at Tucson and Pueblo high schools. Tucson School District superintendent Thomas L. Lee suspended about two hundred taking part in the walkouts over the inequities for Mexican American students. The walkout students gathered at Oury Park and spoke out against racism. The demonstration was described as orderly by police. Baldenegro disputed Lee's claim that adults were using students: "The whole idea [of today's demonstrations] sprang from the kids themselves. They organized everything." The grievances were similar to those in other parts of the country: there were not enough Mexican American teachers in the schools, Mexican cultures were being dismissed by the schools, and they were demanding more bilingual education and the end of racial discrimination. According to Baldenegro, "These students feel that education might be the key to break the whole cycle of poverty."[93]

In September 1969 Baldenegro led a boycott of the Mexican American Studies program at the University of Arizona. MALC, which attracted student activists such as Guadalupe Castillo and Raul Grijalva, accused the administration of tokenism. They said that "the present Mexican-American studies program lacks 'innovativeness' and makes no real reference to 'the Chicano experience in the Southwestern United States,'" and that they would prefer the program to be known as Chicano Studies. In November, Baldenegro represented the Young Mexican-American Association, MALC, the Brown Berets, and American Indian students at the Southwest Council for Bilingual Education, condemning the "'entire educational system as, being racist' to support of the grape pickers strike in California and condemning the Vietnam war."[94] Baldenegro organized the People's Coalition, demanding that El Rio Golf Course be converted into a park. Barrio residents saw something inherently wrong in their children having to play in the dusty streets while outsiders had a lush golf course.[95]

Labeled an outside agitator, Baldenegro was targeted by the city council. These demonstrations led to the establishment of El Rio Neighborhood Center and Joaquín Murrietta Park. In 1971 he formed La Raza Unida Party, saying, "As a matter of fact the two major parties are active and conscious collaborators in the racist society which keeps the Chicano in a position of colonialism." Baldenegro narrowly lost his race for the city council, refusing to moderate his positions.[96] Until the present day, Baldenegro has remained a gadfly in opposition to injustice and a strong advocate of student and community control of Mexican American Studies.

The movement for Chicano Studies in Washington began in the Yakima Valley, generated by Chicana/o students at the University of Washington and other campuses by local chapters of UMAS, the Brown Berets, and later MEChA. Once on campus they brought their issues to the table—that is, the UFW grape boycott, El Centro de La Raza, and demands for more recruitment and Chicano Studies. Many began at Yakima Junior College, with many moving to the University of Washington in 1968, when thirty-five Chicanas/os were recruited mostly from Yakima College. The new students brought the university's Mexican population to 60, or 0.19 percent of the student body of 31,913. New arrival Erasmo Gamboa said, "There were more people in the HUB than there were in my hometown." These recruits brokered the entrance of other Mexicans from their hometown. At the Seattle campus, the BSU occupied the president's office.

The group had close ties to the UFWOC grape boycott, organized in 1967 by Guadalupe Gamboa and Tomás Villanueva, from Yakima Valley Junior college. In 1968 José Correa, Antonio Salazar, Eron Maltos, Jesús Lemos, Erasmo Gamboa, and Eloy Apodaca, among many others, formed the first chapter of UMAS in the Northwest. In 1968 and 1969, they led a successful grape boycott. It was the four-year struggle over grapes that gave UMAS an identity, a moral cause. Erasmo Gamboa recalls "we were energized by the fact that the University at the time was pliant, if you will—we were able to move the University relatively easy."

UMAS also founded La Escuelita in Granger in 1969, which in turn led to the creation of the calmecac project (Nahuatl school), a program that taught history and culture to Chicana/o youth in Eastern Washington. Some of the members participated in the Chicano Youth Liberation Conference as student chapters spread. By 1970 the Brown Berets had been formed, and Chicana/o students in 1972 participated in the El Centro de La Raza takeover of an abandoned Seattle school district plant.[97]

Chicana/o students enrolled in other Washington colleges, where they pushed for the admission of other Chicana/o students. In October 1969 Mexican American students at Washington State University organized MASA, which changed its name to MEChA. Two early leaders were Margarita Méndoza de Sugiyama and Rudy Cruz, who built a network in the Yakima Valley. As at the University of Washington, the UFW's grape boycott galvanized the group. In Pullman, they forced Safeway and Washington State University's Dining Services to stop selling nonunion grapes. Mechistas formed alliances with the Black Student Union, Native American student group, and radical white students. In January 1970 faculty and students wrote a proposal for a Chicano Studies program, which the administration dismissed. After mass protests, the Washington State University president established Ethnic Studies departments and appointed a special assistant as director of minority affairs. In 1971 there were about 100 Mexican American students enrolled in these classes, and Professor Reymundo Marín was the director of the program. As the number of Mexicans grew in the state, they matriculated in greater numbers to other campuses; each formed MEChA chapters and demanded Chicano Studies, recruitment of students, and more Chicana/o faculty.[98]

In the Midwest similar movements began as more students enrolled. In 1970 Chicana/o students in Minnesota organized a summer institute "to explore the feasibility of establishing a Chicano Studies Department in the Midwest. Participants at the conference came from Wisconsin, Iowa, South Dakota, Nebraska, Illinois, Kansas, Indiana, Michigan, and Ohio." The 180 conferees encompassed Chicanas/os from a broad background, including many who were Tejano migrants or their children. The moving force for the conference was the University of Minnesota's Latin Liberation Front (LLF).

The LLF, led by Ramona Arreguín de Rosales of St. Paul, pushed issues such as financial aid, campus employment for students, recruiting, and a Department of Chicano Studies. When the administration dragged its feet, twenty Chicana/o students occupied Morrill Hall on October 26, 1971. Manuel Guzmán told the administration, "If we do not have concrete evidence of the establishment or implementation of a Chicano Studies Department within 72 hours, a vote will be taken to strike against the university administration and its policies." Students rejected a proposal for Chicano Studies to be absorbed into an existing department, because they wanted autonomy. The students held a fast. According to Rosales, "We knew that if we didn't win at that time, that cause, we weren't sure what was going to be the future of Chicano students and Latino students coming to the school. What was the future for your children and our children's children." Chicano Studies opened its doors in the fall of 1972, the first in the upper Midwest. Their example spread throughout the Midwest during the decade.[99]

In Sum

The energy of the Chicana/o generation nationwide was incredible. Here were first-generation college students from immigrant or immigrant-family backgrounds, from working-class families with poor education backgrounds. Many of the young women had to overcome family cultural taboos, and they accomplished what other generations had failed to do. The *Los Angeles Times* ran an article on April 25, 1969, that listed fifty-seven colleges with Chicano classes. The list was somewhat complete, with California State, Hayward, offering the most classes—eight. The next largest was the University of Southern California with six; San Jose State and Dominguez Hills with five; and Fresno State, San Diego State, and San Fernando State with four apiece. In all, twenty-five institutions had at least one Chicano Studies class.[100]

While this profile is informative, it does not tell the entire story. The push for Chicano Studies began in the fall of 1968 at a time when most four year colleges only had a couple dozen Mexican American students. This changed in the fall of 1969 as the seed of the Chicano activism bore its first fruit. For example, Valley State already had forty-five course proposals approved by the Educational Policy Committee and was scheduled to offer twenty-four sections. In May it formally receive departmental status though the trustees, which was approved by the Educational Policies Committee. CSCLA had substantially more classes than reported by the administration, and although they had not been put through committee, they did have a commitment from the college president. Most state colleges had departments or programs within the year.

Rojas says, "Although black studies may have started in teaching colleges such as San Francisco State College and Merritt College in Oakland, the degree granting black studies program is most commonly found in research-intensive institutions. Furthermore, the spread of black studies programs among research universities depends on a combination of . . . black student protest and a 'follow the leader' effect."[101] The experience of Chicano Studies was different.

CHAPTER 4

In the Trenches of Academe

What happened at Santa Barbara in April 1969 has become legend, and legends are assumed to be fact.[1] Today El Plan de Santa Barbara is one of the most posted documents of the era, and legend is that a small group of faculty members, students, and Brown Berets founded Chicano Studies. University of California, Los Angeles, Professor Reynaldo Macias offers a more staid perspective, "Like any document, there is both a grounding and a contextualization in the time and location in which they are created, and certainly the impact of El Plan de Santa Barbara in the early '70s immediately after it was published was significant in a couple of ways." According to Macias, it was important because it was printed, it was "an authoritative voice on what the desires of the Chicano Movement . . . with regard to higher education . . . [and it] was reporting on what was being done in different institutions in the state."[2]

Without minimizing the contributions of those at the three-day conference at Francisco Torres Hall, Macias does have a point.[3] The meeting was called by Chicano Coordinating Council on Higher Education (CCHE), which had been formed at the Crusade for Justice, sponsored by National Chicano Youth Liberation in Denver, to discuss how the community and the students could increase educational access to higher education. The only professors on hand were Gus Segade, Jesús Chavarría, Juan Gómez-Quiñones, Gracia Molina Enríquez de Pick from Mesa Community College, and me. Most of the four dozen or so participants were from the Los Angeles and southern California region. CCHE published El Plan de Santa Barbara in October 1969, sending the message to universities and colleges that Chicanas/os demanded a quality education.[4]

Many attendees were from departments, institutes, centers, and other models ready to be launched in the fall of 1969. So what happened would not change what had been set in stone. The department at San Fernando Valley State College was scheduled to start in September 1969; it would offer summer classes for first-year and transfer students.[5] It was ready to go and had made its way through the numerous college review committees.

59

The motives of the participants varied. Many were caught up in the emotions of the time, having recently returned from the Crusade for Justice's Chicano Youth Conference. Cliques of mostly graduate students existed in what seemed to be an alliance of the Universities of California at Los Angeles and Santa Barbara. Players from Los Angeles State College and those who wanted to be players also attended. The major personas were definitely Juan Gómez-Quiñones (UCLA) and Jesús Chavarria (UCSB). They were tied to most of the participants.

At thirty-five, I was older than most of the participants, some of whom knew each other, and I felt like an outsider. I already had my course of study developed, so I was not there to learn. I agreed with the thrust, which was for the most part ideological, and I saw the urgency of forming alliances with the community as absolutely essential. As mentioned, I had been active in the Mexican American community in the San Fernando Valley since the early 1960s and understood how Chicano Studies could become a power base on campus and a way to recruit and keep Chicanas/os in school. Relations with the community were essential, and the plan addressed this aspect of department building.[6]

As Macias points out, it was in print, one of the few books on the area of Chicano Studies. A Proquest search of dissertations reveals that only two theses have been written on the topic, and they are more reviews of individual programs than critiques of the area of Chicano Studies. CSCLA Professor Michael Soldatenko recently wrote a book on the discipline, an important work, but one that concentrates on Chicana/o Studies at research institutions.[7] The most appealing feature of the plan is its passion, speaking to aspirations of a generation and to those who believe that change can come about. It is a manifesto that follows the pattern of a long line of revolutionary manifestos in Mexican history. The influence of Juan Gómez-Quiñones, trained as a Mexican historian, is all over the document—the mixing of Spanish and English and allusions to Mexican history, the philosophical tone.

> For all people, as with individuals, the time comes when they must reckon with their history. For the Chicano the present is a time of renaissance, of renacimiento. Our people and our community, el barrio and la colonia, are expressing a new consciousness and a new resolve. Recognizing the historical tasks confronting our people and fully aware of the cost of human progress, we pledge our will to move. We will move forward toward our destiny as a people. We will move against those forces which have denied us freedom of expression and human dignity. Throughout history the quest for cultural expression and freedom has taken the form of a struggle. Our struggle, tempered by the lessons of the American past, is an historical reality.[8]

The leaders sought to centralize management of the various California Chicano Studies programs. They foresaw the development of departments taking place at every campus with high Chicano population concentrations. Coming out of the conference, everyone expected UCLA, Los Angeles State, and San Diego

State to be the centers of this movement, since that is where most of the heavies were housed.

What was unforeseen was the resistance to their leadership at other campuses and the factionalism that set in almost immediately after the conference. The document was East Los Angeles centric, and communities such as the San Fernando Valley, Ventura County, Orange County, and the northern part of California had their own identities and were often resentful of Los Angeles proper, where the movement seemed to begin and end. Over the years some campuses, not in the vanguard orbit, became much larger than the big three. Consequently, they would not accept the centralism proposed by the organizing committee.[9] Moreover, the overall numbers of Chicana/o students was not large enough to shift the paradigm.

Much has been made of the nationalist language of the document. MEChA was organized at the conference and over the years has inherited the animosity of racists and xenophobes who have distorted the plan. However, much of the plan's critique of society is still valid today. It says, among other things, that for decades Mexican people in the United States struggled to realize the "American Dream."[10] Surely anyone conversant with American history will agree that few have achieved the dream. The manifesto continues: "But the cost, the ultimate cost of assimilation, required turning away from el barrio and la colonia. In the meantime, due to the racist structure of this society, to our essentially different life style, and to the socio-economic functions assigned to our community by Anglo-American society—as suppliers of cheap labor and dumping ground for the small-time capitalist entrepreneur—the barrio and colonia remained exploited, impoverished, and marginal."[11] And it says that the goal of "self-determination of our community is now the only acceptable mandate for social and political action; it is the essence of Chicano commitment."[12] How much different is this than what was being said by Martin Luther King?

Critics argue that MEChA is ipso facto racist because it is mostly a Mexican American organization that excludes others. Its logo says "*La union hace la fuerza*" (Unity makes for strength or power). These accusations are ill informed. MEChAs are university chartered associations that cannot exclude anyone (and from my experience never have) from membership. The critics are just not probative. Are fraternities sexist because they admit only males? Are the Hillel groups racist because most of their members are Jewish? Or are the Newman clubs racist because most members are Catholics? No one raises these arguments with these and other groups. These same critics look at the plan through an epistemology that has been formed by their own xenophobic legends and fail to see the contradiction of their wearing a flag pin.

The plan makes it clear that:

> . . . the institutionalization of Chicano programs is the realization of Chicano power on campus. The key to this power is found in the application of the principles of self-determination and self-liberation. These principles are defined and practiced in the areas of control, autonomy, flexibility, and participation.

Often imaginary or symbolic authority is confused with the real. Many times token efforts in program institutionalization are substituted for enduring constructive programming. It is the responsibility of Chicanos on campus to insure dominant influence of these programs. The point is not to have a college with a program, but rather a Chicano program at that college.[13]

It can be argued that this goal has never been achieved because higher education is not democratic, and changes are rare.

The plan goes into specifics: (1) organize a *junta directiva (board of directors)*; (2) how to analyze the functional operation of the institution; and (3) "secure from the institution the commitment that it will give the highest priority to the needs of the Chicano community, not because of morals or politics, but because it has the obligation as a public institution charged with serving all of society." It is not so much what the document says but how it says it. It does not make students feel stupid but rather feel that they are somebody—*que si se puede.*[14]

The importance of the plan is that it places students at the heart of Chicano Studies. Beginning with the manifesto, it is a demand for Chicano autonomy calling for a new era, for self-determination, and for social and political action. The plan changed the name of the movement to "Chicano," expressing the community's aspirations and the centrality of higher education to its goals. It proposes a process to control the structure and to establish autonomy within the structure. The duty of students is to recruit others—cultural identity must be an integral part of every activity. The plan also offers a course of study for Chicano Studies and includes examples of programs in progress. Finally, it charges Chicano programs with building political consciousness, political mobility, and developing tactics.

UMAS became El Movimiento Estudiantil de Aztlán (MEChA). Symbolically changing the name from English to Spanish made this movement different. It was not assimilationist. It was not every person for him- or herself. The name "Aztlán" merely recognized the indigenous roots of Mexican Americans and the fact that they were here before Euro Americans.

In retrospect, the selection of Santa Barbara as the site for the conference was a stroke of good fortune and genius. The document could not have been put together without the leadership of a few, and if the conference had been held at Los Angeles State College or UCLA it would have attracted competing forces, and the dissention would have damaged the product. No one felt threatened, and the published monograph captured the spirit of the disparate workshops and in some cases is an almost verbatim transcription. The clarity of the document has served as a model for future generations, and it is one of the most duplicated documents in Chicano Studies.

For many, the plan is proof of Chicano nationalism—that is, *Chicanismo.* But the plan and MEChA are products of a time when students cared and wanted to build a better world. Critics rarely speak to the failure and racism of American education and the almost total exclusion of Mexican Americans from higher education. The times demanded strong denunciations of racism and exploitation and expressions of unity. The question of identity and racism cannot be dismissed or papered over. As Rubén G. Rumbaut writes, self-identity is subjective, shaped by historical context. It has much to do with how people are treated and punished. He gives the following as an example:

> Ted Williams, universally known as one of baseball's greatest hitters but not as a Latino player: his mother, May Venzer, was a Mexican American Baptist who married a soldier named Samuel Williams and moved to San Diego. May came to be known as "the Angel of Tijuana" for her Salvation Army work there. In his autobiography, Ted Williams (2001) wrote that "if I had had my mother's name, there is no doubt I would have run into problems in those days, [with] the prejudices people had in Southern California.[15]

Most would agree that history is an evolutionary process, and as Carlos Muñoz, Jr. says, "Chicanismo partially resolved the question of identity and propelled the movement." As discussed in the previous chapter, it motivated a few thousand students to do what previous generations and the present generation have not been not been able to do.[16] What many fail to recognize is that *Chicanismo* was not an ideology, although some perceived it as such.

Much of the spirit of the plan was moved by the poetry of Alurista, who invoked metaphors such as the spirit of Aztlán, an indigenous past that romantically tied Mexicans to their roots. It countered a history of Americanization in the United States. The preamble to "El Plan Espiritual de Aztlán" said, "In the spirit of a new people that is conscious not only of its proud historical heritage, but also of the brutal 'Gringo' invasion of our territories, we, the Chicano inhabitants and civilizers of the northern land of Aztlán, from whence came our forefathers, reclaiming the land of their birth and consecrating the determination of our people of the sun, declare that the call of our blood is our power, our responsibility and our inevitable destiny."[17] Alurista intertwined myth, identity, and struggle, catching the imagination of the Chicano generation. The product of nationalism, it inspired pride in one's people—like most poetry does. Ironically, many Americans who condemn Chicano nationalism do not criticize Walt Whitman poetry for justifying the invasion of Mexico and, according to him, bringing civilization to Mexico.

Often the same people who criticize the plan and the Chicano generation for their nationalism celebrate their artistic expressions. For instance, the murals in Chicano Park are highly nationalist, but serious scholars consider them state treasures. Art historians Martin Rosen and James Fisher write that the murals were painted "at the height of Chicano political activism," which

> occurred between 1969 and 1975 and not only dictated the specific social and economic issues the movement dealt with, but also coincided with the most productive period of Chicano muralism. . . . keeping with a long tradition of Mexican art as resistance, murals became the art form of choice, silent sentiments and creative yearnings that were vivid and eye-catching, explosions of lights that vanquished the shadows while merging the past and the future with

the present. They spoke to the ever-increasing social consciousness of the barrio and Chicano sensibilities and reflected issues and symbols that ranged from Aztec icons to the United Farm Workers black eagle, combining the Spanish and Indigenous heritage, a significant source of California's history.[18]

Historian Richard García accentuates that

the Mexican American mentality of integration, Americanism, and acculturation was in question, if not in crisis, in the late 1960s. The youth of Mexican American communities were promoting a Chicano Renaissance that was reminiscent of the Black Renaissance of the 1920s. The young activists of the Mexican American communities attempted to give rebirth to the energy of "lo mexicano" in a world in which many people of Mexican American descent found themselves becoming more a part of the culture of "lo americano." This period gave rise to a new consciousness of nationhood that was promoted by the radical youth who had begun to identify themselves as Chicanos rather than as part of Mexican American communities.[19]

My contribution to the conference was a draft of the Mexican American Studies major and minor. The notion of a Chicano Studies major was a new concept almost revolutionary in nature. Disciplines generally take generations to evolve, and they are offshoots of other disciplines, such as history, the granddaddy of them all. Area studies such as American Studies and Latin American Studies were consequently considered illegitimate children and second rate when compared to the mainstream disciplines. Area studies supposedly confused academic identity and the nature of the specific skills and methods that were developed within the discipline. Hence, if scholars were trained in an area studies they were not really historians or whatever and had no identity—even if most of their course work was in history or some other discipline. At the time, most Chicana/o graduate students were shaped by the biases of their discipline and proposed classes such as Chicano psychology or Chicano sociology. The real question was how the corpus of knowledge that composed Chicano Studies was going to be taught and researched in multidisciplinary fashion. The reality is that no such thing as Chicano psychology existed, just like there was no Chicano paradigm. For me, it was the best vehicle to teach and study the untapped knowledge and at the same time build Chicano Studies.

The Return to San Fernando Valley State College

The meeting at the University of California at Santa Barbara took time away from department building. The prime value was for outsiders to get known. Many of the participants became familiar faces and soon took jobs at institutions other than the ones that they were at in 1969–1970. The leapfrogging cost programs stable leadership. I never felt any need to try to mentor other campuses after they hired their directors. I felt that as professionals they either succeeded or failed as individuals—which in retrospect was a mistake and short-sighted.

The Education Policy Committee at San Fernando Valley State College approved the formation of a Mexican American Studies department in late April 1969, at which stage it went to the California State College Board of Trustees. The strategy was to get everything done in the first ninety days, realizing that as time went by it would become more difficult to get courses passed through faculty committees. At the time, I also proposed a change in the institution's general education policies to make these courses more accessible to the new minority students and departments. The culture of the institution was working against Chicanas/os—while some faculty empathized with blacks they could have cared less about Mexicans. Part of the indifference was due to most professors being trained outside the Southwest. Allegedly in order to avoid intellectual incest, colleges hired outside the area. SFVSC had more than its share of Ivy League graduates, which it believed was a mark of distinction. In committees faculty members reminded anyone who would listen that they were from prestigious institutions. This gang ritual is punctuated at graduations, where professors wear regalia with the colors of the universities from which they received their degrees.[20]

Pan-African Studies had sailed through the process. The fly in the ointment for Chicano Studies was the Spanish department, which challenged many of the Chicano Studies proposals. The department chair, Carmelo Gariano—singled out in the twelve-point demands as a racist—kept challenging the department's proposals. Thankfully, he was neutralized by friendly faculty. Knowledge of blacks is rooted in history. Nearly everyone had studied the Civil War, and a number of them had supported the civil rights movement. However, Mexicans were considered foreigners, the people who killed Davy Crocket at the Alamo.

Besides turf wars, the principle objection to a Department of Mexican American Studies was that it was not a discipline, which was essential to becoming an academic department, according to purists. A particular methodology distinguishes a field. A corpus of knowledge is researched using a particular methodology. For example, while history has developed alternative theoretical models, at the core of the historical method is the use and vetting of documents. A scholar who does not use documents is not a historian. This principle is so exacting that at most research institutions the rule of thumb is that a historian does not become an associate professor unless she has published one book in an academic press—two books to move to full professor. I conceded that Chicano Studies was not a discipline and argued that it was an area studies that housed multiple disciplines under its administrative wing.

The question of a corpus of knowledge defining the Mexican experience was touchy at the time of the formation of the department. If the term "Mexican American" had been separated from the Mexican experience, it would have been difficult to make the case.[21] Almost no literature was readily available on Mexican life experiences in the United States in print; it was a time before digitalized documents.[22] If Chicano Studies had limited its corpus of knowledge to the existing literature in print, it would have narrowed itself to being part of American Ethnic Studies, which at the time was almost entirely sociological, about immigrants (mostly European) and African Americans. The available Mexican American literature in print was sparse. This dilemma was partially resolved by including the Mexican experience. This transition was facilitated because the academy had very few courses on Mexico, an area that was equally neglected. For instance, outside of history no courses were offered on Mexico at San Fernando Valley State. The Spanish department had courses on Iberian literature and on the literature of the Rio de la Plata (Argentina), but none on Mexico. This was a failure that worked to Chicano Studies' advantage.

Many of these obstacles were overcome by categorizing Chicano Studies as an area. Fortunately, because of the student turmoil, the counter arguments were garbled, and only a minority of the professors on campus was rigid enough to hold up the process. Chicano Studies was also fortunate because of white fear of African Americans. (Chicano Studies owes the African American community a huge debt because it blew the door open. The blacks' continued presence created a tension Chicano Studies was able to exploit.) While the great white fathers grilled me, the members of Educational Policies Committee approved almost everything and anything that Pan-African Studies put on their plate. Yet, we knew as a matter of fairness, the committee members could not approve Pan-African's proposals and reject Mexican American Studies.[23]

Area studies developed as a reaction to the tyranny of the disciplines. Since the early nineteenth century, reformers have argued that the disciplines should not determine the areas of studies. They challenged the tyranny of the disciplines and posited that disciplines should emanate from the area. This led to the development of area studies programs similar to those in American Studies and Latin American Studies, which were in great part products of the cold war.

Area studies became popular after World War II, at a time when few scholars were interested in studying topics outside the United States. The Central Intelligence Agency and Ford Foundation, the Rockefeller Foundation, and the Carnegie Corporation of New York began funding them because they were the best way to train specialists in an area. The only kicker was that the foundations limited the definition of area studies to international programs. Many institutions developed American Studies, Latin American Studies, Asian Studies, and African Studies graduate degrees in order to break narrow specialization. I went through a Latin American Studies program. After a period of study we determined that this model was also applicable to domestic models, and it was the quickest and surest way to develop interdisciplinary Mexican American courses and ensure the hiring of Mexican American faculty members in the disparate disciplines, and to short circuit racism in hiring Chicanas/os. The uniqueness of the SFVSC program was that it was a department of area studies with a core tenured faculty the department hired. They were not joint appointments.[24]

The selection of an area studies model served another purpose. Chicano Studies are, above all, a vehicle to educate Chicana/o students from poorly prepared backgrounds. My generation was greatly influenced by John Dewey, who was one of the first to propose that pedagogy be recognized as a university discipline.[25] Dewey recognized that the university could not adequately research a corpus of knowledge without being a discipline or being recognized by the academy as one. The reason for Chicano Studies was to teach student skills by using a relevant knowledge base that would motivate them.

Proponents of Chicano Studies argued that if the college was color-blind, it would already have courses in Mexican American Studies in every department on campus. Logically, if the departments would have hired qualified professors to teach and develop those specialties there would have been no need for Chicano Studies. But, due to racism and the resistance of faculty to the acceptance of courses on Mexicans, the university neglected that corpus of knowledge. As a result of the exclusion, the colleges were failing in their mission of objectively seeking the Truth. Thus, initiating a department was very essential to the "objectivity question."

Chicano Studies was therefore not one discipline but many disciplines within an area examining a common corpus of knowledge. Chicano Studies used this logic to argue that it should be considered an area when appropriating credit for general education. When the institution certified Chicano Studies, the certification became a contract. Based on this contract, the department hired scholars according to their discipline, which was not in Chicano Studies but in art, history, music, and other fields of study. This was the argument Chicano Studies made to expand its offerings in general education and liberal studies.

Aside from being good historians and the like, faculty members were expected to develop an interdisciplinary world vision. Tenured faculties were encouraged to teach lower division classes that were outside their field. For instance, Chicano Studies 100 was supposed to include history, culture, and literature. Faculty members were supposed to know each other's disciplines, as doing so bred respect and a sense of community. This has not happened, and many Chicano Studies professors look elsewhere for legitimacy. A case in point, more Chicana/o sociologists attend the American Sociological Association's conferences than the National Association for Chicana and Chicano Studies.

The Hiring of a Faculty

The first task was to hire faculty members. Numerous candidates with terminal degrees were contacted who rejected the positions out of hand. They were not enamored with the prospect of teaching four classes at a teaching institution. The load of four courses a semester was too heavy, and the pay was low in comparison to research institutions (the preference of almost every scholar). The candidates also had to go through interviews with a committee composed of students, community, and faculty. The Mesa Directiva made it clear that it was asking for an eight-to-five commitment, five days a week. One prospect told the committee that he had not studied for twenty years to end up at a community college or glorified high school. Moreover, the number of PhDs available was limited, and those who qualified were for the most part not the types that would go to the Santa Barbara conference or want to teach in a state college. Anyone who knew academe and the changing demographics knew that due to the small number of Chicana/o PhDs available that it would in the future become a sellers' market. The dramatic growth in the Mexican and Latina/o populations would make their degrees more marketable with time.

Finally, most available Chicana/o scholars were not hustlers. Ideology, education, and commitment are not the only traits that prepare a scholar to develop a program in hostile waters. Therefore, the strategy at SFVSC became to hire good teachers with intellectual potential. That is why we called state colleges and universities to get the names of Chicana/o college graduates who ranked high in their graduating classes while at the same time seeking seasoned high school teachers. The tactic was to hire candidates as instructors—often at low salaries—with the understanding that the new professors would continue their education. No one thought a terminal degree was unnecessary. In fact, to get tenure and be promoted, instructors would have to have a terminal degree. This so-called elitist standard can be blamed not only on the institution but also on society. The world is title driven, especially capitalist and socialist societies. Moreover, once the students graduated, they wanted jobs with the department, justifying their qualifications with the fact that their professors did not have advanced degrees. In an interview, a former student told the selection committee that he was prepared to teach Chicano history because he had taken my class and had taken copious notes.

The importance of teaching experience cannot be overstated. I had done my student teaching at SFVSC in 1958 at what was then a satellite of CSCLA. When putting programs together, students and Chicana/o faculty members at other institutions made the mistake of concentrating on hiring personalities rather than building programs. For example, at California State Fullerton, the program was allocated four faculty positions to start the department, which was generous in comparison to other colleges. Its chair, Roberto Serros, boasted that Fullerton had the most qualified Chicano Studies faculty in the country because all of them had PhDs. However, they all had doctorates in Spanish literature, and two of them were Iberian specialists. They all had degrees from the University of Southern California. They presumed that because they had terminal degrees and Spanish surnames that they were qualified to teach Chicano Studies, which would have probably been true if their degrees were in different fields. Valley State took another approach and built the department much the same as a baseball team. The central consideration was the team and the skill of each player to play her or his position. (We assumed that the hires would grow into the position and get their doctorates along the way.)[26]

Many founding faculty members were former high school teachers, which was in keeping with the pedagogical mission of the department. Students entered college without proper preparation. Most of the Mexican schools did not have college prep classes at the time. High school teachers were conscious of teaching skills and had experience in developing courses. They knew what a lesson plan was and how to incrementally develop units. For example, Gerald Reséndez, one of our first faculty members, was a former vice principal at Cathedral High School. He developed capstone courses, such as Children's Literature in Translation and Religion and the Chicano, and was an excellent teacher and stable force in the department. Carlos Arce did not have a teaching background, but he was brilliant, and during the first year he attracted a strong cult following. However, he left after the second year due to personal problems and pursued a doctorate at the University of Michigan.[27]

The next faculty member hired was José Hernández, originally from Eagle Pass, Texas. Hernández had a master of arts from Ohio State and was in a doctorate program at the University of Cincinnati. He was a student teacher supervisor at the university level. The committee flew him out for an interview, and despite a split vote it was decided that a position should be offered. He had a family and was anxious to move back into *Chicanolandia*. Rafael Pérez-Sánodal was the only PhD the committee initially hired. He was known to the committee members, many of whom had worked with him in the Latin American Civic Association. Pérez was attractive on several scores: he had a terminal degree, he was a Mexican national who would appeal to the Mexican-born, and he was a task master. He developed a particular constituency—those attracted to the intellectual.

The department also made an effort to hire women teachers, which was difficult for a number of reasons, one of which was that they did not have, for the most part, the flexibility that males had to move. Indeed, the second person offered a tenure track position was a Chicana who accepted the offer but withdrew several days before classes started. At the dissertation stage of her PhD in anthropology at UCLA, she had had a traumatic experience while in Bogota, Colombia, as part of a private sector Peace Corp–like program. She had been gang raped and was stranded there without any type of support from the organization. As the semester approached, she panicked. She felt that she was not emotionally ready to assume full-time teaching duties. Alicía Sándoval, a high school teacher, taught during the first summer. She became a host of her own program on KTTV (Channel 11) and was later the editor of the NEA (National Education Association) journal *Thought and Action*. In retrospect, it would have been ideal if SFVSC would have made gender a distinct category within the program, since this would have created the need to hire a specialist in Chicana Studies.

The administration allocated Chicano Studies six positions instead of the seven demanded. When the first female candidate dropped out, the department hired Tony Ortiz as an interim appointment. The enrollment was so successful the first semester that the administration allocated Chicano Studies a seventh line to teach part time and serve as a special assistant to the president. The specification was that the candidate have a doctorate in hand. The mesa directiva selected Joe De Anda. He had a doctorate and was active in LACA. He was also a teacher at Valley Junior College and a former high school Spanish teacher in the Valley.

THE ESTABLISHMENT

Relations with administrators were always tenuous and that was good. The only thing that kept them from booting the chair of the department was the threat of a student backlash. After an initial confrontation with the first dean, things improved when Mal Sillars became the interim president and later the dean. Despite his flaws, he was a decent human being. However, the administrator that the department worked most directly with was David Benson, who belonged to the most conservative faction on campus. Associate Vice President Benson, who later became vice president, greeted me with, "I do not believe in Ethnic Studies programs, but I'll do everything in my power to see that you are successful." Benson was a Barry Goldwater Republican. Worse than that, he was a former jock, an issue that not only the liberal but also the conservative faculty would often raise. Benson, however, was a man of his word and facilitated a lot of our early projects. Unlike Jerome Richfield, later the liberal dean of the School of Letters and Sciences whom Chicano Studies later worked with, Benson did not play blacks and browns against each other. Moreover, he made key concessions: he agreed to widen the Chicano Studies net in general studies and accepted the principle of area studies. The students had already established that EOP students could take their writing and Title V government requirements in Mexican American Studies. Benson posited that limiting credit in these areas to Chicana/o students could be interpreted as discriminatory toward non-EOP students, so the EOP prerequisite was dropped.

Logically, if Chicano Studies was interdisciplinary, the area studies program should be given credit across disciplines. Valley State had a liberal arts charter, and many professors in departments such as English had terminal degrees in American Studies, avoiding the bias of mainstream departments. Benson also advised the department to study geography's offerings and its use of mode and level. I suffered through a short meeting with Richard Lamb, an opinionated and gruff man. Nevertheless, his design was a work of art, crafted to take advantage of every college regulation in the books. Its mode and level guidelines, for instance, richened the allocations to the department to the point that it had one of the lowest student teacher ratios in the college. Each class, depending on whether it was designated as a lecture class or a field studies class, would be designated seminar status and/or other combinations. In a lecture class, the teacher-student ratio may be as high as one to thirty-five, whereas in a three-unit field the ratio would be one to nine. Lamb made almost everything field study, seminars or labs.

Chicano Studies followed Lamb's model, and most of the classes built in field study, lab, or seminar components. Almost immediately enrollment justified far more faculty than was assigned. Chicano Studies was so successful that the university changed the rules by temporarily suspending them. We soon learned that what was good for the all-white geography department was not necessarily good for Chicanas/os.[28]

Jerome Richfield became dean of letters and sciences in 1972. He was self-described intellectual and infinitely more liberal than David Benson. Yet he never understood mode and level or curriculum development. In fact, when he saw the formula propelling Chicano Studies, he dumped mode and level and used head counts, which worked against the department because it had a number of art and music classes. Richfield was very loyal to his former department, philosophy, and subsidized it at the expense of the rest of the school, not just Chicano Studies. Richfield at the time was paternalistic and benevolent on the human level. He protected our political rights but never understood the intricacies of the Chicano Studies curriculum. He considered us to be a notch above Religious Studies faculty members, which to him were wannabe philosophers. Richfield was liberal, but he socialized with and subsidized the research of the most reactionary professors on campus because he considered them his intellectual peers. On a personal level, I liked Richfield and appreciated that politically he protected me. If it had not been for Richfield, I probably would have been suspended or fired. But he was not forthcoming, and his lack of fairness in curriculum matters and faculty allocations set the department back. He rationalized his actions by saying that if Chicano Studies was rewarded, he would have to lay off faculty from other departments, and that would be unfair.[29]

Finally, Richfield encouraged dissent among faculty members and departments within the college. On one occasion he volunteered that a Chicano faculty member was intellectually limited but said that the person needed help because he was not trained in a discipline and only had an EdD. At the same time, he volunteered that the professor gave him expensive tequila. He was also down on a female professor in Chicano Studies because she had an EdD. Nevertheless, Chicano Studies classes continued to increase in enrollment with no augmentation in staff.[30]

The Importance of the Educational
Opportunity Program

A department can have the soundest theoretical base. It can have the best teachers in the world. But if it does not build a support network, it will not grow. EOP is essential in building this network. Students, no matter how lacking in college preparation, think that they can make it. They believe in American myths of equality. Many of the first students recruited from barrio high schools were A and B students who, while they did not take academic subjects in high school, were told they were superior students. They believed that they were prepared to excel in college. However, the truth was that an A or a B was not the same in a Chicana/o or black Los Angeles district high school as it was in a white school. Most political Chicana/o students had no illusions and just wanted the chance to attend college. Many believed that the professors would help them, which is why they took Chicano Studies. Some came to college because of the military draft; others came for the stipends and thought it was a free ride. Still others just wanted out of their lives, wanted something better. When I asked young Chicanas what they wanted out of life, many responded that they did not want the lives their mothers had.

Proper counseling is essential to improving the success rate for students from poorly prepared and underfunded schools. At schools such as Roosevelt High, Garfield, San Fernando counselors discouraged most students from taking college prep courses. Hence, once in college the students were unprepared and had no idea about what the school required. College counselors would load them up with fifteen units of hard time, often taking combinations that students were not prepared for. Fortunately, EOP had its own counselors to guide students into Chicano Studies, where they could be incubated and could notify EOP what they lacked.[31] Often they would get special help with assignments and have the benefit of follow-up counseling. Chicano Studies also pressured the counseling office to hire psychologists trained to work with Latinas/os.

Tragically, many of those who did not go through EOP tried to take heavy loads in other majors and failed. After an initial shock, they would come to Chicano Studies for help. Because it reached out, a lot of students were saved, but we also lost some. Chicano Studies' philosophy was that even the ones who failed gained, because everyone has the right to succeed, and everyone also has the right to fail. Chicano Studies had to seed a generation or two. Students still approach me and ask me if I remember their parents who attended CSUN (aka Valley State). I always say yes, but in some cases the parents or parent only attended for a semester or less. The important thing was that college showed them something better, gave them pretensions, and they passed on this memory to their children.

Without EOP many students would have floundered and they never found their way to Chicano Studies. They would have remained isolated in some *rinconcito*, a small corner of the university, arguing whether there was a Chicano paradigm. Tragically, Chicano Studies programs often isolate themselves from EOP and even go into competition with it. In these cases, the students suffer. In the first years the Chicano Studies department was fortunate because it had a Chicano and a black EOP. The two units were consolidated about five years later. By that time the departments were rooted. These programs were all consolidated in the name of integration in 1972, but like Ethnic Studies, integration does not always produce a positive outcome.[32]

More recently, EOP has been pressured to mainstream and recruit students from parochial and magnet schools. This helps the university's retention and graduation numbers. At the same time, Chicano Studies faculty members begin to think of themselves as members of the community of scholars at the academy. They forget that they were hired to teach working-class Chicana/o students. EOP staffs begin to serve the interest of administrators, who blame the lack of retention on students being unprepared, and they become more selective about who they recruit. They want "quality."

In this equation, students are essential to keeping everyone honest. SFVSC was fortunate, since after the twelve-point agreement EOP was divided into a Mexican American EOP and a black EOP, which allowed them to concentrate on the needs of their respective groups. It also minimized the competition between Mexican

Americans and blacks—keeping conflict at a minimum. It gave the Chicanas/os and blacks a feeling of autonomy.

THE INTERNAL LOGIC OF CHICANA/O STUDIES

Like every other field in academe, Chicana/o Studies follows an internal logic and rhythm. The system develops student skills and ensures the interdisciplinary area of study. It attempts to build on a general knowledge of a particular discipline within Chicana/o Studies, progressing to more specialized courses. For example, first-year courses are introductory, while in the sophomore year it is assumed that the student has some knowledge of the subject matter. The third year is not technically an introduction but more general than the fourth year. The student by this time should have a prerequisite background to permit more specialized studies. For example, the "History of Mexico" belongs in the 300 series, whereas the "History of Mexico in the 20th Century" belongs in the 400 sequence.

An interdisciplinary program organizes the disparate disciplines in a way to complement each other. This overview and more specialized scheme is even evident inside the lower and upper divisions, with the 100 classes being breadth classes and the 200 being depth. In the upper division, the 300 courses introduce an area of study, whereas the 400 is more content based. The first Mexican American Studies offerings generally followed this pattern. An exception was that in the beginning the SFVSC program eliminated the 300 level courses because Chicano Studies wanted to push for a master of arts program in which only 400 classes were accepted—junior (300) level classes' could not be used for graduate credit. The numbering system for upper division classes is as follows:

    300–399 or 400–499
    00–09, culture or anthropology
    10–19 visual arts and music
    20–29 economics
    30–39 education classes
    40–44 geography
    45–49 history
    50–59 religion, philosophy, and thought
    60–69 politics and community study
    70–79 sociological theory, the family, and urban institutions
    80–89 literature and linguistics

Based on this logic, Chicano Studies resisted the temptation to hire friends. Faculty members were hired to meet the curricular needs of the department's course of study and not the professors' preferences. Specialization was essential. An instructor could be a good sociologist, but that did not qualify him to teach about children or upper division art. It would have been impossible for the core of professors to teach all the courses in Chicano Studies. The clear distinction in the individual disciplines forced the department to hire specialists to teach in each of the disciplines. This ensured, for example, that Chicano Studies did not have too many historians or too many literature specialists.

The Chicano Studies major had four options: humanities and the arts, social science, education, and community studies. At one time the education component was for the purpose of expanding Chicano Studies' autonomy and offering pedagogical offerings. The department wanted to offer education classes and eventually credential teachers to teach in elementary and secondary schools. Hence, a numbering sequence was essential.

THE MONOPOLY GAME

At research and teaching universities, turf is extremely important. Teaching institutions, unlike research institutions, which are heavily funded and endowed, operate on an academic marketplace. A Monopoly board determines the successes and failures of new fields of study. Therefore, to survive in the game the new department has to get a piece of property. This is easier said than done, since the "Boardwalks" and all of the prime property on the campus is owned by the founding departments. The operators are good capitalists; they don't give an inch, and when they do it is a pittance. The disparate Ethnic Studies programs are thrown into the minority ghetto to compete for three units with the other misfits. The former nerds who were knocked around in high school and live in fear of rebellions protect their turf through committees that configure general education and other mandatory programs. They work deals that force students to take their courses. To stay in the game and get a degree, students must land on designated properties. This becomes really insidious, since the board determines the size of the faculty, the size of the offices, secretarial help, and resources.

They justify adding to the requirement and maintaining their monopoly by using politics to argue their case. For example, the requirement that students take a year of Western Civilization has been a sacred cow. Any attempt to change this requirement has met opposition. Just changing the focus from Western Civilization to World History produced cultural wars that still rage in academe. At Northridge, white faculty members and administrators had a hard time accepting that a history class taught in Chicano Studies class by a trained PhD in history was the same as a history course taught in the history department by a white historian, even though the history department's class was often taught by a teaching assistant. The same rule applied to art, dance, sociology, and the like.

The most important battle after getting the department approved was general education. General education is the breadbasket of teaching universities and colleges. Even more so than majors, the portion of general education that a department cuts out determines its growth: "One common purpose of general education programs is to ensure that students have a secure foundation in prerequisite skills that will be essential for upper-level and disciplinary major courses. On most campuses, these foundation skills include mathematical understanding, written communication, and computing and information technology."[33] This principle adheres to the liberal arts tradition that pretends to produce a well-rounded student.[34] General education has been almost eliminated in prestigious small liberal arts colleges. However, in public institutions, especially community colleges, general education is "key" to ensuring that "ill-prepared" students receive a "proper" education.

Again research and teaching institutions differ, and the disciplines and tradition play a more important role at the former.[35] At teaching colleges, a strong department is essential for getting a share of general education and liberal studies. Without a department, Chicano Studies could not play on the Monopoly board, and they would be at the mercy of majors within the disparate disciplines. As it is, the department has had to battle for properties such as Title V (U.S. history and government requirements), English, literature, economics, etc. Chicano Studies often used students to stack Educational Policies Committee meetings and the Subcommittee of General Education with students. It often got ugly.

CREATING THE LEGEND

Academe is a microcosm of society. It creates illusions of self-governance. Throughout the 1970s the institutions that established Ethnic Studies programs told minority scholars that to survive the programs had to attract students to carry their share of the load. In order to survive, they had to enroll students in order to justify the classes. The same rule applied to research institutions that spent millions of dollars to establish and support Medieval Studies centers that served a half dozen students. But the Ethnic Studies center had to scurry around for soft money to pay their way. In reality, not all of the animals were equal.

The illusion is that the administration is fair—it is the victim's fault for its community not wanting Chicana/o Studies. The reality is that institutions of higher learning prioritize what courses students should take. At the community college level, the first classes to fill are the general education classes that are transferable to four-year institutions. The same pattern follows students into the upper division. Most colleges have set general education courses that are negotiated by departments and administrators. Over the years, it takes what amounts to a constitutional amendment to change them. Counselors tell their students to get the general education classes out of the way, even before they decide on a major. The result is a monopoly game that students play, and new departments are expected to survive.

Who gets what depends on what the professors on a labyrinth of committees think is important. Generally, senior professors are elected to these committees. They know each other, drink each other's merlot, and often sleep together. At teaching institutions, general education is a big deal because departments are allocated professors and other resources on student enrollment. There is an illusion of inclusion based on the legend of faculty governance.

There are openings, however. For example, San Fernando Valley State College was established as a complement to Los Angeles State College, which had a general charter that allowed it to offer technical programs, such as nursing and industrial arts education. SFVSC, in contrast, had a liberal arts charter in the tradition of a Harvard. The liberal arts curriculum essentially revolved around history, philosophy, abstract sciences, and language—disciplines that scholars believe foster general intellectual ability. The curriculum entails classical learning as distinct from specialized or vocational training. The fundamental principle of any liberal study is the notion that society's quality of life depends on rational thought. However, as mentioned, universities are far from being rational and are more like theological centers than academies. It is difficult to introduce new knowledge when everything is deduced from accepted knowledge. It is in these instances where other knowledge must be induced through disruption.

A basic flaw with most studies on Chicana/o Studies and Latina/o Studies is that researchers have not looked at the epistemology of the field. I would posit that Chicana/o Studies is not yet fully developed as a research field, and that its development as a teaching field has been thwarted by being housed in disparate disciplines. We are on the road toward developing a content field, but we still have not arrived. The basis and justification for the area is more pedagogical than it is theoretical. Everyone has the right to know how to read and write. So, we must concentrate on being superior teachers.

A serious flaw in the formation of the SFVSC was the failure to address the gender question and homophobia. Many naively believed that education and political action alone would transform society, and that all forms of inequality would disappear. Others were just plain patriarchal and homophobic. What most failed to recognize was that activism alone would not transform society as a whole. That could not happen without a constant critique of the social order and a correction of its imperfections. For many, this was the pedagogical mission of Chicano studies: to empower Chicana/o students and the whole community through the act of critical thinking. This was what San Francisco State, the Chicano walkouts, and the establishment of Chicano studies was about. The stemming of the dropout problem was essential to this mission.

CHAPTER 5

The Building of Chicano Studies

The years 1969–1973 were critical to the formation of Chicano Studies. Students took advantage of a window of opportunity to form Chicano student organizations that were able to negotiate and disrupt when reason failed. The opportunities closed rapidly at the end of the Vietnam War, and any goodwill that Chicano students had dissipated quickly. After this point, the high priests moved to reassert *their* control over *their* institutions.[1] The adrenaline boost infused by the movements of the sixties was gone. The only possible advantage was the decline in white enrollment. The end of the white baby boom led to a loss of 12,000 students in the Los Angeles schools in 1971, and the birthrate in the state slowed down another 6 percent that year. The crisis would have devastated the schools if it had not been for the rise in minority enrollment, which since 1967 had increased by 50 percent. The decline in the white student population was offset by the rise in the Latino student population at the K–12 levels.[2]

However, Chicanos were not in a position to exploit these events, because they were not used to thinking in these terms, and because most Mexican Americans were still not prepared academically to go to college. Unofficially over 60 percent were still pushed out before finishing high school, and the quality of the schools remained separate and unequal. What changed was the attitude of a minority of students that learned from the Chicano movement that *si se puede*, and more blamed the crappy schools instead of themselves. What had not changed was institutional racism and the attitudes of many educators who denied the glaring inequality in the schools. In 1973 many educators still attempted to explain the educational disadvantaged by saying that their culture bred poverty.[3] Denial was still the main strategy for not ending education inequality—a strategy that had changed little since the early 1960s when the strategy to end the dropout rate was to end "cultural disadvantage."[4]

EDUCATIONAL OPPORTUNITY PROGRAM AND NUMBERS

The name of the outreach efforts varied from state to state. The best known was the California EOPs. California was important because it had 9.8 percent of the national population, 15 percent of all students in higher learning, and 12 percent of federal EOP funds.[5] The programs

> varied at each level of California's tripartite system of higher education, the student recruitment and retention program focused primarily on increasing access to higher education and to servicing the academic and financial needs of minority and low income students in an effort to redress educational inequity. Whereas EOP at the UC and the state college system was known as the Educational Opportunity Program, at times it was referred to as the Equal Opportunity Program in the community college system.[6]

The California Master Plan for Higher Education (1960) designated the University of California campuses as research institutions and the state colleges as teaching institutions. According to the plan, the University of California selected its freshmen students from the top one-eighth (12.5 percent) of the high school graduating class, and California State Colleges picked from the top one-third (33.3 percent). The junior colleges were supposed to take the leftovers. Without EOP, the growth of Chicano and Black Studies would not have been possible. EOP was the frontline; it admitted, motivated, funded, and retained students. In order to achieve this goal they were engaged in recruitment, counseling, tutoring, and retention. Hence, where strong EOP units emerged, strong Chicano Studies programs followed.[7]

Without a doubt, the expansion of these programs benefited from the large African American population. According to Harry Kitano and Dorothy Miller, California's population was comprised of 11.1 percent Chicanas/os and 7.2 percent blacks—but only 11.0 percent of the community colleges, 3.8 percent of the university enrollment, and 5.8 percent of the state college students were black or Mexican American. In the fall of 1968 black Americans comprised 1,456 students out of 66,857 total University of California students and 960 EOP students, whereas Mexican Americans made up 1,186 students and 550 EOP students. In 1969, 4,216 EOP students attended the state colleges—59 percent were black and 34 percent had Spanish surnames.[8]

In 1968 the University of California president's office reported that the EOP had 1,948 students enrolled, compared with 1,090 the last year and 472 two years ago. There were 918 blacks and 500 Mexican Americans.[9] Numbers tell the importance of the EOP network. In 1964–1965 there were about 100 EOP students in the UC system. According to the University of California by the fall of 1969 there were 5,300 EOP students, 4,200 were undergraduates. In November 1969, the *Los Angeles Times* wrote, "Berkeley's EOP program was the first in the states and is now one of the largest in the nation, having grown from a handful of students four years ago to 1,166 this fall. . . . About 55% of the EOP students at Berkeley are black, 25% are Chicano with the rest divided among American Indians and low-income whites and others."[10] Sixty-three University of California, Berkeley, EOP students graduated in the four-year period. Despite a promising record, the program was threatened by state and federal cutbacks and students had to resort to fundraising. The gains were miniscule in comparison to the state population, and in June 1970 Gil García, the director of the UCLA Mexican American Cultural Affairs Center, pointed out that UCLA had more foreign students than Chicanas/os on campus, numbering about 600 out of 31,000. Out of a faculty of 1,800 only five were of Mexican origin.[11]

Like the University of California, the state colleges concentrated on low-income and first-generation college students. In 1966, 86 EOP-type students attended the California state colleges; by the fall of 1969 the enrollment was up to 3,150. EOP admissions were limited to 2 percent of the total college population (later raised to 4 percent). Established at Sacramento State College in the spring of 1968, EOP operated a tutorial center. According to Frank Navarrette, "The biggest problem our Educational Opportunity students face is the cultural shock of entering college and learning what the college—and particularly the professors—expect of them for success." Despite the obstacles, Sacramento State lost less than 10 percent of its students.[12] This was a similar problem at each of the state college campuses, where often struggles between Chicanas/os and blacks for control of the programs often got out of control. The success of enrollment for fall 1969 motivated the more political Chicano student organizations that had been hampered by their low numbers. Also, it must be repeated that, unlike white radicals and even black students before 1968, Chicano students were first-generation college students with little organizational experience.

The state colleges at this point lagged behind the University of California. When Kitano and Miller conducted their survey, only twelve of the nineteen EOP directors responded.[13] Although there was some improvement in the numbers of minority students entering the state college campuses, out of 13,759 *qualified* to enter, some 3,780 entered as freshman in 1969–1970, only 27 percent of those educationally eligible versus 60 percent of white high school graduates.[14] A major problem aside from recruitment was the filling out of applications, bad high school counseling, and disillusionment.

At the junior colleges, Chicano Studies departments were never able to dig trenches deep enough to withstand the assault of not only their administrations but also the faculty governing bodies. Students at two-year institutions turn over every two years. It is tough to a build leadership base and programs within that short space of time. Moreover, white faculty members have more rights at the two-year college level. In addition, faculties are unionized and therefore unions play a much greater role in the politics of the district. Through political action, which means money, the unions have been able to elect a majority of the trustees to community college boards, who often do the unions' bidding. Unfortunately, many white union members have seen—and still see—Chicano Studies and professors as competitors.[15] Community colleges have also had to overcome the stigma of being minority ghettoes. The state spent $800 per student at community colleges, compared to $1,500 per student at state colleges and $2,500 at universities.[16]

What pushed outreach were Mexican American student organizations. The community colleges did not formally begin an EOP until January 1970. Prior to 1967 Mexican American organizations lacked political trajectories and functioned as support groups aimed at motivating students. MASA at East Los Angeles College initially worked on community projects, including tutoring in the public schools and supporting Chicano politicos. By 1968 the organization became increasingly active on campus. While less than 2 percent of the Mexican American student population attended the University of California and state college campuses, about 8 percent were enrolled at junior colleges. These numbers made new student organizations possible.[17]

DEPARTMENTS OF CHICANO STUDIES: A CRITICAL VIEW

The best way to grow the area of Chicano Studies is a department. Centers, institutes, and programs are not full members of the academy. Moreover, only through a department can Chicano Studies achieve a balanced curriculum and stability. A single discipline does not address the wide range of disciplinary approaches that make up the totality of the study of the Mexican peoples in the United States.[18] Chicano Studies departments developed more easily at the state colleges because of their organizational structure. In considering this equation, distinctions must be made between a teaching college and a research university.

CALIFORNIA STATE UNIVERSITY, LOS ANGELES—THE MEXICAN MECCA

At the big three, Los Angeles, Long Beach, and San Diego, Chicano student relations with their administrations were initially cordial. Over the next three years these relations deteriorated. Everyone expected CSCLA to hit the ground running when Ralph Guzmán was appointed to head up Chicano Studies. Guzmán had been an associate director of the UCLA Mexican American Studies Project and had attended East Los Angeles College before graduating from CSCLA on the GI Bill. In the 1960s he was finishing up his PhD at UCLA. A columnist with the *Eastside Sun* and the *Los Angeles Free Press*, Guzmán worked for La Alianza Hispano Americana and the American Civil Liberties Union. During the Vietnam War, Guzmán did the first research on Latino casualty figures and found that Chicanos from the five southwestern states were being killed and wounded at twice the rate of their numbers in the general population.[19]

According to Gilbert Cárdenas and Phil Castruita, Carlos Muñoz led the anti-Guzmán faction (Cárdenas and Castruita supported Guzmán). A dispute seems to have begun over his proposal for Mexican American Studies, which did not include a demand for a department. Muñoz described it as too mainstream—too much like Latin American Studies—which is ironically what most successful programs evolved into. According to Muñoz, "the proposal for a Mexican American studies program had an emphasis on traditional academic and professional training." He called it an unfortunate student-faculty struggle. Meanwhile, under student leadership, the *Los Angeles Times* reported a total of five classes would be offered during the winter quarter.[20]

Yet, even after the coup of Guzmán, CSCLA and Chicanos had cordial relations with college administrators, who gave Chicano Studies departmental status in name only, appointing a procession of graduate students to run or try to implement Chicano Studies.[21] From a May 1969 report it is clear that the Chicano Studies Department was still under development. Like other programs of the day, it was very much a service unit—a coequal with EOP—and was responsible to the UMAS. What stood out about the report was the absence of information on the Chicano Studies program and its progress. Also surprising was the high level of participation of students throughout the Southern California area as consultants for Chicano brokers. Witness the Long Beach conference—especially since most were so critical of Chicano establishment figures—calling them *vendidos.*

Another letdown was the failure of Chicano Studies to control Chicano space— that is, Chicano-related courses and programs. From the beginning at Valley State, the department insisted that all courses and programs related to Chicanos be routed through Chicano Studies during the vetting process. (In theory, every department has the power to flag courses related to its discipline.) For example, in June 1969 CSCLA announced a five-year million-dollar U.S Office of Education grant to train teachers to teach Chicana/o students. The grant was administered by Charles F. Leyba, associate chair of the secondary education department, and forty-one students received a $200 monthly stipend. The remainder went toward administrative costs and fees, professors' salaries, clerical assistance, and space rental. This grant took the focus away from Chicano Studies and UMAS.[22] Being in the heart of the Mexican barrio, the School of Education had mapped out an area of interest in Mexican American education, and numerous conferences were held on campus. CSCLA was known as the minority school, with 20 percent of its 20,000 students being Mexican American or black. In March 1968 it received a $135,000 grant from the Rockefeller Foundation—this was on top of a $165,000 grant for an experimental project at Locke High School, a predominately black school.[23]

The Los Angeles chapter of UMAS on June 4, 1969, sponsored a forum at CSCLA; graduate student Gilbert González had taken over for Carlos Muñoz Jr. At least in the press, CSCLA President John Greenlee gave lip service to Chicano gains. However, the climate was changing as Chicana/o students pressed the administration to recruit more students. Ultimately, the Chicano faculty leadership could not equal the savvy (and ruthlessness) of administrators like Deans Leonard Mathy and Don Dewey who did not share the interests of Chicano Studies. Another factor contributing to California State's turbulence and factionalism was that it was in the eye of the storm—in the center of Los Angeles' largest concentration of Chicanas/os, with a surplus of student leaders, many of whom became prominent scholars, lawyers, journalist, medical doctors, and teachers. The intense activism of the times also contributed to factionalism. There was no stable organizational structure to socialize incoming or current Chicano students. The disorganization was predictable because the bulk was first-generation college students from working-class families not privy to the organizational experiences that many white and African American students had. Another factor that is not often mentioned is that a core of white faculty members felt threatened by the large Chicano population immediately outside the campus' walls; hence, faculty opposition was intense.[24]

Nevertheless, CSCLA was a center of information during the Chicano movement. Speakers such as César Chávez, Dolores Huerta, Corky Gonzales, Reies López Tijerina, Bert Corona, Sal Castro, Alicia Escalante, Joe Razo, and David Sánchez drew sizable crowds. Additionally, CSCLA produced a large number of academics, including Gilbert Cárdenas, Carlos Muñoz, Gil González, Feliz Gutiérrez, María Elena Gutiérrez, Monte Pérez, Vicky Castro, María Baeza, Becky Reza, Mary Pardo, Phil Castruita, and Oscar Martínez. The EOP student population went from 133 students in the spring of 1969 to 593 in the 1969–1970 academic year.

SAN DIEGO STATE COLLEGE: IN THE SHADOW OF LOGAN HEIGHTS

The San Diego State College's Chicano Studies program came about through the activity of the Mexican American Youth Association (MAYA), which formed in 1967. MAYA organized an ad hoc committee to develop the department and the Centro de Estudios Chicanos (Mexican American) and classes on the Mexican American experience. The committee consisted of two professors, an administrator, and MAYA students. The program offered its first classes in the spring of 1969.

The notion of a Chicano Studies department at San Diego State received a boost from the Plan de Santa Barbara. It began as a Chicano program and blossomed in 1969. In the early 1970s it "launched a full–fledged Chicana and Chicano Studies Program," which Chicanos called a department. The acting chair, Gustave V. Segade, worked part time in the department. José Villarino, Ruth Robinson, Rafael Estupinian, and Alurista were instructors. David Weber taught a class, as did historian Juan Gómez-Quiñones, who left for UCLA in the fall. Queta Vásquez, Evangelina Bustamante, and Carlos Vélez-Ibañez were among the part-timers. Rene Nuñez, who arrived in fall 1969, was not one of the original organizers or developers of the department. Vélez-Ibañez became the chair in 1970.

The program received departmental status circa 1971 when Vélez-Ibañez revised the curriculum. It was not part of the College of Liberal Arts and Science, reporting to the assistant vice president for Academic Affairs. According to Vélez-Ibañez, the strategy was to improve access to resources, which would have been problematic if it had been a department. Hence, they made the conscious decision not to incorporate within the college structure. The administration initially allocated four positions to the program in the fall of the 1969–1970 academic year, and 6.5 faculty positions for the spring.[25] However, it did not have official departmental status. The next academic year the program reached 10.75 teaching positions, serving about 1,100 students and offering thirty-nine sections per semester.

The center was established after the department and did not play a major role in curriculum development. It served as an umbrella for the various organizations to develop Chicano programs. The center under Nuñez's leadership did bring ideological intensity; however, the fallout eventually destroyed a highly functional department. Students during Vélez-Ibañez' tenure did not make hiring decisions or vote, but they did participate in the interviewing of candidates. By 1971 the department had begun to implode, and Vélez-Ibañez resigned and returned to graduate school.

According to Nuñez, he was hopeful of getting a Chicano school. His reasoning was that Chicanos could achieve more autonomy through not being part of the college structure preferring to rely on the good faith of President Love. For San Diego State College administration, this arrangement was profitable: Nuñez obtained a Department of Health Education and Welfare grant to fund the Centro and Barrio Stations. Because the program thrived, the administration was relieved of the responsibility of providing hard money for its operation.[26] Moreover, the fact that the department was not part of the institutional structure left faculty members vulnerable: faculty members were not granted tenure and served at the whim of the administration.

Meanwhile, factions developed that vied for control—an all-out struggle raged from 1970 to mid-1974. One faction wanted to consolidate into a department and into the college structure in order to combine its growth and stabilize its programs. Another, led by the October League, wanted self-determination. Nuñez eventually followed this path. Considerable discussion occurred on how San Diego State could remain consistent with the goal of self-determination as articulated in El Plan de Santa Barbara. The consensus was that student leadership should remain involved in all aspects of departmental affairs. MEChA assisted in running the department, helped make policy, hired and fired faculty in consultation with Mexican American Studies faculty, and helped develop curriculum. Theoretically, that participation would transform students. "It was felt that the highest level of education was in an individual's participation in transforming his/her own condition. The process that was established allowed students to be involved in controlling their own programs." By the mid-1970s the Marxist contingent was in decline, and in 1977 Mexican American Studies joined the College of Professional Studies. Two years later, it transferred to the College of Arts and Letters.[27]

No doubt the internecine struggles hurt the department and the entire Chicano operation. By 1980 the department shrank to five positions, with an enrollment of 482, seven fewer spots than in 1971. In San Diego one of the most promising Chicano programs all but disappeared. Slowly the department recovered during the 1980s, but it never fully recovered its 1970 high. Thirty years later Timothy McKernan wrote the following:

> A faction of faculty and students with a Marxist philosophy—those who wanted that "definite policy-making relationship" that they perceived as part of the self-determination precept put forth in El Plan—struggled against members of the Mexican-American community to control the direction of the young department. The Marxist faction dismissed the Chicanos as reactionary; the Chicanos felt the Marxist approach smacked of a betrayal of the culture the department was created to perpetuate.[28]

Much of the energy evaporated after Nuñez and others left. He represented the enthusiasm of El Plan de Santa Barbara—its sense of revolution. Knowing the times, however, it is naive to blame the Marxist, or the nationalist, or the assimilationist. This is too simplistic. Nuñez in many ways got caught up with his own idealism, and the early success blinded him. A former military officer, he should have realized that even revolutions have to be consolidated. Moreover, revolutions are made in the streets, not on college campuses.

The October League was not the only player. After 1972 San Diego became a battleground between the Social Workers Party, Marxist Leninist, nationalists, and others. It became so chaotic that Vélez-Ibañez, a stabilizing force, left for the University of California, San Diego, to complete his PhD. A positive aspect of the whole affair was the self-critical sessions. Positive changes took place in the students themselves. Feminists Enriqueta Chávez from Calexico and Felicitas Nuñez from Brawley, played constructive roles during the whole process. Alurista, the poet of the Chicano movement at the time, built a sense of community and a sense of idealism.[29] For a time, the department and the Centro had done extremely well. They opened a library and a community tutoring center, and they administered internships. In addition, San Diego State students were involved with Chicano Park and other grassroots activities.

CALIFORNIA STATE COLLEGE AT LONG BEACH:
IN THE SHADOW OF THE ANGELS

California State College at Long Beach (CSCLB) is south of downtown Los Angeles. In 1969 it had a student body of 27,000 students who were overwhelmingly from moderate and white middle-class families. According to Dean of Students George Demos, only fifty to seventy-five students belonged to Students of a Democratic Society (SDS), which nevertheless kept the pot boiling on campus, promoting the issues of war and educational equity. Without this agitation, college officials would not have implemented reforms. The dean said of the SDS that he felt that he had been in combat. According to Demos, one member of the SDS told him that when they took over they were going to put him against the wall and shoot him. One demonstration drew as many as 2,000 students. Demos admitted that because of the demonstrations and sit-ins, Black Studies, Mexican American Studies, Native American Studies, and Asian Studies came about, but added they would have happened without the protests.[30]

Recruiting was successful. Long Beach had 244 EOP students in the spring of 1969 and 484 in 1969–1970. The Mexican American Studies program at CSCLB was informally launched in the spring of 1969 when Phil Móntez and Richard Alatorre taught part-time classes in the program—no doubt benefiting from the political climate at Long Beach. Armando Vásquez, chair of MEChA 1970–1971, recalls that despite the tensions of the times the relations with President Stephen Horn and the CSCLB chapter of MEChA were excellent.[31] Indeed, the administration had allowed UMAS to designate Frank Sándoval, the student chair, as the department's first chair and appointed other students to professorships.

In May 1969 UMAS received a grant from the Department of Health Education and Welfare for a three-day conference.[32] The presenters were Chicano professionals outside Chicano Studies. Frank Sándoval, twenty-nine, and Frank Sánchez, reputed to be the brains of the operation, had excellent relations with Armando Rodríguez, the chief of the Mexican American Affairs Unit of the United States Office of Education, who keynoted the conference.[33] Rodríguez was a Washington insider who brokered many of the early grants.[34] In the summer of the following year, Sándoval and others sponsored a three-day conference at Harbor College with the purpose of setting up a Chicano Institute to consult with other studies programs in California and the Southwest. The National Endowment for the Humanities funded the programs.[35] Sándoval used movement rhetoric to perfection. "How can a man who's gotten his Ph.D. after 10 years of study relate to the problems of the Chicano barrio—particularly 'if he's white?'" he asked. "On THE OTHER hand, we'd be destroying ourselves if we hired someone just because he had a brown face."[36]

Long Beach MEChA ran a federally funded Chicano Mobile Institute that supposedly had flying squads of educators to help Chicano Studies in California, Arizona, New Mexico, Texas, Utah, and Colorado grow. Problems began to develop in 1973; that year the Mobile Institute was run out of New Mexico Highlands University in Las Vegas, New Mexico. The original grant had been through MONTAL Educational Systems in Los Angeles, with funding through the Education Professions Development Act. Aside from Long Beach, much of the leadership came out of Phoenix, Boulder, New Mexico, and Texas. Its focus was the cultivation of state and local elected officials.[37] In Long Beach, the Chicano Studies Institute was administered by Louis Rosales, twenty six, and it allegedly helped develop leadership programs elsewhere. The campus run projects, according to Vásquez, were successful.[38]

The role of outside funding was unknown to other campuses. The Chicano movement as a whole was puritanical in regard to federal projects, labeling the operators poverty pimps. Meanwhile, Frank Sánchez took employment with the Department of Health, Education and Welfare, working out of Washington D.C.[39] Sánchez, who obtained a PhD from George Washington University, used his contacts to acquire McDonald's fast-food franchises in Downtown Los Angeles and in East Los Angeles. Sánchez stated, "In 1982 I was chosen as a franchisee to open a McDonald's in East LA. Although this was dramatic change in my professional career, I decided to take the opportunity. It was a business opportunity, but I also felt that McDonald's was a company that would also allow me to work for family and community so that I could continue community activities that I had developed."[40] Criticism of the student activities was based not so much on the programs or that most people were making money from them, but that MEChA and Chicano Studies were being used as covers for the operations.

In 1971 because of pressure from the administration, and criticism from some Mechistas who were dissatisfied with Sándoval, Sánchez, and company, an outside search was conducted for a chair. They hired Frank Cruz, a Sonoma State professor who had taught in the Los Angeles Schools.[41] Problems developed when, according to Cruz, the cabal worked to hold on to control of the department and exert influence using the leverage that the grants gave them with the college administration. The group chafed as Sándoval and other former student leaders were let go after a protracted struggle. Cruz set about professionalizing the department, an action which did not always have positive results.

Cruz denied that student control was a problem. According to him, the conflict was about a small group of individuals who wanted to control the department and increase the influence of Chicano corporations that brokered government funding. While Sándoval, Sánchez, and others had been students, they were no longer students, and they were older than most Mechistas. My opinion was clouded by a phone call that I received from Sándoval in which he started to harangue me for allegedly supporting Cruz. The real reason for his call was my opposition to his attempts to bring federal projects to Valley State, something that would have relieved the administration of having to deal with the department, since it could turn around and say that it was already dealing with Chicanos. Further, these projects would not be subject to Chicano faculty, student, or community governance. Had it happened, the growth and moral authority of the department would have been seriously impacted.[42]

When I pushed back, Sándoval put Mike Montes on the line. This infuriated me, since it strained my relationship with Mike, who was the driving force behind the Latin American Civic Association, and I had worked with him for years. Montes, a dentist with excellent activist credentials, had been a member of the State Board of Education, a Congressional Advisory Committee on Bilingual Education, and several charitable organizations. He was also the president and principal stockholder of Montal Systems Incorporated, a taxable California corporation organized in 1969 to engage in Mexican American educational activities. Our relations had been cordial, occasionally strained by his close relationship with Phil Móntez, a close friend of Sándoval. It became evident that Montes did not understand why I opposed the grant that Montal wanted to run through San Fernando Valley State. I explained that it was not about Montal but my distrust of people such as Sándoval who used Chicano Studies as a vehicle for their own economic interests. After this point, my relations with Long Beach and Montes were strained.

Without a doubt, the grants initially bought the cabal favor with the Long Beach administration. The college received a 20–40 percent cut from grants for administrative purposes. The grants funded Mobile Institutes at Long Beach, who in turn sponsored research studies. But Sándoval was not satisfied with running programs through Long Beach and sought to influence other programs.

Some of the projects and people associated with Sándoval cannot be dismissed out of hand. They supported the East Long Beach Neighborhood Center, Centro de la Raza, which housed Chicano artists and was funded by the Long Beach Commission on Economic Opportunity. It included a Chicano Pride School, summer day camps, and English-as-a-second-language classes. These projects were the brain children of Armando Vásquez, who was the director of La Escuelita, a special preschool on the Eastside and president of the Neighborhood Center's board of directors.

By 1974 a decline in Chicano student enrollment at Long Beach State was apparent. An EOP study showed 1,435 Chicano students at the Long Beach campus—the third annual decline since 1972, when it had a high of 1,561 students. The Chicanos' grade-point average was about 2.1, while the non-Chicano students' was 2.2. A comment on the study asked, "If the university, which graduates 10 percent of the teachers in the state, cannot create and implement more effective educational programs for Chicanos, how can we expect the high schools and elementary schools to likewise close the gap?" At nearby Long Beach City College there were 1,238 Chicanos enrolled.[43] In November 1975, Frank Cruz became a television news field reporter for KABC, and the department went into survival mode.[44]

FRESNO STATE COLLEGE: IN THE LAND OF THE COWBOYS

With mostly white faculty and students, Fresno State had a student body of 13,000 in the late sixties. The school started as Fresno Normal in 1911 to educate young men and women interested in teaching. It became Fresno State College in 1935 and its Chicano Studies program was the first in the state to declare itself a department in the 1960s.[45] The year 1968 brought the outside world to Fresno, as campus-wide protests ripped the campus apart. Fresno State President Frederic Ness had denied tenure to English professor Robert Mezey despite positive evaluations from his department and the dean of the School of Arts and Sciences. In November 1967, Mezey had participated in a "Panel on Pot." Mezey commented that the laws against marijuana were ineffective and unjust. These remarks caused a public uproar, and the termination of Mezey brought student and faculty protests.[46] Meanwhile, Ness poured oil on the fire with the clumsy hiring of Marvin X, a black Muslim.

Pressured by California State College Chancellor Glenn Dumke, Ness refused to hire the charismatic poet. In turn, Marvin X defied Ness and Dumke, touching off a thunder of protests. This led to Ness's resignation in the fall of 1969. The *Los Angeles Times* reported:

> Black Muslim Marvin X appears to be the most powerful man at Fresno State College.... He teaches despite orders to the contrary from State College Chancellor Glenn S. Dumke. He caused the institution's respected president to quit.... Marvin X doesn't care much about chancellors and presidents. His dedication is to black people.... "I don't want to teach," the wiry, 25-year old told *The Times*, "but black people have to do what is necessary to get their people out of hell."[47]

The Marvin X standoff led to a boycott of classes supported by the student senate. Acting president Karl Falk introduced a radical reorganization of the college structure, replacing many administrators. Falk then curtailed funds in the Experimental College, the Ethnic Studies Program, and EOP, which eventually implemented layoffs.

In late May 1970 about one hundred black and brown students allegedly destroyed a $1 million computer with fire bombs. Falk banned all public assemblies not approved by his office. Militant students violated the order and held a noon rally. Two hours later, about fifty Chicano and black students marched to the library and shattered thirteen large windows. City police were placed on standby call, and Phillip Walker, the acting dean of arts and sciences, recommended that eight of the twelve instructors, among them Richard Keyes, the chair of Black Studies, and Eliezer Risco-Lozada, the chair of La Raza Studies, be terminated.[48] Risco-Lozada was a Cuban national and founder of *La Raza* magazine in Lincoln Heights. La Raza Studies was a program within the department of Ethnic Studies and as such had strong ties to Black Studies. It actively supported Marvin X's appointment.

On July 14, 1970, Norman Baxter became the president of Fresno State College. In September, Baxter refused to reinstate the eight Ethnic Studies professors, blaming them for the May fire bombings and disturbances. Falk then canceled La Raza classes for fall 1970, one week before they were to start, claiming that the program had not hired qualified faculty and that La Raza Studies had refused to adopt an academic model that met his approval. The real reason was that Baxter considered the leadership radical and yielded to pressure from the business community and the Chancellor's Office to terminate it.[49]

La Mesa Directiva of Fresno demanded that the program be reinstated and that the administration be given status similar to what was given to the Fresno Black Council from Higher Education. Baxter refused the demands.[50] About 125 mostly Mexican Americans disrupted the fall registration. They blocked the men's gym, and a protestor shouted to the registrants, "You might as well go home. You are not our enemy." Violence broke out as the security forces confronted the protestors. Jess Quintero, chairman of the Fresno County Council of Mexican-American Organizations complained that they had come "to communicate the frustration and despair over the cancellation of the La Raza studies. . . . Black and Chicano students attempted to demonstrate their concern at registration," and the demonstrations were peaceful and orderly until police provoked them by encouraging students to cross the picket line. In December La Raza Studies was reinstated consequent to community pressure.[51] The cancellation of the Fresno La Raza Studies program sent ripples throughout the state.

THE LEGACY OF SEGUNDO BARRIO: THE CHILDREN OF ROSALES

El Paso, the Gateway City, is also known as Chuco. It houses some of the best historical museums and city libraries in the nation, as well as an active community college and the University of Texas, El Paso, all of which have excellent archives on Chihuahua and local history. The El Paso campus was founded in 1914 as the Texas State School of Mines and Metallurgy, changing its name in the mid-1950s to Texas Western College. In 1967 it became the University of Texas at El Paso (UTEP), and it continued a long tradition of white borderland studies. Meanwhile, many white scholars resented the rise of Chicano Studies and its revision of *their* history.

In 1969 over 44 percent of the city's population of 322,262 residents had Spanish surnames. UTEP had the largest Mexican origin student population in the nation, numbering more than 3,000. Frequent anti–Vietnam War campus demonstrations politicized a core of the student population that joined 11,000 other students in marching on the Texas state capitol at Austin. The campus had a small black student population and an emerging black student movement.[52]

The heart of Chuco was El Segundo Barrio, El Paso's oldest neighborhood, a strip of land bordering Mexico and the United States. As one resident of Segundo Barrio said in 1971, "The movement knows no generalization, socio-economical class or other attributes. It involves individuals who are cognizant of the inequities that affect the poor to the poverty-stricken MA [Mexican Americans]."[53] A sense of moral outrage ignited on January 4, 1967, when three children from "the Miguel Rosales family died of asphyxiation when a fire swept their small upstairs apartment [on] South Mesa street."[54] A spontaneous Chicano protest march broke out as some thousand pickets paraded "around City Hall angrily demanding housing code enforcement, higher wages, and a slum clearance program."[55]

At the forefront were Abelardo Delgado and El Huevo Ramírez, who had formed MAYA and an adult program, the Mexican American Committee on Honor, Organization, and Service (MACHOS). Delgado had contact with the emerging student movement there. In the early 1970s Delgado taught in the program. A minority of Chicano students attending the university were from El Segundo. Since 1967 many of these students had joined organizations and had a sense of the inequities in society.[56]

The El Paso faculty responded to demands for Mexican American Studies by submitting their own proposal that would be composed of existing courses and taught mostly by white faculty members. Mechistas, Bert Hernández, José Antonio Medina, José Antonio (Tony) Parra, Carmén Morales, and Patricia Sutton led the students. They objected to the administration's lack of consultation and led protests. University President Joseph Smiley blamed the Vietnam protests for the demonstrations and threatened that he would "stand for no disruptive activities on campus, and if such were to happen he would ask El Paso police to aid campus police, if necessary." Students had the right to dissent, according to Smiley, but nondissenting students had the right to go to classes. Smiley ignored the emerging Chicano identity and calls for reform. Everything was just fine, said Smiley: Mexican Americans had more elected officials than in 1950, and more money had been allocated for campus buildings. Evidently Smiley thought he had solved the problem when Mexican American and Black Studies minors were approved in December. In Smiley's eyes the course of study was legitimate because it had been pulled together by a black vice president.[57] What Smiley did not take into account was that Chicanas/os wanted to give input and were tired of the paternalism at the university.[58]

Throughout the spring of 1970 Mechistas worked toward the autonomy of Chicano Studies. A dialogue took place with black students softening the friction that had occurred the prior semester when a fight broke out at an intramural football game. By August MEChA had developed its own proposal for Mexican American Studies. The Mesa Directiva vetted the proposal. Meanwhile, I was among several speakers who appeared at UTEP and answered student questions. The university did not help financially, and the speakers stayed at students' homes. The UTEP newspaper, *The Prospector*, endorsed the student proposal, pointing out that 30 percent of the students were Chicano and that the poor quality of education made the program a necessity. Chicano Studies, according to the *Prospector*, was recognition of the importance of the Chicano community. According to Philip Ortego, "Chicano Affairs Programs are vitally important in order to help us eliminate the inaccuracies we've become accustomed to about Mexican Americans and, hopefully, to lessen the debilitating effects of prejudice, the most crippling of American maladies."[59]

In April students met in a closed session with Smiley. For two days they discussed rumors that MEChA would takeover of the administration building if its demands were not met. From all accounts the students were calm and polite. Smiley responded that despite fiscal restraints he believed Chicanos had made progress. Finally, on November 29, 1971, MEChA presented Smiley with its written demands. The present "watered down" program was not acceptable; it wanted a department. The irony of the Texas system having "Slavic Studies" on its trustees agenda did not escape the students.[60]

In early December 1971, Chicana/o sealed off the front entrance of the administration building after their demands were not met. Thirty students were arrested when they tried to take over the administration building.[61] The demands of the students resembled those at other campuses: Hire more Chicana/o professors and administrators, reconsider the rejection of Lidia Aguirre as assistant dean of students, and get rid of the hostile administrator that MEChA said discriminated against Chicanos.[62]

The action was successful, and Carina Ramírez, an instructor in the linguistics department, was appointed director of Chicano Studies. The appointment increased the interest of students, and enrollment jumped 51 percent (there were 392 students enrolled in courses taught by twelve faculty members). Ramírez planned a major in the area; however, the enthusiasm soon began to wane. In 1974 an article summed up the situation: "Four years ago a group of Chicanos had a dream of UT El Paso being the Chicano Studies capital of the world. They felt the University had the educational and cultural resources to rejuvenate diplomatic and cultural relations between the United States and Latin America. . . . The group imagined the University evolving into a bilingual-bicultural institution serving the needs of both countries, with Chicanos as mediators." They began working sessions on a Chicano Studies program that was the first step toward their vision. "The program was designed to build Chicano cultural awareness on campus and to establish a base to combine their dreams with reality." They wanted a Chicano Studies department, but the administration held firm. Still, progress was made as plans were made to establish more courses, community information centers, bilingual-bicultural teacher training, a Chicano advisory board, more Chicano faculty recruitment, and a major degree program. Alfredo Vásquez noted how "[some] officials felt CSP [Chicano Studies program] would precipitate a racial schism on campus while others expressed little confidence in the program." Even after the director was appointed, the administration continued to drag its feet. Wynn Anderson, assistant to the president, admitted that more faculty members and resources were needed to implement the plan. He added that funding was needed, but "it is unfair to extract money from department budgets and use it in the community. . . This is an academic institution with the student its main concern." Guillermo Camacho, chair of MEChA's Chicano Studies committee, countered, "If Chicano faculty rock the boat, the system weeds them out."

Despite the administration, class enrollment gradually increased from 560 students in spring 1972 to 684 in spring 1974. In December the first Chicano Studies major was expected to graduate. Ramírez pointed out that the Chicano Studies proposal met the academic standards of the university.[63] Ramírez was reportedly enthusiastic. She was the codeveloper of the university's Child Studies program and authored a proposal for a major in Chicano Studies. In a Fort Worth, Texas, speech before the American GI Forum titled "Chicano Women in Society," she told the group, "You've come a long way, Baby, but we still have a long way to go," referring to the fact that she, unlike many Chicanas, had made the grade, educationally and professionally. She talked about the "double handicap" of being "a woman of a culture in which the male, by tradition, is dominant, and second, being Chicanas, who have not attained equal educational or employment levels in our society." Ramírez had a bachelor of arts in Spanish from the University of South Dakota, a master of arts in linguistics from UTEP, and a PhD in linguistics from the University of Chihuahua. She was married and had one child.[64]

Frustrated with what they termed a snail-paced progress, MEChA and the Mesa Directiva held a press conference on June 18, 1976, and asked for Ramírez's resignation within forty-eight hours. Fernando Chacón and David Rascón, speaking for the groups, said her resignation was necessary to "alleviate the program's stagnation." In other words, there had been a communication breakdown between Ramírez and students, community, and faculty members. According to them, she had failed to organize the faculty, and she resigned her faculty sponsorship of MEChA, cutting ties with students. There was also a lack of new courses and monies directly benefiting the program. They requested the resignation in January.[65] The administration never relented. Chicano Studies, although a respected unit, was never given the status of an autonomous department.

The administration said that it was not bound by the decision of the students and La Mesa Directiva, and MEChA did not have the authority to choose a new director, saying that only faculty members had the authority to recommend on such matters. "The president made it clear he was pleased to have input from MEChA or La Mesa Directiva but that he cannot recognize them as authoritative groups." Meanwhile, most faculty members were wary of associating with La Mesa, who, anticipating Ramírez's resignation, chose an interim director of Chicano Studies. Ricardo Sánchez, a widely known Chicano poet from El Paso, was not nominated by the faculty. According to the administration, "No one on the present faculty wants to be director." The reluctance, they said, was that "the professors would rather be studying and advancing their careers. . . . We are sort of at a stalemate right now."[66]

After resigning, Ramírez continued teaching at UTEP for a couple of years. When she was not granted tenure by her home department, she left for Juárez, returning to El Paso, where she taught English as a second language at El Paso Community College and was the president of the faculty senate. She also had a consulting firm specializing in technical translations.[67] Few facts are known about the UTEP program. The Alfredo Vásquez article is a window. According to it, the expectations were high and the administration meddlesome. What is for sure is that the administration manipulated tensions.

SAN FERNANDO VALLEY STATE COLLEGE: BREAKING OUT

According to a *Los Angeles Times* article published October 5, 1969, "Nearly 700 students, 532 of them new to the college, are enrolled in the program. . . There are 385 black students (268 new and 117 continuing), 296 Mexican-Americas (252 new and 45 continuing) and 13 others, all new."[68] San Fernando Valley State College had 15,000 students. The number of regular admissions is difficult to estimate, since they were listed as Spanish-surname. Valley State was not an aberration among the state colleges. Fortunately, a goodly number of the EOP students, some 350 black and brown, had attended a summer program that allowed the department to acclimate some incoming students.

Because most veteran student leaders had left, the first task was to build a student organization and identity. The department knew that it had to play an active role in the education and politicization of the incoming students. It had to build pride, a sense of purpose, and community. This could not be done by isolating the students from the progressive student movements on campus. They had to become the leaders on issues such as the Vietnam War and the draft. Despite the risks, it was decided that a "them and us" mindset would help forge a strong sense of unity and community.

Black students were under the fire of the trial of twenty-four Black Student Union members arrested on November 4, 1968, on felony charges of conspiracy, kidnapping, and false imprisonment.[69] The associate chair of Pan-African Studies, Bill Burwell, reasoned that the group had sacrificed more than its share and decided not to expose the Black Student Union to further attacks. This decision left a vacuum. The department discussed the situation with leaders from the previous semester, and it was concluded that activism was necessary to keep pressure on the administration and faculty bodies. It also concluded that the actions of the white radical students should not determine the Chicanos' destiny. As a result, the decision was made to encourage MEChA to get at the forefront of the student movement on campus. This militancy would give it an identification, increased pride, and a sense of power.

Chicano Studies achieved autonomy and growth because of Chicana/o students, and Chicana/o faculty continued to depend on the strength of the organization.

MEChA was given the power to work together with faculty, and Chicana/o students oversaw the administration of the department through the Mesa Directiva. This oversight led to policies that were student friendly. Faculty members were supposed to keep the doors of their offices open so students could enter at will; they would be on campus five days a week to build a communitarian spirit.

Chicano Studies and Pan-African Studies were given a choice of offices, the nicer and more spacious of which were on the third floor of the administration building. Although Chicano Studies won the toss of the coin, it chose the first floor because the students would have easier access to its offices. Pan-African Studies put up a counter so secretaries could monitor access of students to faculty members' offices. The free flow environment of the Chicano Studies office space created a student lobby, and although the noise level was deafening, it gave students a sense of community. Students often brought their guitars and would sing or hang out. The faculty members' offices were cramped cubby holes, but the accessibility was a big drawing card.

In most cases student power is an ideal that is never achieved. As a rule, students are only called in when someone is denied tenure or when the administration bucks at giving faculty members something they want. In this case, student sacrifices produced the department, and the presence of students made the department possible. Moreover, the department was a spin-off of the San Fernando/Pacoima community and the activism that had taken place during the 1960s. A goodly number of the founding students were from those communities, which over the years provided the department with the stability other programs did not have. Therefore, new hires agreed to the principle that they served at the pleasure of the students and community.

The hiring of the first faculty members was a group consensus. The chair and the Mesa Directiva interviewed the faculty members, and MEChA as a whole also interviewed them. Understanding that individual faculty members could become free agents once they were hired, they promised that if the Mesa Directiva recommended their termination, and a majority of MEChA members approved the decision, they would resign, as a matter of conscience. Some feared that students would abuse this power, and the anarchy of other campuses would become the rule at Valley States. It seemed as if at some colleges vying factions would conduct regular purges. Quite the contrary, student power gave Valley State stability and also a high degree of faculty accountability. It drove home the point that faculty members were accountable to the students rather than the institution.

However, this does not mean that faculty members were the puppets of the students. In the first year of the program's operation, the Kickass Committee, which included some of the younger and more militant students, wanted to terminate one of the professors because he was supposedly *tapado* (intellectually constipated). The committee members met in my office and reminded me of the policy of Chicano Studies—that it would follow the decision of the students.

While I agreed that the professor had weaknesses, especially in his classroom performance, I also recognized that Chicano Studies had recruited him from the

Midwest and that he had moved his family at considerable expense. Chicano Studies was an emerging field of study, and not everyone was going to be at the same level. I reminded the ad hoc Kickass Committee that it had to go through channels. It had to go to the Mesa and the Chicana/o students. If MEChA agreed, then I would have to comply. I added, however, that I had to follow my conscience, and I would tender my resignation if the professor was terminated. Three months was just not enough time to evaluate a professor; he had a wife and two daughters. A compromise was worked out, and the department used its meager budget to bring in speakers to enrich the professor's classes, something that was continued the second semester. The professor in question was on his own the second year, and then he was reviewed by the retention committee.

Unfortunately, student governance lasted only until the early 1980s, when it was eliminated at the administration's behest by the chair of the department. In fairness, however, it suffered a slow death—students failed to keep the process going by attending committee meetings. As a result, faculty members became more institutionalized and insisted on being treated as faculty members, and some resented the degree of student participation. In all, it was a fantastic experience that generated a sense of community that has not been replicated since the late 1970s.

The student meetings always revolved around music. Everto Ruiz, who was then a student, assembled a *conjunto* called Conjunto Aztlán that played at college events and at the Chicano Moratorium. They often accompanied Violeta Quintero. Ruiz became a professor, and his students spawned over a dozen student mariachi groups in the San Fernando Valley and Ventura County. Students put together a student newspaper, *El Popo*, and Sergio Hernández had a comic strip named *Porfi*. Hernández and Oscar Castillo worked with *Con Safos*, a community magazine. The other artists left a living treasure of murals that exist to this day. When they were painted, the college threatened to whitewash them. Today, guests are toured through the facilities by the administration. These activities, along with the demonstrations and protests, created a community that was essential to the department's survival. It not only encouraged students to take Chicano Studies classes, but it also gave them a stake in the department.

Aside from the internal pressures, the department had to contend with other campuses. After Santa Barbara, most participants entered a twilight zone, and Chicanos in general had to constantly justify themselves as purer, more Chicano, than the others, because they thought themselves more committed. Even though most knew that the plan had little to do with the establishment of disparate programs, the legend had already become fact. The California Committee of Chicanos in Higher Education that had called the conference to compose the Plan of Santa Barbara sought to maintain a common vision by holding other conferences and trying to stimulate communication. Rene Nuñez, a committed activist, was its John the Baptist. Nuñez had moved to San Diego State College to set up a Chicano Studies department. Chicanos in Higher Education visited the various campuses, and many of the emissaries became dogmatic.

The Chicano Coordinating Council on Higher Education (CCHE) attempted to impose its model on Valley State. When CCHE held a conference at the Northridge campus, it merely refused to participate. Valley State resented criticism from Chicanos in Higher Education. For example, they proceeded to tell Valley State students and faculty that they were too nationalistic and directed them to abolish their mariachi classes and other Mexican cultural classes. Valley State students, many of whom belonged to Marxist study groups, resented this intrusion and resolved not to participate in the Chicanos in Higher Education organization. In retrospect, Valley State was wrong, because a lot of marginal programs suffered from the lack of discourse and would have benefited from help with curricular strategies. On the other hand, the dialog was turning ugly. San Fernando Valley at the time was physically isolated, and many community groups heard about outside groups coming onto what they considered their turf, and they wanted to respond.

However, the blame for the failure of CCHE cannot be placed on Nuñez's shoulders or on the nonparticipation of one program. Differences existed between junior, state, and research institutions, and programs often competed. Many Chicano graduate students and professors flaunted where they had received or were getting their PhDs. Personalities and competing ideologies emerged and played a role in preventing communication. The lack of participation of Valley State hurt, because aside from San Diego State, it was the largest Chicano Studies department in the state. By 1976 it had fifteen positions and was consolidating its gains.

Northridge was fortunate because a veteran group of Chicana/o students transferred there for fall 1969. José Galván from Los Angeles City College (LACC) was originally from San Antonio, Texas. José was elected the first chair of MEChA. Also from LACC was Carlos Reyes, a giant of a man and also from San Antonio. Rosa Martínez, a brilliant journalist, came with that group. They were a bit older than the other incoming students who arrived from the San Fernando Valley, East Los Angeles, South Central Los Angeles, Ventura County, and the San Joaquin Valley. Some of them had been farmworkers, while others had lumpen tendencies. The group also had a core of stoners and *vato locos* who were trying to turn their lives around.

Under Galván, MEChA stayed together, and it was not uncommon to have over a hundred students at the weekly MEChA meetings, along with a handful of white students who were looking for a home. The *chisme* (gossip) factor was kept to a minimum. A group of women students maintained a balance, forging a unity among themselves. Many, like Rosa Martínez of Puerto Rican ancestry, had worked on the Chicano student newspaper *El Machete* at LACC. María Terán, who would later become the first MEChA female chair, was one of the leaders. She was from Valley Junior College and was very close to Marie Acosta, who later worked with the San Francisco Mime Troupe. Oscar Castillo, one of the most talented photographers in the movement, arrived with that group. Teresa Orozco was from Roosevelt High School; Avie Hernández was from Oxnard. The Chaparro sisters, Linda and Loraine, who became a PhD in psychology and an optometrist, were from Oxnard. Yvonne Aguirre was from Santa Paula, and Delia Pérez, whose parents were longtime activists, was from San Fernando. Pérez's father, Reyes, was a member of the United Autoworkers. They formed a small community of students and countered some of the craziness that sometimes took place.

There are many success stories, such as Diana Hernández, a former San Fernando High School UMAS chair, who returned to her school to be a teacher, counselor, and dean. Dr. María Vásquez from Lincoln Heights is an elementary principal in the Clark County Schools in Las Vegas, Nevada. Tony Gaitán was the first Chicano principal of Santa Paula (California) High School. Another Tony, son of San Joaquin Valley farmworker parents, arrived with a dream to become a medical doctor. Although his education was deficient, he spent hours in the skills lab and is today a medical doctor. Rafael Vargas practices medicine in Chicago. Dr. Frank Meza of Frogtown in Los Angeles founded Chicanos for Creative Medicine and is an administrator at Kaiser Permanente.[70] Federal Judge S. James Otero, who graduated in 1973, took Chicano Studies classes and obtained his law degree from Stanford. Joe Martínez, who came to Valley State with a 0.8 grade point average, later earned a doctorate at the University of California, San Diego. Richard Alarcón from Sun Valley served as a state assemblyman and senator and is now a member of the Los Angeles City Council. The late Frank del Olmo from Pacoima, a founder of *El Popo*, became an editor of the *Los Angeles Times*, a Pulitzer Prize winner, and founder of the Chicano News Media Association. Countless others became attorneys, PhDs, medical doctors, teachers, and community organizers.

There was no shortage of artists: Sergio Hernández, a cartoonist and muralist; Guillermo Bejarano, a muralist who studied under Siqueiros; Joe Bravo, Ramón Holguin, and dozens of others. Dr. María Ponce Adame from Pacoima was an award-winning novelist. I mention these students to correct the lies told about Chicano Studies and particularly MEChA. These individuals are part of a core of less than 250 Chicano students who arrived in the fall of 1969 as the result of the activism of two dozen students.

MEChA, along with the student senate, pressured the administration to fund a Valley State Chicano community house. Irene Tovar, the first director, was well known to students. A graduate of Valley State, she was a founder and president of the Latin American Civic Association. Irene was the lead person from Valley State and the San Fernando Valley in organizing Chicanos on August 29, 1970. She and Chicano Studies student Charlie Pérez organized the San Fernando Valley Chicano Moratorium Committee, which sponsored a march and rally that drew almost a thousand protestors during the second week in July. During the moratorium she coordinated a legal team that bailed out hundreds of people, including me.[71] The storefront opened in January 1971, and there were high hopes that the college would finally operate programs in the San Fernando community. When conservative student senators came in, however, they did not acknowledge the budget and would not pay the bills of the center. This angered MEChA, who packed senate meetings. After this, the community center suffered a slow death.[72]

The next major issue came up about 1973. Instructional faculty was being moved out of the administration building that housed Chicano Studies. Vice President

David Benson told Chicano Studies that it would be housed on the third floor of Monterey Hall or fourth floor of Sierra Towers. The offices had ample space. Benson wanted the department faculty to vote on the alternatives. These locations would have been nightmares: inaccessible to students and few elevators. We suggested that Benson assign Chicano Studies the first floor of Sierra North, which was being vacated by audiovisual services. When Benson ordered the department to follow his orders, Jorge picked up the phone to call Abbey Rents, with the intention of setting up our offices on the lawn. Benson acceded to the department's demands. The first-floor location allowed Chicano Studies to maintain its free flow of students and furnish a student lobby. But, like everything else, the allocation was based on a formula, and in order to have the luxury of a student lounge, faculty office space was reduced.

The administration did not help. It did not rein in the campus police, who too often acted like cowboys. Next, Dean of Students Ed Peckam and others hit on the scheme of paying off the debt on a new dorm by requiring EOP students to rent rooms in the new dorm or have their financial aid package reduced.[73] Consequently, a large portion of the residents were minority students. Black students had a difficult time renting apartments in the surrounding community, as did darker-skinned Mexicans—particularly males. To make things worse, the dorm was nine stories, and students had to crowd into elevators. Some 600 students were crammed into the building. The dorms were coed, causing tensions between the groups. Further, Mexican parents were not enthusiastic about their daughters living in a coed dorm.

Fights broke out between blacks and browns, with a knifing taking place, and students began arming themselves. The concentration of students in a single dorm building attracted outsiders who came to party, many of whom were drug pushers posing as students. This caused an epidemic of drug use circa 1971–1972. Along with a student named Joe Chacón, I went into the dorms and paid calls to known drug dealers and told them to leave or Chicano Studies would report them. Red pills were flushed down the toilet. The department then advised students and parents to break their contracts and move out of the dorms.

Peckam was infuriated and said that Chicano Studies was acting unprofessionally and was encouraging students to break the law. The campus police could deal with the problem—creating a catch-22. The students, according to Peckam, had signed contracts. But the issue was public safety. If he did anything to discipline Chicano Studies, the department would call a press conference and air the facts. Peckam backed off. The dispersal of students throughout the Northridge and Reseda communities made life easier for the time being. Over time, students learned to live together in dorm areas, and Chicano and black staff who knew the situation were hired.

The burning of the Chicano House on May 5, 1970, caused a major crisis on campus. The cause of the incendiary was unknown, but at the time believed to be the work of right-wing extremists who were reacting to the lowering and burning of the American flag by CSUN students on campus. The students were angry over the Ohio National Guard shooting down four white students at Kent State. They were also protesting the invasion of Cambodia. Almost every campus had demonstrations, to the point that Governor Ronald Reagan closed the state and university campuses for two days. As with almost every campus in the state and nation, student protests rocked the campus communities.[74]

Mindful that the BSU would participate peripherally I warned Galván to be careful—to let the white student radicals be the shock troops. As the day ground down, the students got angrier and angrier. They marched on the flag pole in front of the west entrance of the administration building. Infuriated by the flag that was the symbol of the invasion of Cambodia and the killing of the students, the protestors moved to take it down. At this point, the white students stepped back, and the Chicanos rushed to the forefront, taking down the flag and burning it. I was furious with the Chicano leadership for being suckered. It led to one of the few disagreements that I had with Galván.

However, it was no time to get dramatic, so I warned students that the police investigators would be around and they should keep quiet. I then had photos confiscated. Soon afterward, the investigators showed up and started to ask me questions. No, MEChA was not involved! They showed me photos of the flag burners, and I responded that I did not know them. They then showed me photos of the flag burning. Did I know any of the students? No! They then proceeded to name the suspects. I chuckled. They were not even close. I realized that all Mexicans looked alike to them, and we should just deny, deny, deny. They never apprehended who did it.

Satisfied that the crisis would blow over, I went to Rincón Hall to give a Cinco de Mayo talk. Half way through the speech, someone told us that the Chicano House was on fire. The group rushed to the house, but it was totally consumed. The police and the firemen were gruff. They had arrested two Chicanas, Yvonne Aguirre and Monica Medina, for trying to go into the house to see if anyone had fallen asleep. I knew Monica's father, Monico, so I knew that everything would be cool with him. However, we drove to Santa Paula and told Yvonne's parents, very nice people who owned a mom-and-pop store. The next morning, instead of letting the students join the campus protests, the department and MEChA organized a silent march through the campus. Everyone wore a brown arm band and did not say a word. An onlooker said, "When those Indians are hollering it's bad, but their silence is eerie." The march solidified the group. It gave it an identity. The white students continued protesting. In a couple of days, after discussion with MEChA, it was announced that the department would reopen in the fall semester. The department and MEChA immediately set up a community meeting at Las Palmas Park in San Fernando. It was attended by hundreds of community folks, many of whom were parents. A special edition of *El Popo* was printed and distributed throughout the Valley.[75] In the interim, Mechistas had taken over student government.

Meanwhile, another crisis was brewing. A slate supported by MEChA and the BSU won ten of seventeen offices in student government, as well as the presidency. Chancellor Glenn Dumke and Governor Ronald Reagan asked for an investigation, alleging MEChA-BSU had used EOP facilities to print and send out campaign materials. The Reseda and Northridge chambers of commerce called for the expulsion of revolutionaries. President Cleary responded that he did not know any revolutionaries.[76] The inner city had come to the Valley paradise, and the first radical student government had been elected at Valley State. Fights with the administration followed as students grappled to control the budget, which the president was accustomed to dipping into.[77] They wanted funds for an experimental college and a student-owned bookstore. They objected to the Greeks, who were 5 percent of the students receiving 25 percent of the funds.

The events of the first year had given me too much visibility and power. If the department was to grow, more faculty members had to get involved in the administration of the department. Few of them knew how the college functioned. After consulting with the Mesa Directiva, it was decided that I would step down after the first of the year and that the chair would be rotated on an annual basis. This is easier said than done. Just exposing faculty to how academe functions does not give them insight into the institution. Every faculty member would serve for one year, and I naively assumed that the former chairs would join a personnel board to establish continuity. The Mesa did not accept my nomination of Joe De Anda and selected Carlos Arce, who had a bachelor of arts degree from Berkeley (Arce later received a doctorate from the University of Michigan).

In Search of Aztlán: Alternative Colleges

The sixties were a time of idealism—maybe utopianism. Chicano students were no different than their black, white, and Asian counterparts, and as soon as they began entering the colleges and universities, they sought alternatives to what they considered a corrupt and unequal system. Many Chicano organizations hooked up with progressive colleges, such as Antioch College in Yellow Springs, Ohio, that had a history of supporting progressive causes. Founded by Horace Mann, Antioch opened its doors in 1852 in an era of American Utopianism. Racial and sexual equality, independent study, and independent thinking were integral parts of Antioch College. In the aftermath of World War II, it reached out to the Nisei and formed a Central Education Fund for room and board for former Japanese internees. From 1959 to 1963, it reached out to black students, and by the late sixties it reached out to Puerto Ricans and Chicanos.[78] Another institution that worked with Chicano organization was Goddard College, which started as a women's seminary in Vermont in the 1840s. Goddard became a college in the 1960s, expanding during the decade.[79]

Antioch innovated and developed a new Adult Degree Completion Program, which was dubbed the University Without Walls. Students could take classes close to home while earning a BA or BS. The model was developed in association with Antioch centers—Juárez Lincoln University, Philadelphia Graduate Center, and Antioch–New England (the Keene Center). Juárez Lincoln offered a fifteen-month program leading to a master of education degree. The Mexican American College emphasized bilingual and multicultural education and community involvement. Juárez-Lincoln was originally part of Jacinto Treviño College, splitting into two factions in 1971. Juárez-Lincoln was led by Leonard Mestes and Andre Guerrero. In 1975 Juárez-Lincoln became an affiliate of the Antioch Graduate School of Education, changing its name to Juárez-Lincoln University. Four years later, Antioch removed its accreditation and it closed in 1991.[80]

Colegio Jacinto Treviño emerged from a 1969 MAYO state conference in Mission, Texas. The conference took place in the midst of high school walkouts throughout the state. They were looking for models that emphasized community control and Chicano Studies. Antioch College agreed to lend its name to the development of a degree in education through its University Without Walls graduate program. Jacinto Treviño published *Semillas de liberación* (Seeds of liberation), a book of poetry. After the 1971 split, the more militant faction, led by Narciso Alemán, twenty-two, continued until the mid-1970s.[81] According to Alemán, "Large-scale protests were the impetus for both the founding and the closing of the college." Many of the local residents labeled them pinkos. The college grew to about forty students, and the founding graduate students became the core faculty for an undergraduate program. "The school issued Masters of Art in Teaching, Masters in Education and Bachelor of Arts in Interdisciplinary Studies degrees." It attracted professors such as Victor Moheno, of the University of California, Berkeley, who served as dean of the graduate program. "While the school was successful in securing traditional scholarships and loans for its students, its educational project failed," said the *Valley Morning Star*. The college had a successful theater troupe, El Teátro Jacinto Treviño, that raised money for operational costs.[82]

Students participated in protests. At Pharr City Hall, local police, state troopers, and Texas Rangers broke up the demonstration with gunfire and tear gas, arresting Efraín Hernández, a MAYO activist. Jacinto Treviño remained open until 1976, when the Texas Higher Education Coordinating Board denied it certification. Jacinto Treviño was subjected to intense red-baiting. Weslaco School Superintendent Otto Longoils objected to a grant application, saying, "If Jacinto Trevino College gets involved in this school district it will become involved in all school districts in the Valley."[83] Texas newspapers ran bylines such as " 'Hate' Is Taught at Chicano College." Reverend Oliver W. Summerlin, pastor of the First Baptist Church of Mercedes, called the college "an outpost of radical thought." Summerlin was at the center of the storm, encouraging Police Chief L. R. Park and his deputies to attack its members, to the point that the American Civil Liberties Union filed a complaint.[84]

César Chávez College was a college without walls in Mount Angel, Oregon. It was established in 1973 but closed in 1983. The institution was the first accredited, independent four-year Chicano college to receive candidacy status from the Northwest Association of Schools and Colleges in 1975. In 1977 the college granted bachelor degrees to twenty-two Chicano graduates—more than the University of Oregon and Oregon State University for that year. The school took over the facilities of Mt. Angel College, a Benedictine school. By 1972 Mt. Angel College (the predecessor of César Chávez College) had a student body of only 250, only 37 of whom were Mexican American. The school changed its name El Colegio César Chávez and affiliated with the Union for Experimenting Colleges and Universities. It encouraged the participation and collaboration of students, staff, and administrators in creating and implementing the curriculum.[85]

By 1977, the *Walla Walla Union Bulletin* ran a blurb entitled "Students Face Eviction." The message was to either hand over the keys or the Department of Housing and Urban Development would evict them. The faculty and students were outbid by a contractor for the rights to the land when they failed to make payments. The local Chicano community helped but tired of the struggle, and the college was forced to impose tuition on students. Its fate was sealed when in the early 1980s the business community turned on the college and it was audited. According to the *Walla Walla Union Bulletin* "Pola Ponce, a member of the Committee to Rebuild Cesar Chavez, says the school's board, mostly Hispanic businessmen from Portland, has lost touch with the 25,000 Mexican-Americans who work on farms in the area around Mount Angel."[86]

Deganawidah and Quetzalcoatl University (DQU), California's only Native American and Chicano college, was established in 1971, seven miles west of Davis, when students claimed an unused military yard. After a lengthy struggle, DQU was given title to the land. It closed in 2005 when it lost its accreditation. Three years later, U.S. General Services Administration moved to take the land. It had a culturally based education, one that included Native American history, language, culture, and spirituality to help prepare Indian students for the multicultural world. DQU was a member the first American Indian Higher Education Consortium. "The concept is that Indians and Chicanos will have opportunities to receive college-level educations oriented to their needs, with the institution and courses administered by Indians and Chicanos." Notable professors such as Jack Forbes, Powhatan Indian and professor at University of California Davis, and Luis Flores served on the faculty. Forbes was very supportive of the inclusion of Chicanos. According to the *Albuquerque Journal*, "At its inception DQU had around 150 students, predominantly Indians and Mexican-Americans who painted the drab Army installation with colorful murals and turned the barracks into classrooms."[87]

As in the case of other idealistic alternative schools, it began full of hope, only to have the realities of a brutal society take over. It did not have enough money, and most students were not willing to support institutions not valued by society. There were dozens of smaller ventures that sprouted up, sharing a millenarian spirit and demanding control of their schooling, their culture, and their lives.

CHAPTER 6

Growing a Program

While the number of Chicanas/os has grown, their access to academe has become more problematic. In 1955 the California college and university systems were the envy of the nation. More than half the 86,000 high school students graduating that June took advantage of the close-to-home campus arrangement. They had their choice of sixty public junior colleges, ten state colleges, and the giant University of California, with eight campuses. Fifty private four-year colleges and six private junior colleges were also available to those who could afford them. The educational code prohibited public junior colleges from turning away students, so everyone had a chance. The junior college education was free, the state college students paid no more than forty dollars a year, and the University of California tuition was eighty-four dollars.[1]

By the mid-1960s, Republicans clamored for raising fees for out-of-state residents to pay for rising professor salaries. To shift the cost of social production to the students' families, Republicans proposed raising resident fees by $100.[2] The California Taxpayer's Association called for a $200 annual fee per student attending state colleges, as well as drastic cuts in wages of the University of California professors. They also called for deep cuts in poverty programs and adult education.[3] In 1967 the legislature cut 10 percent of the budgets of state colleges and the University of California.

Meanwhile, Governor Ronald Reagan dismantled California's mental health system. Reagan put more pressure on legislators to impose tuition to make up for the shortfall in the state colleges and the University of California system. While higher education resisted the tuition hikes, the University of California Regents, appointed by the governor, proposed cutting student enrollment. Aware of student discontent, Reagan proposed money for scholarships for low-income students and raising student parking fees. He called the backlash to his proposal of raising fees from $200 to $400 "shocking." Reagan's approach was to "get rid of undesirables. Those there to agitate and not to study might think twice before they pay tuition. They might think twice how much they want to pay to carry a picket sign," he said.[4]

Reagan's actions mobilized thousands of public school teachers and college and university students against his policies. Reagan asked the state's 169,000 workers to forgo their Lincoln and Washington holidays and kick back their usual extra pay. In reaction, 3,000 University of California students marched on Sacramento. Educators countered that education was a good investment, with graduates paying more taxes. Indeed, if fees were increased, the University of California would be the fifth most expensive public system in the nation.[5]

The Democrats in the legislature blocked the proposal. Some legislators blamed the crisis on the acceptance to four-year colleges of "unprepared" minority students. At best this was simplistic. *Los Angeles Times* reporter Mary Barber showed other factors: "From Claremont on the east to California State College at Los Angeles on the west, San Gabriel campuses are inundated with a new species—the woman over 35 who is returning to school after devoting several years to home and family." The trend of women enrolling in institutions of higher education statewide and changes in the economy were making the two-salary household a necessity. Moreover, younger women were no longer willing to be subsidized in education and enrolled in better paying majors leading to medical and law degrees.[6]

Reagan proposed a plan of deferred tuition. It was opposed by California State Chancellor Glenn Dumke and University of California President Charles Hitch. Assemblyman John L. E. Collier (R-Pasadena) labeled the Reagan plan "learn, earn and reimburse." UC fees would have increased from $330 to $1,330 a year.[7] The privatization of higher education had begun: In 2009 California State University undergraduates paid $4,155 per year and rising. The tuition for the University of California undergraduates cost about $8,720 annually. (In 2010 it would be over $10,000.) The solution to the shortfall was one way of eliminating the poor and the dark-skinned students from four-year universities and colleges.

CHICANISMO AND THE GROWTH OF CHICANO STUDIES

Part of the attraction of Chicano Studies to working-class Chicana/o students was identity. In California the growth was based on the Educational Opportunity Program making education affordable. In the late 1960s this was less so in Texas because of a lack of financial aide. However, both states drew students who wanted Chicano Studies or at least a course on the Mexican American experience. The common denominator between these states and others was Chicano nationalism, although it differed in California, Texas, and Colorado.[8] Chicano Studies contributed to a flourishing arts and poetry movement. Chicano Studies not only employed artists and literary folk but also gave them broader forums and markets. Chicano Studies programs differed in their level of participation. As a general rule, those housing the multiple disciplines under a single department made greater transformations than those with disciplines that were dispersed throughout the academy.

The presence of a Chicana and Chicano identity was richest in the visual arts. Numerous Web sites are a testament to this productivity. Undoubtedly, it was influenced by the Mexican art tradition, especially the muralists of the Mexican

revolution. Vibrant colors in Chicana/o art date back to the Mesoamerican civilizations.[9] In a very short time span, Chicana/o art went from the public walls to
the museums and into the homes of collectors such as Cheech Marín.[10] Colleges
and universities also collected private exhibits. During the 1960s and 1970s, the
Chicana/o mural movement spread throughout the Southwest, Northwest, and
Midwest. It became part of the urban landscapes of Los Angeles, San Diego's
Chicano Park, San Francisco, Seattle, Chicago, and San Antonio.[11] In San Antonio,
the Community Cultural Arts Organization was funded by an agency established
in 1979, producing more than two hundred murals by 1992 at public-housing
projects in the West Side barrio. In 1984 the Guadalupe Cultural Arts Center—
featuring the visual arts, music, literature, film, theater, and dance—was founded.
By the mid-1970s, Chicano art became less political.

Chicano Studies programs hired Chicana/o artists, many of whom were art
historians. One of the best known is Malaquias Montoya, who was born in
Albuquerque, New Mexico, and raised in the San Joaquin Valley of California.
Since 1989 Montoya has held a professorship at the University of California, Davis,
teaching in the departments of art and Chicano Studies. His brother José Montoya
is an internationally known poet, musician, and artist and a founding member of
the Chicano Royal Air Force, based in Sacramento, California.[12] Initially named the
Rebel Chicano Art Front, the organization formed in 1969 to advance the Chicano
civil rights and labor organizing movement of the United Farm Workers. Other
collectives formed, such as Asco, led by Harry Gamboa, Gronk (Glugio Nicondra),
Patssi Váldez, and Willie Herrón.[13] A whole colony of artists emerged, including
the internationally known Carlos Almaráz, Diane Gamboa, Margaret García,
Carmén Lomas Garza, Gilbert "Magu" Luján, Leo Limón, Marta Sánchez (San
Antonio), Nephtali de León (San Antonio), John Valádez, Yreina Cervantez, and
Alma López.[14]

A Renaissance also took place in prose and poetry, which was inspired by
nationalism and the poems of Alurista. Street poets such as Abelardo "Lalo"
Delgado and his "Stupid America" inspired youth.

> stupid america, see that
> chicano
> with a big knife
> on his steady hand
> he doesn't want to knife you
> he wants to sit on a bench
> and carve christfigures
> but you won't let him . . . [15]

Abelardo captures the political mood of Chicana/o literature and cultural
expression of the time. *Quinto Sol* gave Chicana/o literature a firm push by publishing many of the early writers. Rudolfo Anaya, Sandra Cisneros, Gary Soto,
Luis Váldez, José Montoya, John Rechy, Luis Omar Salinas, Denise Chávez, and
dozens of others were early voices. The genre has grown as the number of Mexican

Americans and Latinas/os has increased. The selection of politically oriented pieces has decreased in recent years; the present literature lacks the punch of the poetry of Alma Cervantes. It is not a cliché to say that the number of Chicana/o writers is just too large to mention, let alone critique. A contribution of Chicano Studies created the market for Chicano literature, giving space to many student and local writers with messages.

Finally, music played a huge role in uniting many Mexican Americans, who began to increasingly appreciate *lo mexicano* and incorporate it into the present. This transition began in the 1930s and 1940s with swing bands bringing young Mexican Americans to dance floors. The postwar years saw the urbanization and growth of second- and third-generation U.S.-born Mexican Americans. Jazz influenced Latin sounds, as did rock 'n' roll. Garage bands sprung up. Among the first was Ritchie Valens (Richard Valenzuela), from Pacoima, who revolutionized rock with the adaptation of "La Bamba."[16]

In the sixties, in places like East Los Angeles and Texas, consequent to the growth of the youth population there was a renaissance of art, music, and politics. Groups such as Cannibal and the Headhunters, Thee Midniters, and others popularized the California car culture. In the Rio Grande Valley of Texas and San Antonio, Tex-Mex music acquired greater influence. Conjunto bands featured an accordion, bajo sexto, bass, and drum and entered into a period of experimentation. Breakthrough artists such as Freddy Fender and Flaco Jiménez and the Texas Tornados influenced the sounds of white Texas musicians. The evolution of Tex-Mex, Tejano and Chicano music brought a growth of a Chicano identity that was not always embraced by the immigrant generations. But, by the late 1960s, these differences began to narrow as Chicanos began to look increasingly to Mexican music for inspiration, and groups such as Los Lobos, with Francisco González, created a bridge—ironically, again with "La Bamba."

What spurred interest in Mexican music was the growth of the Mexican immigrant population. In 1970 Mexicans were 7.9 percent of all immigrants. Ten years later they were 15.6 percent. By the same account, Mexicans were 1.5 percent of the population in 1970 and 10.2 percent by 2005. Groups such as CASA, the Chicana/o left, and Movimiento Estudiantil Chicanos de Aztlán became the conscience of the community and instilled a sense of duty to protect the rights of the foreign-born. Consequent to their presence there was a dramatic growth of Spanish language media. In this context the popularity of Mexican and Latino culture grew—with Los Lobos crossing bridges between Chicanos and immigrants.[17]

The Chicanas/os' sense of Latin American identity grew. In the 1960s that identity revolved around Cuba—Fidel and Che were icons. That identity was expanded with a dirty war in Chile in 1973, when General Augusto Pinochet ousted democratically elected President Salvador Allende in a CIA-backed coup d'état in Chile. The United States during the decade dealt with military juntas in Uruguay, Chile, Ecuador, Bolivia, and Argentina.[18] During the 1970s, close to 900,000 Chilean expatriates left Chile, and about 110,000 came to the United States. Some of their children joined MEChA and, in turn, many Mechistas and Chicana/o activists were politicized by groups such as Chile Democrático, which had a large number of communists and socialists. They were exposed to *nueva canción* (the new song), which spread from the southern tip of Latin American to Mexico, Central America, and Cuba. Many refugees were political and sought support from the Chicano community. The *nueva canción* conveyed the pain of exile expressed in the poems of Pablo Neruda. The Chileans left their imprints. Jaime Corral was a student in the early 1980s and a member of MEChA. His father, two brothers, and sister were tortured by Pinochet's butchers. He radicalized many Chicana/o students around him.

SAN FERNANDO VALLEY STATE: SUBVERSION AND INFANTILE DISORDER

Considering the positive aspects of the cultural renaissance that Chicano Studies helped create, it is a wonder why police agencies sought to disrupt it. Many Chicano Studies programs were lost in their infancy. For example, San Fernando Valley State College had its share of agent provocateurs. The case of Miguel Valenzuela stands out. Valenzuela was a drug addict who came to the college to turn his life around. He was a student assistant in Carlos Arce's Language of the Barrio course; his *retórica*, the use of *chuco*, was poetic. In another life Valenzuela would have been a linguist, a university professor. One day he looked despondent, so I asked him, "What's happening?" He confessed that he had done a terrible thing, according to him. The Devonshire police had taken him in and, in his words, "sweated him." They knew he had a monkey on his back. They wanted him to tell them about me and the department. Valenzuela said that he played loose with the truth because he wanted his fix. A week after the conversation, Valenzuela overdosed in a Pacoima gas station restroom.

In 1969 Fernando Sumaya, twenty-three, attempted to infiltrate the SFVSC UMAS. Chicano students grew suspicious of him and ousted him. Meanwhile, Sumaya infiltrated the Brown Berets. On April 24 he was at the Biltmore Hotel and joined Mexican American activists in protesting a speech by Governor Reagan to 400 Mexican American educators. According to some of the activists, Sumaya agitated the protestors and was provocative. According to the *Los Angeles Times*, "Sumaya, who grew a beard and posed a dedicated rebel in his dangerous undercover role, also in a companion case in which three others were indicted in the May 10th fire-bombing of a Safeway market in East Los Angeles."[19] Based on Sumaya's testimony, a grand jury indicted the Chicano activists. The trial of two of the activists ended in a mistrial, and their second trial was dismissed for insufficient evidence. Seven of the eight were never tried, and Carlos Montes took off, fearing police reprisals. When he came back in 1979, he was acquitted for lack evidence.

On November 11, 1972, at a statewide conference at San Fernando Valley State, Mechistas caught Lt. Don Yelverton, a black campus police officer, hidden behind a vending machine, secretly taping the proceedings of the conference. The campus police recorded the conference at the behest of the Devonshire Division of the

Los Angeles Police Department. Senior class President Ben Saiz presented a resolution in the student senate to investigate the incident. Meanwhile, President James
Cleary denied the incident happened. He explained that Yelverton had taken the
tape recorders to a storeroom in the cafeteria where the conference was being held,
and that he was just testing them. He "flatly asserted that campus security had been
given no order to 'bug' the meeting and no 'bugging' was done." Assemblyman-elect
Howard Berman promised to take the case but dropped the ball.[20]

The next incidence of known surveillance of the Northridge department came
to the surface during an American Civil Liberties suit against the Los Angeles
Police Department for unlawful surveillance of activists and organizations.[21]
MEChA and several California State Northridge professors were plaintiffs and had
access to documents yielded in discovery. The Los Angeles Police's Public Disorder
Intelligence Department (PDID) was an unlawful intelligence gathering unit associated with right wing groups. Chief Daryl Gates knew about the agency violations.
When it became evident to the public that the unit was operating beyond the pale
of the law, PDID officers hid documents in cars and garages, in many instances
handing over documents to a ring of right-wing cohorts. Because of the American
Civil Liberties Union suit, the spy unit was disbanded and a new unit formed that
would only investigate "terrorists."[22]

According to the *Los Angeles Times*, three officers spied on MEChA and the
BSU from 1974 to 1979. The discovery documents that were not open to the public
were even more damning and suggest that there were at least six undercover officers taking Chicano studies classes. The officers lived in the campus dorms. PDID
officer Donald Rochon spied on the BSU, and Officers Augustine "Augie" Moreno
and Joe Ramírez infiltrated el Movimiento Estudiantil Chicanos de Aztlán and the
La Raza Unida Party. "To support their contention, the student leaders and their
lawyers released about 100 pages of police reports apparently written by one of the
undercover officers who attended MECHA meetings from 1976 through 1978."[23]

As a plaintiff, I reviewed the discovery documents. I ran across an item filed by
Rochon. According to his report, a meeting with black and brown students took
place at a Jack in the Box fast-food franchise near the campus. Rochon named
members of the League of Revolutionary Struggle. I knew them, they were friends.
According to Rochon, they talked about assassinating me. The plaintiffs were not
supposed to discuss the reports other than with other plaintiffs. However, I had
known some of these people since they were teens, and I sought one of them out
and confronted him with the information. He admitted that the meeting had taken
place and that there was criticism of me; however, he denied any conversation of
assassinating me or doing me bodily harm. After about two hours of going round
and round, I calmed down. Today this individual is one of the most positive forces
in the movement.[24]

It is evident that Rochon was embellishing a story for his own purposes (and
those of the LAPD). Moreover, if the alleged conspiracy had taken place, why
hadn't the police informed me or campus authorities? If true, it would have endangered not only my life but the lives of students. The story does not end there. I met

Los Angeles Sheriff Lee Baca at a fund-raiser in Arcadia in the 1990s; he admitted spying on the Chicano Movement and on me. Baca said in retrospect that there was no cause, although the culture of the police at the time justified it.[25]

The relationship between police surveillance and the growth and stability of student organizations and Chicana/o Studies must be more fully explored, since it still continues and will increase. For example, on September 2, 2009, CSUN MEChA was holding its first meeting on the lawn between Jerome Richfield Hall and Barman Hall—an area called Manteca Park—when the students and faculty in attendance observed more than a dozen older men with backpacks looking at the students. At first it was thought that they were Minutemen, since they had intended to disrupt the Chicano graduation in late May. However, their plans fell through when they showed up at the College of Humanities graduation. Overwhelmed by the numbers, they backed off. MEChA President Abraham Ramírez and the community liaison Felicia Rivera grew concerned: "We saw this guy rushing us, coming toward us really fast," Rivera said. "We were backing them. At the corner of our eye we saw that his group caught up to him and restrained him." Ramírez said, "We heard them say something to him like, 'It's not time yet.' Then they huddled up again." According to associate chair of the Chicano Studies department, Gabriel Gutiérrez, "As the meeting continued, it was announced that the meeting would be moved to the Chicano/a house . . . In the mean time, the group that had at this time taken what appeared to be a rather aggressive posture toward the participants of the MEChA meeting gathered their belongings and proceeded on the walk going north along the library." There was a brief encounter, during which the group identified themselves as LAPD officers from the Devonshire division. The campus police confirmed that they were from the LAPD and that the Minutemen-looking group was conducting a training exercise.[26]

MEChA and Chicano Studies decided not to hold a press conference until all of the facts were collected, a decision that Mechistas on other campuses criticized as going soft. However, the facts that came in made things worse: the Devonshire division denied that the officers were acting in an official capacity. They were being trained by a private vendor or contractor. The commander of the San Fernando Valley, Deputy Chief Michel Moore, called and apologized to the university, admitting that the officers were off-duty LAPD working under a private contractor and said it would not happen again. CSUN Campus Police Chief Annie Glavin said Moore assured her that MEChA was not targeted and that there wasn't any profiling involved. She stressed that there was no intention to involve the members of the organization in the training exercise, but that LAPD was "wrong and had no business doing what they were doing. . . . It was an amazing irony that these officers wandered into territory where MEChA happened to be meeting. These officers had no clue who they were dealing with," she said. "Needless to say, they do now. I'm sure they are highly embarrassed and thus the apology from the LAPD, a very sincere apology." Also coincidental was that Northridge MEChA had been at the forefront of the July demonstrations at the California State University Trustees and was part of a statewide coalition opposing tuition hikes. Meanwhile, several e-mails to the editor of the *Sundial* were printed, most of which were hate literature blaming MEChA.

In January 2010 Chicana/o Studies and MEChA met with Assistant Chief Michel R. Moore, now director of the Office of Special Operations and the head of Intelligence for the LAPD. They apologized, but we are still waiting for information on the vendor and the extent to which vendors are being used. It was learned that they are funded by federal antiterrorist funds. The American Civil Liberties Union was present and has submitted a formal request for information.[27] Meanwhile, CSUN and other campuses are receiving funds from the CIA to conduct classes and seminars on their campuses. As with Reserve Officers Training Corp (ROTC), administrators have caved in to the almighty dollar. As for MEChA, the controversy has hurt it. The organization has lost two-thirds of its membership. They are intimidated.

The point is, if it happened to Northridge, then there is a strong probability that it happened at Cal State LA, San Diego, El Paso, and other Chicano Studies programs.

BALANCING THE NUMBERS

Were there revolutionary groups on campus? There is supposed to be; this is the nature of the university. Academe is a chalice, a vessel of competing ideas. At Northridge there was a mixture of ideological currents, often at cross purposes. It never occurred to the leadership of Chicano Studies to push a single dogma. Beginning in the early 1970s, mostly through the leadership of Gilbert Cano, one of the leaders of the Chicano Moratorium and a SFVSC student, the department was involved with Padres Asociados para Derechos Religiosos, Educativos, y Sociales (PADRES) and Las Hermanas (the sisters) at the Mexican American Cultural Center (MACC), on the northwest side of San Antonio. The brainchild of Father Virgilio Elizondo, MACC was a national center for pastoral education and language studies for ministry to Mexican Americans. MACC was very involved with liberation theology. I gave several lectures and a weeklong seminar for priests and nuns, meeting liberation ethnologists and Father Patrick Flores, who later became an archbishop. Through this contact I met Father Juan Arzube, who was later an auxiliary bishop. He helped the department on occasion. For instance, the department was organizing a parent conference, and administrators in Ventura County red-baited it. Juan was gracious enough to write a letter introducing us as good friends. It came out on his stationery. This also helped us in recruiting Chicana/o students. Cano also brought the Jesuit liberation theologian Jesús García from Guadalajara, who gave a rousing homily to students.

The relationship with left groups differed, not because of the ideas but because of party building. Favoring one tendency invited struggles that deterred from the building of a community and caused tensions within MEChA. Chicana/o students identified closely with a Chicano or Mexican identity—this was even true of left-wing groups such as ATM (the August 29 Movement, later the League of Revolutionary Struggle, or LRS) and Centro de Acción Social Autónoma (CASA), which had

separate takes on the national question and who would be at the vanguard. They
were not unique. For example, visiting Baldemar Velázquez, the president of Farm
Labor Organizing Committee (FLOC) in Toledo, Ohio, in the late 1970s, I found
his staff dejected because they had been preparing for an organization drive of
tomato pickers, and they had invited the Socialist Workers Party to help. The party
had raided the union's latest volunteers and taken them off to be revolutionaries.
The incident did not make FLOC anticommunist, but they would not make the
same mistake. In California many student groups were caught in the crossfire of
these party-building activities.

What was essential was to have a stable MEChA organization. It has become in
mode even among Chicanas/os to criticize MEChA, but the critics forget that the
first group that Chicana/o faculty turn to when they are denied tenure or a position
is MEChA. For example, in May 1974 Carlos Muñoz was denied a position in the
political science department at the University of Washington. About seventy-five
students staged a sit-in to protest and took over the College of Arts and Sciences
offices. "It looks like a hurricane hit the place," one student said after protestors left
about 6:30 P.M. "Dirt was strewn over carpets and desktops in the rooms occupied,
paint was spattered, coffee and dirt was thrown into file cabinet drawers." Students
demanded the hiring of Muñoz. The political science faculty voted against hiring
Muñoz, with or without tenure, and the department chairman, Richard Fiathman,
said that "he would resign as chairman if Muñoz were hired to teach." Roberto
Maestas, director of El Centro de la Raza, mobilized the community. The case dragged
on, and, according to community sources, Muñoz received a cash settlement.
Interestingly, Muñoz did not acknowledge this in his book *Youth, Identity, Power:
The Chicano Movement.*[28]

The Northridge MEChA leaders made it a point to remain neutral in the LRS-
CASA struggle since many students and faculty had close ties to the Oxnard area.
The Santa Barbara campus was in constant student turmoil due to resistance to
reforms. In 1976 the Santa Barbara history department denied historian Jesús
Chavarria tenure. A senior member of the department, Richard Oglesby, said,
"Some guys spend a lot of time in public service which if they are assistant professors, they are dummies for doing." The truth is that the two Latin American specialists were out to get Chavarria, who was a respected scholar and later went on to
publish *Hispanic Business.*[29]

In 1975 the Santa Barbara student newspaper wrote, "flakjacketed, helmeted
law enforcement agents cleared the multi-million-dollar computer center at the
University of California at Santa Barbara early today, about three hours after
students seized it to protest university policies toward minority students." The sit-in
of some 100 students was led by Arnulfo Casillas, twenty-nine, a wounded Vietnam
veteran. Casillas was a special kind of activist, intense and ready to go to the limit.
He was accompanied by his brother Arturo, twenty, and a multiracial coalition of
brown, black, and white students called Students for Collective Action to protest
cuts in Chicano and Black Studies. They demanded among other things the resignation of Raymond Huerta, the affirmative action officer, who was in collusion

with the administration.[30] Upon getting arrested on Cinco de Mayo at one in the morning, a crowd of over five hundred students chanted "[Chancellor Vernon] Cheadle must go, Cheadle must go." Many of these activists at Santa Barbara had family at Northridge.

Some critics derisively called the Chicana/o student movement at Northridge cultural nationalist because it had a Raza Unida contingent and a very strong music and art program with a *mariachi*, a *jarocho conjunto*, a dance group, and several artist collectives. However, the critics were simply not organizers. When the first large wave of students arrived, the department decided to open its doors to diverse groups and diverse ideologies. Knowing that many of the students were Catholics, it worked closely with the Catholic Neumann Club on campus, which was staffed by a progressive priest and nun. Irish Father Paschal Hardy from St. Euphrasia in Granada Hills, who had strong ties with the Irish Republican Army, sought out the department and ministered to the spiritual needs of a large sector of the students. He used to invite nuns to campus to visit the office of President Jim Cleary, a Catholic, to pray for his soul for mistreating Mexicans.[31] At the same time, Pierre Mandel, a Communist Party USA member, ran Marxist study groups.[32] At the other end, a professor who had worked many years in the Chicano community held study groups using the Redbook (a book popular among Chicano youth).

Determined to keep an open environment, the department could not avoid the struggles with CASA, the Socialist Workers Party, and others. Differences with these groups were not ideological but due to an insistence that all groups operate under MEChA, the central Chicano student body. Groups could not be banned from a state university campus, because that would have been undemocratic. They were just not welcome to use or work within department facilities.

Nevertheless, it would be disingenuous to say that students in the La Raza Unida Party (RUP) did not receive special help. The department paid for speakers such as Corky Gonzales and José Angel Gutiérrez to speak on campus and in the community. Carlos Reyes, a member of MEChA, went to Crystal City, Texas, to organize, and over the course of two-three years the department sent more than a dozen students to live and organize in the spinach capital. They were given two semesters of college credits, worked in the *Voluntario* program, and got free food and lodging. Many of these students had never been out of California, and they met Tejanos and others—even the Texas Rangers. In San Fernando, and to a lesser extent in City Terrace, RUP organizers received credit for community service—many of these activists remain in the community to this day. This was a feat since most of them were from East Los Angeles and other parts of the state. Indeed, any student that had a project could write up a proposal and get college credit.

With time, scholars have created myths about the nature of MEChA, Chicano Studies, the RUP, and other Chicana/o nationalist organizations—myths that have been repeated by nativist organizations such as the American Patrol. For example, there is the myth that white people were unwanted and unwelcome in these organizations. One of the first fellows of Operation Chicano Teacher was a white male student who spoke perfect Spanish, having been raised in the barrio. A white forty-something single mother of two children was voted into Operation Chicano Teacher. Patricia Hynds received her bachelor of arts in 1977 in Spanish and Chicano Studies from California State University at Northridge. Two years later she received a master of arts in Mexican-American Studies, with a specialty in bilingual/cross-cultural education. In 1980, as an associate with the Maryknoll Society, a Catholic organization, she worked in Nicaragua for six years, advising the Sandinistas. She wrote for *Envio*, a monthly publication on political and social events in Nicaragua. Pat made presentations on the situation in Nicaragua throughout the United States, Latin America, and Asia. From 1991 to 1994, Hynds worked in Lima, Peru, as the director and managing editor of *Noticias Aliadas / Latinamerica Press*, a weekly bilingual publication covering politics, economics, human rights, church, and environment in Latin America and the Caribbean.[33] In Texas, one of intellectual godfathers of MAYO was Professor Charles Cotrell.[34]

The struggle between the LRS and CASA got out of hand and led to bitterness and destroyed many campus organizations. Even after the demise of CASA in the late 1970s, the so-called ideological struggle continued up to 1989. Within this struggle a wide range of left-wing organizations participated. The most persistent of the left groups was the Socialist Workers Party, founded in 1928 by former members of the Communist Party USA who expelled the Communist Party for supporting Russian Communist leader Leon Trotsky against Joseph Stalin. This brought on factional fights in Mexico and the United States, leading to the infamous shootout when Mexican muralist David Siqueiros allegedly assaulted the house of Leon Trotsky in May 1940. Trotsky had been befriended by Diego Rivera and Frida Kahlo.

After World War II, several splinterings of the Trotskyite group occurred. During the 1960s it was involved in the movement against the war, and it targeted student groups on university campuses. The Socialist Workers Party gained inroads to Chicana/o students during the Third World Liberation Front strikes at San Francisco State College, the University of California at Berkeley, and elsewhere in 1968 and 1969. It played a major role in establishing the Mexican American Studies Department at Merritt College in Oakland. It supported the National Chicano Moratorium, La Raza Unida, and Chicano nationalism in its newspaper, the *Militant*. Through taxing its members, it achieved a measure of financial independence. Peter Camejo led a large Chicano contingent. Its influence waned in the Chicano movement after the 1977 San Antonio Immigration Conference, as CASA, MEChA, and other left-wing groups went after it.[35]

The October League was founded in 1971 by several student groups that split from the Students for a Democratic Society (which fell apart in 1969). Michael Klonsky, a student at Valley State, was a driving force in the October League. A leader in the New Communist Movement, the October League broke away from the Communist Party USA and its allegiance to the Soviet Union. Klonsky was at Valley State in 1967 during the period of massive student demonstrations. (In 1968 Klonsky became chair of the SDS and his involvement with San Fernando Valley State lessened.) Between 1966 and 1967, twenty-three blacks and seven Latinos attended the Valley State campus. While the October League was not a force at

Valley State, it was at San Diego State and had a following in the Chicago area. The Communist Labor Party had visibility on Los Angeles campuses—the center of which was California State Los Angeles. It called for black self-determination and a black nation in the south. Founded in 1958, it was composed of mostly black and Puerto Rican organizations. Its leader, Nelson Perry, had a home in South Central and had close ties with the Black Panthers at Cal State LA. At Valley State the Communist Labor Party was low key, but individual members participated in Chicano Studies department forums. I sponsored a study group at my Van Nuys apartment. At the time, members operated the Midnight Special Bookstore, which had the best collection of books on Latin American labor and social movements. Unfortunately, due to low sales it had to close shop.[36]

CASA was a spin-off of Hermandad General de Trabajadores, founded by Bert Corona. Up to the 1970s, CASA was a service organization with about two thousand dues-paying members. In the early 1970s, it was joined by members of Casa de Carnalismo, a Boyle Heights youth organization. Casa del Carnalismo rose to prominence in fighting the police brutality confronting drug dealers in the area. A shootout occurred between Casa del Carnalismo and dealers that led to arrests and a trial. The Committee to Free Los Tres was organized by attorney Antonio Rodríguez. CASA, through the influence of Casa Carnalismo, evolved into a Mexican nationalist party, which further evolved into a brand of Marxism that followed theories of the Mexican Communist Party. The Young Turks under Rodríguez, believing that a militant vanguard could attract a broader membership, challenged Corona, who left CASA. Now a vanguard party, it competed with militant nationalists such as the Crusade for Justice and the La Raza Unida Party, as well as Marxist groups. Meanwhile, it entered into a fraternal arrangement with the Puerto Rican Socialist Party, expanding into Chicago, San Antonio, Colorado, and other areas of California. In Los Angeles there were several hundred participating members by 1977. CASA published a newspaper, *Sin Fronteras.* However, its dues-paying base had fallen from 2,000 to about a 1,000 members. CASA formed the National Coalition for Immigration Rights, which conducted a national campaign in cooperation with other pro–immigration-rights organizations. CASA regarded Mexicans and Chicanas/os as the same people divided by American imperialism, having the right of national self-determination as a single Mexican nation. According to it, Chicanas/os were part of the Mexican, not the American, working class. Most accounts say that by the end of 1977 internal strains and conflicts caused a leadership crisis, and this was the beginning of the end. However, CASA left a well-disciplined cadre that formed the core of future Chicana/o politicos, labor and community organizers, and it made and kept the pro–foreign-born struggle at the forefront of the movement.

The ATM had a lot in common with CASA—both were products of the Chicano movement and were composed of barrio youth, students, and workers. ATM evolved out of the Labor Committee of La Raza Unida Party in Los Angeles. It merged with other groups, forming at a Unity Conference in May 1974, and lasted independently from 1974 to 1978. It then merged with the New Communist

movement, which was influenced by the thought of Mao Zedong and Joseph
Stalin's theories on the national question. The ATM published a manifesto, *Fan the
Flames: A Revolutionary Position on the Chicano National Question*, in 1975. It pro-
fessed that Chicanos in the southwestern United States were an oppressed nation
occupied after U.S. invasions. Its goal was a multinational communist party.[37]
ATM had a strong following in New Mexico, where its chapter entered into the
Chicano Communications Center, a media organization founded by Elizabeth
"Betita" Martinez. It also published a newspaper, *Revolutionary Cause*, and a theo-
retical journal, the *Red Banner*. In 1978, ATM merged in LRS, which lasted until
1990. It also drew political inspiration from the Communist Party of China and
Mao Zedong.

The LRS also integrated the Asian American communist organization I Wor
Kuen and then added the Revolutionary Communist League, a mostly African
American communist organization—making it a major force on the radical left.
The LRS published a newspaper called *Unity* and *Forward: Journal of Marxism-
Leninism-Mao Zedong Thought*. These mergers added to their militancy. Like
CASA, the LRS left big footprints, training the next generation of union and com-
munity organizers—activists such as Bill Gallegos, Roberto Flores, William Flores,
Patricia Recinos (Justice for Janitors), Theresa Montano, and many others. The
groups clashed with Chicano Studies departments and with student organizations.

During the early 1980s the LRS strove to establish hegemony on the campuses.
In conversations with the leadership of the LRS, many admitted that party building was often unnecessary. The reality of American society and the academy was
and is that left movements are only successful when they have sufficient numbers
to disrupt, which was not the case in the seventies and eighties. Egos also played a
part, as did hierarchies, in the case of CASA. As mentioned, the LRS mushroomed
overnight and it had the funds to sustain its activities—*Unity* rivaled the *Militant*
and the *People's World* in quality and sophisticated analysis. For a time, *Sin
Fronteras* represented the best within the movement. In retrospect, the contributions of these groups were enormous to the development of Chicano programs,
introducing alternative and even oppositional points of views. They followed the
path of the Black Berets in Albuquerque that blazed an internationalist approach.
Its main leader, Richard Moore, and others went to Cuba with the Venceremos
Brigade, where they often met with members of CASA and LRS.

MEChA, as well as remnants of CASA and defunct Marxist groups, entered
what resembled a good old-fashioned gang fight. But after 1985 even this fervor
began to ebb. However, a lot of bitterness lingered. Circa 1988 I received a call from
Mechistas at Fresno State who happened to be in the Line of March, which had
a large Filipino membership. It was a Stalinist group. This cadre of Chicano youth
was very young and especially militant in attacking the LRS. They called me to get
dirt on Bill Flores, who was applying for a position in La Raza Studies. They did not
want him because he was in the LRS. I knew Bill, he had been on the other side,
but I knew him to be an excellent scholar. So I asked them about the other two
candidates—did they inquire whether they had ever been in a leftist group? If not,

why not? I found this question much more relevant than if Bill had at one time been in the LRS. Apparently, they dropped their opposition after this teaching moment.

The value of the left groups was that they pushed new ideas on the student groups that, even when opposing them, they learned from the encounter. Opposition is a form of learning. Despite the occasional spurts of infantilism from the left, and the exception of the Communist Workers' Party (CWP), a Maoist group originating in 1973, none of these groups ever lied to me. In the case of the LRS, the Chicana/o cadre was an equal partner in the organization, whereas in the CWP they were subsidiary members. By 1985 the CWP ceased to be a Leninist party and formed the New Democratic Movement so they could become social democrats.

Today one of the few Left Party remaining that is run by a Chicana/o cadre and is still active within the Chicana/o community is the Unión del Barrio, established in 1981, which operates out of San Diego, with chapters in Oxnard, Los Angeles, and Bakersfield. It publishes La Verdad. Its chair, Ernesto Bustillos, has prioritized prisoners' rights, education, and Chicana/o Studies.[38] The organization has participated in the formation of community groups, most notable of which is the Association of Raza Educators, which was organized in 1994 after the passage of Proposition 187. A May 15, 2010, conference drew over 700 participants. While the association is not a Unión surrogate, Unión leadership forms its core.[39]

Many professors denigrate the danzantes, the Aztec dancers, and the indigenistas movements. However, like Marxists, feminists, and gay students, they all have a right to occupy space within the Chicana/o Studies orbit. Before criticizing indigenous movements, the power of millenarian movements and their role in history should be studied. Betita Martínez, a stone materialist, once remarked that the left has always underrated the power of spirituality. From personal experience, I know this is true. While I do not like religion, I recognize its power in healing drug addicts.

LESSONS FROM DELANO: PUSHING THE PARAMETERS

Movement politics were often so addictive that the managers of Chicano Studies programs forgot to take care of the shop. In 1965 I was in Delano, California, and there was tremendous pressure on the left for César Chávez and the National Farm Workers Association not to join the American Federation of Labor and to remain an independent union. When pressed by the delegation composed of Mexican American and white activists as to what he was going to do, César got a faraway look in his eyes, and after what seemed hours, he turned to the group and said, "You see all of those people out there? The union has to feed and shelter them. They depend on us. Farm workers have lost most strikes they have participated in—they deserve to win."

Unfortunately, many academics take pride that their Chicano Studies programs have been eliminated. The losers are the students and the community. Somehow the programs were just too revolutionary. The quest for ideological purity quickly dissolves into an ego trip. One of the strengths of the farmworkers is their rich history of strikes won and lost by Mexican American organizations. Unfortunately, the history of Chicano Studies is missing for individual programs across the country. Establishing a record is simple today in an era of digitalized records. Recording success and failures should be a priority. Every five years departments go through a program review. The process is revealing since meetings take place with the dean, associate dean, and interested parties as to what goes into the review. The department's trajectory is included, as is the administration's view of what it wants the department to be. These records allow a scientific evaluation of the progress of the department.[40]

TURF BATTLES

The first record of an evaluation of the Northridge department was a 1975 draft of its first five-year review. The document reveals that the dean and associate dean were not thrilled about what they considered Chicano Studies encroachments on other departments and units on campus. Departmental representatives had several contentious meetings with Dean Jerome Richfield and Associate Dean Gale Larson and the college's academic council. The English department was huge and controlled the academic council. It would not support Chicano Studies, which it saw as a competitor. Larson was a member of the English department and protected its interests. Moreover, there was the snobbery of mainstream faculty members who would tell anyone who would listen that most Chicano Studies professors did not have terminal degrees.[41] The English department made alliances with Languages, Religious Studies, and Philosophy—giving them a majority of the School of Humanities Academic Council. After the splitting up of the School of Letters and Science, Chicano Studies was assigned to the new College of Behavioral Sciences. It quickly petitioned to be housed in Humanities, as Behavioral Sciences housed the mammoth departments of history, political science, and sociology, which were more political than foreign languages. Pan-African Studies also petitioned to go to Humanities, but it was refused admittance by the council on the pretext that it was not compatible with Humanities. In reality, they were darker than Chicanos, who were the lesser of the evils.

Larson and the council took the offensive at the meeting. Richfield played King Solomon and tried to smooth the waters. The department attempted to move the newly created "La Chicana" to general education, but the academic council checked it. The department argued that the "demographic data clearly made it apparent that anyone vaguely contemplating a career in education must seek adequate preparation for their role as an educator of students of Mexican descent."[42] It argued that Northridge and the Los Angeles community colleges had failed to develop courses or programs to meet the needs of Chicanos. Going on the offensive, Chicano Studies designated English-as-a-second language, child development, bilingual education, liberal studies, linguistics, and the social studies waiver as areas that the department planned to expand into. The administration and the academic council strenuously objected, saying that these courses dealt with pedagogy and not content. A shouting match broke out, with the department accusing Larson and the English department of entering into an alliance with the School of Education.

A case was made for Chicano Studies art and music courses and the failure of the institution to fund them at the same level the university funded mainstream courses.

Jorge García and Rachel Wong, an Oxnard School member, had worked out a teacher internship program with the Oxnard and Fillmore schools. This shook up the School of Education and the Ventura County Schools. The department had assumed some of the responsibility for supervision, and this was viewed as encroachment. Larson again objected to the language of the draft and underlined the passages that said "*the development of an effective English-as-a second language credential program which would emphasize a functional rather than structural approach.*" Adding, "*The creation of Chicano School Counselor program [and] . . . The laying of the groundwork for a Chicano School of Social Work*" as part of the Chicano Studies trajectory. The reviewers put large question marks next to these sections and wrote "*in cooperation.*"[43] Larson believed that this was an attack on the School of Education and that it should be given the opportunity to reply to Chicano Studies' comment that "Our main problem is present personnel within other departments and schools and the convincing of their sectors that it is to their best interest to commence development in those areas. Most critical is the absence of qualified personnel in the School of Education to train teachers to teach in barrio schools." According to Jorge García, the department responded that it would not allow Education to respond to the draft because this was Chicano Studies' report, and it would say what it wanted to say.

The deans and the academic council also wanted to strike out:

> The lack of awareness on the part of other faculty [in other departments] is tragic. For instance, in a county which is approaching majority Spanish-surnamed citizens, faculty members are not making any effort to meet changing needs. The School of Education has only three faculty members who can in any sense of the word be classified as moderately classified to teach teachers to function in the barrio. The Department of Sociology does not have one. And, the Spanish Department treats the area of Mexican literature like a bastard son. In short, the goals set for our five-year plan are attainable—the only barrier is a university which is operating as if it were 1958.[44]

In meetings with Richfield, Larson, and the academic council, they pointed out the weaknesses of the academic credentials the Chicano Studies' faculty members and the fact that the vast majority of faculty were ineligible to sit on university committees. While Chicano Studies objected openly, privately it was concerned that the department's weakness was a problem. It cast a shadow over the students' degree and made it more difficult to defend Chicano Studies and the students' interests, since CHS faculty was excluded from key committees. An obvious flaw in Chicano Studies was that it lacked power to shift the paradigm.

THE SLOWING DOWN OF CHICANO STUDIES

In 1979 former English Department Chair Kenneth Seib published an insightful book titled *The Slow Death of Fresno State: A California Campus under Reagan and*

Brown. His thesis is that the Black Studies and La Raza Studies programs were intentionally killed by far right senior professors, with the support of Gov. Ronald Regan and CSC Chancellor Glenn Dumke, who deliberately dismantled them. The governor and the California State College administration encouraged the appointment of unqualified administrators who violated the law in cleaning out liberals and Chicano and black dissidents. Seib cites the President's Commission on Campus Unrest, saying, "Studies of activist youth reveal that in most cases students become activists through an extended process."[45] At Fresno the surrounding community and power structure intentionally provoked students.

The lesson is that each campus must be judged in context. For example, what sets CSUN apart is the presidency of James Cleary, who, although he was not always supportive, had an appreciation for the university as an institution. Cleary, a native of Wisconsin, earned a PhD in communication and public address at the University of Wisconsin, Madison, where he rose to the position of vice chancellor for Academic Affairs and professor of speech. In 1969 he began his presidency of San Fernando Valley State College. Most of the faculty were delighted because they considered him a true scholar. The only reservation some liberals had was that Cleary had been vice president of Academic Affairs when 10,000 students marched on the capitol in support of black student demands and the National Guard occupied the campus. According to the *Capital Times*, "Early Thursday morning some Guardsmen had bared their bayonets to move demonstrators off University Ave."[46] Under his watch compulsory ROTC had been eliminated at Wisconsin, but Cleary defended its existence.

Cleary looked the part of a president. He was short and white, wore tweed coats, and smoked a pipe. The worse Chicano Studies ever said about him was that he reminded the faculty of Elmer Fudd. Cleary was a player in higher education, and in 1982 he was named president of the American Association of State Colleges and Universities. He retired from Northridge in 1992 after twenty-three years of service. He was a coeditor of *Roberts Rules of Order, Newly Revised* (1970, 1981, and 1990). Although at times authoritarian, he would not blatantly violate the conventions of the academy, and on more than one occasion he supported the departments against political interference. His long tenure at Northridge allowed a settling in period where he got to know Chicano Studies' political preferences and idiosyncrasies.

THE TYRANNY OF WORDS

Aside from police provocateurs, interference by state and university officials, the rising cost of a university education, and the lack of institutional support (based on the nearsightedness of the academy), structural changes were taking place that profoundly affected the growth of Chicano Studies. The year 1978 was devastating for education: the Bakke decision and the passage of Proposition 13 in California accelerated institutional control of higher education.[47]

On June 28, 1978, the U.S. Supreme Court declared affirmative action constitutional but said that racial quotas violated the equal protection clause of the Fourteenth

Amendment—reverse discrimination. The court's isolating the variable of race opened a Pandora's box. For instance, the decision said nothing about legacy admits (the admission of the children of alumni or donors), which often composed a quarter of the freshman class at prestigious universities. Nor did the ruling include religion as a variable. The facts were that the medical school at the University of California, Davis, reserved 16 percent of its admission places for minority applicants. Allan Bakke, a thirty-six-year-old white California resident, had twice unsuccessfully applied for admission to Davis. Bakke was turned down on the basis of his interviews, so in 1974 Bakke sued Davis, alleging his grades and test scores were better than many minority students accepted for admission. Bakke alleged "reverse discrimination" on the basis of race, claiming his denial violated the Civil Rights Act of 1964 and the equal protection clause of the Fourteenth Amendment.[48]

The 1976 California Supreme Court held that Bakke was the victim of racial discrimination because he was denied admission to the University of California, Davis, Medical School. In anticipation that the U.S. Supreme Court would affirm the California State Supreme Court ruling, anti-Bakke coalitions were formed: "The Bay Area Coalition Against the Bakke Decision held its first statewide conference on the UC campus to discuss ways of applying pressure to reverse the decision and maintain and expand existing minority admissions programs."[49] There was criticism of the UC's handling of the case. Assemblyman John Vasconcelos (D-San Jose) charged on the assembly floor that the UC attorneys were dragging their feet and were less than competent. The case also caused tensions in what was previously a liberal coalition of Jewish and minority organizations. The American Jewish Committee and other Jewish organizations supported Bakke. On the other side, assemblyman Peter Chacón (D-San Diego) charged that the University of California was racist. Governor Jerry Brown's office pointed out that less than 1 percent of the state's attorneys were Mexican American. It was no secret that a negative ruling would devastate minority illusions of equal opportunity. Columnist William Raspberry wrote, "The assumption is that large numbers of highly qualified whites are being shunted aside in order to make room for marginal blacks, and that the only defensible approach is now to return to a system where admissions decisions are based solely on relative merit. . . . The truth is that such a system has never existed. Admissions preferences are the rule, not the exception. Sons and daughters of alumni usually are given preference in admissions."[50] Eleven medical schools, eleven separate committees, and dozens of faculty members and medical students had rejected Bakke's application, and the only way he got into Davis was through his suit.[51]

As the U.S. Supreme Court deliberated, in April 1978, "in one of the most militant and massive demonstrations held anywhere in the United States since the civil rights struggle of the 1960s, over 35,000 people, the majority Black, Asian and Latin youth, came to Washington, D.C., today to voice their total opposition to the racist Bakke case now pending before the Nixon-packed U.S. Supreme Court."[52] The march was put together by the National Committee to Overturn the Bakke

Decision (NCOBD). Meanwhile, the Bakke case was put on the calendar for October 1. On October 3 a rally and march started at United Nations Plaza in San Francisco. It was sponsored by the Black Law Students Association in conjunction with NCOBD, the Anti-Bakke Decision Coalition (ABDC), and other community groups. At this point the role of the UC was suspect. It testified in filings that if the special program had not been in place Bakke probably would have been admitted. This testimony did not take into account the disparate committees that reviewed Bakke and had reservations about him. Moreover, thirty-five other applicants who had been turned down outranked Bakke.

As mentioned, the case split the liberal community, polarizing the black and Jewish communities. Normally liberal Representative Henry Waxman (D-Los Angeles) supported Bakke. In Los Angeles NCOBD organized a rally at MacArthur Park.[53] Demonstrations spread to Washington, D.C., where the demonstrators chanted "Bakke says yes; the people say no" and "Down with Bakke; fight for open admissions." At the Capitol they sang, "We won't go back; send Bakke back." On October 12, the court heard arguments. Meanwhile, demonstrations spread to individual campuses where MEChA played a leadership role.

As expected, the U.S. Supreme Court came down on the side of Bakke. It tried to mask its decision by saying that race could be a variable but not the determining factor. The court split 5–4. Justice Thurgood Marshall was livid, "I do not agree that that petitioner's admissions program violated the Constitution. . . . Today's judgment ignores the fact that for several hundred years Negroes have been discriminated against, not as individuals, but rather solely because of the color of their skins. The dream of America as the great melting pot has not been realized for the Negro; because of his skin color he never even made it into the pot."[54] The dissent pointed out that all admissions were arbitrary. Meanwhile, white America applauded the decision. According to the National Association for the Advancement of Colored People (NAACP), 80 percent of white Americans believed enough had been done for blacks. Led by the UCLA Chicano Law Student Association, fifty law students launched a hunger strike protesting the Bakke ruling.[55]

After this point, the mainstream Jewish organizations and the minority communities drifted further apart. For example, the Anti-Defamation League and the American Jewish Committee filed an amicus brief supporting the Bakke decision. However, it must be pointed out that many of the activists opposing the decision were of Jewish ancestry.[56] No doubt this was a blow to African Americans and Chicanos who had relied on Jewish organizations for donations, expert advice, and media networks. After this point, the student movements in these communities had to rely more heavily on leftist organizations that often had more access to media than they did. This was a barrier to Chicano student and left groups. Even though Chicanos had national organizations, there were limited connections between them and student and activist networks.

The NCOBD and the ABDC were forced to fill the void. NCOBD had been launched in April 1977, and ABDC, was formed two months later. The goal was to bring reformist and revolutionaries together in a coalition. Maoist organizations worked within both groups. The ABDC was the most militant, using the issue to party build. It accused the NCOBD, as it was popularly known, of being reformist.[57] The NCOBD included Chicana/o organizations such as CASA-Hermandad General de Trabajadores and local and student groups. One of the leading forces in the ABDC was the LRS. CSUN MEChA decided to not join a particular coalition but to participate in both.

PROPOSITION 13: THE RICH ARE TOO POOR TO PAY

The Reagan administration had brought a not too subtle movement to tighten rules dealing with student behavior associated with large-scale demonstrations and protests. The loss of financial aid for poor students was fatal. As Seib pointed out in his book on Fresno State, the rules of faculty and student conduct resulted in a "dramatic weeding out."[58] Along with increased fees, the budget for financial aid shrunk. In an attempt to win support from white middle-class families, President Jimmy Carter and others included middle-class applicants without adding funds. The outcome was that poor students had less time to study or participate in student activities.

In California, Proposition 13 destroyed the public school system and shifted the burden of higher education to middle-class families and students. The legislation was proposed by Howard Jarvis as an initiative to reduce property taxes, to the point that local school districts lost control of their schools. The municipal budgets were trashed, leading to the laying off of the most recently hired, who were generally Mexican Americans and blacks. Minorities viewed it as a conspiracy to give back control of the bureaucracy to white males. Proposition 13 often divided white and darker people, although, out of greed, some minority homeowners voted for it.[59]

The so-called taxpayers' revolt was particular to California. In more conservative Texas the so-called revolt died in the water.[60] Proposition 13 capped property taxes at 1 percent. It passed and immediately there were cutbacks in public education, with schools cutting summer classes.[61] This led to budget crises, which set the stage for raising University of California and state college tuition. The community colleges were also affected because of the cut in local revenues. Proposition 13 weakened local government and left control of the budget to Sacramento. "Just as the state legislature was preparing to completely revamp the system of school finance . . . this initiative rolled back property tax rates and property assessments, took control of each of these ways from local decision makers, and established formulae to contain growth of each."[62] In 1970 the UC Board of Regents, dominated by Reagan appointees, favored increased student fees and talked about tuition that was opposed by the legislature. Instead they imposed the "education fee" from $50 a year to $300. State universities raised fees to $205, while the community colleges raised them to less than $10.

This along with Proposition 13 ushered the demise of public education in California education. It prevented the raising of taxes by inserting a proviso that the legislature could only raise taxes with a two-thirds majority. Proposition 13 was a boon to commercial property owners whose taxes were limited to their 1978 levels—with large department stores and others often paying lower rates than small property owners.[63] There were also other built in inequities. Although renters were promised that their rents would come down, in truth the rents went up.

Proposition 13 won in a landslide on June 6.[64] Municipalities to raise revenues encouraged the construction of new apartment complexes because the tax rate was higher on new construction, driving up the rents on the old. Rising rents devastated students, whose rents zoomed. It also intimidated politicos. Governor Jerry Brown vowed "No new taxes," an absurd promise that fed Californians the delusion that services could be maintained through fiscal reforms.[65] Ironically, the growing Mexican American vote in Texas put the brakes on the Jarvis-type tax schemes intended to shift the tax burden to the poor and the middle class. With both parties actively seeking the Mexican American vote, they advocated for more education and government services.[66]

By 2006 California ranked forty-seventh in per-pupil spending, nearly $2,400 per student behind the national average. Indeed, the five states that housed the bulk of the Mexican and Latina/o populations in the Southwest, Midwest, and Northwest ranked below the national average. Washington, California, Texas, and Arizona ranked forty-fifth, forty-seventh, forty-eighth, and fiftieth, respectively. All of these states had large Latina/o populations. Mississippi ranked thirty-ninth in the nation.[67] The Rand Corporation wrote, "As recently as the 1970s, California's public schools were reputed to be excellent."[68] In 1970 California spent $400 more per pupil than the national average. The decline took place from the late 1970s through the middle 1990s, when California's support lagged about 1.2 percentage points behind the national average. After this point, the gap widened.[69] This has had a direct affect on Chicano Studies by thinning out the base.

In Sum

The growth of Chicano Studies was dependent on the free flow of working-class students, which was obstructed by intentional flaws in the American educational system. Fifty-three percent of Latinas/os in California did not and do not graduate from high school. "Sixty-eight percent of all California prison inmates did not graduate from high school."[70] This situation worsened with the *Bakke* decision and Proposition 13. Campus police provocateurs and the nonsupport and manipulation of the educational establishment conspired against its growth. It would be easy to blame leftist groups or Chicanas/os for the lack of stability and the demise of many programs, but this would be wrongheaded. The left was essential for advancing the mission of education, which was supposed to be promoting thinking. As mentioned, higher education is supposed to be a vessel where ideas are explored and a search for the truth takes place. In order for this to occur, all available knowledge must be explored. Students also have to have positive self-images in order to gain the skills to enter into the conversation.

CHAPTER 7

The Mainstreaming of Chicano Studies

Fabio Rojas presumed that "a new academic program required hundreds of thousands of dollars for faculty salaries, staff, office space, and equipment. Because an academic program has significant financial needs, university administrators can deliberate for years as they weigh a proposal's intellectual merits and develop new budgets."[1] According to Rojas, the sudden appearance of Black Studies in 1968–1969 took college administrators by surprise. They had not planned for these "unanticipated financial needs." It was, therefore, natural for academe to turn to private foundations such as Ford to pay for research, salaries, and other support. As with other scholars writing on the topic, Rojas does not separate research and teaching institutions. Yet it could be argued that public academies should have been supporting the study of minorities and women all along. It was this misfeasance that caused the "unanticipated financial needs."

The failure of the academy allowed Ford and the federal government to control the agendas of Black, Women, and, to a lesser degree, Chicano Studies. Believing that they could legitimatize the fields by making them academically competitive and earning them the respect of mainstream disciplines, the foundations pursued a hierarchal strategy that supported programs at more prestigious institutions. According to Leslie Hill, "The Ford Foundation has had a long-standing commitment to the development and institutionalization of women's studies, having provided substantial funding since 1972 for fellowships, women's research centers, and projects to integrate the new scholarship on women into the curriculum." The growth of Women's Studies was dramatic—more so than Black and Chicano Studies. The first program was established at San Diego State University for the 1969–70 school year, and in 1970 there were approximately 100 Women's Studies courses being offered at schools across the country. By 1971 more than 600 courses were being taught, and by 1978 there were 301 full-fledged programs in operation. That number more than doubled to 621 programs by 1990. From 1972 to 1992 Women's Studies programs received $36 million from Ford and other foundations. By 1981 they were heavily endowed, and twenty-nine women's research centers

123

operated in the United States. Two dozen years later, more than sixty universities had Women Studies centers. Susan M. Hartmann credits the Ford Foundation with being a substantive force that created the feminist movement.[2]

In forcing these new programs to turn to the nonprofit sector for financial assistance, institutions of higher education forfeited their moral ground. These institutions also profited handsomely by taking the usual 20–40 percent fee off the top for administrative costs. Academe thus *compromised* its vaunted search for the truth and allowed nonprofit foundations to often determine the research topics and their scholars of choice. The Ford Foundation has a long history of social engineering—trying to influence and control social movements at home and abroad.[3] After the big war, Ford was involved in the development of area studies as a quick and efficient way of training specialists in Latin American, African, Chinese, and other regions. Moreover, the CIA often used philanthropic foundations to recruit agents and channel large sums of money to its projects abroad without alerting the recipients as to their source.[4] Ford during the 1950s shifted its focus and cultivated long-lasting relations with the black civil rights movement. In 1963 Ford gave Morgan State College, a historically black institution in Maryland, $175,000 to extend the life of its Institute for Political Education. It would step up this involvement under the Ford presidency of McGeorge Bundy, a former John F. Kennedy adviser.

Ford took an active role in the struggle between the mainstream civil rights movement and black power advocates.[5] The black colleges rejected the growing nationalism of black militants and later stood against Afrocentrism. Ford supported elder statesmen such as Bayard Rustin, a close adviser to Martin Luther King Jr. and a harsh critic of Black Power. For a brief period the Congress of Racial Equality (CORE) flirted with the Students for a Non-Violent Society, and this influenced Ford to look into funding these organizations. CORE's brief turn to the left led Ford to conclude that the Black Power advocates were neither renegades nor opponents of the democratic faith and were deserving of financial help. However, in 1968 CORE took an abrupt turn to the right, supporting Richard M. Nixon in his 1968 and 1972 presidential campaigns. After this, Ford appeared to return to its trajectory of mainstreaming minorities, and Bundy proactively supported the mainstreaming of the civil rights movement.[6]

Ford had a more difficult time adjusting its strategy to the Mexican American community, which did not have a national organization such as the National Association for the Advancement of Colored People (NAACP). The League of Latin American Citizens and the GI Forum were not truly national in scope. In Texas, PASO challenged them, as did the Mexican American Political Association (MAPA) in California and, of course, César Chávez's farmworkers. Youth were also emerging as a force. Churches did not play the leadership role in the Mexican American community that they did in the black community. Ford must have been stung by criticisms of its UCLA Mexican American Project.

Ford appears to have adopted a strategy of creating organizations in the Mexican American community modeled after the black community, such as

NAACP's legal defense fund. To this end, Ford funded the Mexican American Legal Defense and Education Fund (MALDEF) to the tune of $2.2 million to promote the civil rights of Mexican Americans. It created a separate $450,000 fund for the legal education of thirty-five Mexican American law students.[7]

By early 1969 the preliminary data accumulated by the new census made it clear that the Mexican American population was too large to ignore, with major articles appearing in the press.[8] Other than the farmworker movement, Ford had few links to Mexican Americans. Meanwhile, Ford moved aggressively to mainstream Black Studies. The major recipients of Ford grants included Yale, Princeton, Rutgers, Howard, Morgan State, and the National Endowment for the Humanities. Ford also saw the emergence of a feminist consciousness as a potent force, early on funding feminist studies.[9] Ford was not faced with the same problem as it had with Black Studies—that of nationalism. Ford did attempt to promote the participation of women of color in Women's Studies and, according to Leslie I. Hill, encouraged the centers to "integrate women of color into the curriculum at the University of Arizona, Duke University, and the University of North Carolina, UCLA, and Memphis State University." Through the support of women's studies the foundations sought to "extend curricular change beyond 'cultural enrichment' to meaningful incorporation of both materials about and perspectives of women of color into core courses."[10] The Ford Foundation expended funds for course revisions that were in line with its vision.[11]

In an attack on Afrocentrism, F. Champion Ward, a Ford vice president and former dean of graduate studies at the University of Chicago said, "we believe that Afro-American studies should not be fenced off. We do not believe that only white Americans can understand Carl Sandburg or only blacks can understand Leopold Senghor. . . . We are persuaded that these subjects will not achieve the place in the college curriculum that they deserve unless they are designed and taught with regular standards of learning and scholarship. To accomplish this, trained faculty and new course materials must be developed vigorously in the years ahead."[12] While acknowledging that history textbooks needed revision—separatism, according to Ward, was not the way. Ford also instituted a program to fund black, Mexican American, and Native American PhDs and $225,000 to fund farmworkers' counseling centers.[13]

The jury is still out as to whether Ford helped Black Studies in the long run. The judgment depends on one's ideological perspective. At the University of Wisconsin, Craig Werner, chair of the Afro-American Studies department, credits Ford for the growth of African American Studies, which nearly doubled from six to twelve full-time, tenure track professors during the culture wars of the mid-1980s and early 1990s. Generous financial support from the Ford Foundation and strong institutional support allowed the Afro-American Studies department to flourish at Wisconsin. Because of this support, Werner maintains that the Wisconsin program grew despite the hostile environment of the times.[14] The programs at Harvard and Yale similarly benefited.

SOCIAL ENGINEERING AND CHICANO STUDIES

Meanwhile, Chicanos in San Antonio formed the Mexican American Unity Council (MAUC) in 1967 to organize for economic and political empowerment. Its founding board of directors comprised Dr. Charles Cotrell (St. Mary's University), Dr. Richard Caldwell (Kelly AFB), Judge Albert A. Peña Jr. (Bexar County Commissioner), and community activists Mario Compeán, William C. Velásquez, and Juan J. Patlán. Among MAUC's issues was the right to speak Spanish on school grounds. Willie Velásquez, a founding member of MAYO and later founder of the Southwest Voter Registration and Education Project, served as MAUC's executive director. MAYO also had a working relationship with MALDEF and played a role in its formation, including hiring MAYO leader José Angel Gutiérrez. Congressman Henry B. González was threatened by the increased militancy and nationalism of MAYO as well as the potential loss of control of patronage; hence he launched a personal crusade against MAYO.[15]

González launched his attack in April 1969, expressing doubts about the tactics of MAYO. The tone of González's attack caught even moderates off-guard. Considered a maverick, González had been elected to Congress in the late 1950s. He had sponsored and supported civil rights legislation. The right-wing press immediately sided with González, and Ford caught flack over the funding of MAYO projects. However, González took pains not to antagonize Ford: "About three years ago the Ford Foundation took an interest in the Mexican-American minority group. What the foundation saw was an opportunity to help. That opportunity coupled with the best of intentions, had produced . . . a very grave problem in the district I represent. As deeply as I must respect the intentions of the foundation, I must say that, where it aimed to produce unity, it has so far produced disunity; and where it aimed to help, it has hurt."[16]

The San Antonio congressman then tied the Southwest Council of La Raza to violent behavior by attacking one of its projects: "It also created a vague entity known as the Universidad de los Barrios," which the congressman described as a gang operation where there was a murder. According to González, neighbors were terrified. Without missing a beat he tied MAYO to the terrorists. He charged that the Ford Foundation contributed funds to the MAYO, which, according to González, "distributes literature that I can only describe as hate sheets. MALDEF has MAYO members on payroll. . . . I fear very much that the Ford Foundation miscalculated in choosing those who have charge over their grant money." González continued,

> I cannot accept the belief that simple, blind, and stupid hatred is an adequate response to simple, blind, and stupid hatred; I cannot accept the belief that playing at revolution produces anything beyond an excited imagination; and I cannot accept the belief that imitation leadership is a substitute for the real thing. Developments over the past few months indicate that there are those who believe that the best answer for hate is hate in reverse and that the best leadership is that which is loudest and most arrogant; but my observation is that arrogance is no cure for emptiness.[17]

González's hyperbole pressured the Ford Foundation and forced the Southwest Council of La Raza to defund MAUC, and MALDEF to cut ties with MAYO in an effort to isolate the nationalists. (From 1970 to 1990, Ford gave MALDEF $27.9 million in grants and the National Council of La Raza $21.5 million.) During the 1960s and 1970s Ford did not finance LULAC, although it was the epitome of patriotism and middle-class values. However, in the 1970s, when LULAC began espousing what one author calls strident nationalism, Ford intervened and in 1981 funded the organization. Other foundations followed Ford's lead and pulled away from controversy, or at least tried to engineer it.[18]

As mentioned, José Angel Gutiérrez's call for Chicanos to break the Gringo society's control over their destiny riled Congressman González. The Texas representative called for an investigation of Ford's grants to Mexican American organizations connected with MAYO. What triggered the investigation was a speech Gutiérrez gave to about 250 students at the University of Texas, Austin: "To effect meaningful change, we must be prepared to use any means necessary to accomplish our goals . . . resist any and all further encroachments on our dignity." The presentation, sponsored by the Mexican American study group on campus, was welcomed by George I. Sánchez, who criticized González, although not by name. The mood of the participants was nationalist, which was countered by the Progressive Labor Party, who said that unity should be achieved through worker unity and not on the basis of race.[19]

Ford patterned its Chicano initiatives on old immigrant ethnic models or those it believed worked with black Americans. It sought to create respected role models within the Chicano and Latino communities. In a 1973 report it stated, "Possession of the Ph.D. is not essential to begin college teaching, but it is important in being hired by stronger colleges and universities, in promotion, and in obtaining tenure."[20] The report said that fewer than 3,000 blacks and probably no more than 200 Chicanos, Puerto Ricans, and Native Americans held doctorates out of 300,000 PhDs nationally. It funded Julian Samora at Notre Dame. According to Estevan Flores, "Through his work with the Ford Foundation and the U.S. Office of Education, he secured the necessary funding—more than $700,000—to open up graduate school opportunities at Notre Dame for individuals (not just Mexican Americans) interested in graduate study of the Mexican American or Chicano experience. . . . He helped more than 50 students earn their master's or Ph.D. or law degrees." Unfortunately, Ford did not require Notre Dame to institutionalize the program through internal funding—hence, the university profited handsomely.[21]

Ford rarely funded Chicano Studies departments; however, it did fund Mexican American Studies centers at research institutions. In fairness to these centers, many of them would probably not have survived without this support because little institutional funding was forthcoming. From studying documents and speaking to interested parties, it never seemed as if Ford had a handle on the Chicano community. At the initiative of a progressive program officer, it would fund an imaginative program like MAUC and then pull back when it seemed that the programs offended establishment figures or its field officers deemed them too radical. Part of the problem, as mentioned, was that Ford did not know the Mexican American community and never trusted anyone in that community enough to elevate them to positions of power. Ford never understood the subtle differences between the Mexican American and Puerto Rican communities and the nuances within their organizations. An example is William Díaz, who joined Ford in 1983. His world-view was limited to the East Coast, and he did not know the Mexican American community in Texas or on the West Coast.

The Ford aura was further tarnished in 1970 when *Ramparts Magazine* and *El Grito del Norte* broke the story of the cancellation of a $1.5 million loan to a New Mexico group because of nepotism.[22] The money was supposed to go to help 6,000 rural and 750 urban families living below the poverty line in northern New Mexico and southern Colorado. Ford executives glowingly praised the project, which was endorsed by the Office of Economic Opportunity. However, instead of the money going to a nonprofit in northern New Mexico, it ended up in La Jara, Colorado, where the brother-in-law of Boudinot P. Atterbury, a Ford administrative officer for program-related investments, was the principal cattle trader. The article also claimed that "the Ford Foundation entered New Mexico in an attempt to create a 'leadership structure' replacing Reies López Tijerina among the poor Mexican-American people." Atterbury was quoted as saying, "We're going to show those people like Reies Tijerina, we're going to show those advocates that Ford has a better way." The article further charged that the federal government knew about the nepotism.

Ford spokesperson Arthur Trottenberg countered that the foundation made a $1.3 million loan, "not grant, about 18 months ago to establish a feedlot program for poor Spanish Americans in southern Colorado." Ford did not answer the Office of Economic Opportunity report that alleged that the money ended up instead in a feedlot corporation headed by Atterbury's brother-in-law.[23]

A Ford program officer paid a visit to the campus and asked me about the PhD initiative it was contemplating. He became visibly annoyed with my response. As a Latin American history major, I was well aware of the high fertility rate among Mexican women in the 1960s and 1970s. There was no way the country could absorb the high number of youth entering the labor force. It was only logical that large numbers of Mexicans would migrate north. Also given that the median age of Mexican American women was ten years younger than white women, the population explosion promised to continue in the United States. At the same time, the black American population was beginning to stabilize.

I posited to the Ford program officer that if the Mexican American PhD pool was about 100, doubling or even tripling the number would have little impact on the Chicano community. Among blacks that had a pool of about 3,000 PhDs, doubling or tripling that number to 6,000 or 9,000 would have a significant impact. Moreover, the increase of black PhDs would be in locations with large black popu-lations. Sending Chicanas/os to Ivy League Schools may have be good for individual careers, but it was hardly transformative for the Chicano community. I proposed that with Chicanas/os Ford consider focusing on community colleges, where master of arts, not PhD degrees, are required. I was also concerned that sending doctoral students away from home would alienate them, and I proposed that, if they were to move ahead with the fellows program, Ford require the fellows to work summers as interns in labor unions, community organizations, prisons, and Equal Opportunity Programs. What was important was numbers.

An "Advanced Study Fellows Award Fact Sheet" for 1967–1973 listed the number of awards to minorities: 691 blacks, 85 Chicanos, 62 Puerto Ricans, and 37 Native Americans. On a Selection Committee for Advanced Study and Doctoral Fellowship Programs, 1968–1973, out of the ninety-five members only four were of Mexican origin.[24] Not wanting to denigrate the fellowship program, it must be posited that who does the research determines what questions are asked and what conclusions are made concerning the questions. Probably no more than 200 Latina/o scholars had doctorates in the early 1970s. A need for PhDs and EdDs was evident.[25] However, Ford and other foundations did not initiate these programs for altruistic reasons, so it was wrongheaded to apply models used with the black community to the Chicana/o community. The flawed policy was compounded by program officers who did not know the needs of the community.

An incident indicative of the Ford Foundation's paternalism occurred circa 1976. Ford called a meeting in California of American Indian, Black, Chicano, and Puerto Rican scholars. The meeting was with the editors of *Daedalus*, founded in 1955 as the *Journal of the American Academy of Arts and Sciences*. Ford had given *Daedalus* a grant to publish an issue on the four minorities—notably absent were Latina scholars. Leading the meeting was Stephen R. Graubard, a particularly obnoxious little man who in effect lectured us on how prestigious *Daedalus* was and how it would legitimize minority scholarship to be published in his journal. The issue would be based on the model of a similar publication by *Daedalus* in 1965 on blacks. In the preface of the 1981 issue it said, "In planning this issue of *Daedalus* it was agreed that representatives of each of the four minorities should be asked to write about how the events of recent decades have changed the lives of those who belong to these minorities. We urged each to meet and consult, to write individually or collaboratively, as seemed most reasonable and convenient, but to answer a specific set of questions." I do not know who agreed, since I was at the meeting and I raised serious objections to Ford's strategy of anointing *Daedalus*. It was a repetition of the UCLA Mexican American Study Project. I objected to Graubard selecting the scholars or topics, and I insisted that Chicanas/os have their own editorial advisers to assign articles. I would recuse myself as an author. I criticized the fact that *Daedalus* was receiving several hundred thousand dollars from Ford, and it was a paternalistic arrangement. The dialog got heated. I was isolated but others were more than willing to publish in the journal. I learned an important lesson: unity has its bounds.[26]

FACULTY GOVERNANCE

Ford's strategy of buying the acceptance of Chicana/o Studies scholars from prestigious universities may eventually work with Women's Studies, but it is doubtful whether the strategy will work with Mexican Americans and Latinas/os in the near future. For example, the organic links between Ivy League schools and Mexican Americans do not exist. And the population centers of Mexican origin peoples are on the opposite coast.

The first thing that happens when a minority faculty member sues for discrimination is that affirmative action officers and the legal system ask for the available labor pool. The National Science Foundation reports that from 1990 to 1999 Mexican origin candidates earned 0.7 percent of the doctorates in all fields in 1990 (190) and 1.1 percent (344) in 1999. In psychology they went from 0.8 percent (25) to 1.4 percent (44); in the social sciences, from 0.8 percent (19) to 1.2 percent (33); in the field of health, from 0.5 percent (5) to 1.8 percent (19); in the humanities, from 2.6 percent (80) to 2.7 percent (117); in education, from 1.5 percent (84) to 1.7 percent (95).[27] The proportion of Latinas earning doctoral degrees has increased in the past ten years, from 49 percent in 1997 to 56 percent in 2007. Latinas have received more doctoral degrees than Latino males each year since 1999. However, not all is rosy. In areas such as history, Latinas/os earn less than a half dozen doctorates annually.[28] Many graduates have a hard time finding employment. Departments answer charges of discrimination by saying that there are not enough Mexicans or Latinas/os in the labor pool, which is disingenuous. In the CSUN history department of twenty-five historians, there is not a single Mexican American. It has yet to hire a professor of Mexican origin in this century.

In the 1990s Provost Luanne Kennedy blamed the lack of minority hires on the large Ethnic Studies departments. For three years straight she did not allocate positions to Chicana/o Studies and gave them to the so-called mainstream departments on condition that they hire minorities. When they did not, she reversed her policy and began to allocate Chicana/o Studies the positions it was entitled to and the department mushroomed.

The culprit is faculty governance. The functioning of the academy is riddled with peer-group reviews. When faculty members are hired, when they submit their dissertations or articles for publication, merit pay allowances, promotion, tenure, or a grant, there is peer-group review. Discrimination is almost impossible to prove because the reviewers are protected by confidentiality. The plaintiff could not prove discrimination because he or she could not prove what the review committee or the evaluators said. This was partially remedied in *University of Pennsylvania v. Equal Employment Opportunity Commission* (1990). The Supreme Court unanimously rejected a privilege protecting the confidentiality of material assembled for tenure decisions in cases involving discrimination. Although the case focused on sex discrimination, it included race, political, and age discrimination, taking the obvious into account that tenure committees can prevent "smoking guns" from getting in tenure review files and deny access to those files.[29] In the *Pennsylvania* case, Rosalie Tung, an Asian American professor, alleged she was denied tenure because of her sex and her race. The EEOC petitioned the university for access to Tung's confidential peer review file citing the protection of academic freedom. The university refused because it had promised not to breach the confidentiality promised to reviewers.

The abuses of confidentiality are well-known. Peter Novick reviewed letters of recommendation given by Arthur Schlesinger of Jewish candidates. Schlesinger wrote of Oscar Handlin, "[he] has none of the offensive traits which some people associate with his race." Of Bert J. Lowenberg, he wrote, "by temperament and spirit . . . measures up to the whitest Gentile I know." Roger B. Merriman wrote of Daniel J. Boorstin that "[he is] a Jew, though not the kind to which one takes exception." Of Richard Leopold, Merriman wrote, "of course a Jew, but since he is a Princeton graduate, you may be reasonably certain that he is not of the offensive type." Merrill Jensen wrote of Solomon Katz that he was "quite un-Jewish, if one considers the undesirable side of the race." One can only imagine what many reviewers have said about minorities under the veil of confidentiality.[30] Most Chicanos have suffered from similar evaluations, but in a much more overt way. I myself have been described as a fair-skinned Mexican with light eyes and plagued with a Mexican temper.[31]

The review panels for the National Endowment for the Humanities and other foundations choose reviewers who are safe, more often than not who know little about the subject. When I applied for a grant to finish *Corridors of Migration*, which received the Choice Best Book Award, most reviewers sent back jaundiced reviews stating that I would never finish the proposal. Vicki Ruiz stated in her review that the material had already been covered in Debra Weber's book on the 1933 cotton strike, although only a small portion of the book was about the strike.[32] I got the reviews after badgering the foundation and threatening to sue. Reviews are not transparent, and rarely do scholars have the opportunity to confront his or her accusers or find the smoking gun.

When I successfully sued the University of California at Santa Barbara, the attorneys retrieved a treasure trove of documents during discovery. After receiving the personnel files of Chicana/o and white scholars, a definite pattern emerged: most review panels were composed of white scholars whose biases were clear. Above everything else, being a "good citizen" was the principle requirement for promotion. Caustic remarks were made about the scholarship of Chicano and Chicana scholars whose promotions were questionable until they sided with the administration in my suit against it. It would be interesting to do a before-and-after analysis of the professors' evaluations at the University of California, Santa Barbara (UCSB).

Also revealed was a pattern of sexism. Yolanda Broyles González, who everyone agreed was an exceptional scholar, received a salary and promotions that lagged behind her male counterparts. González ultimately sued UCSB and received a settlement. Without piercing the veil of confidentiality, the lawyers could have never proven discrimination. For example, they learned that three Chicano professors, Ramón Gutiérrez of San Diego, and Raymund Paredes and Rudy Alvárez of UCLA, were collaborating with the UC attorneys.

The committee's statements about my scholarship were used to prove discrimination. The aggregate summary of the July 30, 1991, report said, "*Occupied America* is a 'cult book,'" and it calls me a "cult Professor," saying that I had to be isolated in a large mainstream department because I was dangerous and would corrupt the minds of Chicano professors. The file was full of phrases such as "we do not judge his fiery brand of advocacy appropriate for a professorship in the University of California"; "yet another drawback is found in the fact that Acuña, at the age of 59, has never trained doctoral students"; and "Acuña is a polemicist more than a seeker for truth." There were also remarks that it was the ad hoc committee's duty to shield the "inchoate" Chicano Studies department from my influence. In a deposition the provost David Sprecher admitted that he had not read my files but called the evaluations of leading Chicana/o scholars "not analytical." Despite the numerous smoking guns found in the files, it was difficult to prove discrimination. The UC had deep pockets, which meant millions of dollars of taxpayers' monies.[33]

CHICANO STUDIES ENTERS THE DIALOG

It is not argued or implied that grants are not necessary and that doctoral candidates should be required to pull themselves up by their bootstraps. Upper middle-class families subsidize the education of their children, and indeed this is why so many professors are upper middle class and independently wealthy. However, in growing Chicano Studies and other ethnic studies programs, the applicants must be aware of the effects of mainstreaming and that foundations do not give awards for benevolent ends. They are all engaging in a form of social engineering.

In recent memory, the War on Poverty offers lessons of the positive and negative impacts of large sums of money coming into a community. I belonged to the Latin American Civic Association (LACA) that was composed of community and professional volunteers who set up preschool classes of the mommy-and-me variety. The volunteers went door to door enlisting sometimes reluctant parents to send their children to a local park so they could learn English and acquire basic skills before entering Kindergarten. The members also pressured the schools for reform meetings with school officials. For example, in 1964 LACA met with Valley State Professor Betty Brady and pressed the School of Education for special programs to train Mexican American children. This program was so successful that in 1966 LACA received its first Head Start program grant. Overnight the organization mushroomed, with meetings attracting several hundred people, which would have been ideal if LACA would have become a mass organization instead of a service provider. The grants drove the organization's agenda, and many of the original members dropped out. However, it cannot be denied that Head Start did wonders for preschool students.

The lesson for higher education is that an organization has to be built on hard money to maintain its autonomy. It is the college's duty to support and finance the Chicano Studies department, and the only way for the department to grow is to attract internal funding and resources. At Valley State the decision was also made not to focus on majors but on courses that complemented other programs around campus. Why should Chicano Studies be limited to majors? General education and liberal arts classes would more than compensate for a lack of majors. The growth and survival of Chicano Studies depended on teacher education because realistically this was the largest job market. Few of the first-generation students would become rocket scientists, for example.

In 1970 not a single Chicana/o was enrolled in the SFVSC teacher credential program. As mentioned, two years later Jorge García and Oxnard School Board member Rachel Wong pushed through a teacher internship program for Chicana/o students at the Oxnard and Fillmore school districts. Rachel Wong was one of the greatest community supporters of Chicano Studies from its inception. She was a Chicana married to a Chinese gentleman, and she taught elementary school in the Oxnard schools. She later took classes at Valley State (a.k.a. California State, Northridge). Wong was active in teacher organizations in the district. I teased her because she was a graduate of Immaculate Heart High School in Los Angeles, and I had not met many activists from that school (nor, to be fair, from my own alma mater, Loyola High). I first met her in 1968 or 1969 when I gave talks in Oxnard to teachers on Mexican American education. I was white listed and Rachel came to my defense.

By the early 1970s Rachel was regularly criticizing the district for the lack of Mexican American teachers and administrators. By 1971 Rachel Wong was elected to the Oxnard Schools Board of Trustees, where she continued to fight for Chicana/o children. As a trustee she battled reactionaries on the board who were threatening to pull their kids out of the schools if they desegregated them through busing. When the president of the board threatened to pull his kids out of the district, asserting that as the district was "a ward of the court and no longer a public school, I will take care of my children in some other way." Wong shot back, "Just when was [the district] placed in receivership?" Because of Wong's activism, the board passed the Affirmative Action-Promotion of Employment Practices Resolution, which promised to achieve an ethnic balance in the teacher and administrative ranks as soon as possible. Wong and Armando López addressed the board from the audience and criticized the resolution as a "piece of paper," saying it did not go far enough in hiring minorities. The district's budget for recruitment was $3,000.

Under Rachel's leadership the board proposed a plan to hire "only" minority teachers to fill the first twenty instructor vacancies. Reactionaries alleged the plan was illegal, although it adhered to the mandate of Robert Hints, area administrator of the Fair Employment Practices Commission. Wong complimented the resolution, saying, "We want teachers, not another award."[34] The board adopted a program to hire twenty-eight interns for the fall. Eight teacher interns were guaranteed from San Fernando Valley State College. The other twenty teachers, along with the interns, were "uniquely qualified" to teach the district's minority students. The interns were to have a degree other than education and would receive summer training. Student teaching would be done on the job. Officials acknowledged that the program "was successfully set largely through the efforts Wong because of her rapport with the College Chicano Studies department. . . . Each intern will get the minimum state allowed teacher salary of $6,000. The district will also pay $500 towards the cost of a fulltime San Fernando Valley instructor giving advance guidance to the interns . . . about $6,000 in stipends [would be paid] for the interns for work during summer, and salaries of master teachers."[35]

Up to this point Chicano Studies could not attract institutional support for a Chicano teacher's program—the School of Education resisted the internship program. As mentioned, Fillmore and other districts inquired about the program, and more interns were added. Chicana/o students worked as teachers and satisfied the student teaching requirement on the job. This was a tremendous boost since most Chicana/o students did not have the financial resources to take off during student teaching. Soon other Ventura County school districts were inquiring about Chicana/o interns.[36] The School of Education did not want to supervise the Ventura County interns, preferring to supervise students near campus in the San Fernando Valley. The laziness of the white professors was Chicano Studies' luck.[37] The program was popular since many of the graduates did not know what they were going to do with a bachelor of arts in Chicano Studies—not all of them could go into law or professional schools.

Unfortunately, the internship program was limited, and relatively small numbers could be absorbed by Ventura County. Chicano Studies had conversations with Julian Nava about starting up a larger internship program in the Los Angeles schools, but it was more complex there with the presence of an emerging teachers' union. The void was filled by Operation Chicano Teacher (OCT). As mentioned, up to this point the department followed an unwritten policy of not accepting soft money—that is, grants from the federal government or foundations. Soft money from various government and public sources had suffocated the growth of the Chicano Studies department at Long Beach State College, where students were managers and consultants on government projects. Chicana/o students at other institutions were also distracted by working as paid consultants. At the University of Notre Dame, which attracted large sums of soft money, it failed to build an undergraduate program. More than one government agency offered Valley State soft money, but it was felt that the college had to make a commitment to the department and students. It had to make available hard monies—being part of the line-item budget was essential in the beginning. Growth would follow in the form of tenure track positions, classrooms, and other resources that would be more difficult to cut back or eliminate.

At first Chicano Studies benefited from the anti-intellectual mind-set of the Fisher Act, passed in the early sixties, which downplayed the disciplines and gave Schools of Education a broad mandate. This allowed Chicano Studies to enter an even field. Teacher candidates needed a bachelor's degree in any field, but this changed with the passage of the Ryan Act, which mandated a liberal arts major for elementary school teachers. Unfortunately, the burden of rewriting and restructuring the department to meet the new guidelines fell on a couple of professors. Many other campus Chicano Studies departments did even bother to adjust. Ultimately, the new requirements worked to the advantage of Chicano Studies because of its area studies course of study. It had classes that would fit into every category. Restructuring the department meant not only rewriting course proposals but defending them against the challenges of other departments and committees.

Meanwhile, turf battles raged in committees and behind closed doors, with key administrators and a limited number of Chicano Studies professors taking part. It is impossible to overestimate the importance of the Movimiento Estudiantil Chicanos de Aztlán during this phase of development. The administration feared the student organization and Chicano Studies was able to pressure it by jamming committee meetings with students. These battles had nothing to do with respect or academic excellence or winning the hearts and minds of white folk. They were bitter turf battles.

By the mid-1970s, the department's general education and liberal arts offerings took on their present form. Meeting education requirements always involves the rewriting of classes to standards.[38] Unlike for other departments, the burden of proof is on Chicano Studies to prove that they meet the standards. For instance, it is not assumed that because a historian teaches a class in Chicano Studies that it is a history class. Resistance to Chicano Studies also developed because of the downturn in white enrollment following the end of hostilities of the Vietnam War and the recession. Mexican American enrollment in the public schools had climbed to 22 percent and was rising. After this point, scrutiny of classes became pettier because white departments needed bodies. Another problem was that the administration had allowed departments such as history to overhire, which meant that Chicano Studies could not get additional positions.

The opportunity to expand the Chicano Studies teacher program came from an unexpected source. UCLA professor of education Simón González invited me to a meeting with Ford Foundation Vice President Marshall A. Robinson.[39] I owed González a favor, so I showed up for the meeting. Much to my surprise, I was the only person there and wound up speaking to Robinson by myself. Robinson invited me to lunch, where I ordered water because I did not have money on me. I was skeptical, aggressive, and probably obnoxious in criticizing the Ford Foundation. Marshall was patient, and after hearing me unload, he asked me what I would do if I had a million dollars. What kind of research project I would set up?

My response was that I would not use the money for research, since research in itself does not transform society. It was already the duty of professors to publish. The need of the Northridge program was to graduate more Chicano teachers. The challenge was not to fund a program that would make money for the university and individual professors, but one where outside funds generated institutional change by giving stipends directly to students who in turn took designated classes that generated positions and resources. Chicana/o students would be paid annual stipends of $1,000, and by blocking students into classes the college would be forced to pay for the cost of their education. The plan was to create a demand for certain kinds of classes and generate full-time equivalent students to pay for an assistant director and secretary. (Northridge paid the director's salary).

The plan would also allow the Chicano project to piggy back on the Ford name and attract students who would be Ford fellows to receive their stipends through EOP and other financial aid sources, thereby doubling the number of fellows. This approach would also give Chicano Studies the ability to negotiate with other departments, get them to offer classes that Chicano Studies wanted for their students, and give them the power to name the professor and the time of the class. Over a five-year period the program could graduate 500 Chicano teachers and put in place a program for future teachers. Additionally, it would help Chicano Studies to moderately transform the culture of the college.

The meeting did not hold out much hope, but about two weeks later Robinson called me from Moscow and asked the department to put down its thoughts in a two-page paper. When Robinson returned from the Soviet Union, he called, and this was the beginning of OCT, which lasted until the mid-1990s. The name of OCT came from LACA's Operation Head Start. The target population was the San Fernando Valley Chicano community, which was growing dramatically, and Ventura County.

Instead of the $1 million requested, Ford initially invested $347,000. Chicano Studies had refused to accept soft money, but the Ford grant was structured differently than other programs where the university promised but failed to make institutional changes. (There was no release time or other perks for faculty members.) When Chicano Studies agreed to the program, Robinson told us not to worry about the administration at California State University at Northridge—he had done his homework and President James Cleary had never gotten a Ford grant. According to Robinson, Cleary was ambitious, and every university president wanted a Ford grant on his or her résumé. Jorge García, without whom much of this would have fallen apart, reminds me that President James Cleary, Vice President Harry Finestone, and other administrators, as well as select members of the Chicano Studies department, met with Robinson at Howard Johnson restaurant. When Cleary tried to pick up the check, Robinson snatched it up, saying that Ford had more funds than Northridge. Just before the meeting broke up, Robinson added that no further paperwork was needed, instructing Cleary to call in the institution's Ford number. Cleary looked puzzled, and Robinson added, "Oh, you don't have a Ford number?"

Although the grant was just $347,000, $300,000 was for student stipends, which Chicano Studies supplemented by going after the 10 percent administrative fees that it had negotiated.[40] Several times during negotiations with the administration, Chicano Studies threatened to blow it up and go to the community and hold it up as another example of the bad faith on the part of the university. Chicano Studies paraded Mexican nuns through Cleary's office—he was a devout Catholic—and announced to them that he was anti-Catholic. We had nothing to lose. The institution could not afford the bad publicity, and it would be accused of blowing up a program for the Chicano community.

With the help of Robinson the deal was cut. Admittedly, Cleary was generally supportive, although occasionally he could get petulant. The institution itself remained resistant to change. Unknown to the Chicano Studies department, Robinson encountered internal criticism at Ford. CSUN was hardly the belly button of academe. Abel Amaya said that program officers questioned the wisdom of giving such a large program to a teacher's college, and there was criticism of me and my ties to leftist activists. They did not like my book *Occupied America*. They wanted assurances that I would cooperate with them in their individual projects. To his credit, Robinson never played politics with the department.

The controversial aspect of OCT was the near elimination of service fees to universities and the use of stipends to drive student growth. According to Amaya, the program officer who most vehemently opposed the OCT grant was Ralph Bohrson, who headed the southwestern region, where he was a longtime operative and a leader in Ford's Western States Small Schools Project. New Mexico was at the heart of his empire. He was an empire builder, and in 1967 he hired David Grant, thirty seven, a Chicano regional representative: "Bohrson wanted an indigenous Chicano—but one 'who could live with the Foundation.'" Like most program officers, Bohrson was building a compatible team of loyalists. Bohrson as the voice of Ford carried a lot of weight. However, he had been hurt by the 1970 Atterbury scandal. When CSUN got the contract, he paid me a visit. He wanted to use me as a consultant in New Mexico, where they were trying to sell a project and improve their image. I declined, since I knew they would use me to legitimize their work. Bohrson was none too pleased.

If I had been aware of Ford's New Mexico problems when we entered into negotiations for the OCT, I probably would have pulled out, because I had been played by the War on Poverty and Chicano mainstream politics. Marshall Robinson had just become a vice president, and he was intrigued by the model that in effect would give Ford a lot of bang for the dollar while giving it a more progressive image.

OCT director Tony Ortiz deserves the credit for the success of the program. He sacrificed his career to hold the disparate group of Chicana/o students together. (Not only did he have to supervise the students getting stipends from Ford but also some 200 others with EOP grants.) In the end, Chicano Studies was not able to retain Ortiz because he did not have a doctorate, and lecturers could only be retained for five years. If Ortiz had been kept for the sixth year, he would have qualified for a tenure track position, which the administration was not willing to give without a doctorate. It was a huge loss.

One of the biggest hurdles to the program was credential requirements. Before the requirements were changed, a secondary teacher candidate was not required to be a history major to teach history, and a degree in Chicano Studies enabled the teacher to teach almost any subject. The Licensing and Certificated Personnel Act of 1961, known as the Fisher Act, established new credential guidelines for California, shifting the responsibility for regulating teacher education from the legislature to the State Board of Education. Before 1961 it was possible for a teacher to receive a credential by taking more education courses in the subject she or he taught. The Fisher Act, motivated by post-Sputnik hysteria, shifted the emphasis to subject matter and upped the credentialing requirement from four to five years.

Almost immediately there was a backlash from educationists. Assemblyman Leo J. Ryan (D-South San Francisco) led the charge. As mentioned, Fisher had been opposed by many teacher organizations. The Ryan bill banned the granting of a teaching credential to anyone getting a degree in education, and it drastically limited the "how to do" classes. Among other things, the teacher had to have a bachelor of arts from an accredited university and had to have taken nine units in methods courses. At the elementary level, the primary teacher no longer had to have only a single subject major. The catch-22 was the School of Education, since it frankly did not have professors who were qualified to teach Chicana/o students, who were then about a third of the Los Angeles School District.

Ryan also increased the number of units required for the credential. Education classes that could once be taken after the candidate did his or her student teaching were required before graduation. Under Ryan, the courses had to be taken before student teaching, which in some cases meant the student had to take as many as twenty-two units to meet the deadline. In effect, Ryan added another year to teacher preparation, and students under Ryan would not be able to do their cadet teaching their senior year, delaying it to the graduate year. This would have made compliance with the Ford grant impossible, and OCT would have probably lost some of the fellows. There was no problem with getting students their major requirements—Chicano Studies controlled its courses and allowed double dipping, sometimes even triple dipping. But OCT had to meet the new education prerequisites, which were offered sporadically at the School of Education's convenience. The bill was signed into law in 1970 and went into effect in October 1976.[41]

In order to get many of the OCT secondary teachers under the wire, Chicano Studies had to graduate them under the Fisher requirements, so it literally loaded the first wave of fellows with twenty-one and twenty-four semester units. Since I was a credentialed teacher with a lifetime general secondary credential, I taught the social institutions class through the School of Education as an overload, which delighted Education. That first semester I taught eighteen units, teaching two classes gratis. Carlos Navarro and José Hernández, who were credentialed, supervised the students once they were student teaching. Chicano Studies was also able to get the elementary education candidates under the wire. They were able to take their methods classes and do their student teaching in the fourth year.[42]

The tribulations caused by the Ryan Act in reality helped Chicano Studies. After this point, elementary schoolteacher candidates had to have liberal arts majors instead of a single subject major. OCT gave the department a window into the liberal arts credential program. The CSUN liberal studies major consisted of eighty-four units. Chicano Studies was able to negotiate a package in which students could elect twenty-seven units in Chicano Studies. The liberal studies major would complement the general education package. Most mainline departments saw this as a boon because students had to take over 140 units to graduate. Chicano Studies took another track. It was an area studies program, not a discipline, so it had much more flexibility. The student could take classes that met both the general education and liberal arts requirements and at the same time major in Chicano Studies, so it allowed students to triple dip.

There was no pork in the OCT budget. Yet the program generated about ten to twenty times what Ford granted Chicano Studies in terms of professors' salaries, space, and other resources. The beneficiaries were the students. The budget also

THE MAINSTREAMING OF CHICANO STUDIES

allowed Chicano Studies to manage large numbers of students, which was consistent with the department's commitment to mass education. (In comparison, a local institution got a $1 million grant that trained thirty Chicana/o teachers.)

It is interesting to read the list of the first group of OCT students. Many of them became teachers and administrators in the San Fernando Valley and Ventura County: Alfredo Tarín (principal Los Angeles), Arturo Barragán (principal Ventura), María Vásquez (principal Las Vegas), Mario Muñiz (director at the State Department of Education), José Gaitán (principal at Santa Paula), Lorenzo Moraza (assistant principal Santa Paula), and Diane Velarde (assistant principal at San Fernando), just to name a few. The Ford grant not only impacted the university but also the community (and there is no telling what impact it would had if this funding had continued). The experience also politicized the students. It must be emphasized that very few of these students entered college with high grade point averages, nor had they met all of the requirements for college.

However, the Ford Foundation balked at renewing the Northridge grant.[43] This is puzzling. The California State University system prepares more than 60 percent of the teachers in the state, but it receives less funding than the University of California system for teacher education. Foundations routinely give more funds to research institutions than they do to teacher training institutions, although there is no evidence that they produce better teachers.[44] A major problem is the Chicana/o and other minority brokers at places like Ford adopt the culture of the institution. It looks better on their résumés to fund Ivy League schools than cow county schools. For them, institutional change comes from the top down, so most monies are allocated for research and graduate fellowships (which are important). That said, California State Northridge filed a new proposal that was called "El Nuevo Maestro" in 1976.[45] It was written by Tony Ortiz, with Jorge García and myself.

The proposal is interesting. The numbers are somewhat skewed because OCT carried extra participants that were funded through work study, EOP, and financial aid. However, there had been backlash to the presence of larger numbers of Chicana/o student teachers in the schools. Before OCT Chicano Studies was constantly told that the schools needed more Chicana/o teachers; however, under the threat that teachers would be laid off, many white teachers now saw Chicana/o teachers as competitors. Chicano Studies was also hopeful that education would hire Chicana/o professors. (The school at this point only had two Latinos.) The new proposal made it clear that it was Chicano Studies' intention to institutionalize and reform Chicana/o teacher preparation. The El Nuevo Maestro proposal also emphasized bilingual/bicultural education. Unfortunately, it was not funded.

Despite the setbacks the department was in good shape. It had made institutional changes (e.g., in the liberal studies major). Since I could not get elected or appointed to the Liberal Studies Committee or the Educational Policies Committee, the negotiations were led by Jorge García and Gerald Reséndez, and the negotiations were brutal. The twenty-seven units that Chicano Studies received were scattered in English, the Humanities, and the Social Sciences.[46]

During the initial OCT phase, Chicano Studies majors were pressured to take a minor in English as a second language (ESL). It would be easier for them to get jobs. Fortunately, Chicano Studies controlled ESL, which at the time required a certificate to teach. José Hernández was initially the director, but he bailed out when he went to UC Riverside for a doctorate. Carlos Navarro filled the position for a year or two but bailed. This ended Chicano Studies' control of ESL, since no one else would assume the coordinator position. Nevertheless, the ESL phase had helped Chicano Studies develop a strong linguistic component that the English department no longer controlled.

The focus of El Maestro Nuevo was on mathematics, science, health science, and English. Chicano Studies figured that these were areas of need. Just as important, they involved departments that Chicano Studies wanted to impact. The schools were just starting to feel the effect of the immigrant population. The white student population had plummeted from just over 351,000 in 1966 to about 215,000 in 1976 in the Los Angeles schools, the Latino student population doubled to almost 200,000 during this same period.[47]

Jorge García synthesized the state of the institution in 1976. He hammered home that Ford had not given added funds for faculty income or support. "CSUN has turned out more Chicano teachers in three years than all teacher training institutions in California combined."[48] Jorge points out that through alliances with the anthropology department, they were able to break the monopoly that English and to a lesser extent Spanish had on linguistics. There had been a restructuring, with Chicano Studies becoming a senior partner. OCT also impacted the preparation of white students. "The University Teacher Preparation Committee, along with a special committee on competencies of teachers, has determined that any student who elects student teaching at a school with 25% or more Chicano enrollment must demonstrate competency in language/linguistics, culture, history and contemporary problems of the Chicano."[49] This requirement was important since Education claimed that it was educating teachers to teach all students, which was, and is, ridiculous, since 30 percent of the students were Latinas/os. (Today they are 75 percent of the district.)

After being told by Ford that it was not going to fund the El Maestro Nuevo plan, it relented and gave OCT another cycle of students. No doubt that Marshall played a big role, as did the outpouring of support from school districts. But Chicano Studies could never break through the underlings at Ford. Even Marshall mentioned that there was internal criticism of not the program, but the philosophy behind it. There were also those who criticized CSUN for having a reputation for being militant. Fundamentally, Chicano and Latino representatives at Ford and other funding agencies were no better than their white counterparts. One could sit down with them and eat jalapeños, but they had the same tunnel vision as their white counterparts and wanted to do business with the Ivy League institutions, which many hoped to hook up with in the future. Whatever, but without the Ford money, it became increasingly difficult to carry on the work of the program. The university had made a commitment that it would continue funding the program;

however, this commitment became tentative as time went by. Academe has an extraordinarily short memory when it comes to Chicanas/os. The departure of Tony Ortiz also hurt the continuity of OCT. Four years was not enough time to permanently institutionalize the reforms forced by the program.

OCT remained operational until the early 1980s, when it started to run downhill. An OCT graduate, Mario Muñiz took over for a couple of years and was able to attract a Migrant Corp contract that paid a core of students' stipends. Teresa Orozco served for a short period and administered small grants and kept the students together by sponsoring Saturday workshops, speakers, and the like. When Orozco left, Miriam Ojeda became the OCT director. Problems developed between Ojeda and the incoming chair of Chicano Studies, and the bickering became nasty. There were tensions when she organized Students United for Bilingual Education, a Chicano student bilingual teacher association, and Miriam was forced to take a job with the school of business, where she mentored the Latino Business Association.

During this period, Chicano Studies suffered a blow when Jorge García, who had done a lot of the department's grunt work, left to work for his father's farm in Dinuba, California. The incoming OCT director basically served as an assistant chair, and the program aspect disintegrated. She was a master teacher, but she focused mostly on a core group of Students United for Bilingual Education (SUBE). Meanwhile, institutional support for OCT waned, and it faded away.

The community lost and so did teacher education. It led to a deemphasizing of how to teach the Chicana/o and Latina/o child. The lesson was that foundations give grants to programs, but it is soft money funding, enriching the universities and individuals. A small group of students benefit, while very little institutional change occurs. The truth be told, academe does not want to change. They want total control of the process and reject any kind of *alien* intrusion.

It could be argued that OCT was one of the few instances in which Ford funded a mass education program designed to change an institution; it certainly gave California State Northridge a boost. Playing the game of what-if: a ten-year plan would have radically changed the culture at CSUN, which still caters to the "beautiful people." The San Fernando Valley and Ventura counties would have been changed radically through the infusion of Chicana/o and Latina/o professionals.

TROJAN HORSES

Chicano Studies had its opportunities to expand, but they would have come at a price. For example, it could have taken soft money, which would have totally changed the culture of the department. Even in the case of OCT, it made sure that the monies received would turn hard. Chicano Studies circulated prospectuses to fund other programs but was unsuccessful. One of the best proposals was for a program to train former gang members to teach gang kids and to serve as resource teachers in the public schools. The gang problem was becoming acute, and Chicano Studies had numerous former gang members who had turned their lives around. The inspiration for the gang program came from observing Humberto Guizar, who came to Northridge from Cypress Park. At CSUN he became a teacher candidate, eventually getting his law degree. He could communicate with gang kids—although, during his first years he was a pain in the posterior, because he could not leave the neighborhood in the streets. However, he was brilliant when it came to communicating with his "homies." The same can be said of Frank Estrada from Cuatro Flats, and others.

As much as Chicano Studies tried, it could not get a bite from the foundations for its gang teacher project. However, the Law Enforcement Assistance Administration (LEAA) informally contacted me. LEAA, which was created by the 1968 Safe Streets Act and placed in the Department of Justice, routinely funded educational programs and research. The program officer said he thought LEAA would be interested in this innovative approach, but I opposed any and all contact with the organization. I had witnessed this kind of cooperation during the 1960s, when MAPA and other organizations recommended members to a governmental agency and were then put on an advisory board as a consultant. The recommended person was window dressing that gave the agency credibility and nothing much was accomplished. While the leadership of the organization accumulated chips for grants in the end, the community was not served. LEAA was just moving into this area, but it had already become tainted.

The message was communicated to Mario Muñiz, director of OCT, and several faculty members, one of whom had strong activist credentials. To my surprise, they were all interested. An estimated $3 million would establish Chicano Studies as a leader in the field and create a lot of scholarships. I threatened to resign if Chicano Studies pursued the grant, which would have changed the culture of the department. While the Ford Foundation engaged in social engineering, organizations such as LEAA claimed souls.

CHAPTER 8

Getting It Right

As a rule, more middle-class women attend college than males. This is a trend that began at least by 1870 but slowed down after World War II, when the GI Bill encouraged white males to enter college in large numbers. In 1920 over 60 percent of high school graduates were women. College enrollment among all women climbed steadily during the 1970s and 1980s, and by 1992 women earned 54.2 percent of bachelor's degrees, 58.9 percent of two-year degrees, 51.5 percent of master of arts and professional degrees, and 37.3 percent of PhDs. It should be noted that women have made strides in most industrialized nations. Yet considering the wealth of the United States, its record is not that great. In the United States, 53 percent of college students are women, but only 31 percent are faculty members. In Cuba, 55 percent of students are females and 47 percent are faculty members.[1]

Numbers are important. The number of households headed by Latinas increased from 14 percent in 1970 to 22 percent in 1990. By the turn of the century, Latinas maintained 24 percent of the households without a husband present. In 2000 only 33 percent of Latina/o students eighteen to twenty-four years old were enrolled in college, compared with 42 percent of whites.[2] In 1960 the medians for Spanish-surname people were 8.1 years for men and 8.2 for women. Yet Mexican American women only accounted for 39.1 percent of those who attended college within this category, while white females were 46 percent of all southwestern college students.[3]

In the twenty-first century, education continued to be the main stairway to economic security. According to *Excelencia in Education*, "In 2005, Hispanic students represented 11% of the total student enrollment in higher education—up from 6% in 1990. Between 2000 and 2005, the number of Hispanics enrolled in undergraduate education increased about 30%, compared to only 10% for whites, 28% for blacks, and 16% for Asian/Pacific Islanders." Forty-eight percent of this group was of Mexican descent, 16 percent Puerto Rican, 3 percent Cuban, and 28 percent "other." In 2004, Latinas composed 60 percent of all Latinas/os in higher education. As a whole, Latinas/os received the lowest average federal aid awards of any racial/ethnic group. They averaged $5,415 in federal aid awards, as compared to $6,230 for white students, $6,145 for African Americans, and $5,995 for Asians.[4]

Latinas as a class went from receiving 20.1 percent of the doctorates in the Latino community in 1975 to 45.7 percent in 1986. As a group, Mexican Americans trailed other Latinas/os, with 5.8 percent having college degrees versus 17.0 percent of Cubans and 8.0 percent of Puerto Ricans.[5] The Mexican American family went through dramatic structural changes as education widened the sphere of women's social contacts.[6]

REACHING BACK

Communication exists between the Mexican and Latin American feminist movements on the organizational front. Latin American feminists have been influenced by the American feminist movement. Ironically, the Chicana/o movement as a whole has not been—other than the arts—impacted by Latin America, except for isolated cases such as the Juárez murders. Mexico is a diverse country, with disparate regions differing dramatically on women's rights and their attitudes toward homosexuality. The journal *Fem* covers the evolution of Mexican feminist politics of sexuality in the 1970s, when Mexican feminists borrowed from diverse foreign feminist ideologies and practices. According to Tim Hodgdon, consciously "resisting bureaucratic-authoritarian programs of structural adjustment sharply differentiated their struggles from the *bourgeois* feminism of first-world women, defining their primary task as 'bread first': securing for the masses of women the means to a stable subsistence, recognition of women's social-reproductive labor, and their right to full participation in education, employment, and politics."[7] In the 1970s and 1980s, they strengthened ties with the Latin American self-identified feminist movements.

Mexican feminists formed Mujeres en Acción Solidaria (Women in Concerted Action), which held its first public demonstration in 1971. *Fem* began publication in 1976 to analyze the condition of women in Latin America. It attracted lesbians to the collective and offered a historical analyses, saying that "lesbianism [in the United States] was transformed from a sexual into a political option. This meant the possibility that women's lives need not revolve around men." Thus, the definition of lesbianism was transformed, and the achievements such as rape-crisis and battered-women's shelters, Take Back the Night marches, and the campaign against pornography, with the burning of 'sex shops' and billboards, became standards, which they adopted to combat the Mexican reality. These actions promoted direct action and swelled the ranks of the local collectives. "Fem played a central role in promulgating this raised consciousness of sexual politics."[8]

It is ironic that Chicana feminism has not had more contact with Mexican and Latin American feminists. Patriarchy is inherent in Mexican culture and the Chicana/o movement, and it reinforces sexism.[9] They share large working-class constituencies that struggle with social and economic inequality. Increasingly, gender is being integrated with class in many organizations as "socially constructed differences between men and women and their beliefs and identities."[10] Like class, gender and homosexuality are disruptive because they flout the assumptions that support inequality.[11] Both Mexicans and Mexican Americans share a history of colonialism that formed a mythical view of sexuality: "the organization of the Spanish family and society as a whole, and they affected not only women but men, too." Gendered expectations of behavior became part of culture—sustained by the image of the family and reinforced by the Catholic Church.[12] Culture constructed a distorted image of manhood, which "in Spain has long been associated with *cojones* [testicles]."[13]

Within eighty years the population of what is today Mexico and Central America fell from 25 million to under 1 million.[14] As mentioned, inequalities were perpetuated through a caste system based on race. A gender hierarchy reinforced unequal relationships among women. The Spanish race and gender stratification was important in maintaining discipline,[15] and gender restrictions varied according to class.[16]

Culture, language, and religion are powerful forces in stratifying society. The Spaniards changed Indian culture, and language was a major factor in this transformation, with Spanish becoming the official language. Women were generally unequal, the inequality often depending on the woman's class. Poor women who worked in "peasant marketplaces . . . enjoyed a reputation as institutions that free women from the sexual discrimination and sexual inequality found in other social contexts."[17] Although women merchants had more freedom than elsewhere, the "arenas of feminine achievement . . . seldom directly compared men and women in a marketing context."[18] Under colonialism, women had children at younger ages. In indigenous societies, women generally married around twenty years. The church, with its emphasis on women's chastity, encouraged girls to marry at twelve or fourteen.[19] Even in death, men received preferential treatment and were more likely than women to be buried within the church courtyard.

The colonization also led to the breakdown of the traditional indigenous family system based on an extended family relationship rather than the highly patriarchal nuclear family favored by the Spaniards. This reduced the authority of the elders, and early marriage changed gender relations, reducing the authority of native women within the clan. The age difference in marriage between the husband and wife also widened. "Obviously [a woman of fourteen] did not have the same power base as a woman of twenty wed to a man her own age and surrounded by a network of supportive relatives."[20]

It is said that God was invented to control man. In the same vein, human beings invented cultures that control human beings. Because a *criollo* culture was imposed on the Mexican people, it has passed on its values to most Mexican Americans who are not far from their immigrant past. In time, especially with the urbanization of Mexican origin people in the United States, gender constructs have been changed or at least modified. However, we should be aware of the saying that the past is always with us. As in the case of Latin American women, the Chicanas' struggle has involved the relationship to Spanish and U.S. imperialism and the subjugation of their own societies.[21]

CHICANA AND CHICANO STUDENTS CIRCA 1970

Chicanas and Chicanos attended college before the 1960s; however, as they became urbanized, higher education was more accessible. Mexican American women have always had a small group in college; witness the members of the Mexican American Movement founded by the Young Men's Christian Association (YMCA) in the 1930s that had a small group in college in California and Arizona.[22] The largest number was from parochial schools and Protestant denominations. After World War II, more Mexican American women filtered into the junior colleges and Catholic and Protestant colleges. However, before the late 1960s they were invisible outside of schools with larger Mexican populations. The numbers were largest in Texas and New Mexico, generally among the middle class, where even before the Educational Opportunity Programs (EOP) in California, clusters of Mexican American women sought an education. In the mid-1960s Texas A&I had 1,026 Latina/o students. No more than 20 percent were Latinas, and they were generally from nearby Brownsville and Laredo. Mexicans from Matamoros who attended A&I were in the majority, but they did not identify with Mexican Americans.[23] The advent of EOP-like and outreach programs throughout the Southwest in the second half of the 1960s accelerated the process. Outreach programs were more often student generated than generic products of higher education. This later wave differed from early Mexican American college students, since for the first time Mexican American students did not come primarily out of the middle class. Also, the pool was larger because most Mexican American students were from urban areas.

The 1970 Census counted 2,245,323 Spanish-speaking males and 2,287,112 females. Their median age was nineteen. In 1970, 52.8 percent of Chicanas had high school degrees, and 8.1 percent had been to college. Accordingly, 51.9 percent of Latinas/os had a high school diploma, and 13.5 percent were college students. In 1970, 1.5 percent of four-year college students and 1.2 percent of graduate students were classified as Chicanas/os. These statistics are open to inquiry, because they were not categorized in the 1970 Census but derived from other data. Consequent to this, there was a dramatic undercount, and the dropout numbers usually included those finishing high school and not those who dropped out before the tenth grade. During this period, Latinas/os were largely absent from the statistical profile of the nation.[24]

A clearer picture of the status of Chicanas at the state college level is found in David López-Lee's 1971 report on the student population of California State College, Los Angeles, the school that was for all intents and purposes the flagship of Mexican Americans in the state college system. Fed by East Los Angeles Community College, Los Angeles City College, and over a dozen high schools that were predominately Chicana/o, it provided a good portrait of inequality in 1970. The median grade completed among students from the Eastside was just under the tenth grade.

The principal feeder schools were heavily Chicana/o: Belmont (61.2 percent), Garfield (92.0 percent), Lincoln (87.9 percent), Roosevelt (80.8 percent), Mark Keppel (35.9 percent), San Gabriel (29.4 percent), and Wilson (82.0 percent). Significantly, these feeder schools sent only 17, 57, 37, 11, 19, 14, and 30 students respectively. Incredibly, Roosevelt High only sent 11 Chicana/o students to the campus. Los Angeles State had 18,462 students, claiming that 1,697 were Latinas/os—1,108 males to 589 females. López and Enos reported 195 EOP students—122 males to 73 females. The difficulty in maintaining an accurate count is highlighted by López and Enos, who write, "An extremely high percent of Chicana/o students in the University system are there through EOP (in excess of 70% as compared to 40–50% in the State University and College system)."[25]

Shifts were occurring in the gender composition of Chicana/o college students. By fall 1979, East Los Angeles College reported that 7,543 students, 45.9 percent, were males, and 8,892, 54.1 percent, were females.[26] Just over 65 percent of ELAC's students were Mexican American: 32 percent (3,393) males and 34 percent (3,678) females in the spring of 1979. Only 0.1 percent (10 students) majored in Chicano Studies.[27] In the east area, 35.7 percent of Chicana/o families earned less that $10,000, and 61.5 percent earned less than $15,000.[28]

The Growth of a Gender Identity

The role of Chicana/o Studies in the growth of consciousness of a gender identity has been analyzed in theoretical terms, often ignoring the space created by Chicano Studies for the growth of this consciousness.[29] The same can be said about homosexuality, that, like gender, it is "disruptive of organizing processes because it flouts the assumptions of heterosexuality." The stigma produces disadvantages for lesbians and gays and women, much as race does. "Schooling is one of the most important factors that enhance women's power within relationships. Education provides women with knowledge and verbal skills that directly facilitate their participation in decision-making processes. In addition, it facilitates women's participation in activities outside the relationship, such as involvement in the community, which can also indirectly enhance women's power." Participation is central to undermining patriarchy—lived experiences are important to "creating knowledge and crafting group based political strategies."[30] It could be argued that the change in consciousness of gender and sexuality is due more to the participation in Chicana/o Studies than because of it—Chicana/o Studies broadened the area of participation—and it broke the silence. It can also be argued that the transformation was more rapid in the Chicana sphere than in the white.

The vast majority of Chicanas were and still are first-generation college students. They did not have the role models or advocates within the academy. Women's Studies did not actively recruit them or incorporate them. Latin American feminists were familiar with American writers as early as the nineteenth century. They knew American women who influenced feminist thought throughout the Americas. Early on, this knowledge was not commonly available to working-class Mexican American women. Latin American women were acquainted with Beecher Stowe and had read *Uncle Tom's Cabin*, and her views on emancipation were applied to the emancipation of women. In her journal, Stowe wrote, "I wrote what I did because as a woman, as a mother, I was oppressed and brokenhearted, with the sorrows and injustice

I saw, because as a Christian I felt the dishonor to Christianity, because as a lover of my country I trembled at the coming day of wrath." In 1876 Argentine feminist María Eugenia Echenique (1851–1878) wrote a critique on the role and rights of women.[31]

The breakthrough in the availability of feminist literature came in 1963 with the publication of Betty Friedan's *The Feminine Mystique*, which caused controversy that was distorted in the press about the 1950s housewife. Its statistics were devastating. Three out of ten women would go to college, nine of ten would work at some time outside the home, nine out of ten would get married, and eight out of ten would have a child. However, reporters distorted Friedan, saying that record numbers were enrolled in bachelor of arts and master of arts programs. Ironically, relatively little was reported on Friedan or feminism throughout the rest of the decade. It could be argued that the sixties increased awareness as a result of the civil rights, antiwar, and student movements, and as a result women became more prominent in activism, education, and politics.[32]

The term "women's liberation" was popularized in the 1970s. The number of women in academe and the popularity of the movement eroded the paradigm. A critical mass was demanding a "new and different society." The first line of attack was language. Friedan organized the National Organization of Women (NOW) in 1966, which comprised mostly professional women, middle class and white, who criticized former Vice President Hubert Humphrey's adviser Dr. Edgar Berman. In an exchange with Representative Patsy Mink, Berman claimed that the woman's menstrual cycle limited their potential for leadership. The tone of the Diane Monk article differed considerably from Jean Libman Block's 1963 article. Governor Nelson Rockefeller of New York raised a similar storm when he said that he understood "racism, sexism, repression and war," but that he was puzzled over the objections to "sexism."[33]

Expressions of feminists have been prevalent in Mexican society since the 1860s among the left and the emerging middle class in the form of anarchist thought. In 1879 Carmén Huerta, a Mexicana, was elected president of the anarchist El Gran Círculo de Obreros de México (The Great Center of the Workers of Mexico). "These organizations espoused mutual aid, workers' defense, and a wide range of radical and conservative ideologies."[34] At the turn of the century, Mexican women, seeing the injustices of the system, began to critique them. In 1870 Mexican poet and educator Rita Cetina Gutiérrez formed a group, mostly of school teachers, called La Siempreviva in Mérida, Yucatán. Its focus was educating the poor and establishing a secondary school for girls. The group published a newspaper and was a strong supporter of women's rights, advocating collective action. Yucatán was the center for feminist activity, and later a feminist league was named after Gutiérrez. Three years later, women textile workers in the Federal District organized Las Hijas de Anáhuac. The establishment of a sizable number of feminist groups and newspapers followed that later shared the goals of groups such as the Partido Liberal Mexicano. They saw revolution as a vehicle for social change. Middle- and upper-class women became writers and journalists; they organized feminist and women's magazines and newspapers in which they argued for reform and gender equality.

As more women became professionals, their readership expanded. Feminist ideas evolved into a body of feminist thought. In 1904 Dolores Correa de Zapata, a schoolteacher, Laura Méndez de Cuenca, and Murgía Manteana published the feminist monthly magazine *La Mujer Mexicana*. In Laredo, Texas, Sara Estela Ramírez (1881–1910) edited *La Corregidora* and *Aurora*. A friend and supporter of Flores Magón, Ramírez worked for the Federal Labor Union and La Sociedad de Obreros, Igualdad y Progreso, a mutual-aid society formed in the mid-1880s. Juana Gutiérrez de Méndoza wrote for *El Diario del Hogar* as early as the 1890s, criticizing mining conditions. She served three months in jail for her anti-Díaz activities. By 1901 she published *Vésper: Justicia y Libertad* and soon broke with Ricardo Flores Magón over what she termed "matters of principle." Méndoza died in Mexico City in 1942, poor and forgotten. Teresa Villarreal founded *El Obrero: Periódico Independiente* in San Antonio, Texas, before 1910. The newspaper catered to the proletariat—both men and women. From 1913 to 1915, Blanca de Moncaleano published *Pluma Roja* in Los Angeles, which, according to Clara Lomas, "placed the emancipation of women at the center of its anarchist agenda, adding a new dimension to the politics of the revolutionary struggle."[35] These feminists shared the characteristics of being middle class and activists.

Most Mexican Americans were cut off from this radical tradition because of a lack of access to schooling and political literature. Urbanization and education lessened their cultural chains. As late as the 1960s the emphasis was on identity and racism, leading to critiques on patriarchy and social and physical marginality. At first, some erroneously argued that only "assimilated" Chicanas identified with feminism. This wrongheaded logic was corrected by the growth of the college education of the Chicana, as well as more women working outside the home.[36]

The Prairie Fire: Growth of Chicana Consciousness

The popularity of women's issues was also spread by social agencies and activists who actively promoted Chicana programs. The first national Mexican American feminist conference was organized in Houston in 1970, and from there feminist ideas spread. At the all-women's Mills College in the Bay Area, Chicanas accused the college of "negligence." MEChA demanded that Mills increase the Chicana enrollment to 15 percent; include new Chicana-oriented classes; hire Chicanas for administrative, clerical, maintenance, and residence positions; form an advisory council with a counselor to aid Chicanas; and provide more financial help to the sole American Indian student on campus. Only twenty-five of Mills College's 1,000-plus students were Chicana.[37]

As early as 1969 at the University of Texas, El Paso, the Chicana identity was expressed: "In previous years, she has been the mother, the homebody type. If she was married, her husband wouldn't let her work because of his pride. If she was single, her father had the same feeling towards her. This is true of my mother." Another student said, "The Mexican-American woman hasn't had much of a role." Other sentiments were that the role of the " 'Chicana' is more or less the same as it

is today, to make tortillas and frijoles and as an extremely good maid." The
university was an escape. "The overwhelming majority work as unskilled labor in
factories and packing plants, or in service jobs as maids, waitresses. . . . Particularly
in Texas, Mexican-Americans sometimes get less pay than others for the same
work. Even the few who have some education do not escape discrimination." In
regard to the macho Mexican male, "He also believes the woman is only for loving
and taking care of the home. She is only seen and not heard." Lisa Rivera said,
"Only the Mexicans from Mexico act this way. The average Mexican in the United
States has lost this 'machismo.'" According to the interviewed women, "the
Chicana does no longer feel inferior to the Anglo female," and this, according to
them, improved relations with white women.[38]

Whittier College's Chicanas Independientes in November 1972 sponsored a
conference on women's issues. The keynote speaker was María Gaitán, a well-
known Chicana activist and member of CASA. Other speakers and workshop
leaders included heads of social service agencies. The purpose was to create an
awareness of the changing nature of the role of women in the family, education,
and society as a whole. These types of conferences were relatively new and designed
to bring together working-class Chicanas and college students. Gaitán took on the
question of unity at all cost: "At first I had a very negative feeling about the whole
issue of unity. I felt the Chicano movement can't be separatist. We must have unity
with the movement but still women have problems only women can solve. . . .
Chicanas are asking about unity. Many are worried that the movement will alienate them from men." She then diagnosed the issues that women could change.
"The act of dividing labor, even at home is a political act. Washing a plate is not
important, but if it's political, then it's revolution." Gaitán simplified the process:
"The Chicana movement is going to be dealt with day by day, problem by problem,
defeat by defeat and success by success."[39]

At a 1972 San Francisco conference, Romana Acosta Banuelos, U.S. Treasurer
and a Richard Nixon appointee, extolled the president's appointment of "more
women to high positions than any other president."[40] In 1972 Petia Jiménez was the
first Chicana to graduate from the University of New Mexico School of Law.[41]
In 1973 CSUN incorporated the women's theme on campus in its student outreach
to high school students from the San Fernando Valley and Ventura counties. The
activities were supported by Chicano Studies faculty and student organizations.
By 1978 the dialogue was more widespread. The Chicana identity spread like a
"prairie fire."[42]

The Chicana identification was not limited to California. Wherever there were
poets, novelist, and lawyers, the descriptive term "Chicana" was used. For example,
in Texas, Mujeres por La Raza was a women's caucus within the Raza Unida Party.
Formed in 1971, it represented the merging of Chicano nationalism and Chicana
feminism, and it promoted the political interests of Chicanas. Virginia Múzquiz
served as Raza Unida's national chair from 1972 to 1974, and María Elena Martínez
was the last Texas chair, from 1976 to 1978. Although there were often tensions
between males, there were greater numbers of Chicanas entering politics.[43]

The U.S. Women's Bureau held a conference in Phoenix in 1972. The bureau invited ninety-eight Mexican American women from five states to attend the session, with workshops on employment rights, manpower administration programs, and state legislation. "Spanish-American women are fighting for their own identity," said Narcisa Espínoza of Phoenix. Another member added, "A lot of us felt we were taking a back seat to men. We think women do have leadership ability and we want to encourage it. This doesn't mean that we want to subdue men." However, most delegates were quick to state that they were not associated with the women's liberation movement, adding that it was an "Anglo" movement and that "Spanish-American women do have special problems."[44]

In 1974 in Las Cruces, Ray López wrote, "history has not been kind to the Chicana. As a migrant mother she still works next to her husband and her family as she has always done. And in attempt to break from this mold the new Chicana has infiltrated the colleges and universities. Slowly and stubbornly she will fight the discrimination, prejudice and apathy of the male dominated society. The days of the Chicana being subjugated to the male are almost over. Which is certainly for the best, because she *has* so much to offer."[45] In 1975 a statewide Chicana conference was held in April at Southern Colorado State College in Pueblo. The theme was "La Chicana in Modern Society: Toward Quality of Life." Evey Chapa, executive director of the Chicana Research and Learning Center at the University of Texas, Austin, was the keynote speaker. That same year, a Chicana Awareness Conference was held at Weber State in Oregon with speakers from the entire region.[46]

In 1975 Martha Rodríguez of La Raza Unida at the University of Wisconsin–Madison led a group to Mexico City to attend the International Women's Confab. Rodríguez indicated that Chicanas at the conference felt discriminated by historians who depicted them as "people without history, uncivilized people in need of salvation," who are "lazy, lacking in achievement, non-educationally oriented, emotional, irrational and sexually irresponsible." Although concerned with Chicana identity, Rodríguez also advocated knowing more about Chicanas/os. Racism was a binding issue among students of both genders.[47]

Abortion and the Equal Rights Amendment were defining issues among Chicanas. In 1977 the *Albuquerque Journal* ran a story about a delegation of professional Chicanas en route to Houston for another International Women's Conference. It gave a profile of Patricia Rodgers, who had lobbied the New Mexico legislature for women's rights since 1967. She fought for the Equal Rights Amendment and against the resolution banning women from the New Mexico Military Institute. Although Rodgers personally believed in abortion, she didn't "think I should impose my beliefs on anybody else." She did "not understand homosexuality, but is for doing away with discrimination of any kind."

Teresa Sánchez, a lawyer and deputy director of Southern New Mexico Legal Services, supported the Equal Rights Amendment. "There are already lots of laws that assure women of equality, but once sex discrimination is prohibited by a constitutional amendment, the burden of proof is then on the discriminator rather than on the person being discriminated against." She was going to Houston to represent Chicana interests. Sánchez was for the right to choose abortion. She saw no reason why the gay rights issue should not be included. "They should have all the civil rights anyone else has."

A third Chicana, Pat Luna, was a native New Mexican with a master of arts from University of New Mexico. She served as assistant coordinator for vocational development at the Women's Center. Luna said, "My main concern [at the conference] is low income women whose problems cross all cultural barriers," because few of the attendees were from this sector of the community. Luna believed that the biggest issues at the conference would be abortion and the Equal Rights Amendment. She supported both, as well as the use of federal funds for abortions for low income women. She also believed in rights for gays. "If we want equal rights for women, we want it for all women, period. You can't make exceptions for certain groups because then you leave the door open for more exceptions."[48]

Chicanas were young—21.3 years median versus 30.6 for all women—and less educated—8.6 years of school completed versus 12.4 for all women. In 1978 only 45 percent worked in white-collar jobs versus 64 percent for all women. They earned a median of $5,080 in 1977 (83 percent of what all women earned), and they were poorer. The average family income for all families was $16,000; for Mexican American families it was $11,740, three-fourths as much.[49] The growth of the Latina population and the glaring inequalities heightened awareness of ethnic and gender identity and the students at UCLA grew restless. Seventy-five Chicana students led by MEChA and the Chicano Law Students marched on the office of the *Daily Bruin* when the paper ran an article titled "Youth Gangs and Violence," which quote a fictional Latino gang member as saying, "Kill all white people."[50]

LOST MEMORY

In the spring 1969 at Valley State College there were more male students, and they tended to be a bit older than the females. Little discussion about gender took place, although an awareness existed. The discourse mostly revolved around race and civil rights. Chicanas were active in the selection of the EOP class. The first group of Chicano males recruited for the fall of 1969 were difficult to enlist. There was a high proportion of stoners among the male students; many were lumpen and ill prepared academically. Chicanas generally were better prepared—both in skills and in temperament. Many Chicanas were introduced to each other during the summer of 1969 by Project Move, which was made possible by a $133,000 college-aid grant from the federal Economic and Youth Opportunities Agency. Two hundred students, ages seventeen to twenty-six, were selected for the nine-week program on the basis of high school grades. The students took three classes, or nine units of college credit. The Chicano classes included Mexican American Studies— that is, literature, speech, and written expression. During this period Chicanas began to bond.[51]

When the continuing students arrived, Chicanas had already formed a sense of place on campus. Diana Borrego of Santa Paula, who had been arrested at a campus demonstration on January 9, 1969, continued to work with the fall students. Student leaders such as María Terán, Marie Acosta, Delia Pérez, Rosa Martínez, Leonor and Marta Ramírez, Irma Pardavé, and Avie Guerra developed followings. Many younger students, such as Teresa Orozco, seventeen, came from Roosevelt High School and an immigrant family.[52] This first wave had to battle their parents to stay in school. Faculty members hid some female students in their offices when fathers showed up to campus to pull their daughters out of school. Terán—later the first Chicana MEChA chair—was outspoken and expressed frustration over the lack of Chicana role models. Some had children, so they formed a day-care co-op at the Chicano House, because many could not afford the fees at the college's day-care facility. Acosta and Martínez were very active in community affairs and were among the founding members of *El Popo*—the Chicano student newspaper. They were all fiercely protective of student independence.

These first years were not without controversy. As with other programs, who did and did not receive tenure was a source of controversy. For instance, Anna Nieto-Gómez was interviewed for a position in the spring of 1971, along with Fermín Herrera and other hires. Her selection was influenced by the first wave of women who felt that women faculty were inactive. They had high expectations and supported Nieto-Gómez's agenda and classes.[53] Socializing with faculty leadership and their spouses, she initially seemed integrated into the body. Older faculty members did not socialize much with anyone because of family commitments. However, breaches developed with women student constituencies—more along the line of personalities and tactics—as the first wave of Chicanas graduated. Admittedly, from the beginning students were much more territorial than faculty members and expected to play more than advisory roles.

The second wave continued the tradition of a children's co-op at the Chicano House. Moreover, they sponsored *La Peña* and had a Children's Christmas program. MEChA had a women's committee and a parent co-op. In 1973 it sponsored a women's week and held a women's conference. They reached out to Chile Democrático and in 1977 held a Mujeres Unidas Conference. Within this collage of activities, Chicanas worked with women in the R. G. Sloane strike (1973–1974) and the Skyhorse and Mohawk Defense Committee (1976). At the same time, they were taking on more and more of a San Fernando Valley identity.[54]

The third wave of students brought outstanding activists such as Yolanda Huerta from the San Joaquin Valley, who everyone thought was a niece of Dolores Huerta (she was not), and Norma Jean Solis, a single mother of a four-year-old boy, who arrived in 1974. Norma was from Huntington Park, California, and had not previously been involved in the Chicana/o movement. Solis was like a sponge—she was active in organizing Hermanas Unidas—a Chicana support group. They also expanded the child care cooperative. According to Solis,

> We were able to hold fundraisers at the Chicano House to raise money to feed the children, while we were taking turns going to class. We had two snacks and one hot lunch. We had up to 13 children that were under 3 1/2 years old from parents that were Chicano studies and Pan African studies students. The regular child care center did not take any students under 4 years old.[55]

In 1975 they attended the First World Conference on Women, in Mexico City, called by the United Nations. Solis was involved in police abuse cases. She was chair of MEChA in 1976–1977. During this time, Solis became involved with the anti-Bakke movement, participating statewide. Solis was involved in the formation of the Committee Against Police Abuse (CAPA), founded by former Black Panther Michael Zinzun. Norma also led MEChA in the campaign against apartheid in South Africa and organized rallies in support of farmworkers and helped organize a gang conference that brought 2,000 gang kids to the campus.

Solis was involved in the sterilization cases related to Mexican immigrant women that was exposed by Chicano attorney Ricardo Cruz. Solis represented the National Coalition Against Sterilization Abuse at a National Organization of Women conference and was active in supporting the Equal Rights Amendment.[56]

Solis said of her involvement:

I was part of the Marxist study groups with Enrique Vela, Miguel Pérez, Jaime, Martin Cano and Ms. [Evie] Alarcón. I was a college recruiter and still work with the schools and the colleges to this day to help students attain a higher education. I was involved in educating students and the community about the apartheid in South Africa and got in problems with the school police for putting up a poster in our Chicano Studies depicting the atrocities that were going on with our investments from the CSUN Board. . . . Chicano Studies was our home.[57]

Solis is the kind of student Chicano Studies sought to develop. She attended graduate school and went to work at Centro de Amistad in Canoga Park to counsel and organize gang kids.[58]

Anna Nieto-Gómez alienated Hermanas Unidas and MEChA. Hermanas Unidas had been formed before the Nieto-Gómez controversy. Nieto-Gómez wanted to collapse the group into her group, but after a meeting the Hermanas decided to remain independent and concentrate on student and community issues such as the Third World Co-op. Moreover, the Solis group was reaching out to other minorities on campus. When Yolanda Huerta was elected chair of MEChA, Nieto-Gómez confronted her, asking her if she was going to be a loyalist or follow her. Huerta responded that she represented all the students and was not beholden to faculty. She later accused Nieto-Gómez of trying to divide MEChA.[59]

Some students resisted feminism, which was not synonymous with any one individual. There was sexism, and there is still sexism, within the movement. However, the degree of sexism could not be compared to the homophobia of the times. Homophobia was rampant at every level of Chicano Studies and the movement, and even Marxist organizations that were at the cutting edge of the struggle against sexism were for the most part anti-gay, believing homosexuality to be a product of decadent capitalism. The only possible exception was the Socialist Workers Party that ran articles in the *Militant* criticizing homophobia. Homophobia, at least to my knowledge, was not even an issue at the time of the Nieto-Gómez controversy.

An awful lot goes into building student support, not least of which is effective teaching—which was of concern at the time of the denial of tenure to Anna Nieto-Gómez in the spring of 1976. Nieto-Gómez, without a doubt, made significant contributions to the founding of Hijas de Cuauhtemoc and Encuentro Femenil and raised awareness of the issue of women's equality. Her criticisms of Chicano Studies and the movement had validity. Nieto-Gómez, like early feminist activists of the time, called attention to the gender question. However, it was not her ideas that were controversial among the faculty members; they knew that they had to confront sexism. By 1976 it was a priority of most leftist groups. As mentioned, Nieto-Gómez dissipated the initial goodwill and became a polarizing figure. Many students resented her "my way or the highway" approach.

The decision not to grant Anna Nieto-Gómez a promotion or tenure was made by the department's Promotion and Tenure Committee. The committee, comprised of three students and three faculty members, voted four to two against Nieto-Gómez. The two male professors voted for her, and the four female members voted against her. My sole role was to testify before the committee. I told the members that I personally would vote for tenure because no matter what happened, I would be blamed. Moreover, I pointed out that several male members in the department had equally weak academic records, and they had been passed on by the Personnel, Promotion and Retention Committee.

Many of the faculty who were initially supportive of Nieto-Gómez grew disillusioned. Because we could not attract Chicanas/os with PhDs or even people with a master of arts, the department recruited candidates with the potential to enroll in master of arts and doctorate programs. As early as 1973, the department began pressuring faculty to matriculate in these programs—those with master's were encourage to matriculate into doctorate programs, and those with bachelor of arts, into master's programs. Nieto-Gómez was offered the University of California, Riverside, option. Carlos Cortés had gotten Northridge faculty members admitted to Riverside's graduate programs. Nieto-Gómez protested that she was a single mother, having recently divorced her husband, and that this was a hardship. The department contacted the UCLA Chicano sociology graduate students, and I made an appointment for Nieto-Gómez and went with her to meet with them. The Chicana/o graduate students—despite the fact that she was not academically qualified—made an extraordinary case, and she was provisionally admitted. I wrote Nieto-Gómez a strong letter of recommendation, and the department approached Dean Richfield, who gave Nieto-Gómez six units per semester release time.

Two semesters later, it was learned that Nieto-Gómez had dropped out of UCLA before the end of the first semester. She did not inform the department while taking the release time—50 percent of her load. At this point, if anyone would have been out to get Nieto-Gómez, he or she would simply have had to mention it to the dean. Her actions constituted fraud and were grounds for dismissal. Several members asked Nieto-Gómez why she had dropped out. She replied that UCLA could not teach her anything about Chicanas. She was the expert. The dean was under the impression that she was enrolled in a master of arts program. It was recommended that she at least learn to read Spanish for her research on Mexican women, since the dean was impressed with people knowing multiple languages.[60] Nieto-Gómez replied that this was a cultural-nationalistic request.

In 1974 Dean Jerome Richfield called into his office representatives of Chicano Studies to review future retentions and promotions. He strongly suggested that Chicano Studies pressure every faculty member who did not have a terminal degree to enroll in a doctoral program. He specifically mentioned the Nieto-Gómez situation, since she had been hired with a bachelor of arts with a marginal grade point average. At the very least he wanted proof of progress toward a master of arts. He also mentioned that Nieto-Gómez articles could not be called scholarly. They were opinion pieces. He wanted to see them published in refereed journals. The department relayed the dean's recommendation to the faculty. Richfield made the same point the following year during the faculty review and in numerous private conversations.[61]

From the beginning, students questioned faculty members' lack of credentials. Indeed, a measure of the power and prestige that I had can be attributed to my terminal degree. While liking the faculty members personally, they compared themselves to individual instructors and wanted to know why they couldn't be professors of Chicano Studies. It became apparent that if the area of Chicano Studies was to be respected and the students' degrees to mean something, the faculty had to be vetted in their respective fields. They all understood this when they were hired that they had a window of opportunity. If they wanted to be promoted and retained, they would have to enroll in a graduate program. Francine Hallcom enrolled at the University of Southern California and earned a doctorate in education. She made a point of the fact that she was a single mother and had returned to school. Gerald Reséndez enrolled at UCLA for a PhD in Spanish literature. He earned a second master of arts and is an ABD (all but dissertation).[62] Three other faculty members enrolled at the University of California, Riverside. Two received doctorates, and the third dropped out but got a doctorate in education from Harvard. Other hires were required to have PhDs before they could receive tenured track appointments. Two male professors were granted tenure with bachelors' degrees; however, they were evaluated as musicians. It is common practice in music departments to tenure renowned performers even without even a bachelor's degree.[63] Every faculty member thereafter was required initially to have a master's degree and to later enroll in a terminal degree program.[64]

When the decision was made not to grant Nieto-Gómez tenure, things got ugly. She did not have the support of any Chicana constituency, except for a small group of loyalists who themselves had made enemies. When the committee made its decision not to recommend Nieto-Gómez for tenure, she had the option of appealing the decision to the MEChA body.[65] Instead, Nieto-Gómez went to Dean Richfield and demanded he overturn the Personnel, Promotion and Retention Committee, challenging its legitimacy because it had student voting members on the committee in violation of university policy. University policy prohibited student participation.[66] She proposed that he split the department into Chicano and Chicana

Studies. This infuriated the MEChA body, and a couple of hundred members attended a meeting where only a handful supported Nieto-Gómez. She also lost the little credibility she had with the administration.

Her supporters circulated the unsubstantiated charge that widespread violence occurred. At the time, the department was under heavy police surveillance. If there had been a hint of violence, they would have taken the opportunity to shut down Chicano Studies. As mentioned, at least three Los Angeles police officers spied on MEChA meetings from 1972 to 1978. LAPD officers Augustin Moreno, Joseph Ramirez, and Donald Rochon produced over a hundred pages of documents on the department alone. (Moreno and Ramirez filed reports on the MEChA meetings, which appeared in discovery in the *CAPA v. PDID* [*Coalition Against Police Abuse v. Public Disorder and Intelligence Division*] case.) Police reports mentioned the Anna Nieto-Gómez controversy, but they did not indicate that there was violence or threats of violence. In all probability, they would have led to the closing of Chicano Studies.[67]

Nieto-Gómez's main support came from *La Gente*, the Chicana/o student newspaper at UCLA. When I asked a member of *La Gente* staff why UCLA did not hire her, she responded that UCLA had high standards. Nieto-Gómez lasted as a part-time instructor at Claremont for about two semesters before they let her go. Not a single institution moved to hire Nieto-Gómez, although people not even involved insisted that Northridge hire her. Nieto-Gómez had never published a scholarly article. Her articles were popular newspaper opinion pieces. They were very important but not scholarly, according to the standards of the university.

The Northridge Chicano Studies department made mistakes. It should have been proactive in developing this field of study. The Anna Nieto-Gómez case was a wake-up call. To the department's credit, it did not purge anyone who supported Nieto-Gómez, and it committed itself to hiring strong women with activist and academic credentials. By the end of the 1980s, it consciously recruited at least two gay faculty members, and two-thirds of the faculty members were women. Consequent to this, the culture of MEChA and the students changed and it has since elected at least three gay chairs. Many argue that if Nieto-Gómez had stayed on the faculty this would not have happened, because she was a polarizing figure. Only women who she approved of were qualified, according to her. Years later Nieto-Gómez got a master's in social work; she did Northridge a disservice by not going back to school in the mid-1970s. If she had, there would have been no controversy, and I would have been saved a lot of personal grief.[68]

After Nieto-Gómez left, the Chicana courses were offered regularly and were expanded. The priority of the department was to hire qualified Chicana professors who would commit themselves. The position in history was left open for three to four years, passing over several good male professors. The department was extremely lucky to hire Shirlene Soto, who gave Chicano Studies a bona fide Chicana historian. The most productive addition was Mary Pardo, who worked in EOP and had a master of arts. She is an excellent teacher and built a strong student following in the department—both among Chicanas and students outside and inside the department. She enrolled in a PhD program in sociology at UCLA and has become a leader in the field. The department owes the development of a strong women's contingent to Pardo, who worked on department and university-wide committees tirelessly and became chair of Chicana/o Studies. Most Chicana professors were hired under her stewardship. In spring 2010 the department offered seven undergraduate and two graduate courses that were specific to Chicanas, and eighteen out of twenty-five tenured professors are women.[69]

To Populate Is to Govern

In 1981 *Los Angeles Times* reporter Marita Hernández gave a portrait of the Chicanas attending a Chicana conference at California State University at Los Angeles. Hernández wrote, "Some were lured out of the home by school issues and a concern for their children's education. A few went to college. Others tried their wings in woman's auxiliaries of organizations their husband's belonged to, then formed woman's groups of their own. Still others acquired awareness of the civil rights struggles of the 1960s and the community." According to Hernández, Chicanas began to redefine themselves, "rejecting their stereotype role as docile, unassertive and submissive females, a role thrust on them by culture and, sometimes their own men."[70]

The movement by and large was promulgated among the "socially concerned middle-class Chicanas" and brought a "certain optimism about a 'Chicana Movement' of the growing awareness of issues." Hernández added, "The median number of years of school completed by adult Chicanas was 8.6 compared with 12.4 for all women. The gap was narrower, however, among younger women." About 56 percent were married and living with their husbands. Nearly half of the families headed by Chicanas were living in poverty in 1977—one in five for all Mexican American families and one in nine for U.S. families. The optimism was expressed in the greater visibility of Chicanas in business and the professions and appointments to state boards, commissions, and the municipal court. MALDEF—then based in San Antonio—was headed by Chicanas. "Chicanas are less likely than their Anglo counterparts to blame their oppression on their men than on the system that oppresses them both. . . . While Anglo feminists seem to want to do away with sexual roles altogether in their quest for equality, Chicanas advocate an expansion of choices while retaining the woman's traditional nurturance role and such traditional values as commitment to family, community and ethnic group."[71]

Throughout the 1970s, Chicanas forged a corpus of analytic literature in the social sciences, humanities, education, and the arts. Many careers can be tracked in the *Aztlán Journal*, much the same as can the academic careers of many of the early Chicano male professors. This pioneer generation had it hard because of limited resources and the antipathy in graduate departments toward Chicanas, as well as the lack of role models and mentors. The importance of *Aztlán* is that it was published by a university venue and was refereed. In the 1970s faculty review panels rated articles according to the journal that it was published in. Often excellent articles in the Mexican and Chicana/o experience were rejected because of the bias of the reviewers toward the subject matter.[72]

Early feminist scholar Linda Apodaca identified the omission by Chicano historiographers of the role and situation of Mexican and Chicana women. She accused the movement of being male dominated and tolerating rampant *machismo*. At the time, Apodaca was one of the handfuls of Chicana scholars to make it to graduate school. She and Rosalinda Méndez González taught the first course in women studies, "The History of Women's Oppression," at the University of California, Irvine, as graduate students. Apodaca was active in the collective and academic journal *Latin American Perspectives*, as well as other leftist venues.[73]

Perlita R. Dicochea observes that at a "Chicano Studies (NACCS) conference, a college-age Chicana questioned the near-invisibility of women in the preview showing of the film *Chicano!* One member of the panel presenting the documentary responded, 'Those were traditional times. Women were just not as involved,'" which was not true. After this point, according to Dicochea, Chicana Studies courses nationwide exploded. The change came about through numbers—the growth of the Chicana school population and its middle class.[74] The field of Chicana thought was forged brick by brick through academic publications—and the corpus of knowledge that comprised Chicana Studies grew correspondingly. Another very important aspect was the increase in courses and Chicana/o Studies programs.[75] Singular in the construction of Chicana/o Studies was Adaljiza Sosa Riddell, who sacrificed her own career in building a Chicana/o Studies department at the University of California, Davis. Sosa Riddell was a founder of Mujeres Activas en Letras y Cambio Social (MALCS) in 1983. Along with Rosaura Sánchez and Maxine Baca Zinn, she was a breakthrough scholar.[76]

Although California Chicanas have received most of the attention, new ground was forged throughout the Southwest, Northwest, and Midwest. Texas is a neglected area of study in Chicana scholarship. It differs from California and other areas of the country because the Chicana is more integrated into the political and social fabric of the movement. During the first decade of Chicana/o Studies, the work of activist-scholar Martha P. Cotera stood out. She participated in the electoral revolution led by the La Raza Unida Party in Texas. She was also active in the Colegio Jacinto Treviño and later Juárez-Lincoln University. In 1976 she published *Diosa y Hembra: The History and Heritage of Chicanas in the U.S.*, which was meant to attack the historical amnesia of the Chicana in order to reclaim her identity.[77] The book is what Teresa Córdova would describe as the formation of agency, commitment, and connection. "It was through ideas, therefore, that the Chicano experience could more accurately be defined, thus challenging dominant ideologies and the structured interests they serve."[78] Cotera's work was one of the first to put Chicanas into a historical context. This literature was rounded off by three anthologies, two that were compiled at the UCLA Chicano Research Center and a third edited by Margarita Melville.[79]

Chicanas struggled to forge a presence in the National Association for Chicano Studies (later the National Association for Chicana and Chicano Studies). They presented numerous workshops on Chicanas and sexuality at the NACCS conferences. They had minimal presence in the 1970s but grew exponentially in the 1980s and 1990s, to the point that in 2001 there were sixty-eight panels.[80] The first surge in Chicana presence was in 1981, when many of the Chicana graduate students presented papers. A list of Chicana graduate presenters and new professors includes Guadalupe Fríaz (San Jose State), María Linda Apodaca (UC Irvine), Rosalinda González (Claremont College), Denise Segura (Berkeley), Deena González (UC Berkeley), Shirlene Soto (CSUN), Louise Kerr (University of Illinois), Antonia Castañeda (Stanford), Christine Sierra (Colorado College), Rosaura Sánchez (UC San Diego), Clara Lomas (UC Santa Cruz), Angie Chabram (UC San Diego), Irene Blea (UT Austin), Yolanda Broyles (UT San Antonio), Aida Hurtado (University of Michigan), Sosa Riddell (UC Davis), Beatriz Pesquera (Berkeley), Vicki Ruiz (Stanford), Adela del la Torre (Berkeley), Patricia Zavella (UC Santa Barbara), and Lea Ybarra (Berkeley). The next milestone was the 1984 NACS Conference at the University of Texas, Austin, where there were thirty workshops on the Chicana.[81]

In the winter of 1981 Antonia Castañeda and Ada Sosa Riddell discussed the lack of Chicana courses in the academy. The next spring Chicana/Latina scholars met at the University of California, Davis, and established MALCS. Soon thereafter, they published a newsletter and a journal and held summer institutes. An academic organization that articulates Chicana/Latina feminist perspectives, MALCS's stated goal was to establish an organization that affirmed "the membership's dedication to the unification of their academic life with their community activism." Ada Sosa Riddell, Deena González, and Elisa (Linda) Facio wrote the proposal for the Chicana Summer Institute Planning Session in 1985. Because MALCS has focused the scholarship on Chicanas, this research field has grown. However, much more difficult to measure is its impact on the pedagogical aspect of the area of study.

While the field's growth was driven in great part by the zeal of Chicana lesbians, sexuality did not become a popular topic of study until the 1990s. Without slighting activist feminists such as Emma Pérez, Deena González, and scores of other women scholars, such as Antonia Castañeda and Cynthia Orozco, who tirelessly pushed the Chicana agenda through professional organizations and their respective disciplines, the work of the late Gloria Anzaldúa is singular in Chicana/lesbian and feminist scholarship. Anzaldúa crossed over into mainstream scholarly literature and was a leader in postmodernism. As an unrepentant modernist who believes that the truth must always be tested by documents, in my opinion Anzaldúa's work shows that the vetting process can be done through various forms. Paradigms are not necessarily deconstructed through a deductive process, and documents can come in various forms. Theory is only one way to find the truth, no matter what its name—because identities are fluid.[82]

Anzaldúa was teacher—spawning a generation of Chicana feminist scholars. The renowned historian Emma Pérez wrote,

> Decades ago Gloria Anzaldúa comprehended what many of us spend our lives attempting to grasp—that colonization may have destroyed our indigenous

civilizations but colonization could not eliminate the evolution of an indigenous psyche. That world still persists inside our community's psychic, material lives. We wear it on our bodies, our flesh, our *mestizaje*. The mixed racial bodies and minds that we've inherited usher that past into the present and, more important, into the future. She devised her theory—*la conciencia de la mestiza*—as a method, a tool that offered us hope to move from a bleak present into a promising future. *La conciencia de la mestiza*, mestiza consciousness is that transformative tool.[83]

In 1981 Anzaldúa coedited a groundbreaking anthology with Cherie Moraga— *This Bridge Called My Back: Writings by Radical Women of Color* in 1981. The formation of a Chicana identity is central to her work, one that places the Chicana at the center of the Third World and provides "an intellectual framework" of identities based on race, ethnicity, and sexuality.

Anzaldúa's identity differs from that of her cohort, Cherie Moraga. They represent two separate worlds—Texas and Los Angeles. Anzaldúa is Valley—South Texas—and Moraga is from a mixed environment with a white father and Mexican mother. This is a reality—the fixation with color—in which many Chicanos and Chicanas in Los Angeles find themselves; for instance, at Northridge, students have formed a *hapa* club (Hawaiian word for mixed race). Moraga seeks a Queer Aztlán—one capable of embracing a "full range of racial diversities, human sexualities, and expressions of gender."[84] Culture is more natural in Anzaldúa's work, which often has a sense of a person who has suffered exiled.

Anzaldúa was a border person. Her ancestors arrived in the Rio Grande Valley in the seventeenth century, and she lived most of her life in Hidalgo County. It was an area where code switching was the rule—the mixing of Spanish and English that broke the constraints of formal language—changing not only words but syntax. In the preface of *Borderlands*, Anzaldúa writes, "the actual physical borderlands that I am dealing with in this book is the Texas–U.S. southwest/Mexican border. The psychological borderlands, the sexual borderlands and the spiritual borderlands are not particular to the southwest." In her essay "*La conciencia de la mestiza*: Towards a New Consciousness," Anzaldúa writes about the mestiza lesbian on the borderlands, about the clash of cultures: "Cradled in one culture, sandwiched between two cultures, straddling all three cultures and their value systems, la mestiza undergoes a struggle of flesh, a struggle of borders, an inner war." She challenges traditional American as well as Mexican culture, both of which she found repressive. "But it is not enough to stand on the opposite river bank, shouting questions, challenging patriarchal, white conventions." She is stuck in the middle of two cultures—dependent on American institutions, knowing that she lives in the United States, but she is spiritually a Mexican and rebels against the encroachment of Anglo values. Further complicating this identity quagmire is her gender and sexuality, which she accepts on her own terms. As with her language, Anzaldúa superbly switches her metaphors, using Nahuatl concepts and images to underscore the tensions of the two cultures and identities. She writes,

> Within us and within *la cultura chicana*, commonly held beliefs of the white culture attack commonly held beliefs of the Mexican culture, and both attack commonly

held beliefs of the indigenous culture. Subconsciously, we see an attack on ourselves and our beliefs as a threat and we attempt to block with a counterstance.... Because the counterstance stems from a problem with authority—outer as well as inner—it's a step towards liberation from cultural domination. But it is not a way of life.[85]

Fundamental to this mestiza consciousness is a spirituality that is the product of conquest, marginalization, and resistance. According to Anzaldúa, mestiza spirituality fosters an oppositional consciousness that calls attention to injustice colonialism. This mestiza spirituality prepares Chicanas to recognize the ethical pitfalls and moral dilemmas and allows for healing.

By the time Anzaldúa died of cancer in 2004, Chicana as a research area of studies was well established. It is difficult to determine the number of classes on the Chicana that are being offered, not only at research institutions but also at teaching universities and community colleges. Chicanas serving as chairs of Chicana/o Studies are more common. Yolanda Broyles-González became the first woman of color to be tenured at the University of California, Santa Barbara (1985). Six years later she became the first native Chicana woman to chair an academic department within the University of California system, and she was one of the first Chicanas to be promoted to full professor at a major research university. Under her leadership, the very first proposal for the Chicano/a Studies doctorate degree in the nation was created, and under her leadership a Mexican America Studies department was initiated at the University of Arizona.

Longtime activist and scholar Adelaida del Castillo became the first woman chair of the San Diego State University Chicana/o Studies department. Mary Pardo was the second female chair of the CSUN department, and Juana Mora was the first. As mentioned, Sosa Riddell founded the Davis program. Alicía Gaspar de Alba is chair of the UCLA Chicana/o Studies department. Deena González headed the Loyola Marymount Department. Chicana control of Chicana/o Studies will increase steadily in the coming years. The proportion of Latinas earning doctoral degrees has increased—from 49 percent in 1997 to 56 percent in 2007. Latinas have received more doctoral degrees than Latino males each year since 1999. Interestingly, "by the year 2009 the majority—over 51 percent—of K–12 students in California's public schools [were] Latina/o." Yet by 2000, Latinas/os as a whole represented 0.4 percent of those receiving doctorates in 2000. At the time they were over 10 percent of the population.[86]

RETURN TO BEAN COUNTING

Bean counting was a very necessary exercise during the civil rights movement—raising questions such as "How many Mexicans are attending college?" "How many courses are being offered on Mexican Americans?" As mentioned, MALCS came about because two Chicana scholars asked "How many?" Today there are plenty of areas for growth. For example, at CSUN only one of the nine sections on

Chicanas is currently offered online, which is a shame since four sections would easily fill up. Online courses more than meet their target, and they are rarely canceled. No matter how unfair it may seem, teaching institutions of higher learning and community colleges are driven by enrollment. The number of clerical assistants and even pencils are determined by how many. If it is the mission of Chicana/o Studies to teach Chicana students, it must reexamine its priorities. According to Daniel G. Solórzano, Martha A. Rivas, and Veronica N. Vélez, "studies show that about two-thirds of all Latina/o students begin their postsecondary career in community colleges." However, "even though 71% of Latina/o students who enter a community college desire to transfer to a four-year institution, only 7% to 20% end up doing so." Community colleges are vitally important. Chicanas/os are more likely than any of their counterparts to have attended a community college—23 percent versus 10 percent overall, 10 percent of blacks, 11 percent of whites, and 3 percent of Asians. This figure will certainly grow as cost of four-year institutions skyrockets. Extended-day or online classes are routine at the community colleges.[87] This book posits that community colleges are central to the growth of Chicana/o Studies. Without a doubt, the leadership and the future of Chicana/o Studies is with Chicanas. They are earning a majority of the graduate degrees among Chicanos, and it does not take a rocket scientist to deduce that most hires in Chicana/o Studies programs will be Chicana. This has its good and bad points, because if these hires are concentrated in research institutions, the impact of Chicana Studies will be limited to a few.

CHAPTER 9

Resisting Mainstreaming

The role of philanthropic foundations such as the Ford Foundation in the development of Chicana/o Studies is a mixed bag. Columbia University Professor
Manny Marable notes that the Ford Foundation joined with Harvard in the 1980s
to shape Harvard's African American Studies and Black Studies programs nationally "in their own liberal multiculturalist image." Ford funded a comprehensive
nationwide survey of Black Studies conducted by Harvard's Nathan Huggins and
used its money to fund compatible African American programs. Marable says that
it packed these programs with "inclusionists who always assumed that blacks
had to succeed in the context of white institutions and Euro-American standards."
The lesson, according to Marable, is that Ford's intervention no doubt helped for
the moment, but the flip side is that such support "often comes with political and
ideological costs." Along these lines, Indiana University sociologist Fabio Rojas says
Black and Women's Studies programs at research institutions experienced growth
during the 1980s consequent to the foundations funding these centers during
the "culture wars" of that decade and that some would have perished without
that support.[1]

There is no study that I know of that assesses the influence of Ford on Chicana/o
or Latina/o Studies. Hence Marable and Rojas's generalities cannot be mechani-
cally applied to Chicano Studies departments, perhaps because so few of these programs were located at research institutions. In the 1980s these departments were in
their infancy, and most did not receive foundation support. What kept Chicano
Studies alive was that the surge of Latina/o student enrollment added to how effectively the numbers were used by Chicano Studies. The one thing for sure is that
intervention generally reproduces hierarchies.

Unlike the late sixties and early seventies, a perfect storm did not take place during
the 1980s. During this decade the issues of immigration and the wars in Central
America literally put the community under siege and consumed the Chicana/o and
Latina/o communities. The political revolution and the election of Latino politicos
also distracted this generation, and racism on campuses was more subtle and

therefore less urgent. Racism did not produce the same moral outrage that had forged Chicano unity in the past.

As mentioned, in the 1960s a large number of black students were admitted into predominantly white institutions. In 1950 about 75,000 black students were enrolled in colleges and universities; by 1970 that number had grown to 700,000—three-quarters of whom were now attending predominantly white academies. By 1971 some 500 colleges and universities had African American Studies, which peaked at 800 in the early 1970s and declined to about 375 by the mid-1990s as financial support diminished. This new state of affairs, however, did not spark the moral outrage among blacks that it had in the 1960s; without this energy, the perfect storm did not come about, because there were not enough Latinos enrolled in college. Meanwhile, the differences between Black, Women, and Chicano Studies can be partially explained by location, numbers, as well as economic and social class differences. The nagging fact exists that the growth in Chicana/o students would not produce the same exponential results in Chicano Studies as it did in Black and Women's Studies programs.[2] There were other differences, such as the cluster of Black and Women's Studies centers was in the eastern part of the country, close to the centers of financial and political power.

The Decade of the Hispanic

Ronald Reagan's presidency witnessed the last wars between black revolutionary nationalists and cultural nationalists. The prestigious centers were mostly immune to these internecine struggles, and established and recognized scholars directed them.[3] They were not organic institutions like San Francisco State College. The world looked much different from the shade of Cambridge than it did from the shadows of Oakland. Chicano Studies followed a less conventional path. Generally, most Chicano Studies programs were situated close to Mexican American communities, they were more influenced by local events and issues than academic trends in the Ivy League orbit.

Progress in the academy was slower than in what some observers caustically called the real world. The 1980s were labeled by Latina/o leaders as the "Decade of the Hispanic," which generally meant the decade when the Sleeping Giant would awaken and Latinas/os would become a political powerhouse. There were political victories during the decade, which did help since legislators of all colors began to pay some attention to the large pool of Mexican American voters. In turn, there was more attention paid to Mexican American issues. For instance, the *Los Angeles Times* reported that Chicana/o and some white legislators called the number of Chicana/o faculty "dismal."[4] In turn, the presence and rhetoric of Latina/o politicos emboldened Chicana/o professors. However, the lack of support within the institutions isolated the studies programs, and administrators generally ignored them. While complaining about the lack of Chicana/o faculty members, no one pinned down the administrators, and institutions were allowed to give lip service to the hiring and retention of Latinas/os. The status of Chicanas/os in higher education was important, but it never made it to the top of the political priorities of Latina/o politicos.

Distance between the programs made communication difficult. For instance, California and Texas were over a thousand miles apart. Other enclaves such as the Pacific Northwest and the Midwest could not be reached easily by land transportation. Most meetings were regional, and they seldom extended beyond a radius of 500 miles. For example, in 1986 Richard Griswold del Castillo at San Diego State called a conference to discuss the decline in Chicano Studies. The attendance was local.[5] Meanwhile, research centers had very little impact on the departments. Even when in the same city, research universities did not communicate with state colleges, which in turn had little contact with neighboring community colleges. The arrival of millions of Mexican and Central American immigrants made the situation even more challenging.

In 1982 the Latino directors of research centers met to discuss the status of university-based Latino research. The centers included the Mexican American Studies Center at the University of Texas, Austin; the Centro de Estudios Puertorriqueños at Hunter College at the City University of New York; the Chicano Studies Research Center at UCLA; and the Stanford Center for Chicano Research at Stanford University. They agreed to reduce their separation and encourage cooperation and collaboration. A year later the Inter-University Program for Latino Research was established to increase the amount of Latino-focused research and the pool of Latina/o researchers. In February 1984, under the auspices of the Inter-University Program for Latino Research, thirty-five scholars met at Stanford University to assess the state of knowledge of the Latino population of the United States. This activity, however, did not include teaching institutions. A Ford Foundation grant facilitated the cooperative program, providing seed funding for the working groups and serving as a catalyst for other research through a competitive grants program for public policy research and contemporary Latino issues. The number of centers expanded to nine. In 1999 the Inter-University Program for Latino Research moved to Notre Dame's Institute for Latino Studies. While the program increased communication among the research centers, the isolation of the departments at teaching institutions widened.

Movimiento Estudiantil Chicanos de Aztlán

The 1980s brought a change in the academic and professional preferences of students. In the 1960s, the core was idealistic, whereas in the 1980s they turned to business and the like. Chicano Studies programs were reduced and even eliminated at many colleges. According to the National Chicano Council on Higher Education, at least three hundred colleges offered courses in Chicano or Puerto Rican Studies (not necessarily programs). In New York area, thirteen campuses of City University and a half dozen private colleges had majors in Puerto Rican Studies. In the Great Lakes region, Wayne State University in Detroit, Northern Illinois University, and the University of Wisconsin at Milwaukee, among others, had Latino Studies programs. In reality, there was only a small core of programs, and they were constantly under siege. Reflecting a greater participation and influence of Chicanas, on March 1984 nearly a thousand scholars met in Austin, Texas, for the twelfth annual conference of the National Association for Chicano Studies, where they proposed changing the name of the National Association for Chicano Studies to the National Association for Chicana and Chicano Studies. (This change took place in 1995.)[6]

While communication decreased between programs, it increased between students. The Movimiento Estudiantil Chicanos de Aztlán remained the premier student organization. Various campus chapters held regional, statewide, and national conferences that were attended by thousands of students. Some departments, in the name of fiscal responsibility, were absorbed into Ethnic Studies programs or departments. Others, such as San Diego State, witnessed a slow but steady comeback. Much of the comeback at San Diego and other campuses were made possible by a de-emphasis on majors and servicing of students regardless of majors. Consolidation and expansion was difficult in part because of the scholarly ambitions of many Chicana/o faculty members.

Teaching institutions are wannabe research institutions that resent the latter for receiving bigger budgets, having reduced teaching loads, getting research subsidies, and funding for frequent sabbaticals. Many state university professors publish more and are compensated at a lower rate. But most of all, they feel put upon that their students come from inner-city schools and often lack the proper academic preparation. They delude themselves into believing that only the brightest will understand the complexities of their lectures. They rationalize that if these students lack skills, then it is the failure of the lower grade school to prepare them. This mind-set says more about the competency of college and university professors than it does about students or Chicana/o Studies. Nevertheless, the pretensions of faculty members are important in the building and maintenance of Chicana/o Studies.

CALIFORNIA STATE LOS ANGELES: STRUCTURAL FLAWS

According to the *Los Angeles Times*, the NACS held its conference in 1978 at the Claremont Colleges: "The sixth annual conference talked academic—as opposed to Chicano—issues for the first time, forming committees to investigate the problem of tenure for Chicano Studies teachers and the status of female teachers in the discipline." A low attendance was attributed to a competing conference on minority studies at Stanford. Claremont lost practically its entire Chicano faculty, who resigned over the issue. Ed Quevedo—who was criticized for not resigning—saw it as a stage in the development of the discipline, laying the foundation for future growth. The Claremont program had grown to about forty courses, but after the dispute it was down to twenty-five.[7] Unfortunately, NACS did not follow the trajectory of monitoring programs such as the Claremont Colleges.

The next year, Richard Santillán was denied tenure at CSULA. An assistant professor, he had offered classes since 1972. His case had been pending since 1974. Santillán had been active in La Raza Unida and later worked for the Rose Institute at Claremont. The department voted 3–2 not to retain him. The case was explosive since James Rosser had been appointed president of CSULA over Julian Nava. The 3–2 vote was overturned by an appeals committee, which was then overturned by Dean Donald O. Dewey. A grievance committee supported Dewey.[8]

The split in the Chicano Studies department was symptomatic of a structure of failure that made future ruptures inevitable. The CSULA department was dysfunctional, and the university kept it that way. Five tenured professors split into several factions. The Santillán case was about maintaining balance. According to Times reporters Kenneth Reich and Henry Méndoza, "Although census figures show that 19% of California's population is Latino—a 60% increase over the last decade—the Latino push for more political clout in this state continues to be fraught with difficulty."[9] Even after Santillán went away, the department continued to fester. By August 1982, the *Los Angeles Times* reported, "Professors of the Chicano Studies Department at California State University, Los Angeles, have found their cars set afire, brakes cut and tires slashed, during a period of bitter faculty in-fighting over jobs and tenure. . . . Faculty members have been feuding for several years over dwindling job opportunities in the department which has been hit by budget cuts and declining enrollment."[10]

The source of the friction was administrative policies that encouraged the hiring of part-time faculty members. The administration could squeeze out five classes from one position versus four from full-time faculty members. Part-timers at the Los Angeles campus outnumbered the full-timers and had an equal vote. The university administration was manipulative and encouraged tenured faculty versus part-time tensions that worsened with the budget cuts. After the administration got rid of Santillán, the two factions fought for the spoils with four full-time members pushing for another full-time appointment, while the other sided with the part-timers, who wanted to protect their positions.

Bert Corona, the foremost Chicano activist in the Los Angeles area, headed the twelve part-timers who opposed the acquisition of another tenured track professor and the promotion and tenure of another. The Corona faction successfully opposed the tenure of Roberto Cantú, who alleged that Corona told him "to be man enough" and to abide by the consensus and not appeal the decision. Cantú accused Corona of accosting him and threatening him, saying, "What happened to your car is nothing." Corona denied the allegations. He said he spoke to Cantú but denied having been involved in the burning of his car. Corona told him: "We can get rid of you by getting the community against you. You may have tenure but you're not going to have peace." Corona's supporters claimed that Cantú was motivated by fear that his tenured position would be eliminated if part-time positions were maintained. The two other professors who opposed Corona were Hector Soto-Pérez and Lou Negrete. Corona had supported them during the Santillán case.[11]

Corona taught at Valley State from 1969 to about 1972. There was a dispute with the administration, that would not consider Corona for a tenure track position because of a lack of a degree. However, after heated negotiations, the administration agreed to hire Corona as a lecturer at a full professor's salary. Bert agreed to this arrangement. Circa 1972 he received an offer from CSCLA, and the Valley State agreement set precedent for his rank and salary compensation. Corona was a popular instructor of Community Studies courses. I asked him whether he was certain that he wanted to go to the Los Angeles campus, and he replied that the drive to Northridge taxed him. I was under the impression that he hoped for a full-time appointment.[12]

Corona was CSULA's link to the community. Tensions heated up in June 1982 as the summer classes of Corona and two other part-timers—Rudy Holguin and Mary Méndez—were canceled.[13] They sued, but a superior court judge turned down the case until other issues were resolved. At this point, Manuel de Ortega sided with the part-timers when he was denied his position as associate chair.[14] The case meandered through the court. In May the court ordered the university to pay the plaintiffs $9,000 for the lost summer classes but refused to reinstate them. The judge held that the department had properly notified the plaintiffs of their dismissals. The media contributed to the confusion with a lack of analysis. It was clear that if there was any proof of violence, it would have come out in discovery.[15]

KEEPING THE ACADEME WHITE

Chancellor W. Ann Reynolds took over the nineteen campuses of the California State University system in 1982. A provost at Ohio State, she was a respected biologist and a welcome relief from Chancellor Glenn S. Dumke. Female faculty members were ecstatic at the prospect of a woman chancellor; however, Chicano Studies professors were concerned that she was not from the Southwest. Further, the system was entering into collective bargaining negotiations with the professors' union, nearly 19,000 strong.[16]

The hype had it that she was "very bright," "a quick study," and a "real doer."[17] Danger signals soon emerged when some faculty at Ohio State called her "Queen Ann" or simply the "queen." CSUN President James Cleary had been in the running, and many hoped he would get the chancellorship. But, as one trustee put it, the board took a risk in wanting a woman and a member of the establishment. A national recession caused a budget crisis that saw some community colleges cut classes by as much as 40 percent, which directly affected Chicano Studies. The rising costs at the University of California also had consequences, accelerating the drift toward privatization as more of its faculty salaries were supplemented from outside sources. The California State University fees jumped from $230 to $650 per student a semester. Meanwhile, the state universities signed a collective bargaining pact with the teachers' union.[18]

Reynolds was imperious and she demanded deference. Her reign over the California State system was contentious, with the Board of Trustees finally urging her to mend her ways or resign.[19] Most Chicana/o faculty tried to stay out of her way until she pushed a plan to raise the admission standards to the state universities. Her reasoning was that by raising admission requirements the public schools would raise their standards and offer more college bound courses, thus removing the burden of remedial classes from the state universities. This was putting the chicken before the egg. Minority students came from schools that did not have the requisite number of required math and science courses. California was in the throes of a tax-cutting binge, and it did little to address the dropout problem among Latinas/os, which was over 50 percent. As a consequence of the recession, the budgets of the public schools were ravaged.

When Reynolds moved to implement her plan to raise requirements, I sent a letter to the editor of the Los Angeles Times on January 25, 1985, which began a battle with the chancellor and the Board of Trustees.[20] The Movimiento Estudiantil Chicanos de Aztlán, along with community organizations and left organizations such as the League of Revolutionary Struggle (LRS), jammed the California State University headquarters. Campuses took busloads of students to the trustees' meetings.[21] Reynolds was sure of herself as Claudia Hampton and Vice Chancellor Herbert Carter (both African American) defended Reynolds's plan. Hampton and Carter were adept at getting African Americans into administrative posts, but they showed a lack of vigor in maintaining the flow of black students into California State Universities. My letter began, "I am appalled at Chancellor W. Ann Reynolds' Dec. 15, 1984, letter thanking *The Times* for its editorial support (November, 1984), 'Cal State: Quality With Equality.'" I went on to attack the assumption that raising requirements would improve education and would threaten the gains made to date. Northridge had increased its enrollment of Chicanas/os from less than 75 to 1,300 Mexican American students in a student body of 28,000. However, at this point, Mexican Americans were more than 40 percent of the Los Angeles Unified Schools. I wrote, "We are not satisfied with this record, Chicano faculty and staff realize that without special programs, i.e., special admissions and retention, that this record would be even worse." I called the new policies "exclusionary racist policies of the pre-civil rights days when unrealistic requirements (in view of society as it was) effectively kept minorities out." I concluded that "Chancellor Reynolds' proposal will force many of us to resume agitation to 1960 levels to prevent the exclusion of our peoples."[22]

Incredibly, the CSU faculty senate defended the chancellor's plan and sent a response to the *Los Angeles Times* attacking me. The response letter said that the signers believed the Republican legislature, Republican Governor George Deukmejian, and Superintendent of Public Instruction Bill Honig that, by requiring more rigorous high school graduation standards for all California high school students, the public schools would meet the challenge. They wrote: "We do a disservice by admitting poorly prepared students who are likely to fail."[23] The signers—good liberals—concluded, "In his preoccupation with predictions of 'doom,' Acuña failed to note that the students could attend a community college and have every opportunity to qualify for later transfer to a university."

During this period I came under personal and professional attack. President Cleary received a call from the Chancellor's Office. Cleary defended Chicano Studies and MEChA's right to protest. It got so heated that my former student, columnist, and assistant *Los Angeles Times* editor Frank del Olmo wrote a column defending

me and endorsing my credentials. Del Olmo went on to point out that the state
university system produced 50–70 percent of California schoolteachers and that

> part of the problem might be that the institution training most of our teachers
> also is doing a less-than-satisfactory job. . . . statistics released last week by the
> Los Angeles Unified School District indicate that Latinos represent 52% of
> the public-school students in Los Angeles and 63% of those in kindergarten.
> In light of those numbers, 5% [students in CSU] is not good enough. Cal State
> officials had better be sure that their own house is in order, as Acuna suggests,
> before shifting the responsibility for improving public education to the state's
> high schools.[24]

Del Olmo's column saved part of my posterior.

Reynolds aggressively defended raising admission standards and appeared
before women's groups, where she was gaining traction. Carter and Hampton
continued to defend her interests in the black community.[25] By 1987 Reynolds was
again under fire, and in 1990 she was forced to resign. Latinas/os composed 25 percent of K–12 students in California's public schools, but they made up only one-
tenth of the state university students. Reynolds's plan would have shrunk this
number.[26] Her base of support was the American Council on Education's Office of
Women in Higher Education, which salvaged the careers of white women administrators. ACE's initiative to promote women PhDs began in the 1950s. Reynolds
was a 1958 ACE Fellow. According to American Council on Education, the number
of female presidents increased from 148 in 1975 to 286 at the end of 1984—an
increase of 93 percent.[27] Reynolds often spoke about recruiting more minorities,
but her policies contradicted her actions, as she failed to reach out to Latinas.
Chicano Studies lacked networks, making the support of del Olmo and politicos
such as Assemblyman Richard Alatorre all the more vital. At the time, the only
Chicano University of California chancellor was Tomás Rivera, who was appointed
to the Riverside campus in 1979. Rivera died in 1984. Miguel A. Nevárez was
appointed president of Pan American University (Texas) in 1981, and Tomás
Arciniega was president of California State Bakersfield College in 1986, where he
served for twenty-one years.

In 1987 Reynolds received a negative rating from the trustees. By 1990 Reynolds
came under renewed attacks for her lavish lifestyle and the hefty increase in her
salary and the salaries of her immediate subordinates. This led to Reynolds's
abrupt resignation, which the *Orange County Register* called the "Abdication of the
queen."[28] Incredibly, within a couple of months Reynolds was named to head the
twenty-one-unit City University of New York system, which had been beset by
student protests over programs for minorities and proposed budget cuts. Many
observers attribute her rehabilitation to ACE connections.[29] She got into similar
problems at City University of New York. After months of attack by the trustees
there, she left for the University of Alabama at Birmingham. After four years at
Alabama, Reynolds was again forced to resign.[30]

AROUND THE UNIVERSE

As mentioned, Chicano Studies was frequently threatened by the consolidation into Ethnic Studies programs. At the University of Washington, President William Gerberding in 1984 approved a plan to consolidate three Ethnic Studies programs into a single department, but students protested. According to Gerberding, he wanted to unite Afro-American, Asian American, and Chicano Studies into a Department of American Ethnic Studies, and he had strong support from faculty members and senior administrators. Chicana/o student leaders charged that "students fear that the programs will wither away, as in similar mergers in two other Washington universities, or blend into a department of 'beige studies,'" James Wong, commissioner of the Asian Student, said that the president "didn't take us seriously." Only Lauro Flores, director of the Center for Chicano Studies, who was on tenure track, went along with the merger that would combine services such as secretarial.[31]

University of California, Davis, in 1987 attempted to engineer Ethnic Studies departments. Assistant Vice Chancellor of Academic Affairs Francisco J. Samaniego convened a review committee at the Davis campus to make recommendations on the status of the four Ethnic Studies units at Davis. I was the only reviewer from a teaching institution. Among the reviewers were Ron Takaki of the University of California, Berkeley, and Nathan I. Huggins, the W.E.B. Du Bois Professor of History and coordinator of Afro-American Studies at Harvard University. There were no prominent Native American scholars in the mix. The finding was supposed to be part of a report by an internal UC Davis workshop on the state of Ethnic Studies.[32]

It was soon apparent that the targets were Asian Studies and Indian Studies and that the Davis administration wanted to clean house. I was surprised that Takaki and Huggins were eager to go along with the agenda. The administration did not like a Pilipino scholar in Asian Studies who they called weak; however, I felt that he needed time and Davis should invest in him. How many Filipino scholars were available at the time? Takaki said that the scholar was not up to "UC Standards," an assertion I challenged. Much of the discussion devolved around the Indian Studies program, and a remark was made about a woman scholar who also happened to be a Chicana. The reviewers alleged that she was not really a Native American or "UC caliber." The discussions grew tense. Takaki was deferent to Huggins, with whom I got into a heated argument about the role of education. At one point, I said that maybe minority communities could not afford pampered scholars, which remark he took objection to. The final straw was when Samaniego and the others made the comment that the problems in Indian Studies would take care of themselves because a couple of their scholars were elderly and would die off.

The committee published a 124-page report that generally went along with the Davis administration, incorporating the recommendations of the task force I served on. However, I responded in a minority report, dated May 13, 1987, in which I criticized the task force: "My main concern is that the panel members, who are in their majority members of minority groups, in taking care not to offend the Administration and faculty at Davis, may very well give the impression that the ethnic programs caused their own problems. Nothing could be further from the truth." It went on to enumerate the generalizations about the four programs: "The result is that the Report infers that the programs are weak, and that they are staffed with mediocre personnel." The major obstacle was "UC Davis and its hostile attitude and failure to meet the curricular needs of the programs—instead it played to the culture of that particular community. The Spanish Department's offerings in Mexican literature are inferior to most California community colleges. And, the history department does not have a Mexicanist to develop this area."[33] The minority report recommended that a team of minority scholars be formed to revise the university's curriculum. It attacked the assumption that Davis could not attract quality minority scholars. The minority report recommended that courses in the minority programs be given general education credit. It also cautioned Davis not to consolidate the departments into a single Ethnic Studies unit.

The minority report concluded that senior faculty must be recruited but that respect should be shown to the senior faculty already at Davis who were not fully accepted. "Some of the Panel members were shocked by the lack of respect shown to the Native American studies program in not allowing it to fill vacancies, expressing the sentiment that most of the present staff would not be there in a couple of years, and it could appoint people it considered qualified." Perhaps I should not have reacted so impulsively; the whole affair was disappointing, since up to this point Takaki and Huggins were among my favorite scholars.[34]

BLACK-BROWN TENSIONS

Contributing to black-brown tensions on college and university campuses was the worsening economic times. In the previous decades, tension had been minimal because of the size differences of the two populations, with African Americans outnumbering Mexican Americans and Latinas/os. Due to the huge growth of the Latino population, the two now often competed for jobs, housing, political offices, and attention. Numbers stimulated the Mexican American leadership to demand a larger share of prestigious posts. This competition came at a time when black political leadership was at its height. In Los Angeles, Mayor Tom Bradley was running for governor and Speaker Willie Brown reigned over the California Assembly.

In 1979 the vacancy of the CSULA presidency was announced. The university is adjacent to the country's largest Mexican American population. Mexican American organizations, leaders, and the community wanted one of their own appointed. The logical candidate was Julian Nava, who had graduated from Roosevelt High School in nearby Boyle Heights and attended East Los Angeles College, Pomona College, and Harvard University, where he earned a doctorate. A history professor at CSUN, Nava was elected to the Los Angeles School Board in 1967. Since school board elections were at large, Nava had to run at large in the City of Los Angeles and parts of the county, and receive more votes than the mayor of Los Angeles.[35]

Nava was promised the support of Chancellor Glenn Dumke and Claudia Hampton, a black trustee. The only fly was friction between the black and Latino communities as to who would take Nava's place on the board.[36] Despite strong support, the CSU trustees appointed black educator James Rosser, vice chancellor of the New Jersey Department of Higher Education, to the presidency by an 8–7 vote. The Chicano Caucus in the legislature immediately called for another vote. State Senator Joseph Montoya threatened to cut the budget of CSULA. Latinos argued that East Los Angeles was predominately Mexican American, while the university was 16 percent Latino, 15 percent Asians, and 14 percent black. Claudia Hampton, the new chair of the trustees, although she had made commitments to Nava, said she had no intention of reviewing the vote. According to Hampton, she did not vote because she was advised by counsel to recuse herself because she worked for the Los Angeles Schools, where Nava had been an elected official.[37]

The loss of the presidency was a serious blow to the Chicana/o community's pride. Nava would have been a symbol, and it was believed that he could have controlled the bureaucracy and chaos at the university, as well as the antipathy of many faculty members and administrators toward Chicano Studies. At CSUN he had been supportive of the department. His academic experience was the equal of Rosser's. Nava had worked with the budget of one of the largest school systems in the nation, taught for twenty years, published, and run major political campaigns. Prior to his New Jersey post, Rosser had been an associate vice chancellor for academic affairs at the University of Kansas in Lawrence. His PhD was in health education administration and microbiology from Southern Illinois University at Carbondale.

The failure of the Chicana/o community touched off a series of setbacks at other universities. At San Marcos, in the northern part of San Diego County, Chicanos were hopeful they would get the presidency, high-ranking administrators, or at least be among the founding faculty. They were disappointed. In a *Herald-Examiner* op-ed piece of October 6, 1989, I wrote: "The California State University system is pledged to racial, cultural and program diversity. Yet the selection of San Marcos, in northern San Diego County, as the site for its newest campus and the appointment of Bill Stacy as the founding president raise serious doubts about the system's commitment to live up to its promises."[38] When the new campus did not search for a Latina/o president or sufficient numbers of Latina/o faculty members, Chicano legislators were livid. Not only had heavily Latino areas such as Ventura County been passed over, but Latina/o faculty members constituted 3.6 percent— or 426 people—of the 11,731-member system's faculty in 1987. According to a report of CSU trustees, "CSU ought to 'give the highest priority' to hiring Hispanic presidents, vice chancellors, vice presidents and deans. The report urges establishing affirmative-action plans for the chancellor's office and for individual campuses and appointing a task force to monitor compliance." The twenty-person team even proposed an all-Latino university as a possible solution.[39]

The California State University system, because of pressure from the Chicana/o community, the deteriorating public schools, and elected officials, was forced to modify Reynolds's regulations and institute remedial courses. Funding was so top heavy that MEChA recommended that the state's funding formula be reversed, with the public schools getting the lion's share of the budget. The lag in Latino college enrollment was critical nationwide. According to the Bureau of the Census, "the number of Hispanic people who are 18 to 24 years old—the age group where college students are concentrated—grew by 62 percent over the last decade, from 1,551,000 in 1976 to 2,513,000 in 1986. The number of Hispanic people in that age group enrolled in college increased by only 43 percent, to 433,000 from 309,000." The tensions in Texas were so critical that the University of Texas, along with Texas A & M, opened recruiting centers in Laredo, Houston, Dallas, and the Rio Grande Valley.[40]

In 1989 Los Angeles Times reporter Marita Hernández wrote, "After more than a decade of struggling to survive, Chicano Studies programs at universities throughout the Southwest are becoming the focus of renewed interest, coinciding with growing public attention to the Latino population boom." Even so, the troops were restless. A 1987 national survey of 240 Chicana/o professors conducted by Santa Clara University said that Chicano Studies professors felt like they were treated as "second-class" and "illegitimate" on their campuses, and that their research was undervalued by their universities. In the University of California system, Chicana/o students accounted for only 3.4 percent, yet they were about 25 percent of California. Even so, Rick Malaspina's statement that UC President David Gardner "long advocated developing a faculty more reflective of the state's minority and female population" sounded hollow.[41]

Fresno State, which in the spring of 1970 had fired eight of the twelve faculty members in the La Raza and Black Studies programs, made a comeback. In 1975 the community and students sat in at President Norman Baxter's office. They believed that the administration was trying to keep the La Raza program from becoming a full-fledged department. In May 1975 the entire La Raza faculty signed letters of resignation. By 1989 the department was called Chicano and Latin American Studies and had over a thousand students enrolled, experiencing a 50 percent growth from 1983 to 1988, partly based on the new Ethnic Studies requirement.

A Stanford survey found nearly half of the African American, Latino, and American Indian students believed that most white students were racially prejudiced. Racial tensions were on the rise at many campuses, including the University of Michigan, the Massachusetts Institute of Technology, UC Berkeley, and Stanford University. Hate crimes were common. According to a Los Angeles Times article published April 10, 1989, titled "Racism Still Plagues Campus Life,"

> On most campuses the faculties are barely integrated. Few students attend classes taught by minority professors. The course work also is barely integrated beyond a few separate Afro-American history or Chicano studies classes. Few students take even one class about another facet of American culture. Yet most minority students spend their academic careers engrossed in the dominant white American culture. . . . Blacks, Latinos and Asians will make up the majority of the population in nearly 20 of the nation's largest cities by the year 2000.[42]

THE CASE OF TOMÁS ARCINIEGA

Born and raised in El Paso, Tomás Arciniega graduated from the University of New Mexico and returned to teach at the University of Texas, El Paso. He was appointed dean of the College of Education at San Diego State, provost at Fresno State, and then served as president of California State University, Bakersfield, for twenty-one years. A respected scholar and an expert on bilingual education, he served as a trustee of Carnegie Corporation of New York Foundation. *Change* magazine selected Arciniega as one of the top 100 academic leaders in American Higher Education. Arciniega was a quiet man who by no means could be considered a radical. As I mentioned to him, he should have sued the CSU system.

After serving four successful years, Arciniega applied in 1990 for the vacancy at California State University, Fullerton, east of Los Angeles in Orange County, which served a large and growing Mexican American and Latino population. There was hope, since the pious lip service of state authorities and the CSU administration about the pressing need for Mexican American administrators and faculty members had reached crescendo levels. Fullerton had a struggling Chicano Studies department that experts in the field believed had the same potential as campuses with larger Chicano Studies departments.

Many were surprised when Arciniega, a sitting president, was passed over in favor of Milton A. Gordon, a vice president for academic affairs at Sonoma State University, a campus that was not much larger than Bakersfield. The appointment of Gordon was justified by liberals, who pointed to the fact that Gordon was black and that the appointment brought the number of black CSU presidents to four. A press release said that "Fullerton is a very proud institution." In researching the controversy for a possible op-ed article, I found the similarities to the Julian Nava snub at CSULA striking. The selection had nothing to do with qualifications or even a black president. The general feeling of the Fullerton California Faculty Association and the faculty governance was that they did not want a Mexican American president. The large Mexican American community would give him or her an independent political base.[43]

In 1991 at Fresno State an almost all-white search committee eliminated all Chicano or Latino applicants from its finalist pool, including Tomás Arciniega. According to the *Ukiah Daily Journal*, "The 1990 census shows that at least one-third of the populations are Hispanic in the four central San Joaquin Valley counties—Tulare, Fresno, Kings and Madera. But a Fresno Bee survey of 1,168 valley elected officials found that only 10.8 percent are Hispanic."[44] Trustee Ralph Pesquera reopened the search to include new applicants, and members were added to the search committee. Assemblyman Richard Polanco, chair of the state legislature's Hispanic Caucus, introduced a bill putting the trustees in charge of selecting presidential selection committees in order to ethnically balance them. Latinas/os and Chicanas/os led by MEChA and Chicano Studies packed the trustees meeting demanding that the search process be aborted and the Chair of the Trustee William Campbell, a member of the presidential selection advisory committee, resign. Campbell had been the de facto head of CSU since Reynolds resigned. The student and faculty members carried signs reading "Ya Estuvo" and "CSU Trustees Are Racist."[45]

In 1992 Arciniega applied for the presidency at San Jose State, where he was once more a finalist. The alumni association was upset because all of the finalists were women and minorities. Again Arciniega was passed over. The committee favored Ruth Leventhal, dean and provost of Pennsylvania State University, Harrisburg, since 1984, with no experience with Chicano issues. At this point Arciniega had been a sitting president of a CSU campus for six years. The usual protests were heard, but the trustees declined to act.[46]

THE TRANSITIONAL 1980S

Most of what many Chicanas/os learned about the gay and lesbian movements was from progressives outside academe. At Northridge, a large contingent of gay professors taught in departments throughout the university. However, they never called attention to the question, and more often than not they sided with the most reactionary elements on campus. A version of "Don't Ask, Don't Tell" operated. The tragedy of AIDS shook many faculty members. Chicanas/os preached about the strength of the Mexican family, but we learned of mothers and fathers who refused to acknowledge their gay and lesbian children. Some young kids died of the dreaded disease without the comfort of their parents. This was inhumane. Gays were as much Chicana/o as any of us.[47]

At CSUN, the debate was forced by queer students. The *Los Angeles Times* reported, "Today, the 60 members of Strong Queers United In Stopping Heterosexism [SQUISH] find themselves at the center of a stormy debate at Cal State Northridge that has provoked emotional demonstrations, angry confrontations and threats of violence and death." SQUISH members strove to "gain basic human rights by fighting what they call 'heterosexism,' the belief that only heterosexuals are whole, legitimate people." They challenged the notion that homosexuality was "unnatural and evil." They were confrontational, which is the only way to challenge an entrenched paradigm. They staged a "kiss-in" and covered a campus billboard with messages such as "I thought all straight men were rapists" in an attempt to show the dangers of stereotyping. However, flyers were distributed offering free baseball bats for a 'gay bashing and clubbing night.'"[48]

SQUISH was the brainchild of gay rights activist Mat Rodieck, one of the brightest student activists I've known. I met him when he showed up in my class as a student. Most of the students thought he was a white jock, which, aside from his color, made him stand out. The students liked him because he was more outspoken against injustices than they were. One day he showed up to class wearing a T-shirt reading QUEER and most males were flustered. One day he asked me to come to a demonstration to admit gays in ROTC. My first reaction was, "Why the fuck do you want to go into ROTC?" He answered that it was his choice. So I showed up to the demonstration and was surprised that the only other professor,

John Clendening, a heterosexual, was present. I was also surprised that a couple of gay professors I had clashed with came up and privately thanked me.[49]

At another rally, "The confrontation began about noon when four students criticized Father David Walsh of the Newman Center, a campus Roman Catholic institution, for joining the 'die-in,' arguing with him that as a priest he should not be supporting what they called unnatural conduct. The students were 'yelling and screaming' at him, said the priest, who said he was not defending homosexuality but protesting against hate." The campus had to call in reinforcements.[50] I lost track of Rodieck during this period because I had begun my suit against the University of California, Santa Barbara, and had to travel to New York and around the state to drum up legal support. However, SQUISH had a lasting effect on the department. In 1992 Queer Latinos Unidos formed as a CSUN MEChA standing committee. The intent was to create space for the group and to combat homophobia. The leadership of MEChA was changing, and articles appeared in the Chicano student newspaper, *El Popo*, which went beyond a dialogue on AIDS. MEChA chair Gabriel Buelna, a heterosexual, was very instrumental in bringing about this change, encouraging other chapters to discuss the question and sponsoring workshops on the topic. Consequent to this change, Chicana/o homosexuals became more visible and many did not feel compelled to defend their homosexuality. This caused splits in MEChA, with many members leaving the organization. Within the group, sexism and homophobia was equated with racism—how could Chicanos discriminate against others and complain about racism? It can be argued that the militancy of SQUISH and Queer Latinos Unidos were instrumental in this change in state of mind. However, Chicana/o gays and lesbians also contributed to the change.[51]

Mary Pardo advanced the discourse. In October 1992, along with Mujeres de Aztlán, Pardo hosted a Chicana conference of several hundred female college students, high school students, college faculty, and community members, and they raised the topic. They discussed AIDS, sexuality, and domestic violence. The following year, Juana Mora became the first Chicana chair of the department. Mora's becoming chair had a lot to do with the changing of the composition of the department, which had become mostly Chicana. Meanwhile, not all was smooth sailing with MEChA. There was opposition, especially with the growth of Latino fraternities and many members attributed the loss of membership to admitting gays. The student leadership under Buelna, Miguel Paredes, and Filiberto González held firm. Long discussions took place and department members supported this course. Meanwhile, Enrique Castrejon emerged as the leader of Queer Latinos Unidos. He questioned the sincerity of Chicanas/os in their advocacy for equality. Castrejon, although a strong leader, did not have the confrontational nature of Rodieck, but nevertheless led confrontations. As a junior in the fall of 1995 he led a protest against Governor Pete Wilson on the Northridge campus.[52]

In *El Popo* Castrejon wrote, "The continued silence of not recognizing and accepting us, the denial of our existence, only contributes to hate, fear, suicide, and HIV infection of our *gente*. Yes Raza, we are killing each other off because we fail to discuss, address, or take any action to end the homophobia that affects our *gente* and communities."[53] Enrique was especially hard on gay males for not coming out and credited lesbians for gains. He became MEChA chair for a brief period but resigned. No doubt, pressures and his desire for change wore him down. He had nevertheless contributed to a transformation in the body, which has elected at least two other gay chairs since.

Getting a Chicano Studies Department
the Old Fashion Way

UCLA MEChA students Marcos Aguilar and Minnie Fergusson in 1988–1989 were intent on establishing a Chicano Studies department at UCLA. It was their passion in life. At meetings our conversations would invariably return to the topic of Chicano Studies, what it was, and what students could do to get a department that would give them the best vehicle for student and community power on campus. They had been recruited to the fight to preserve Olvera Street by their teacher, UCLA historian Juan Gómez-Quiñones.

At the time that I got involved with the Olvera Street struggle, I was a columnist (aside from being a professor) for the *Herald Examiner* and *La Opinión*, two Los Angeles dailies. I had not thought much about Olvera Street, since for years it was a tourist trap that no self-respecting Chicana/o would frequent. However, through contacts with community leaders such as Frank Villalobos of Barrio Planners and of the Mothers of East Los Angeles's crusade to prevent the building of yet another prison in East Los Angeles, my view of urban planning broadened. Frank showed me his plans, commissioned by the Olvera Street Merchants' Association, to develop the street, data that I shared with my Chicano Studies classes.[54] I published my first piece on Olvera Street in the summer of 1987: "The fate of Olvera Street, Los Angeles' oldest, is up for grabs. Earthquake laws, historic preservation, the pimping of Mexican culture and a political power struggle over who will control El Pueblo de Los Angeles Historic Park, all are playing a role." Now, developers had descended on Olvera Street and were threatening to convert it into a Taco Bell.[55]

Olvera Street was meant to showcase Los Angeles's Mexican heritage. During the Great Depression, a mural critical of American capitalism—*America Tropical* by David Siqueiros, the great Mexican muralist—was whitewashed. In 1953 California established El Pueblo Park, and Olvera's merchants, mostly small vendors, had great expectations. These hopes were dashed when state bureaucrats insisted on basing the history on buildings rather than people. This meant that it would highlight the history of Italians and Chinese, lessening the focus on Mexicans. Although every major ethnic group in the city had a museum, Mexicans did not have a place in Los Angeles or in southern California that marked their extended presence.[56]

How to preserve Olvera Street got tangled in the ambitions of council members Gloria Molina and Richard Alatorre. The city was promoting a "Fantasy Heritage" reminiscent of Old Town San Diego, where white merchants dressed in Mexican costumes ran the franchises. The Olvera Street vendors were not perfect, but their families had worked Olvera Street for up to fifty years. The leader was Vivian Bonzo, owner of La Golindrina restaurant.[57]

By 1989 Chicanas/os formed the Mexican Conservancy. Minnie Fergusson and Marcos Aguilar were among the group that wanted to preserve the history of Olvera Street. A fight loomed as Latinos and developers jockeyed for a piece of the street supported by Richard Riordan, head of the Los Angeles Park's Commission, and Alatorre. During one confrontation, I asked Riordan if he wanted Olvera Street to become another McDonald's, Riordan answered yes. Riordan wanted to privatize Olvera Street and everything else in Los Angeles, including the schools and libraries.[58]

Jean Bruce Poole, the curator of the El Pueblo de Los Angeles Historic Monument, was paternalistic and intent on neutralizing the Mexican presence on the street. She enlisted the support of the Italians and the Chinese by promising them a piece of "Old Mexico." I wrote in an article titled "History Is People, Not Bricks," published in the April 2, 1990, *Los Angeles Times*:

> For 12 years, Poole and her gaggle of Anglo historians have been plotting to impose their Mexican-less vision of Olvera Street. Their opportunity for success came when administration of El Pueblo Park passed from state to the city Recreation and Parks Commission. Eager to renovate, the commissioners put together a proposal. Since they and the Recreation and Parks Dept. lack the expertise to make historical recommendations, Peter Snell, an architectural historian, was paid to make proposals some. Snell is a close friend of Poole and has acted as a consultant for El Pueblo Park."[59]

The Recreation and Parks Commission voted 4–0 vote to proceed with plans to put Olvera Street out for bids. This action was supposed to end the wrangling over the status of Olvera Street. This angered the Mexican Conservancy that marched on City Hall and packed the commission meeting. Five hundred supporters of the conservancy jammed the Los Angeles City Council chambers, stomped their feet, and clapped their hands over assertions that the commission had authority over Olvera Street. Riordan did not show up to the meeting.

After three hours of debate, it authorized the restoration of a community hall and museum for Italian-Americans. "This is simply not acceptable," screamed Vivien Bonzo, president of the Olvera Street Merchants Association. And I added that "we're not anti-Italian. We have a Chinese museum at one end and now we have an Italian museum on the other . . . Who is going to stand up for us?" Luis Váldez, founder of the Teatro Campesino, told the commissioners that the proposal was full of "little tricks that are meant to bring in the McDonald's . . . to bring in Taco Bell."[60] Historian Gloria Ricci Lothrop said the Italians wanted to take back important historic sites, sites they had built after they uprooted the Mexicans who had occupied the space before and after the Italian occupation.[61]

Eventually, Alatorre and Molina agreed to support a seven-member "authority" to oversee the park, ending the control of the parks commission.[62] Slowly, the Mexican American community lost space on the street, with their historical past bartered away by white and brown politicos in city hall for the political support of Italian, Chinese, and other interests to further their careers.

GREEKS AND LUPE

Every successful mobilization is driven by moral outrage. For example, in October 1992 a staff member in charge of Greeks at CSUN alerted me to his attempts to punish the Zeta Beta Tau after he discovered a flyer announcing a party dedicated to "Lupe," a song in a fraternity songbook about a preteen Mexican whore. When the student adviser attempted to get Zeta Beta Tau to withdraw the flyer, the fraternity president became defiant, saying that it was their constitutional right to hold the party. I alerted Chicano Studies and MEChA and held a rally that drew more than a thousand demonstrators.

In November CSUN suspended the Zeta Beta Tau fraternity until January 1994 for distributing the party flyer. It violated campus rules against sexism and racism. Scott Krivis, a Zeta Beta Tau alumnus and spokesman for the fraternity, said the penalty was too harsh and threatened to sue. "The UCLA fraternity that actually had the song in their songbook was suspended for less than one month. . . . We are going to fight this decision." Tensions grew as more rallies were held. Complicating matters was the fact that Zeta Beta Tau was a progressive Jewish fraternity established because of racism toward Jews in the Greek system. The Hillel rabbi was more than cooperative and condemned the actions of the fraternity.

Los Angeles Times columnist Al Martínez wrote an article titled "'Lupe' and the Guys." It started with tongue in cheek, "College humor, as everyone knows, has never been based on goodwill, honesty, spiritual enhancement, parental love or family values." This was tested in the discovery of the UCLA songbook. "Lupe was a 'hot . . . Mexican whore' who lost her virginity early and 'finished her life in a welter of sin,' most elements of which are described in blunt, less than lyrical terms."[63]

CSUN President Blenda J. Wilson, a black woman, began having second thoughts and pressured the Chicano Studies chair, Gerald Reséndez, to support cutting the fourteen-month suspension on the grounds that defending the suit would cost too much. Attorney Vilma Martínez, the former MALDEF general counsel, supported Wilson as did the CSU's general counsel who was also Mexican American. MEChA and Chicano Studies refused the offer, but Wilson did what she wanted and settled with the Zeta Beta Tau.[64]

Most faculty opposed the settlement, but Wilson defended it. When the faculty senate considered a resolution to boycott the Zeta Beta Tau and the legal settlement, Wilson spoke against the resolution, saying, "They're young people. They come here to learn, to grow and develop, and they can't do that if your view is to punish. . . . You can condemn, but don't punish." Cynthia Rawitch, the publisher of the student newspaper, the *Sundial,* said, "There's enough retribution and punishment going on at the campus right now without my adding to it."[65]

Unknown to us at the time was just how far Wilson and the CSU attorneys and Martínez had capitulated. They panicked when it was learned that David Horowitz and his Center for the Study of Popular Culture were going to front the costs of a free-speech lawsuit. To add to the insult, Wilson and the CSU agreed to pick up the costs of the ZBT's attorney fees and the publication of the apology. The outrage over the Lupe Song preceded the hunger strike by two months.

A CHICANA/O STUDIES DEPARTMENT

The formation of the UCLA Chicana/o Studies department was historic and proof that individuals can make a difference. Throughout the Olvera Street struggle, Minnie Fergusson and Marcos Aguilar had been active in organizing conferences and politicking for support for their dream. They wanted a department because they thought that the Chicano Studies Research Center was inaccessible to students and that Chicana/o faculty was too dispersed and disengaged to listen to them. Generally, research centers are aloof. There are exceptions, like the University of Houston, where under the directorship of Anastacio "Tatcho" Mindiola Jr., the center functions as an interdisciplinary academic program, a watering hole that brings students and faculty together. Assistant director Lorenzo Cano is directly involved with students, and he has coordinated a minor program in Mexican American Studies. The long tenure of Mindiola and Cano has contributed to stability and a sense of community.[66]

At UCLA many professors did not like MEChA and started other organizations, which frustrated student unity. Some were blinded by a dislike of Juan Gómez-Quiñones. UCLA was the flagship of Chicano Studies in Los Angeles, and it had to have a strong program in order for the area of studies to flourish. It was difficult to understand how Chicana/o professors could put their likes and dislikes above the good of the community. Each also had their own ideas about what form the department should take. One Latina sociologist with little experience in building student power wanted an Ethnic Studies unit and saw a department as a personal threat. Finally, Associate Vice Chancellor Raymund Paredes stood in the way. Paredes did not have ties to the Chicano movement, and greatly resented Gómez-Quiñones.

Minnie Fergusson was from Lincoln Heights and Marcos Aguilar was from Mexicali. They were tall and thin and very serious. Aguilar was intense to the point that his intensity intimidated people. They became *danzantes* and sought answers through a study of their indigenous past. They were not fanatical in trying to impose these views on others. Nevertheless, some faculty members were intimidated by the intensity and single-mindedness of their views of Chicano Studies. They resented that they were not deferent to their professors, who in turn responded by spreading rumors, such as that Aguilar was a macho, a chauvinist, and a nationalist. Knowing both Aguilar and Fergusson and dozens of other friends of theirs, I knew that they were not. Indeed, he did not chase, drink, or take drugs. The faculty who criticized Fergusson were sexist and took her lightly because she was a woman. But Fergusson was as persistent as Marcos was intense, a combination that challenged many of their peers.

For four years they worked through MEChA, chairing a committee to draw up curriculum. They held Saturday conferences in which faculty, community, and students were invited. Matters became critical in 1990 when the faculty senate recommended that Chicano Studies be suspended. The administration relented when MEChA and faculty members protested. The interdisciplinary courses had been popular on the campus for twenty-one years. The justification the senate gave was that only twelve students majored in the field in 1989 and no Chicano Studies courses had been offered for a quarter.

Chancellor Charles E. Young called a closed-door meeting with Chicana/o and white faculty members and vice chancellors. The meeting bypassed the Chicano Studies Committee. The chancellor agreed to new funding, and the Committee to Administer the Chicano Studies Major was given one staff member, one researcher, office space, and supplies. The committee had had an operating annual budget of $1,500. Marcos Aguilar protested: "This meeting is a deviation from the process we began ourselves." The issue was respect for the students who were most affected by the program.[67]

Young invited Los Angeles lawyer Ralph Ochoa, president of the UCLA alumni association, to calm the waters. Ochoa had few ties to the community and less credibility. He always sided with the University of California system, with whom he did business. Students were enraged when Paredes publicly opposed the department. According to Paredes, UCLA had higher admission and curriculum requirements than the state universities. Paredes lobbied mainstream community leaders and the editorial staff of the *Los Angeles Times*. Meanwhile, Young would not answer the calls of Vivien Bonzo, president of the Olvera Street Merchants Association and a member of the Mexican Conservancy.

The United Community and Labor Alliance demanded that Chancellor Charles Young meet with its members to discuss the future of a separate Chicano Studies department. Juana Gutiérrez, Councilwoman Jackie Goldberg, and State Senator Art Torres (D-Los Angeles) were part of the alliance. The committee also demanded the end to the harassment of students. Ferguson charged at the press conference that the university faculty was trying to intimidate students and "work against us in terms of getting recommendations for graduate school." Paredes, true to form, said students seeking a Chicano Studies department did not represent the majority of the 4,000 Latina/o students on campus; they "are not taking courses in Chicano studies. They are majoring in the conventional fields like English, history and science."[68]

Paredes in *The Hispanic Outlook in Higher Education* called the accusations against UCLA unfounded, writing, "Very clearly, the needs of most Chicano students are best addressed in established departments . . . with non-Chicano students, many of whom need to learn that Chicanos are capable of far more than the menial tasks generally assigned to them in American films and television." Paredes claimed that many of the Latina/o professors opposed Chicano Studies and considered it regressive. On the UCLA campus the issue ignited emotional confrontations.[69]

MEChA was polarized. Many followed the lead of Chicana/o faculty members, who urged the organization to abandon the issue and concentrate on other affairs.

Some Mechistas were concerned about the growing alienation with faculty and other Chicana/o student organizations on campus. MEChA had a rule that graduate students could not participate in the organization. Fergusson was enrolled in the master's program in Urban Planning. Aguilar and Fergusson argued that MEChA had committed itself to a goal, so "let's complete it." The organization ousted Aguilar and Fergusson. This did not dissuade them, and they continued to work with community groups.

After three years of controversy, Chancellor Young announced on April 28, 1993, that Chicano Studies "will not be elevated to an independent department at the Westwood campus."[70] Young's decision came on the eve of the funeral of César Chávez. Aguilar and Fergusson acted and began contacting allies.[71] They formed a group called Conscious Students of Color. They decided to strike the citadel of faculty power and take over the faculty club. A rally began at noon on May 11 that attracted about 200 participants. About eighty students began a sit-in inside the club. Many were first-time freshman and people who had never been involved. The campus police were assisted by 200 LAPD officers who arrested eighty-nine students on felony charges. The arrests drew support. On the second day, a crowd of a thousand people gathered in front of Royce Hall. The arrests awakened students.

The Los Angeles Times editorialized that "it seems only logical that there should be a Chicano studies department at the most prestigious public university in the city with the nation's largest Mexican-American community."[72] Times reporter George Ramos supported the creation of a department. "The protesting students at UCLA sounded familiar to me. Full of ethnic pride, they have marched and sat in to dramatize their demand that a Chicano studies department be created on the Westwood campus. They believe in the correctness of their position. Campus administrators also said things I've heard before. They reminded me of their predecessors from the 1960s, saying they wouldn't be bullied by demonstrators into changing their decision not to elevate Chicano studies to department status. UCLA administrators have hurt themselves by ignoring the growing public support for a Chicano studies department."[73]

After the arrests, a meeting was called by Vivian Bonzo. Fergusson and Aguilar attended, along with a select group. The students wanted feedback. The prospects were grim because finals were about to begin, and people would be leaving for the summer. Young probably made the late announcement knowing that it would be impossible for the students to mount a prolonged counteroffensive. Several alternatives were discussed and it was concluded that only a miracle could sustain the movement.

On May 25, 1993, six UCLA students, a high school student, and an assistant professor began what would eventually be a fourteen-day hunger strike, vowing to stay until they extracted a promise to create the department. "This is not a symbolic act, this is not a political statement. Either we get a department of Chicano studies or you will see us die before your eyes," said Jorge Mancillas, a biology professor in the medical school. A tent city was pitched in the quad closest to

Murphy Hall. Urban Planning Professor Leo Estrada was the faculty spokesperson. Leo was the perfect choice, soft spoken and respected by all sides.[74]

The mother of striker María Lara was there daily. "I'm really sad and really scared," Bertha said. But she did not did not discourage María to quit the water-only hunger strike. "It's my daughter's decision," she said. UCLA junior Joaquín Ochoa, twenty-one, was in a wheelchair, weakened after a week without food. Cindy Montañez, nineteen, and her sister Norma, sixteen, were among the hunger strikers. They were from San Fernando, and years later Cindy became a city councilperson and an assemblywoman. From San Fernando High, Norma said, "I know I'm a minor, but this is my decision . . . I really strongly believe I am doing the right thing. I am willing to die for it. . . . In high school, junior high school and elementary school, they don't teach you anything about us and our people. . . . We have been ignorant of our culture for a long time, and I think it is time they teach us who we are, where we come from and what our history is." Mancillas told reporters that the hunger strike had been inspired by César Chávez.[75]

The chancellor's decision not to establish a Chicano Studies department was considered a slap in the face of the Latino community. Rallies called to support the new department included Latino politicians, striking janitors, gang members, and community activists. The Rodney King rebellions in South Central Los Angeles were fresh in the minds of all. The denial of a department came at a time of heightened awareness of Latinas/os and their history. According to Saul Sarabia, a community member, the hunger strike was a symbol of the lack access to quality education; therefore, it made sense to expect the state's public universities to research and teach what is relevant to Latinas/os.[76]

María Lara, twenty-one, was a Roosevelt High School graduate who rode a bus from her South-Central neighborhood for the 1 1/2-hour trip to UCLA. Lara joined the hunger strike when she saw that the mass arrests had not moved the UCLA administration one iota. A political science and education major, she said, "I started to crystallize in my mind that there's racism in this university, but other than the individual racist acts, the institution serves the purpose as a racist institution. . . . A lot of people seem to think that the Mexican culture is at fault for many students not coming to a university, that the Mexican students are not serious. People have told me they heard that people live in the barrios because they want to. The fact that we don't even have certain classes on campus sets the tone for that."[77]

A twenty-mile march from Olvera Street to UCLA took place on the twelfth day to pressure the UCLA administration to meet with the hunger strikers. A meeting with high-ranking officials followed. Young had refused to meet with students or the community, or to discuss the matter, for over four years. Negotiators failed to reach a resolution. A desperate Paredes kept calling columnists such as Frank del Olmo to lobby them. He disparaged the research of Gómez-Quiñones and my contributions to the field. Paredes seemed to be oblivious or not to care what would happen if one of the strikers were hurt. Among the negotiators were Senators Art Torres (D-Los Angeles) and Tom Hayden (D-Santa Monica).

The nine-hour march had an impact, and many Angelinos remember it as a defining moment. I was a monitor and among the organizers. The march was arduous and hot. And, while it was peaceful, it was attended by many different factions that were not used to working together. Long Beach elementary schoolteacher Rosa Aderon-Salinas pushed her two-year-old daughter, Lumino, in a stroller past MacArthur Park. She said, "Our kids don't know who they are. They have no role models. They see no leaders in their schools who are like them." José García, a construction worker, said, "We have roots. We don't want to lose them . . . If people don't have roots, they don't have an identity. They are lost. They fall prey to gangs that can offer them an identity, and drugs." Several hundred people welcomed over a thousand marchers.[78]

Two days later a compromise was reached. The César Chávez Center for Interdisciplinary Instruction of Chicano Studies was established which would function as a department but would not be technically a department.[79] While not a department, it would have much more autonomy, according to the administration. The protesters argued that an independent department, with its own faculty and budget, was more appropriate for the most prestigious public university in the city with the nation's largest Mexican American community. Supporters, worried about the strikers' health, urged them to take the compromise. Knowing Aguilar and Fergusson, I had no doubt that they would go the limit.

Chancellor Charles E. Young was asked if he felt beaten up by elected officials who were pressuring him to give in to the protesters' demands. "You bet," he replied. "I'm sitting in there with people who have power over me and are threatening to use it." Professor Robert Dalleck repeated the old myth that the Irish and other ethnics made it in America.[80] Chicanos responded that Dalleck should read history and the Irish's use of political power. As for Young, he remained insensitive to the end, saying, "their hunger strike accomplished nothing."[81]

Paredes remained the fly in the ointment, and the administration dragged its feet even after the compromise. Hunger striker Balvina Collazo, twenty, said, "I personally feel very frustrated and angry with the administration. . . . I don't know what they think—that the hunger strike and protests were just a one-time thing and once we got an agreement we would all go away and forget about it? Well, they better think twice." History professor Juan Gómez-Quiñones echoed Collazo, saying that he was disappointed. "It seems like a bowl of jelly. . . . The least [university officials] could have done was have a director or chair appointed by now."[82]

Finally, in early 1994 UCLA appointed a chair, Carlos Grijalva, an associate dean who had been involved in the negotiations for the department. Jorge Mancillas and Marcos Aguilar criticized his appointment as inadequate. An associate dean and associate professor of psychology, Grijalva did not know the area of Chicano studies. Marcos said that they were using his Spanish surname to silence criticism. From this point on, it was a slow process of mainstreaming Chicano Studies. Through this formative period, Paredes controlled the faculty appointments and the development of the center. From 1996 to 1998 he also served as chair of the César Chávez Center for Chicano Studies. This de facto administrative control was not reversed until Rey Macias became chair and asserted more autonomy. Since then the center has achieved departmental status and regularly celebrates the hunger strike.

Minnie and Marcos today run a charter school, the Academia Semillas del Pueblo. The school has about 600 students serving K–9 mostly Latino working-class students. The school teaches Spanish, Nahuatl, and Mandarin and has student exchanges with China. Despite these accomplishments, they continue to be harassed by right-wing extremists, and their reputations are smeared on KABC radio.[83]

In an August 2009 interview, Marcos revealed without rancor that he has never been invited by the César Chávez Center to celebrate the commemoration of the center. He attended a celebration that honored Juan Gómez-Quiñones, who the couple is still close to. I asked him whether he had any regrets about the hunger strike. He replied that they should have hung in for one to three more days and maybe they could have negotiated their vision of the department. I told him that I doubted whether this would have changed anything because of Paredes. He replied in a matter-of-fact manner. "We should have waited longer."

THE AFTER SHOCKS

The UCLA hunger strike showed what a large and politicized youth population, community, and political representation can add to the potential of transforming higher education. The strike succeeded because all of these factors came together in a perfect storm. It was not solely the strike but also the forces that it released. What would have happened if Latinas/os would have begun a sympathy strike?

Even before the UCLA hunger strike, students were restless. On April 22, 1993, students at Williams College in Massachusetts staged a three-day fast to protest a lengthy search that failed to find a tenured Latina/o professor to teach United States Latino Studies. MEChA students at St. Cloud's in Minnesota began a hunger strike issuing thirteen demands, among which were the establishment of a Chicano Studies major. At Cal State Long Beach, La Raza Student Association occupied the lobby of the acting president's office in September 1993 and demanded the appointment of a Latina/o as his executive assistant. That same month Chicana/o students demonstrated at Berkeley for a separate Chicano Studies department. The demonstration ended after students pulled a fire alarm and broke a window in a campus building. The same day, police arrested six students. They used pepper spray to break up a melee of 300 high school and college students who had met to press demands and celebrate Mexican Independence Day at Fullerton Community College. About 270 students from Sonora High in La Habra, Anaheim High, and other Orange County schools joined the Fullerton College demonstration to protest the lack of Chicano courses in their own curriculum. In 1994, at the University of Colorado, Boulder, thirty-eight Chicana/o students began a hunger strike to demand a Chicano Studies department. They also struck in defense of sociology professor Estevan Flores, who was being denied tenure, declaring that they were "starving for diversity" on campus. Three Chicana/o professors requested transfers out of the sociology department, claiming racism.[84]

On April 27, 1994, nine members of the University of California's El Congreso began a hunger strike to support a community center for low-income families and to enlarge the Chicano Studies department. One of the strike leaders, Raquel López, twenty-one, said, "This is just part of a larger picture of how people of color are treated in institutions across the nation." The strike ended on May 6, with the administration committing to a doctoral program and to double the faculty assigned to the department by 1997. Frustrated in 1998, Chicana/o students took over the administration office and demanded a doctoral program. In 2003 the program was initiated.[85]

In Texas the progress was slow. José Ángel Gutiérrez, a founder of the Mexican American Youth Organization and La Raza Unida, was a political science professor at the University of Texas, Arlington. Gutiérrez had a PhD from the University of Texas, Austin, and a law degree from the University of Houston. He founded the Mexican American Studies Center at Arlington in 1994. In 1996 Arlington President Dr. Robert Witt removed Gutiérrez and, shortly afterward, the center's coordinator, Diana Flores. The usual charges of mismanagement were hurled by Witt and company. Gutiérrez, supported by the Mexican American community, filed a suit. In September an agreement was reached whereby he was reinstated and he became a special adviser to Witt, heading up a special library committee charged with purchasing library and archival materials. However, the administration violated the agreement, and in February, Gutiérrez filed a lawsuit against the University of Texas System, accusing Witt of violating the out-of-court settlement by removing him as special adviser before the appointment was supposed to end. In the summer, Texas settled the lawsuit with him, costing the university more than $100,000. While on leave, Gutiérrez was the lead attorney on *Rosalie Lopez, et al. v. Tucson Unified Schools* (1997) that successfully resulted in establishment of the Mexican American Studies program.[86]

GROWING PAINS

A reoccurring theme of this book has been that numbers have driven the growth of Chicano Studies. The rapid growth rate of Latinas/os living in the United States was dramatic during the 1970s and gained steam in following two decades, changing the Mexican American student population and its priorities in higher education dramatically. The Latino population grew by 61 percent between 1970 and 1980; at the same time, the Mexican American population nearly doubled. From 1990 to 2004 the Latino population grew from 22.4 million in 1990 to 41.3 million.

Latina/o students faced obstacles similar to those they had in 1968. They were more likely to come from impoverished schools with fewer certified teachers. By this time a backlash had set in to the reforms of the early 1970s. There was a shift from knowing the child to academic performance. Teaching aptitude and competency to colleges of education increasingly meant grade point averages of the teacher training candidates. No longer was it requisite for teachers to know about the culture and history of the students they taught, as if learning occurred in a vacuum.

Meanwhile, the dropout rate that had originally motivated the drive for Chicano Studies spun out of control, and 21 percent of Latinas/os between the ages of sixteen and twenty-four, dropped out of school in 2000, compared to 7 percent of white students and 12 percent of blacks. The Latino graduation rate was 53 percent, well below the national average of 68 percent. Within this context, the dropout rates for immigrant students were influenced by country of origin, age at time of immigration, and whether they were from first-, second-, or third-generation immigrant families.

These growing pains overwhelmed the Chicana/o scholars in academe. During this period, the differences between Mexican Americans at teaching and research institutions widened. It was natural that Chicana/o scholars trained during the 1970s would aspire to teach in research institutions where, for the most part, they taught in traditional departments. The Chicano Studies departments that were established at research institutions are a credit to student activism. Programs were under siege, and many were consolidated or eliminated. During my suit against the University of California, Santa Barbara, white reviewers said openly that I would be better controlled in a mainstream department than in an inchoate Chicano Studies department. In most cases, this is what happened to Chicana/o scholars.[87]

Epilogue

In the March 2010 issue of *Hispanic Business*, "The Supplier Diversity Squeeze: How the Downturn Affects Minority Contracts" reported that the amount of money spent on minority women-owned contractors shrank in 2009, to $30 million from $45 million the year before. According to the article, the reason was that "when corporations are looking for places to cut, they look around for areas not generating revenue, and one of those places is sometimes supplier diversity."[1] A similar process plays out in academe: during the budget crises of the early 1980s and in 2008, white administrators and faculty bodies cut programs they deemed nonessential. They slash their budgets of Ethnic Studies programs by consolidating or eliminating them. Apparently, unlike the banks, Latinas/os are not too large to fail.

THE LIFE LINE OF CHICANA/O STUDIES

Chicana/o Studies has survived because of the sacrifices of Chicana/o and Latina/o students, not because of the vision of the academy. The growth of Chicana/o Studies has been dependent on a large activist base that has been fragmented by the downturn in the economy, increases in tuition and living costs, and the lack of a leftist media to document the activism of students. While MEChA and its clones continue to play a key role in the development of Chicana/o Studies, not much is known about these contributions because of a lack of media attention.

Having the advantage of hindsight, I remember the difference between then and now. Weekly MEChA meetings at Valley State in 1969 drew 100–150 students in Engineering 100. It was a time when we had less than 300 Chicana/o students. Today many MEChA meetings are down to a couple of dozen students organized by idealistic peers who still believe in Chicana/o Studies. One of the causes for this decline is the incessant lies spread by the right wing, which portray supporters of Chicana/o Studies as terrorists who want to take back the Southwest.

For example, right wing organizations point to the MEChA logo that reads, "*Por La Raza todo. Fuera de La Raza nada*" (Everything for the people. Everything outside the people, nothing). Distortions of the meaning of *por la raza* shows that critics know nothing about Mexican culture and even less about the Spanish language. The term *la raza* is often mistakenly translated into English as "the race." Like many other words, *la raza* cannot be literally translated. A much closer translation is "the people." *La raza* is much the like the word *paisano*, which when I was a kid referred to your countryman. *Paisana* would mean countrywoman. The MEChA logo merely affirms the organization's purpose to improve the lot of the Mexican people in the United States and to rid society of racism and inequality. Aside from being a bad translation, the mistranslation is mendacious, and it is not a standard that is applied to Jews, Catholics, or any other group in this country.

It is important not to base assumptions on limited experiences or evidence, which is something even Chicana/o scholars do. I have heard Chicano professors accuse MEChA of being too nationalistic, as if they were progressive. This wrong-headedness has become a source of misinformation, and it weakens the mainstay of Chicana/o Studies. Putting things into perspective: when labor and teacher organizations want support on campuses, MEChA is generally the first group they contact. When Chicano and Latina/o professors have problems with the administration, they run to these student organizations for support. The problem is that in recent years there has been very little room for corrections because of a lack information.

Absent is a national press covering these events. In the 1970s the reporting of the left press filled this void. Today, there is no left media covering the daily work of student groups. In order to form a time line of the activities of MEChA, we have randomly selected articles in the Socialist Workers Party publication the *Militant*, which is one of the few leftist presses with a national readership. The *Militant*'s coverage represents the opposition to the American Patrol—a far right Web site. Because the *Militant* is one of the few newspapers chronicling the Latino communities, its coverage is very important.

The following articles in the *Militant* during 1996 include "Tear Down Clinton's Wall!," "Thousands Protest at GOP Convention," "200 Defend Abortion Clinic," "March to Border for Immigrant Rights," and "Chicano Youth Lead Protests." In each of these events, Chicana/o youth were active. MEChA was singled out by the articles.[2] On April 22 of that 1996, the *Militant* reported on a MEChA conference: "In the Río Grande Valley, Texas more than 200 activists who had gathered for a national conference of the Chicano student group MEChA discussed how to fight anti-immigrant attacks."[3] On July 1, the publication reported on immigration raids in the Yakima Valley: "three members of the Chicano student group MEChA met [Laura] Garza for dinner and discussed their recent victory at Yakima Valley Community College, where the administration agreed to a Chicano Studies department. Student Sara Carrion was helping organize for the national immigrant rights march in Washington, D.C., on October 12."[4]

On the August 5, the newspaper reported on an affirmative action march. Patrick Sánchez-Powell, a student at Delta College in Stockton and president of MEChA, was a main organizer for La Marcha through the Valley to Sacramento.

Sánchez-Powell said about the issue, "This proposition is anti-affirmative action. They purposely misnamed it to throw people off. I encourage people to use their ballot as a bullet on this issue." There was heavy participation of Mechistas on this march.[5] On December 16, the Center for Mexican American Studies, MEChA, Latina Coalition, Mexican American Student Organization, and the Hispanic Student Association sponsored a conference promoting the campaign against the *Hopwood* case (Affirmative Action). MEChA chapters attended from throughout Texas.[6]

In 2000, University of Arizona Chicano students rallied against the English Only Act: "On November 6 students at the University of Arizona held a hunger strike against the proposition and camped out on the campus overnight . . . to defend bilingual education. That evening about 35 people marched around campus in heavy rain." Erik Ortiz, of MEChA said, "This is not the first or last attack on minority groups, not only here in Arizona but in the United States. This is the most racist proposition I've heard of."[7] In 2001 Deborah Liatos in Oakland, California, wrote that MEChA participated in an immigration march sponsored by a multi-national coalition:

> Many signs and the speeches at the march were in English, Spanish, and Chinese. . . . Twelve students came from the Santa Clara University chapter of the MEChA. Alejandra Lizardo, 18, heard about the demonstration in her parish. "I think people that come here and work have the right and privilege to become citizens," Lizardo said. 'We're very inspired by the demonstration. We didn't know it would be this big. I think our MEChA chapter should become more political."[8]

In 2003 the *Militant* published an insightful interview with Joel Britton, a Socialist Workers Party candidate for California governor who joined the Young Socialist Alliance (YSA) in spring 1962, at the age of twenty. The interviewer asked about Chicano Nationalism and accusations that MEChA was a terrorist organization: "Members of the YSA and Socialist Workers Party took part in the Chicano youth conferences in Denver, organized by the Crusade for Justice that took place in 1969 and 1970." Britton called these accusations outrageous and spread by the scandalmongers.

> That document was a program for the mass mobilization of Chicanos for community control. MEChA is a Chicano student organization with chapters on campuses throughout the Southwest and other parts of the country. In recent years, MEChA chapters in Southern California helped organize speaking tours for Cubans to tell the truth about the Cuban Revolution. These included Carlos Tablada, the author of *Che Guevara: Economics and Politics in the Transition to Socialism*, and Cuban revolutionary youth leaders. This past summer a number of the young people who took part in the Cuba-U.S. Youth Exchange trip to Cuba were members of MEChA who traveled there to see Cuba for themselves. . . . The attacks on MEChA as a 'racist' organization are a reactionary

slander. MEChA, like other Chicano organizations, supports demands aimed at combating the oppression of the Chicano people. You can't identify the nationalism of the oppressed with the nationalism of the oppressor. I was taught this when I joined the communist movement.

This statement comes from a spokesperson for a group that has not always been in agreement with the Chicano student organization and has even been expelled from campuses.[9]

The accounts in the *Militant* contradict the ad hominem remarks of some Chicana/o scholars. Just like it cannot be said that all white people are racist, it cannot be assumed that all Mechistas are the same. Granted, the articles in the *Militant* were in part meant to win over recruits to the organization; however, they also showed the extent of the loss of the left in 1989, and how the absence of left newspapers has skewed knowledge of the movement. Isolated to individual campuses, knowledge is localized, and more and more we rely on faith based on the theory or assumptions of the sages. Unfounded opinions often allow right-wing kooks to take isolated opinions, distort them, and formulate them into anti-MEChA-Mexican diatribes.[10]

THE CHILDREN OF IRCA

Employer sanctions are a favorite tactic if Republicans, nativists, and now Democrats use them to stem undocumented immigration. The principal is to poison the water hole—that is, make it unlawful for an employer to knowingly hire or recruit illegal immigrants so that society can starve them out. Employer sanctions oblige employers to attest to their employees' immigration status. Liberals fought this proposal on humanitarian grounds but compromised, allowing for the punishment of employers in return for amnesty and a mechanism to legalize the status of undocumented immigrants who had entered the country before January 1, 1982, and had resided here continuously since that time.[11] Hence, Congress passed the Immigration Reform and Control Act of 1986 (IRCA).

An estimated 75 percent of those receiving amnesty were born in Mexico. Of the estimated 3 million people receiving amnesty, 1.7 million lived in California. Legal status, according to most accounts, allowed the new green card recipients to find better employment and to discourage the rampant discrimination they suffered. The act also provided funds to teach those receiving amnesty U.S. civics, history, and English proficiency in an effort to Americanize them. IRCA allocated $1 billion a year to fund these classes, which went to public schools and organizations as Hermandad Mexicana Nacional and One-Stop Immigration. Over the next years, the number of people affected by IRCA grew. There is evidence that higher percentages of Latinas/os became citizens when eligible than previous immigrant waves.[12]

Meanwhile, U.S. policy encouraged further undocumented immigration from Mexico and Central America. The United States financed wars in Central America and pushed political refugees into the country. The economic circumstances in Mexico deteriorated as U.S. policy pushed privatization on Mexico, making billionaire Carlos Slim Helu the richest man in the world. Trade agreements such as NAFTA (the North American Free Trade Agreement) accelerated the decline of the small farm in Mexico, as well as the rush to the cities and movement *al norte.* Mexico's vaunted $37 billion trade surplus went to the creation of billionaires like Slim while accelerating the uprooting of millions of Mexicans. Finally, the U.S. market fueled the drug trade through most of Central America and Mexico, leading to civic instability and growth of drug cartels—which will have grave consequences in the future.

Latina/o students nearly doubled from 1990 to 2006. The growth accounted for 60 percent of the total growth in public school enrollment, as well as the assaults on immigrant rights, affirmative action, and bilingual education. There are approximately 10 million Latina/o students in the public schools—about one-fifth of public school students nationally.[13] This struggle hardened the children of undocumented immigrants, who took ownership of their lives. Even in the face of a well-financed and militant nativism, they fought back. In California, they took part in mass demonstrations, beginning with the anti-187 marches in 1994 that saw over 100,000 demonstrators in Los Angeles alone. They continued during the protests against Propositions 209 and 227 and their clones in other states.[14]

On April 10, 2006, millions of immigrants and their supporters took to the streets in 140 cities across the nation. Tired of being afraid, intimidated by ICE (Immigration and Customs Enforcement), and called terrorist by "minutemen," they marched. H.R. 4437 criminalized not only unauthorized immigrants but also anyone who helped them. Over a million marched in Los Angeles, 900,000 in Dallas, and upwards of 300,000 in Chicago.[15] They had no other choice but to fight back. Most of the students, while not born in the United States, were products of American schools. Most grew up hearing words such as "democracy," "equality," and "human rights." Many considered higher education a right that they had earned as a consequence of hard work, study, and good citizenship. They took the initiative and compromised their safety by fighting for the Development, Relief and Education for Alien Minors (DREAM) Act, which would give them the opportunity to contribute to society. These immigrant youth have lobbied for the bill since 2001, often traveling to state capitols and Washington, D.C., at their personal risk and cost.[16]

SORTING OUT NATIONALITY

Few Central Americans lived alongside Mexican Americans prior to the 1990s. The largest group and the fastest-growing cluster among Central Americans in the United States is the Salvadoran. In 1960, 6,310 lived in the United States; in 1970 there were 34,000; in 1980, 94,447; and in 1990, 565,081. The number grew to 823,832 in 2000. In 1991, the U.S. government settled the *American Baptist Churches (ABC) v. Thornburgh,* a class-action suit that ruled the United States practiced discriminatory treatment of asylum claims made by Guatemalans and Salvadorans. Rightfully, Guatemalans and Salvadorans in the United States before October 1, 1990, and September 19, 1990, respectively, were granted a new interview and asylum decision. Before this, Cubans and Nicaraguans had received preferred treatment because they were fleeing so-called communist governments.

In 1997 Clinton signed the Nicaraguan Adjustment and Central American Relief Act, which gave immigration benefits and relief from deportation to specific Nicaraguans, Salvadorans, and Guatemalans. It also extended these benefits to Cubans and persons from the Soviet bloc countries and their dependents. (From 1984 to 1990, 25 percent of the 48,000 Nicaraguan applicants were granted asylum. This compared with only 2.6 percent of the 45,000 claims from Salvador and 1.8 percent of the 9,500 claims from Guatemalans.) The United States was supporting the quasi-fascist Salvadoran government. By November 2004, an estimated 290,000 Salvadorans, 80,000 Hondurans, and 4,000 Nicaraguans were benefiting from temporary protected status.

The 2000 census counted just over 2 million Central Americans.[17] Salvadorans had 765,000 foreign-born students. Only Mexicans had more, with 7,841,000 students. "By 2008, there were about 1.1 million Salvadoran immigrants in the United States. Salvadorans are the country's sixth largest immigrant group after Mexican, Filipino, Indian, Chinese, and Vietnamese foreign born." Two-thirds of Salvadorans were foreign-born versus less than 40 percent of other Latinas/os; some 28 percent were U.S. citizens.[18]

By 1990 Central American students began filtering into the Chicana/o Studies classes, and this led to the inclusion of Salvadoran and Central American history. They came from families on the various sides of the civil war—pro-government, pro-FMLN (El Frente Farabundo Martí de Liberación Nacional), and neutral. By 1990 they were pressing Chicana/o Studies for their own classes. They asked why Mexican Americans had a department and they didn't. They seemed perturbed when I explained that they did not yet have a critical mass of students and that the administration was not supportive of the notion. Many Chicano activists— including myself—hesitated. We did not want to open Pandora's box. For some twenty years Chicano Studies had discussed the possibility of a Latin American Studies program. However, the stumbling block was that the Spanish Department was comprised of the most reactionary elements on campus. Elías Ramos—a Venezuelan—thought it was his fiefdom. Irresolvable ideological differences broke down talks. Ramos told a class that the most fortunate thing that had happened to the Americas was that Spain had brought its language and culture, as well as its religion, to the Indians. The Spanish department formed an alliance with the history department and helped block a progressive Latin American Studies program.

The only visible Central American professor on campus—Alberto García, a Nicaraguan and Sandinista—taught in Chicana/o Studies, and he was open to Latin American Studies. However, García was not an astute bargainer, and Spanish would have had the votes to do anything it wanted if a Latin American Studies program had been formed. Chicana/o Studies also did not want to cut organizational ties with Central American students, considering the Central American students family. The president and the provost told Chicana/o Studies in no uncertain terms that they would not approve further studies programs. Lastly, the talks with Central American students—mostly Salvadoran—were stalled by my suit against the University of California at Santa Barbara and the 1994 Northridge Earthquake.

Chicana/o Studies was aware of what had happened at East Los Angeles College. The Chicano Studies department proposed a class called "Central Americans: The New Chicanos." The Social Science department challenged the right of Chicana/o Studies to incorporate the class despite the demographic shift of Los Angeles. The tussle pitted Sybil Venegas, chair of the Chicano Studies department, and Consuelo Rey, chair of the Social Science department. Many considered the competition to be part of a personal feud, as they had competed previously within Chicano Studies. Both chairs claimed ownership of Central Americans. According to Rey, East Los Angeles College had a Latin American Studies discipline, and Central Americans belonged to it. Similar struggles were taking place throughout the country.[19]

By 1997/1998, the Central American United Student Association (CAUSA) had grown. Albert García was the faculty sponsor; he had kept the small group together since 1990. There was a new mood developing. Ramón Rivera—half Filipino and Salvadoran—was a leader of CAUSA. Siris Barrios had arrived in 1997, and the organization under Siris's leadership renewed its push for a Central American Studies Program. Siris attended what was probably the worst high school in the city—David Starr Jordan in South Central Los Angeles. She was hungry to learn and was one of the five most gifted student leaders that I have encountered. She formed a friendship with MEChA—especially with Miguel Paredes and Astrid Martínez, who were internationally minded and very progressive. In 1998 a protest took place on La Semana Salvadoreña, in which Siris took the leadership. In 1999 CAUSA sponsored a Salvadoran Youth Conference for high school students, in which María Hernández, a senior who later enrolled in a doctoral program at the University of Wisconsin, along with Siris, took the lead. By this time CAUSA was women-led organization.[20]

Siris's passion was a Central American Studies program: "I wanted to go to college . . . to help me understand what had happened in El Salvador." Barrios was a victim of the violence in that country. When Siris was five, she was hidden inside a spare tire well in a car trunk and smuggled across the United States–Mexico border to join her parents. Three years later, her mother had to return to El Salvador to obtain her U.S. residency card. Siris went with her, but she had a hard time returning—forced to live several months in El Salvador with an aunt during the height of the civil war. She experienced a frightening and embittering experience.

Meanwhile, the situation on campus was deteriorating, and CAUSA students were growing desperate. They talked about a takeover or a hunger strike. Some Chicana/o Studies faculty and students were of the mind that CAUSA students should not have to make this sacrifice and that it was the duty of Chicana/o Studies not only to support but also to facilitate the creation of a Central American Studies program. However, the battle field was strewn with landmines.

The first landmine was that Chicana/o Studies could be easily perceived as big sister, and many remembered how they felt playing second fiddle to blacks on campus. Also discussed at length was the notion that if Chicana/o Studies undertook supporting the establishment of Central American Studies, Chicana/o faculty members would have to refrain from any public criticism or interference with the decisions made by Central Americans, no matter how much they disagreed. A big advantage was that Jorge García was the dean of humanities and he could talk directly to the provost.

The biggest talking point was that it was not going to cost the university money. Universities are rarely moved by moral arguments. Chicana/o Studies was willing to kick in faculty lines—at the time it had about thirty tenured positions. The administration was not about to take positions from foreign languages or other departments that would have screamed to high heaven, which is ironic since Chicana/o Studies had carried foreign language for years. At every step of the way, Chicana/o Studies conferred with the CAUSA students, and MEChA leadership supported them. Criticism began filtering in from alumni and off-campus groups. The department was accused of giving away resources fought for and won by the community. Alberto García was appointed the interim chair, and his line was paid for by Chicana/o Studies. Secretarial support was committed to the project.

Siris remained the driving force that kept the formation of a Central American Studies minor in focus. In her words, the students had taken ownership, which meant responsibility. The Chicana/o Studies department advertised for a coordinator for Central American Studies with a tenure appointment in Chicana/o Studies. CAUSA students and members of Chicana/o Studies sat on the selection committee. The Chicana/o Studies faculty members would rubber stamp the student selection. Good candidates applied, but emotionally the students were loyal to García. His charge was to draw up a minor. After some time, the students grew disillusioned because of a lack of product. García had been a great mentor; however, he did not have the experience in drawing up course proposals or curriculum. His writing skills were marginal, and he moved slowly.

Fearing that the project was losing momentum, the department moved to employ part-timers. At the suggestion of Marta López Garza in 1999, it hired Roberto Lovato to teach a class in *barrio* studies. Marta and I had known Lovato from the solidarity movement. He was an ideal choice because he was raised in the Mission District of San Francisco; he was a *pocho* who knew racism and culture conflict and would be in touch with the youth. More important, he had strong writing skills, and he was not afraid to work. Lovato was fast moving and got frustrated with García, who seemed paralyzed. An all-out effort was made to push through curriculum. Jorge García assigned his associate dean Gregory Velazco y Trianosky, a Puerto Rican, to work with the Central American Studies curriculum committee.[21] Meanwhile, Alberto García was coming up for review, and the college and university committees were critical of his lack of publishing progress. García would have to strengthen his publication record, and Chicana/o Studies took administrative responsibility from García and told him to concentrate on getting tenure. The department would recommend him, but he would not make it past the college and university committees if he did not have several publications.

By this time, Lovato had taken charge. The only caution to him was to always remember that this was a Central American Studies program, not a Salvadoran program. The minor was the first step toward a major and a department. Lovato renewed the spirit of *si se puede* in the students. In 2000 he contracted Carlos Cordova of La Raza Studies at San Francisco State University to conduct a workshop on Central American Studies curriculum-building. The committee decided that the new Central America course of study would emphasize four themes: (1) the role of violence—personal and institutional, (2) a transnational approach connecting the circuits between the two roles of violence, (3) the relationship between technology and reality, and (4) a schematic of history culture. Lovato also recruited part-time faculty that included Hector Aquiles Magaña, Rossana Pérez, and Joaquín Chávez, who had been involved in peace accords and were experts in violence prevention.[22] Under Lovato's stewardship, Central American Studies hired Douglas Carranza Mena. A high level of enthusiasm existed among Central Americans.

CAUSA felt a surge of pride when the group pushed through the creation of a Research Institute that began in 2002–2003. Lovato and company had gone to Sacramento and gotten Antonio Villaraigosa and Tom Hayden to hold up funding for the system until the California State University system allocated the funds. (This was a political victory, but it ticked off the bureaucracy. Chicana/o Studies felt it would have been better to spend getting the minor. The members of the department did not say anything because it would have been divisive.) The inner core of students consisted of Siris Barrios, Monica Novoa, Julie Monroy, and Shirley Virgil, a Guatemalan. They were later joined by Oriel Sui. They successfully created a Central American Studies minor.

Lovato was told that it would be impossible for him to get a full-time appointment. He did not have a graduate degree. Magaña, who had become the director of the institute, could have possibly been considered because he was a doctoral student in regional and urban planning at UCLA. Meanwhile, Chicana/o Studies began to worry about what would happen to the program without faculty leadership.[23]

Beatriz Cortez, a Salvadoran and a member of the Spanish department, had gotten involved in Central American Studies. A respected scholar, she had strong academic skills; however, tension developed between her and some of the students and faculty. Meanwhile, her situation in the Spanish department worsened. The Spanish people resented her commitment to Central American Studies and made it clear to the provost that she would not get tenure. Remarks such as she was hanging around communists in Chicana/o Studies alienated the provost, who moved to protect her. Jorge García and the provost made a deal. If Chicana/o Studies agreed to take Cortez, the department would review her for tenure. The only problem was that Chicana/o Studies had to eat the position and did not get a new line. It insisted that the foreign language people be at least penalized, which never happened.[24]

Meanwhile, Lovato went on to greater things. He is a columnist with New America Media and a regular contributor to the *Nation*.[25] Siris pursued her dream and is a lead community organizer for the Community Coalition in South Central Los Angeles. Cortez is currently the coordinator of the interdisciplinary program, which has four tenure track positions on its way to eventual departmental status. In February 2007, the program was granted a bachelor of arts in Central American Studies, the first in the nation. It is now independent from Chicana/o Studies and has its own lines. There is no doubt that the experience taxed the department. Its tenure track allocations declined by five, and it has been unable to replace its retirees. However, everyone would have lost if Central American Studies had fallen into reactionary hands, become a puppet to the ambitions of individual Chicanas/os, or failed. Its existence proves that Central Americans care about their education and their identity.

COMPETING MODELS: CHICANA/O STUDIES IDENTITY

By the 2000s the term "Chicana/o Studies" was preferred west of Chicago. East of the windy city it was "Latina/o Studies." A dispassionate discussion of the two terms is difficult, since most people in the area have different interests and percep-tions. One of the few studies attempting to make sense of Latina/o Studies is University of Illinois at Urbana-Champaign by Professor Pedro Cabán. In "Moving from the Margins to Where?," Cabán asserts:

> Latino Studies has evolved from its insurrectionary and somewhat turbulent origins as Chicano and Puerto Rican Studies into its current incarnation as a multidisciplinary academic field that explores the diversity of localized and transnational experiences of Latin American and Caribbean national origin populations in the United States. . . . I draw a distinction between Latino Studies as a field of study and Latino Studies as an academic unit of instruction and research in the university.[26]

Cabán divides the transition of the area into the Enclave, Transgressive, and Absorption periods. Briefly, the Enclave is when Chicano, Mexican American, and Puerto Rican Studies units "operated as marginalized, underfunded programs or departments that were politically tolerated, but academically disparaged within their respective institutions," and academies were content to let them exist on the margins. "Chicano and Puerto Rican leaders realized the indispensability of these programs for retention by improving the self-image, confidence, and academic capabilities of those poor urban youth who were fortunate enough to attend college. The struggle for Chicano and Puerto Rican Studies was steeped in political urgency and would have a major impact on the advancement of their communities."

The Transgressive period gave rise to "academic ethnic studies units that have acquired a degree of intellectual authority and political standing within their respective institutions" with Latino Studies, Latin American and Latino Studies, or

Chicano and Latino Studies. . . . during the 1990s, the refusal of university administrators to consider seriously the reasonable student calls for Latino Studies provoked strikes, building takeovers, and militant activities in a number of Ivy League
colleges and prestigious research universities." According to Cabán, the role of
Latino Studies in higher education remained a commitment to democratizing the
academy "by broadening the scope of inquiry and instruction."[27]

Cabán's third period is characterized as "an effort by the university administration to redefine the academic function of Latino Studies and to manage its
incorporation into hierarchically ordered centers for research and instruction.
These are most commonly American Studies Programs and Centers for the Study
of Race and Ethnicity."[28] The 1980s and 1990s, according the Cabán, was a period
of significant academic maturation and professional development. The professionalization was aided by the Ford, Rockefeller, Compton, and Mellon Foundations
that awarded fellowships to the Tomas Rivera Policy Institute and the Julian
Samora Research Institute. It took place mainly during the mid-1980s as validating
the academic presence of Latinos and Latinas in the academy.

Cabán describes Ethnic Studies as umbrella academic units that incorporate
autonomous programs in African American, Asian American, Native American,
and Chicana/o Studies. The two Ethnic Studies programs are the College of Ethnic
Studies at San Francisco State University and the Ethnic Studies department at the
University of California, Berkeley, formed in 1969. This was the preferred model of
university and college administrators who thought along the line of killing a flock
of birds with one stone. He warns that the Ethnic Studies model is fraught with
landmines. There is internal struggle within Ethnic Studies among the groups that
battle over restricted resources and the selection of faculty—that is, which unit gets
the new hire or the replacement—often between the sociological and humanities
aspects of Ethnic Studies.

The Making of Chicana/o Studies has argued that administrators favor the
ethnic studies model because it saves them money and they can more easily manip-
ulate the disparate groups in one category. Although the failure to adopt new
Latino Studies provoked strikes at prestigious research universities during the
1990s, few new programs resulted—the notable exceptions being UCLA, Arizona
State University, University of California, and the University of Arizona departments. A partial explanation posited by this book is that the moral outrage of
students had not reached a sufficient intensity and was localized. Organizational
problems also emerged with the development of Latino professional and social
organizations that diluted political energy.[29]

According to Cabán, "Public colleges in urban settings are subjected to a particular set of instructional demands and political pressures that differ from those in
elite private universities, and consequently are, in principle, more amenable to
support ethnic and race studies programs." Which raises the question of how effective was the policy of Ford and other foundations in institutionalizing and serving
Latina/o students. At Harvard, Latina/o faculty are 2.3 percent of the faculty, up
from 1.98 percent in 1988.[30] Latina/o graduates represented 7 percent (123) of total

bachelor's degrees, and "more Latinas received doctoral degrees than did their male counterparts (13 to 10)."[31] In the meantime, urban Chicanas/os have had to do it in their own way.

Research institutions serve a small part of the Chicana/o and Puerto Rican student population. Latino populations at public state universities far outnumber those at the Ivy League schools, but not one was named in the top twenty-five schools.[32] Latino research is not the priority of teaching institutions, although many professors at teaching institutions do excellent research. A measure of this disparity is that California State University or the University of Texas at El Paso has more Latina/o students than all the twenty-five schools combined. CSUN alone has over 10,000 Latina/o students out of 33,000 students.[33] In 2000–2001, almost 10,500 teachers graduated from twenty-one California State campuses, with the system preparing about 60 percent of the teachers in the state, and about half the bachelor's degrees and a third of the master's degrees awarded annually.

Another work that deals with Latina/o and Chicana/o Studies is Michael Soldatenko's *Chicano Studies: The Genesis of a Discipline,* which is more theoretical than Cabán's essay. It concentrates on mass education, pedagogy, and the use of Chicana/o Studies as a vehicle for power within the institution. It has no illusion, or delusion, that it is possible to create a Chicana/o utopia within this capitalist institution. Chicana/o Studies are a tool to teach Chicanas/os skills and mold their perspectives and commitments so they can make intelligent choices. A subtle difference exists between the course of study comprising the area and individual disciplines.

Soldatenko's review of the literature is the most comprehensive treatment to date. Like Cabán, Soldatenko divides Chicano Studies into categories—the Perspectivist and Empiricist visions. According to Soldatenko, the Perspectivist Chicano Studies became peripheral and fragmented in its intellectual agenda during the 1970s and 1980s. Empirical Chicano Studies settled into the prestigious institutions, and its works became the canon of Chicana/o Studies. In this view, Perspectivist writers were progressively pushed toward peripheral journals or self-publication. The Empiricists, in their pursuit of hegemony, disciplined the field, and they portrayed the Perspectivist approach as "a quaint romantic vision," irrational and apolitical. Soldatenko ties the intellectual origins of Chicano cultural nationalism and Chicanismo to the Perspectivists. One bridge was University of California, Berkeley, anthropologist Octavio Romano, who exemplified the Perspectivist epistemology in contrast to social science empiricism.[34]

According to Soldatenko, El Plan de Santa Barbara called for action—the academy was to be used as a weapon to emancipate the Chicano community. The goal was to control programs and achieve a relative autonomy in academe.[35] Many activists developed a perspective that was concerned with the direction of Chicana/o Studies and how it would differ from the mainstream. (The weakness with this argument is that the actual writings at the time came from a small group that was limited to research institutions. The contributors were mostly graduate students. For example, the 1970 Stanford summer program did not make an effort to include most state and junior colleges. Other conferences, such as at California State College, Long Beach, received heavy funding from the U.S. Department of Education. And even these conferences were invitation only.)

Chicanismo evolved as a philosophy, according to Soldatenko. Quoting Eliu Carranza, who supposedly developed the philosophic framework for Chicano perspectivism, Carranza espouses a return to Chicanos' heritage and values: "The Mexican American has had to return to his own, his parent's, his grandparent's values. This is what has made the *movimiento* a reality."[36] Chicanismo was the start of a cultural revolution, and Carranza supposedly declared war on empiricism, defending the uniqueness of Chicana/o Studies. By the early seventies, according to Soldatenko, few Chicano academics questioned the emerging empiricism. Alternative visions emerged, including Western Marxism, that changed the project. The Empiricist Chicana/o Studies emerged as simply being more palatable to academe. Soldatenko writes, "empiric scholars, who molded Empirical Chicano Studies . . . visualized these programs as part of the overall political struggle for Chicano self-determination."[37] They achieved hegemony "by exorcising all possible competitors and critics."[38] Their success in professionalizing Chicana/o Studies resulted in its institutionalization. Soldatenko claims that the first expression of empiricism was the Plan of Santa Barbara. "El Plan . . . suggested an articulation of a Chicano intellectual academic project."[39]

The Probable Future of Chicana/o Studies

The Making of Chicana/o Studies argued in the opening chapter that Chicana/o Studies is expected to grow because of the increasing size of the Chicana/o population in the United States. According to Kathy Matheson, in "Prestigious Colleges using Spanish to Attract Latinos," "Some venerable East Coast universities are trying to ease that burden—and tap the booming pool of Hispanic students—by offering Spanish translations of their admissions and financial aid material."[40] Matheson points out that between 1995 and 2005 Latino college enrollment increased 66 percent. In order to attract Latina/o students, some universities were even recruiting in Spanish.

Yet society and academe seem to have learned little from history—Hispanics are still waiting for the Decade of the Hispanic. Universities and colleges across the country have not addressed the grievances that caused the campus disruptions of the 1960s. California institutions of higher learning have returned to the shell game of counting Mexican Americans and Latinas/os on whether their names end in vowels. They purposely confuse the terms "Latino" and "Hispanic" and widen their definitions. At CSUN, Penny Jennings, the associate vice president of faculty affairs, tells anyone who will listen that the university has made dramatic strides in hiring "minority" faculty members. The demographic count includes Hindi, Eastern Europeans, and the like, while more than 75 percent of the departments do not have a single professor of Mexican origin. The informal inventory of Latino programs found that a county in Texas had only one institution that employed a single faculty member of Mexican extraction, and many two-year schools did not have a single Mexican American course.

After California, Texas is the largest recipient of Mexican Americans in the United States. Texas differs from California in that the principal organizational base for research and teaching Mexican American Studies is the center. Fortunately, these centers have maintained good relations with Mexican American legislators. The Mexican American Legislative Caucus in 2008 comprised 43 members of the 150 Texas House of Representatives. MALC members vote as a bloc on consequential matters for Latinas/os. Voting in a bloc they control the 74-member Democratic Caucus and are also influential in Texas politics because Latinas/os are a force in statewide and local elections where Republican representatives do not want to offend them.

Texas public colleges and universities were established by legislative mandates that were accompanied by funding. Tatcho Mindiola at the University of Houston, David Montejano at the University of Texas, Austin, and José Ángel Gutiérrez at the University of Texas, Arlington, went to the Mexican American and Hispanic Legislative caucuses and received extra funding because the legislature included them as separate line items on the budgets of their universities.[41] In 2003 state Representative Roberto Alonzo, according to his Web site, succeeded in

> passing legislation that directs all junior college governing boards in the state to determine the need for and demand a program and/or course work in Mexican-American Studies. Working closely with Rep. Fred Hill of Richardson, as well as with officials and students from Richland College, a branch of the Dallas County Community College District, Rep. Alonzo offered legislation which permits Richland College to become the first junior college level institution in Texas to offer such a program. With such a thriving Hispanic community in the Dallas metroplex area and in Texas, Representative Alonzo made it a priority to ensure that educational opportunities exist for all students to be able to study the history and culture of this vital ethnic group in the state.[42]

This type of legislation has not been popular with university and college administrators, who resent what they call political interference.

In 1993 the Texas legislature introduced the Common Course Numbering System for community colleges. Four years later, Senate Bill 148 adopted several lower-division field of study curricula, among which is Mexican American Studies, that meet the requirement of the associate of arts in teaching (AAT) degree for thirty-nine community college districts. The Coordinating Board also approved over fifty field of study curricula in areas such as Mexican American Studies. Although the community colleges are still not meeting the mandates, there is mounting pressure from the legislature that will grow as the numbers of Latinas/os increase in the legislature.[43] Going directly to the legislature has in rare instances been employed in California, much to the chagrin of university officials who want to control the programs.

The greatest threat to Chicana/o Studies is the current attack on two-year colleges. They are the lifeline of Chicana/o education, but an area where very little attention has been paid. In all probability, the numbers taking Chicana/o Studies courses at the community college will grow based on the fact that the numbers of Latina/o students are so overwhelming, and they are close to home and more affordable. There are also programs such as the Chicana/o Studies department at Los Angeles Mission College that increase retention of Latina/o students. However, as mentioned, Chicana/o participation in community colleges is low in terms of instructors.

There is little doubt that the present economic crisis has rocked California as well as other states. This has shaken the optimism that many expressed before the 1990s. For instance, in 1995 Orcilia Zuniga-Forbes, vice president for student affairs at the University of New Mexico, said that the University of New Mexico had no choice but to recruit and retain Latinas/os: "The population is located here. Thirty-eight percent of the state's population is Hispanic." Latino-oriented centers and programs helped ameliorate the alienation of Latina/o students. At Texas A&M University in Corpus Christi, Tito Guererro, provost and vice president for academic affairs, said, "Previously, we offered only upper-class programs. Now our programs have expanded to include a new first-year-student and sophomore cur-riculum and doctoral degree granting programs."[44] In this opening there was some movement toward Chicana/o and Ethnic Studies programs. In the Orange County area of California, the popularity of Chicana/o Studies spread to high schools and the University of California, Irvine, where 31 percent of the county was Latina/o. In the early 1990s, UC hunger strikes and sit-ins had won recognition for ethnic programs.[45]

During the George W. Bush years, before the crisis of 2008, the *Denver Post* reported that "ethnic-studies professors and deans nationwide are feeling that they are under a microscope as the scholarship and background of University of Colorado professor Ward Churchill are scrutinized across the country." According to Carlos Muñoz, professor emeritus at the University of California, Berkeley, "Now, all of a sudden, because of one individual professor we have to undergo this absurd process as a legitimate academic enterprise, and that is grossly unfair. . . . There are radical professors in other departments, and if they speak out there is not the same reaction." They opened attacks on relevancy studies programs.[46]

The trend toward eliminating the gains of the 1960s and a return to the American Dream of the 1950s was accelerated by the financial crisis of 2008—the worst economic disaster since the Great Depression. The Greek Chorus sounded the alarm that American society could not afford to pay for higher education—students had to bear the burden. According to the chair of the California State University, Northridge, Economic department, "artificially low fees attract some students to higher education who simply aren't suited to the academic rigors of a university. Ultimately, the presence of these lower-achieving students hurts those who are more academically inclined, as they end up in watered-down courses in which professors have to focus on bringing the low achievers along."[47]

The news media did not make the counterargument that the middle class had been assuming this weight since the 1980s, when tuition began its upward spiral. The public developed historical amnesia as to why we could not afford to neglect education. Meanwhile, during the Bush years, the country fought two wars on a credit card and refused to tax citizens for maintaining the nation's infrastructure. State legislatures failed to meet their duty to be fiscally responsible, refusing to raise taxes to pay for a sociopolitical and civil society. The crisis left the economy in shambles, and the first to be hit were the poor and the universities.

FIGHT BACK AGAINST GLOBAL CAPITALISM

For the past forty some years, Chicanas/os have fought for access to the universities and colleges, only to be told that everything is equal. However, success depends on parents' income, parents' education, school attended, and SAT and ACT scores. Latinas/os and other working-class people are getting screened out of the system. For the past forty years of Chicana/o Studies' existence, the burden has been partially lifted by programs such as EOP, Pell Grants, and, in the case of California, Cal Grants. However, this funding has become endangered by downsizing and an increase in tuition, fees, the cost of books, and the cost of living. Many students must borrow money to take the GRE (Graduate Record Examination) and other exams to enhance their scores. But even these grants and loans are under constant attack by Republicans and so-called Blue Dog Democrats.[48]

In 2008 thousands of German students took to the streets to demand smaller class sizes and more teachers. At that moment, tens of thousands of students and teachers across Europe protested the privatization of education. In Italy teachers and students protested a $10.2 billion cut in education and research funds and the elimination of 11,200 jobs, with the probability of another 13,500 to go in 2009.[49] The next year, students again took to the streets, this time protesting the "Bologna reforms" that were designed "to have a common European education system, following the Bachelor's and Master's system." They also protested the cost of tuition, which was roughly $750 per semester for Swiss students, in Germany €100–500 (about $135–$675). Swiss think tanks suggested raising it to $5,000 per semester. Students showed their discontent with privatization of education.[50]

Reminiscent of 1968, protests burst out in Potsdam, Cologne, Munich, Dresden, Tubingen, and other cities in Germany. At Freie Universitat and Humboldt University students slept in tents and sleeping bags. At least 6,000 students and community members demonstrated peacefully through the city's heart, with signs reading "Bildung Statt Banken" (education instead of banks). A nationwide education strike took place, following protests in Austria, where students and university workers demanded a stop to the privatization of education, a raise in student-aid monies, and an increase in the percentage of students accepted into master's programs.[51]

In March 2009 students at Hunter College walked out over increasing costs. When the rise in tuition was announced in November 2009 at the University of

California, Riverside, student Veronica Hernández, who grew up in East Los Angeles, said, "It took a long time for minorities to increase their numbers at the University of California. Now those numbers are going to go down." Twenty-six students were arrested at San Francisco State University as students barricaded themselves inside a building to protest budget cuts and tuition increases across the state's public university system. Similar protests took place at Michigan State University in Lansing. In Arizona, two tuition hikes within five months added $1,000 to the burden of incoming freshman. Fees and tuition were spiked 20 percent to $6,840 a year. At Chapel Hill, North Carolina, students protested a plan to raise tuition 5.2 percent for undergraduates. At the University of Wisconsin, students protested a hike in tuition, claiming corporate greed, tax breaks for the rich, and wars in the Middle East had caused a crash that students were paying for.[52] The antiglobalization movement gained steam in the United States, although the rhetoric was not as precise and sophisticated as in Europe.

Without a doubt, faculty furloughs and cuts in classes motivated faculty members and students. Further demonstrations broke out at the University of Wisconsin, Milwaukee, which turned violent. Some fifty students rushed an administration building. More than 100 campuses nationwide participated. Rallies continued at the University of Texas–Austin, the University of California, the University of Illinois–Chicago, the University of Minnesota, the University of Connecticut, the University of Maryland–College Park, the Virginia Commonwealth University in Richmond, and the University of Illinois. There were also protests in Washington State, Oregon, and Alabama.[53]

Meanwhile, in the Philippines and in Europe students protested the effects of rising tuition costs. "More than 5,000 students from York University, University of Toronto, Ryerson and George Brown College gathered at Convocation Hall before marching to Queen's Park to send the province a clear message: Drop student fees."[54]

On March 4, 2010, a National Day of Action saw tens of thousands of students, parents, and public school and university faculty members across California protesting increases in tuition and cuts in state financing.[55] Instead of raising taxes, which would have been the responsible thing to do, the state furloughed University of California and California State University faculty and staff, in effect cutting wages by 10 percent. The University of California Regents raised tuition by 32 percent. In 2000, state university students paid $1,800 a year, increasing nearly $2,600 since Schwarzenegger took office, and doubling in 2010. The state university chancellor projected enrollment limits and said the system would accept 40,000 fewer students over the next two years, a cut that fell hardest on Latinas/os, blacks, and the working class. Similar cuts were made in K–12. The first UC tuition hike raised undergraduate tuition to $8,373, and a second hike raised it to $10,302.[56]

At CSUN, over a thousand students, faculty, public school teachers, and community participated in the Day of Action. Lilia Tejeda, a psychology major, said, "[A tuition increase of] 10 percent, 30 percent, 32 percent? That is not right. What's going to happen next year?" The day began with several students gathering at tables set up by the Coalition of Students and Teachers (COST) in front of Manzanita Hall and the Oviatt Library. Students from BSU and Students for Quality Education (SQE) gathered on the fourth floor of Sierra Hall with signs reading "Stop the Cuts" and chanting "Student Power." The Asian Americans for Community and Talent (AACT) and MEChA also played prominent roles. MEChA had laid the groundwork, leading a statewide demonstration at the Chancellor's Office. The events went smoothly, and the California Faculty Association held a rally on campus.

Off campus about sixty people supported a sit-down. The LAPD, the Highway Patrol, and the CSUN Campus police poured in with over fifty squad cars. Sensing trouble, Karren Baird-Olson, associate professor of sociology and American Indian Studies, was afraid for her students and believed her presence would calm the police. "Students were sitting down blocking the intersection," Baird-Olson said. "And as an experienced activist, I could see the tension in their [police] eyes." Instead, a Los Angeles police officer hit her in the face. José Juan Gómez at that point moved to shield the professor and stepped in between the officer and Baird-Olson, taking blows that knocked him to the ground. Baird-Olson was thrown to the street, and a police officer stomped on her arm, breaking it. "I ended up on the ground and saw a big black boot coming at me," Baird-Olson said. "It was police." The next day she underwent surgery to have steel rods placed in her arm. "They shattered my humerus bone. They brutalized me. Now I have steel rods in my arm," Baird-Olson said. University President Jolene Koester released a statement saying she was "disturbed and saddened by the less responsible actions of a few." (Was she referring to the police?) Olson was disappointed with the president's statement: "We are not the bad guys. The bad guys should be held responsible."[57]

Defending Chicana/o Studies

Administrators are not afraid of faculty. Faculty are vulnerable. What they are afraid of is idealistic and organized students. The crisis awakened many students who had not yet taken to the streets. However, many more students work full time than in the 1960s, at jobs paying marginal wages. They are hanging on by a shoe-string, and some have become disillusioned and dropped out. Slowly, however, students are learning through marches and protests that education is not a luxury. It is a right. It is a lesson that they are not learning through the media, which does not centrally report on student unrest. For example, the beating of Olson-Baird, a seventy-four-year-old professor, was almost totally ignored. The entrance of faculty into the struggle has brought some moral authority. Almost universally, students are drawing the correlation between what is happening on Wall Street and what is happening in the state capitals. The overreaction of police has further enraged and politicized them.

Most of this generation has not experienced public protest and collective action. The demonstrations have put many students in solidarity with groups such as MEChA. The protests have given them a taste of student power. Meanwhile, they have no alternative to fight back. The crisis has also made sectors of the public more receptive. The American public can understand that these are not a bunch of white middle-class kids, that what they are fighting for is against another form of unemployment. Chicana/o Studies must take advantage of the situation and form a progressive alliance, push its case, defend the gains of the past forty years, and, indeed, expand.

Lastly, I would like to make the point that students are experiencing racism firsthand. In April 2010 Arizona passed SB 1070, which makes it a state misdemeanor crime for an alien to be in Arizona without carrying registration documents required by federal law. State and local law enforcement was given the power to enforce federal immigration laws. Arizona is a polarized state with many retirees and backward whites who exhibit xenophobic reactions as the state turns increasingly Latino. The simple fact is that nativist Arizonians are targeting Mexican-looking people. Recognizing that the city councils of Flagstaff and Tucson have condemned the law, the sheriff of Pima County has sternly criticized it, as have law enforcement agencies throughout the country.

The Arizona legislature has also passed HB 2281, signed by the Arizona governor, which attacks Ethnic/Raza Studies. It states "that any course, class, instruction, or material may not be primarily designed for pupils of a particular ethnic group as determined by the State Superintendent of Instruction. State aid will be withheld from any school district or charter school that does not comply." This act affects the Tucson Public Schools' highly successful La Raza Studies program and outlaws books deemed critical of the United States. Superintendent Tom Horne has singled out my book *Occupied America* as being un-American, based largely on the title. However, the title has to do with the occupation of the Americas and is not specifically referring to the United States. What Horne has not learned is that Chileans are Americans, as are Venezuelans, Central Americans, and Mexicans.

QUO VADIS: ONE MORE TIME

As of November 2010, Chicana/o Studies, or, for that matter, all Ethnic Studies programs, are under siege. In Arizona, superintendent of public instruction John Huppenthal called for the ban on La Raza Studies at the K–12 level be extended to the colleges and universities of the state. This fear-mongering strategy is being financed by the likes of Rupert Murdoch, the U.S. Chamber of Commerce, and reactionary billionaires Charles and David Koch. Other states have expressed interest in similar measures that are driven by a desire to save money for capital.

The original intent of Chicana/o Studies was to do something about the horrendous dropout rate of Latina/o students and to prepare large numbers of Mexican American students for success in higher education. However, money buys considerable influence in the cash-strapped halls of ivory, where learned scholars sell their posteriors and write position papers that are subsequently quoted by right-wing politicians and pundits churn out xenophobic and right-wing research.

The purpose is to shift the cost of higher education to the middle-class and the poor. These groups care little about inciting a race war, the dropout problem, or education.

History matters. It matters when a student reaches full potential. Chicana/o Studies has a rich fund of knowledge that should be shared with everyone. It holds the key to the dropout problem that Chicano Studies set out to stem. Xenophobia occurs where there is ignorance of others. A negative self-image occurs when we undervalue ourselves. Ignorance costs. Everyone has the right to learn. The tragedy of what has beset Chicana/o Studies, and indeed the education of the Chicana/o, is that ignorance is winning out. History has been erased, and over fifty years of research on how to teach Mexican Americans has been ignored. It is very similar to the assault on science; it is as if Nicolaus Copernicus never lived.

We must never forget the words of a thirteen-year-old Mexican American student who wrote in 1965:

> To begin with, I am a Mexican. That sentence has a scent of bitterness as it is written. I feel that if it weren't for my nationality I would accomplish more. My being a Mexican has brought about my lack of initiative. No matter what I attempt to do, my dark skin always makes me feel that I will fail.[58]

The events in Arizona have returned us to 1965.

Notes

PREFACE

1. Throughout the book the term "Chicano Studies" is used to refer to programs before 1995, when the National Association for Chicano Studies changed its name to the National Association for Chicana and Chicano Studies. After this date "Chicana/o Studies" becomes the rule. The change from the gender-neutral "Chicano" was brought about by the struggles and sacrifices of Chicana scholars and students who emphasized the partnership of women in building the area of study. The term "Chicana/o" is used throughout the text to refer to the Mexican American people and Latinas/os as a whole.

2. "Acceptance and Latino-Jewish Relations in Arizona," *Latino Perspectives*, http://latinopm.com/opinion/my-perspective/acceptance-and-latino-jewish-relations-in-arizona-781 (accessed November 15, 2010). "Horne Resigns from Board of ADL," *Jewish News of Greater Phoenix*, March 5, 2010 http://www.jewishaz.com/issues/story.mv?100305+horne (accessed November 15, 2010).

3. José Martí to Sr. Manuel Mercado, "Campamento de Dos Ríos," May 18, 1895, http://www.embacubalebanon.com/marti180595s.html (accessed June 6, 2010).

INTRODUCTION

1. Raw Story, "Poll Finds Americans Trust Fox News More Than Any Other Network," January 26, 2010, http://www.wdkp.com/health/tips/poll-finds-americans-trust-fox-news-more-than-any-other-network/8935.html (accessed November 7, 2010). One of the first authors to use the notion of "becoming" is George J. Sánchez, *Becoming Mexican American: Ethnicity, Culture, and Identity in Chicano Los Angeles, 1900–1945* (New York: Oxford University Press, 1995).

2. "Brian Bilbray, GOP Rep., Claims Clothes Identify Illegal Immigrants," *Huffington Post*, April 22, 2010, http://www.huffingtonpost.com/2010/04/22/brian-bilbray-gop-rep-cla_n_547710.html (accessed November 7, 2010).

3. "Myths and Truths: Three Main Myths About TUSD Ethnic Studies Programs," SaveEthnicStudies.Org, http://www.saveethnicstudies.org/myths_and_truths.shtml (accessed November 20, 2010).

4. "Arizona Bill Would Permit Confiscation of Books Opposed to American Values Like Capitalism," *Infoshop News*, May 5, 2010, http://news.infoshop.org/article.php?

story=20080421170146735 (accessed November 8, 2010). For discussions of SB1070 and HB2281 see http://forchicanachicanostudies.wikispaces.com/Arizona (accessed November 7, 2010). One of the charges made by Pearce and Superintendent of Public Instruction Tom Horne is that my book *Occupied America: A History of Chicanos* (New York: Longman, 2010), is unpatriotic and lies because it says that the United States invaded Mexico. A fact that most historians would concede.

5. Leo Anchondo, "Top 10 Myths about Immigration," *Center for Community Change*, http://www.communitychange.org/our-projects/firm/our-work/general-information-on-immigration/top-10-myths-about-immigration (accessed November 8, 2010).

6. Haya El Nasser, "U.S. Hispanic Population to Triple by 2050," *USA Today*, February 12, 2008. A. Francesca Jenkins, "Students: A Statistical Survey," *Hispanic Outlook in Higher Education* 19, no. 7 (January 5, 2009): 54.

7. "U.S. Hispanic Population Surpasses 45 Million, Now 15 Percent of Total," U.S. Census Bureau Press Release, May 1, 2008.

8. *CIA: The World Fact Book*, https://www.cia.gov/library/publications/the-world-fact-book/docs/profileguide.html (accessed May 5, 2010).

9. *U.S. Census Bureau, State and County Quick Facts*, http://quickfacts.census.gov/qfd/states/27000.html (accessed June 22, 2009).

10. State and County Databases, *Pew Hispanic Center*, http://pewhispanic.org/states/ (accessed May 5, 2010).

11. Richard Fry and Jeffrey S. Passel, "Latino Children: A Majority Are U.S.-Born Offspring of Immigrants," *Pew Hispanic Center*, May 28, 2009, http://pewhispanic.org/reports/report.php?ReportID=110. Richard Fry and Felisa Gonzales, "One-in-Five and Growing Fast: A Profile of Hispanic Public School Students," *Pew Hispanic Center*, August 26, 2008, http://pewhispanic.org/files/reports/92.pdf (accessed May 5, 2010). Richard Fry and Jeffrey S. Pasel, "Latino Children: A Majority Are U.S. Born Offspring of Immigrants," *Pew Hispanic Center*, May 28, 2009, i, http://pewhispanic.org/files/reports/110.pdf (accessed May 6, 2010).

12. Latino identity is used in most statistical studies. The two largest Latino groups with the longest history in the United States are the Puerto Ricans and Mexicans. Clara Rodríguez, *Changing Race: Latinos, the Census, and the History of Ethnicity in the United States* (New York, New York University Press, 2000). Roland Chilton and Gordon F. Sutton, "Classification by Race and Spanish Origin in the 1980 Census and Its Impact on White and Nonwhite Rates," *American Statistician* 40, no. 3 (August 1986): 197–201. Generational differences between the disparate Latino groups also affect their identity as well as the proportion of study devoted to their country of origin versus their stay in the United States. "Survey Brief: Generational Differences," March 2004, Pew Hispanic Institute, http://pewhispanic .org/files/factsheets/13.pdf (accessed November 8, 2010)

13. Patricia Gándara, "Chicanos in Higher Education: The Politics of Self-Interest," *American Journal of Education* 95, no. 1 (November, 1986): 256–272. Thomas J. Cottle, "Run to Freedom: Chicanos and Higher Education," *Change* 4, no. 1 (February, 1972): 34–41. Shirley Achor and Aida Morales, "Chicanas Holding Doctoral Degrees: Social Reproduction and Cultural Ecological Approaches," *Anthropology and Education Quarterly* 21, no. 3 (September 1990): 269–287.

14. Amy Stuart Wells, "Hispanic Education in America: Separate and Unequal," *ERIC/CUE Digest No. 59, ERIC Clearinghouse on Urban Education* (New York: 1989), 1. Ralph Guzmán, "The Gentle Revolutionaries," *Los Angeles Times*, January 26, 1969, W9.

15. Teresa Watanabe and Hector Becerra, "Native-born Californians Regain Majority Status," *Los Angeles Times*, April 1, 2010, 1.

16. Proquest, Dissertations, and Theses, California State University, Northridge, Electronic Data Base (database accessible through college libraries).

17. A groundbreaker, one of the first scholarly journals in Mexican American Studies was Octavio Ignacio Romano-V, ed., *Voices: Readings from El Grito, a Journal of Contemporary Mexican American Thought* (Berkeley, CA: Quinto Sol Publications, 1968). Carlos Cortés, ed., *The Mexican American* (New York: Arno Press, 1974); Carlos Cortés, *The Chicano Heritage* (New York: Arno Press, 1976). Arno Press reprinted almost ninety volumes of books showing that there was material—white scholars had just not read them.

18. Ronald E. López, Arturo Madrid, Reynaldo Flores Macias, *Chicanos in Higher Education: Status and Issues* (Los Angeles: Chicano Studies Center Publications, University of California, 1976), 132.

19. López, Madrid, Macias, *Chicanos in Higher Education*, 142. One of the major fights that we had at San Fernando Valley State was for administration to define what a Spanish-surnamed person was. With faculty, they counted spouses of Mexican Americans, Italians, Portuguese, etc. When they narrowed the definition to Mexican Americans, the actual number was cut in half. The statistics are skewed because there was no precise standard. The number was based on Spanish surname, which often meant the name ending in a vowel.

20. López, Madrid, Macias, *Chicanos in Higher Education*, 149.

21. "Students of Color Make Dramatic Gains in College Enrollment but Still Trail Whites in the Rate at Which They Attend College," *American Council on Education* (October 30, 2006), http://www.acenet.edu/AM/PrinterTemplate.cfm?Section=Home&TEMPLATE=/CM/ContentDisplay.cfm&CONTENTID=18734 (accessed May 6, 2010). Richard Fry, "Latinos in Higher Education: Many Enroll, Too Few Graduate," *Pew Hispanic Center Report* (September 5, 2002), http://pewhispanic.org/files/reports/11.pdf (accessed May 6, 2010). López, Madrid, Macias, *Chicanos in Higher Education*, 69. Angelina Kewal Ramani, Lauren Gilbertson, Mary Ann Fox, and Stephen Provasnik, "Postsecondary Participation: Status and Trends in the Education of Racial and Ethnic Minorities," *National Center for Education Statistics* 30, no. 1 (Fall 2007): 28.

22. "Survey of Earned Doctorates. Fact Sheet," *National Science Foundation* (2007): 4, http://www.norc.org/NR/rdonlyres/B40E56EC-9A4F-4892-B871-E330BB689CD9/0/SEDFactSheet.pdf (accessed May 6, 2010). The 2007 survey round includes data on U.S. doctorate recipients who graduated between July 1, 2006, to June 30, 2007. "Vanishing Minority Historians," *Ph.D. in History*, http://phdinhistory.org/wordpress/?p=226 (accessed May 6, 2009; now inactive), post for April 28, 2008. At California State University, Northridge, the history department has no professors of Mexican origin. Three-quarters of the departments do not have a single Mexican American professor.

23. "Students Storm UCLA Building to Protest Expected UC System Fee Increase," *Los Angeles Times*, November 19, 2009.

24. "The Latino Electorate," Pew Hispanic Center/Kaiser Family Foundation National Survey of Latinos, October 3, 2002, 4, 8, 9, http://pewhispanic.org/reports/report.php?ReportID=12 (June 4, 2009). Tom Corfman, "Voting Rights Act Arms Latinos for Congressional Remap Fight," *Chicago Reporter*, May 1991, http://www.chicagoreporter.com/search/index.php?author=Tom+Corfman&criteria=all&pagename=2 (June 4, 2009).

25. "Students Storm UCLA Building to Protest Expected UC System Fee Increase," *Los Angeles Times*, November 19, 2009. "The Latino Vote in the 2010 Elections," Pew Hispanic Center, November 3, 2010, http://pewresearch.org/pubs/1790/2010-midterm-elections-exit-poll-hispanic-vote (accessed November 20, 2010). "In California's gubernatorial race, Democrat Jerry Brown won 63% of California's Latino vote while Republican Meg Whitman won 34%. In Nevada, Latinos supported Democrat Harry Reid over Republican Sharron

Angle by a greater than two-to-one margin—69% vs. 27%. Latino voters in Arizona, Nevada and Texas similarly supported Democratic candidates over Republican candidates in Senate and gubernatorial races." Much of the Latino vote was solidified by the anti-immigrant hysteria in Arizona and Nevada.

26. Office of Civil Rights, *Racial and Ethnic Enrollment Data from Institutions of Higher Education* (Washington, DC: Government Printing Office, 1972), 30. U.S. Department of Heath, Education, and Welfare, OCR-74–12, 1974, 79–80, in López, Madrid, Flores Macias, *Chicanos in Higher Education*, 63–64, 67–68.

27. López, Madrid, Flores Macias, *Chicanos in Higher Education*, 49, 50. Office of Civil Rights, *Racial and Ethnic Enrollment Data*. U.S. Department of Heath, Education, and Welfare, OCR-74–12, 1974, 79–80, 14–79, in López, Madrid, Flores Macias, *Chicanos in Higher Education*, 49, 50.

28. Israel Cuéllar, "Traditional Migrant Streams in the U.S.," in "Witness the Yakima Valley in Washington: Mexican-origin Migration in the U.S. and Mental Health Consequences," *Julian Samora Research Institute*, Occasional Paper No. 40 (May 2002), http://www.jsri.msu.edu/RandS/research/ops/oc40.html (accessed May 6, 2010).

29. Sarita E. Brown, Deborah Santiago, and Estela López, "Latinos in Higher Education: Today and Tomorrow," *Change: The Magazine of Higher Learning* (March/April 2003): 15–16, http://people.cs.vt.edu/~depthead/Diversity/Readings/LatinosInHigherEducation.pdf (accessed May 6, 2010). "*HACU Member Hispanic-Serving Institutions (HSIs),*" http://www.hacu.net/assnfe/CompanyDirectory.asp?STYLE=2&COMPANY_TYPE=1,5 (accessed May 6, 2010).

30. Sarita E. Brown, Deborah Santiago, and Estela López, Brown, "Latinos in Higher Education: Today and Tomorrow," *Change: The Magazine of Higher Learning* (March/April 2003): 1. http://people.cs.vt.edu/~depthead/Diversity/Readings/LatinosInHigherEducation.pdf (accessed May 7, 2010).

31. *Brown v. Board of Education of Topeka*, 347 U.S. 483 (1954).

32. Matthew Bigg, "U.S. School Segregation on the Rise: Report," *Reuters*, January 14, 2009.

33. Patricia C. Gándara and Frances Contreras, *The Latino Education Crisis: The Consequences of Failed Social Policies* (Cambridge, MA: Harvard University Press, 2009). Watson Scott Swail, Alberto F. Cabrera, Chul Lee, Adriane Williams, "Pathways to the Bachelor's Degree for Latino Students," *Latino Educational Policy Institute and the Educational Pipeline a Three-Part Series: Lumina Foundation for Education*, Educational Policy Institute, pt. 3, p. 9. http://www.educationalpolicy.org.

34. Michael Stafford, "Ghosts of Proposition 187: Why Embracing Arizona's Immigration Panic May Sink the GOP," *Delaware Tomorrow: A New Perspective on Policy and Politics*, April 28, 2010, http://www.delawaretomorrow.com/ghosts-of-proposition-187-why-embracing-arizonas-immigration-panic-may-sink-the-gop/ (accessed May 9, 2010).

35. "The State of Hate: Escalating Hate Violence against Immigrants," *Leadership Conference on Civil Rights*, http://www.civilrights.org/publications/hatecrimes/escalating-violence.html (accessed May 7, 2010).

36. Brentin Mock, "Immigration Backlash: Hate Crimes against Latinos Flourish," *Intelligence Report* (Winter 2007), http://www.splcenter.org/get-informed/intelligence-report/browse-all-issues/2007/winter/immigration-backlash (accessed May 7, 2010).

37. Sean D. Hamill, "Mexican's Death Bares a Town's Ethnic Tension," *New York Times*, August 5, 2008, http://www.nytimes.com/2008/08/05/us/05attack.html?_r=1 (accessed May 7, 2010).

38. John Ross, "The Big Scam: 'How and Why Washington Hooked Mexico on the Drug Trade,'" *Counter Punch*, April 28, 2010. Jorge Castañeda, "Mexico's War on Drugs Is a

Disaster," *Christian Science Monitor*, March 25, 2010. "Only the U.S. Can Win War on Drugs," *Dallas News*, February 24, 2009.

39. Rodolfo F. Acuña, "The Ox Bow Incident," *Reader Supported News*, May 1, 2010, http://readersupportednews.org/opinion/124-124/1629-the-ox-bow-incident (accessed May 7, 2010).

CHAPTER 1 — BECOMING CHICANA/O STUDIES

1. "Genetic Makeup of Hispanic Latino Americans Influenced by Native American, European and African-American Ancestries," *Science Daily* (May 31, 2010), http://www.sciencedaily.com/releases/2010/05/100503161421.htm (accessed June 1, 2010). George J. Sánchez, *Becoming Mexican American: Ethnicity, Culture, and Identity in Chicano Los Angeles, 1900–1945* (New York: Oxford University Press, 1995).

2. Robert McCaa, "The Peopling of Mexico from Origins to Revolution," in *The Population History of North America*, ed. Michael R. Haines and Richard H. Steckel (New York: University of Cambridge Press, 2000), 252–256, 263. 277. Gonzalo Aguirre Beltrán, *La Población Negra de México* (Mexico City: Fondo de Cultura Económica, 1972), 237. Austín Cue Cánovas, *Historia social y económica de México (1521–1854)* (Mexico City: Editorial Trillas, 1972), 134.

3. Ellen Yvonne Simms, "Miscegenation and Racism: Afro-Mexicans in Colonial New Spain," *Journal of Pan African Studies* 1.2, no. 3 (March 2008): 233.

4. Rodolfo F. Acuña, *Corridors of Migration: The Odyssey of Mexican Laborers, 1600–1933* (Tucson: University of Arizona Press, 2007), 25–27.

5. Identity and the theme of racism was expressed by the Apostle of Cuban Independence, who lived for many years in the United States and, confronted with racism, grew very bitter. José Martí, "'My Race,' April 16, 1893," *José Martí: Selected Writings*, ed. and trans. Esther Allen (New York: Viking Penguin, 2002), 318–321. "Letter from José Martí to Manuel Mercado, May 18, 1895," *Selected Writings*, 346–349. Disillusioned he wrote of the United States, "I lived in the monster, and I know its entrails."

6. For an excellent discussion of the power of place, see Dolores Hayden, *The Power of Place: Urban Landscapes as Public History* (Cambridge: MIT Press, 1997).

7. Gonzales uses the spelling "Texano" instead of "Tejano." The *x* is the Mexican spelling that sets Mexicans apart from Spaniards. It is "México" in Mexico and "Méjico" in Spain. Trinidad Gonzales, "The World of Mexico Texanos, Mexicanos and Mexico Americanos: Transnational and National Identities in the Lower Rio Grande Valley during the Last Phase of United States Colonization, 1900 to 1930" (PhD diss., University of Houston, 2008), v, 1–6. Gonzales cites o. Douglas Weeks, "The Texas-Mexican and the Politics of South Texas," *American Political Science Review* 24, no. 3 (August 1930): 606–627. Jovita González, "America Invades the Border Towns," in *Southwest Review* 15, no. 14 (Summer 1930): 469–477. Américo Paredes, *George Washington Gómez: A Mexicotexan Novel* (Houston: Arte Público Press, 1990), as works indicative of the México Texano identity. Note again that Gonzales spells "Texano" with an *x* rather than a *j*. The use of the *x* further distinguishes the identity.

8. *CIA–The World Factbook*, https://www.cia.gov/library/publications/the-world-factbook/ (accessed May 19, 2010).

9. Anthony DePalma, "Income Gap in Mexico Grows, and So Do Protests," *New York Times*, July 20, 1996.

10. Robert B. Kent and Maura E. Huntz, "Spanish-Language Newspapers in the United States," *Geographical Review* 86, no. 3, Latin American Geography (July 1996): 446–449.

Traveling by land through Mexico from Central America is exceedingly dangerous given the wars of the drug cartels.

11. Edward Lee Walraven, "Ambivalent Americans: Selected Spanish-Language Newspapers' Response to Anglo Domination in Texas, 1830–1910" (PhD diss., Texas A&M University, 1999), iii, 150–151, 165. Nicolas Kanellos, "A Historical Perspective on the Development of an Ethnic Minority Consciousness in the Spanish-Language Press of the Southwest," *Ethnic Studies Review* 21 (April 30, 1998): 27.

12. Robert B. Kent and Maura E. Huntz, "Spanish-Language Newspapers in the United States," *Geographical Review* 86, no. 3 (July 1996): 446–449.

13. Kent and Huntz, "Spanish-Language Newspapers," 450, 454. Gonzales, "World of Mexico Texanos, Mexicanos and Mexico Americanos," 11.

14. Raquel R. Márquez, Louis Méndoza, Steve Blanchard, "Neighborhood Formation on the West Side of San Antonio, Texas," *Latino Studies* 5, no. 3 (Autumn 2007): 288.

15. Christopher A. Airriess, *Contemporary Ethnic Geographies in America* (Lanham, MD: Rowman & Littlefield, 2006), 187.

16. "Compulsory Education," *New York Times*, February 28, 1872, 4.

17. "Redlands," *Los Angeles Times*, September 6, 1903, 10. "State School Law," *Los Angeles Times*, May 14, 1904, 12. "Lax Parents to Be Prosecuted," *Los Angeles Times*, September 6, 1908, V18.

18. "Political Tips," *Los Angeles Times*, March 16, 1913.

19. The article based on a report of Leonard P. Ayres, the Russell Sage Foundation. "Washington Leads All States in Free Education," *New York Times*, January 5, 1913. Raymond E. Callahan, *Education and the Cult of Efficiency* (Chicago: University of Chicago Press, 1964), 165–167. Foundations, William J. Breen, "Statistics, and State-Building: Leonard P. Ayres, the Russell Sage Foundation, and U.S. Government Statistics in the First World War," *Business History Review* 68, no. 4 (Winter 1994): 454. "The Russell Sage Foundation was one of the oldest general-purpose foundations: it was established in 1907 with an endowment of $10 million. For the first forty years it was oriented toward the development of social research and social welfare policy."

20. Guadalupe San Miguel Jr., "Culture and Education in the American Southwest: Towards an Explanation of Chicano School Attendance, 1850–1940," *Journal of American Ethnic History* 7, no. 2 (Spring 1988): 5.

21. Ibid.

22. Mark Wild, "So Many Children at Once and So Many Kinds: Schools and Ethno-racial Boundaries in Early Twentieth-Century Los Angeles," *Western Historical Quarterly* 33, no. 4 (Winter 2002): 456.

23. Ibid., 457, 458.

24. Ibid., 462, 463.

25. Dianna Everett, "The Public School Debate in New Mexico: 1850–1891," *Arizona and the West* 26, no. 2 (Summer 1984): 107.

26. Ibid., 107.

27. Ibid., 109–110.

28. San Miguel, "Culture and Education in the American Southwest," 6.

29. Allen Pace Nilsen, ed., *Dust in Our Desks: Territory Days to the Present in Arizona Schools* (Tempe: Arizona State University, College of Education, 1985), 2, 4. Elise DuBord, "Mexican Elites and Language Policy in Tucson's First Public Schools," *Divergencias: Revistas de estudios lingüisticos y literarios* 1 (October 2003): 5, http://www.coh.arizona.edu/divergencias/archives/fa112003/Mexican%20Elites.pdf (accessed May 10, 2010).

30. "Spanish in Our Public Schools," *La Sonora*, November 30, 1879.

31. Allen H. Rogers, "Character and Habits of the Mexican Miner," *Engineering and Mining Journal* 85, no. 14 (April 4, 1908): 700–701. Linda Gordon, *The Great Arizona Orphans Abduction* (Cambridge, MA: Harvard University Press, 1999), 177–179, 187, 194, 198. "Arizona House Good to Schools," *Los Angeles Times*, February 17, 1917, I4. The segregation of Mexicans up to this point was more de facto than de jure. Blacks were legally segregated. Mary Melcher, "This Is Not Right: Rural Arizona Women Challenge Segregation and Ethnic Division, 1925–1950," *Frontiers: A Journal of Women Studies* 20, no. 2 (1999): 190–215.

32. "The Popes," *New York Times*, March 21, 1874. Frank J. Coppa, "Pio Nono and the Jews: From 'Reform' to 'Reaction,' 1846–1878," *Catholic Historical Review* 89, (October 2003): 671–695. "The Popes," *New York Times*, March 21, 1874.

33. Jean A. Meyer, *The Cristero Rebellion: The Mexican People between Church and State 1926–1929* (New York: Cambridge University Press 2010).

34. See Everett, "The Public School Debate in New Mexico," 107–126. The early bishops during the American Period were French. Jean-Baptiste Salpointe, the Reverend P. Bourgade, and others were French and conservative.

35. "The Condition of Spain—The Republican Element," *New York Times*, March 28, 1854. "Debate in the Cortes on the Spanish Monarchy," *New York Times*, June 8, 1870. "Affairs of Spain," *New York Times*, June 11, 1870. Rodolfo F. Acuña, *Corridors of Migration: The Odyssey of Mexican Laborers, 1600–1933* (Tucson: University of Arizona Press, 2007), 184–192.

36. William G. Carr, "The Spanish Revolution," chap. 12, "Pawns in the Game" http://www.biblebelievers.org.au/pawns1.htm (accessed May 10, 2010). The *New York Times* has excellent coverage of the struggle over church control of the state.

37. Peter Anderson, "Why Did the Spanish Civil War Start in July 1936?" *History Review* 48 (March 2004): 36–41. "Martial Law in Madrid: General Weyler, as Captain General, Proclaims It. He May Be Contemplating a Coup d'État—Disturbances in the Provinces Continue," *New York Times*, February 15, 1901.

38. See Everett, "The Public School Debate in New Mexico," 107–126. The early bishops during the American Period were vehemently intent on keeping their privileges among Mexicans.

39. Deborah J. Baldwin, *Protestants and the Mexican Revolution: Missionaries, Ministers, and Social Change* (Urbana: University of Illinois Press, 1990). Mark Tollie Banker, "They Made Haste Slowly: Presbyterian Mission Schools and Southwestern Pluralism, 1870–1920" (PhD diss., University of New Mexico, 1987). Monica Irene Orozco, "Protestant Missionaries, Mexican Liberals, Nationalism and the Issue of Cultural Incorporation of Indigenous Peoples in Mexico, 1870—1900" (PhD diss., University of California, Santa Barbara, 1999). James W. Dow, "The Expansion of Protestantism in Mexico: An Anthropological View," *Anthropological Quarterly* 78, no. 4 (Autumn 2005): 827–851.

40. Carlos Kevin Blanton, *The Strange Career of Bilingual Education in Texas, 1836–1981* (College Station: Texas A&M University Press, 2007), 24–30. Some of the privileges of the Church were returned during the regime of Porfirio Díaz. See Acuña, *Corridors of Migration*, 184–188.

41. Michael Werner, *Concise Encyclopedia of Mexico* (New York: Routledge, 2001), 652–653, 654.

42. Marilyn Cochran-Smith, Sharon Feiman-Nemser, D. John McIntyre, eds., *Handbook of Research on Teacher Education: Enduring Questions in Changing Contexts*, 3rd ed. (New York: Routledge, 2008), 428.

43. Ernestine M. Alvarado, "A Plea for Mutual Understanding between Mexican Immigrants and Native Americans," in Proceedings annual session of the National Conference of Social Work, Chicago, 1920, 264–266. In Rodolfo F. Acuña and Guadalupe Compeán, eds., *Voices of the U.S. Latino Experience*, 3 vols. (Westport: Greenwood, 2008), 476–477.

44. Merton E. Hill, *The Development of an Americanization Program* (Ontario, CA: Board of Trustees of the Chaffey Union High School and the Chaffey Junior College in cooperation with the County Board of Education of San Bernadino College, 1928), 3.

45. R. N. McLean and Charles A. Thompson, *Spanish and Mexican in Colorado* (New York: Board of National Missions, Presbyterian Church in the U.S.A., 1924), vii–x. Ernesto Galarza, "Life in the United States for Mexican People: Out of the Experience of a Mexican," *Proceedings of the National Conference of Social Work, 56th Annual Session* (Chicago: University of Chicago Press, 1929). Robert McLean and Grace Petrie Williams, *Old Spain in New America* (New York: Council of Women for Home Missions, 1916), 155–156, write that there were sixty Mexican Protestant churches in Texas, with more than a thousand in Mexico and Texas, noting that the Methodist Episcopal denomination had established the Frances Pauw industrial school for girls in Los Angeles, the Harwood Industrial School for girls in Albuquerque, another school for girls in Tucson, and a settlement house in El Paso. The crown jewel was the Spanish American Institute, which was a boardinghouse and out school for boys. Focused on vocational education, it opened in 1913, closing in 1971 due to a lack of funds and stricter immigration laws. According to McLean, these boys were a bridge between the churches in Mexico and the United States. Many of the leaders of the Mexican American movement in the 1930s and 1940s were educated at this school located in Gardena, California. The school has attracted students from as far away as South America, with benefactors such as the Maxwell family of Maxwell House Coffee. It started out as a full-time school, but because of economic reasons many academic subjects were taught at the local public school. The boys returned to the institute for their vocational training. Many were orphans or from divorced households. San Miguel, "Culture and Education," 9.

46. According to Lee Stacy, *Mexico and the United States* (Tarrytown, NY: Marshall Cavendish, 2002), 48–49, the Mexican consul in 1923 set up literacy classes for Mexican children. Five years later the Mexican Ministry of Education sent emissaries to help set up *escuelitas* whose aim it was to disprove the popular notion that Mexicans were backward peasants and did not have to be Americanized to be modern. "A History of Mexican Americans in California: Revolution to Depression: 1900–1940," *Five Views: An Ethnic Historic Site Survey for California*," National Park Service, http://www.nps.gov/history/history/online_books/5views/5views5c.htm. In the 1950s League of United Latin American Citizens (LULAC) and the American G.I. Forum sponsored a string of schools, teaching children basic English vocabulary. San Miguel, "Culture and Education," 6.

47. Early theses and dissertations can be found at the University of Southern California Library. Evangeline Hymer, "A Study of the Social Attitudes of Adult Mexican Immigrants in Los Angeles and Vicinity" (master's thesis, University of Southern California, 1923). Alice Bessie Culp, "A Case Study of 35 Mexican Families" (master's thesis, University of Southern California, 1921); William Wilson McEuen, "A Survey of the Mexicans in Los Angeles" (master's thesis, University of Southern California, 1914). Helen Walker, "The Conflict of Cultures in First Generation Mexicans in Santa Ana, California" (master's thesis, University of Southern California, 1928). Mary Lanigan, "Second Generation Mexicans in Belvedere" (master's thesis, University of Southern California, 1932).

48. Carlos Cortes, ed., *The Mexican American* (New York: Arno Press Collection, 1974); Cortes, *The Chicano Heritage* (New York: Arno Press Collection, 1976).

49. O. Douglas Weeks, "The League of United Latin–American Citizens: A Texas-Mexican Civic Organization," *Southwestern Political and Social Science Quarterly* (December 1929): 257–278.

50. Félix Díaz Almaráz, *Knight without Armor: Carlos Eduardo Castaneda, 1896–1958* (College Station: Texas A&M University Press, 1999).

51. In 1931 it published *A Course of Study for Negro High Schools and Training Schools.* Greta De Jong, *A Different Day: African American Struggles for Justice in Rural Louisiana, 1900–1970* (Raleigh: University of North Carolina Press, 2002), 50. Carlos K. Blanton, "George I. Sánchez, Ideology, and Whiteness in the Making of the Mexican American Civil Rights Movement, 1930–1960," *Journal of Southern History* (June 26, 2009), http://findarticles .com/p/articles/mi_hb6532/is_3_72/ai_n29284596/ (accessed May 11, 2010).

52. Hershel T. Manuel, "Results of a Half-Century Experiment in Teaching a Second Language," *Modern Language Journal* 36, no. 2 (February 1952): 76–77. Note the work of Victor S. Clark, who wrote two scathing reports on Mexicans and Puerto Ricans with largely the same racist stereotypes. Victor S. Clark, "Mexican Labor in the United States," *Bureau of Labor Bulletin* no. 78 (Washington, DC: Department of Commerce and Labor, 1908): 467, 472–473, 477, 480, 482, 485–486, 494–497, 501, 503. Victor S. Clark, *Porto Rico and Its Problems* (Washington, DC: Brookings Institution, 1930).

53. Alberto B. Báez, Franklin Delano Roosevelt Library, President's Personal File, Entry 21, Box 22, October 11, 1935.

54. E. S. Bogardus, *The Mexican Immigrant: An Annotated Bibliography* (Los Angeles: Council on International Relations, 1929). Carlos E. Cortés, *Mexican American Bibliographies* (New York: Arno Press, 1974). Ernesto Galarza, *Mexicans in the United States: A Bibliography* (Washington, DC: Division of Labor and Social Information of the Pan American Union, 1942). Carlos E. Cortes, "The Mexican American," in *Spanish-Speaking Americans and Mexican-Americans in the United States: A Selected Bibliography,* ed. Lyle Saunders (New York: Bureau for Intercultural Education, 1944).

55. George I. Sánchez and Howard Putnam, *Materials Relating to the Education of Spanish-Speaking People in the United States: An Annotated Bibliography* (Austin: University of Texas, Institute of Latin American Studies, 1959), 55–58.

56. Dave Cubayens, "School Financing May Become Hot Issue," *Paris (TX) News,* April 22, 1946.

57. Hart, "Making Democracy Safe for the World," 53. "FEPC Head Sees Job Shortage for Minority Groups," *Chicago Defender,* October 21, 1944, 16. Raúl Morín, *Among the Valiant: Mexican Americans in WWII and Korea* (Alhambra, CA: Borden, 1966), 16. Robin Fitzgerald Scott, "The Mexican-American in the Los Angeles Area, 1920–1950: From Acquiescence to Activity" (PhD diss., University of Southern California, 1971), 156, 195, 256, 261. David G. Gutiérrez, *Walls and Mirrors: Mexican Americans, Mexican Immigrants, and the Politics of Ethnicity* (Berkeley: University of California Press, 1995), 120–122.

58. Gunnar Myrdal, *An American Dilemma: The Negro Problem and Modern Democracy* (New Brunswick, NJ: Transaction Publishers, 1995), 573. Myrdal's 1944 study was revolutionary. It showed how Americans discriminated against blacks and then blamed them for their poverty.

59. Clete Daniel, *Chicano Workers and the Politics of Fairness: The FEPC in the Southwest, 1941–1945* (Austin: University of Texas Press, 1991), 8–9. Manuel Ruiz Jr., "Making Public Employment: A Model of Equal Opportunity: A Report of the Proceedings of Regional Civil Rights Conference II," sponsored by the U.S. Commission on Civil Rights in Boston, September 22–24, 1974, 34–35, http://www.law.umaryland.edu/marshall/usccr/documents/ cr12an72.pdf (accessed November 5, 2009). Richard Griswold del Castillo, ed., *World War II and Mexican American Civil Rights* (Austin: University of Texas Press, 2008), 75–78. Robert Garland Landolt, *The Mexican-American Workers of San Antonio, Texas* (New York: Arno

Press, 1976), 76–77, 88–117. Pauline R. Kibbe, *Latin Americans in Texas* (New York: Arno Press, 1974), 161–162. Charles Loomis and Nellie Loomis, "Skilled Spanish-American War Industry Workers from New Mexico," *Applied Anthropology* 2 (October–December 1942): 33.

60. Hart, "Making Democracy Safe for the World," 83. Emilio Zamora, *Claiming Rights and Righting Wrongs in Texas: Mexican Workers and Job* (College Station: Texas A&M University Press, 2009), 126.

61. David E. Hayes-Bautista, Werner O. Schink, and Jorge Chapa, *The Burden of Support: Young Latinos in an Aging Society* (Stanford, CA: Stanford University Press, 1988), 15, 18–21. Mario García, *Memories of Chicano History: The Life and Narrative of Bert Corona* (Berkeley: University of California Press, 1994), 161–163. Rodolfo F. Acuña, *A Community under Siege: A Chronicle of Chicanos East of the Los Angeles River, 1945–1975* (Los Angeles: Chicano Studies Research Center Publications, 1984), 21–106, 275–94, 407–50.

62. Grebler et al., *The Mexican-American People*, 150, 154. Thomas E. Sheridan, *Los Tucsonenses: The Mexican Community in Tucson, 1854–1941* (Tucson: University of Arizona Press, 1986), 235–236. David A. Badillo, "From West San Antonio to East L.A.: Chicano Community Leadership Compare" (Working Paper Series No. 24, Stanford Center for Chicano Research, April, 1989), http://ccsre.stanford.edu/pdfs/wps24.pdf (accessed May 12, 2010).

63. "Hold Meeting on Spanish Education," *Santa Fe New Mexican*, December 13, 1945.

64. *Mendez v. Westminster: A Look at Our Latino Heritage*, http://www.mendezvwestminster.com/ (accessed November 5, 2009). The sixtieth anniversary of *Mendez vs. Westminster*, http://uprisingradio.org/home/?p=1896 (accessed November 5, 2009).

65. *Delgado v. Bastrop ISD, Handbook of Texas Online*, http://www.tshaonline.org/handbook/online/articles/DD/jrd1.html (accessed November 5, 2009).

66. Henry A. J. Ramos, *The American G.I. Forum: In Pursuit of the Dream, 1948–1983* (Houston: Arte Público Press, 1998), 23. Patrick J Carroll, *Felix Longoria's Wake: Bereavement, Racism, and the Rise of Mexican American Activism* (Austin: University of Texas, 2003). American G.I. Forum, *PBS*, http://www.pbs.org/kpbs/theborder/history/ timeline/19.html (November 5, 2009). "A Class Apart," *WGBH American Experience*, http://www.pbs.org/wgbh/americanexperience/class/photoGallery/ (accessed November 5, 2009). "Felix Z. Longoria: Private, United States Army," *Arlington Cemetery*, http://www.arlingtoncemetery.net/longoria.htm (accessed November 5, 2009).

67. Rosales, *Chicano!* 97. Ramos, *The American G.I. Forum*, 23.

68. Beatrice Griffith, *American Me* (Boston: Houghton Mifflin, 1948). Carey McWilliams, *North from Mexico: The Spanish-Speaking People of the US* (Philadelphia: Lippincott, 1949).

69. Guadalupe San Miguel Jr., "Middle-Class Mexican Americans and the Desegregation Campaign in Texas, 1929–1957," in *En Aquel Entonces Readings in Mexican-American History*, ed. Manuel G. Gonzales and Cynthia M. Gonzales (Indianapolis: University of Indiana Press, 2000), 211, 215. Guadalupe San Miguel Jr., *Contested Policy: The Rise and Fall of Federal Bilingual Education in the United States, 1960–2001* (Denton: University of North Texas, 2004), 5, 118.

70. Blanton, "George I. Sanchez," 569.

71. García, *White but Not Equal*, 177. Years later, Sánchez claimed that he and his former student Carlos Cadena, a lead attorney on the case, had come up with the class-apart argument, saying that he and Cadena had outlined the brief. James de Anda refuted this claim, saying that it was his idea.

72. Blanton, "George I. Sanchez," 569.

73. Carlos K. Blanton, "George I. Sanchez, Ideology, and Whiteness in the Making of the Mexican American Civil Rights Movement, 1930–1960," *Journal of Southern History* (August 1, 2006): 569.

CHAPTER 2 — THE SIXTIES AND THE BEAN COUNT

1. Leo Grebler, Joan W. Moore, and Ralph C. Guzmán, *The Mexican-American People: The Nation's Second Largest Minority* (New York: Free Press, 1970), 150.

2. Grebler et al., *Mexican American People*, 16, 106, 126, 143, 150, 185, 236, 251. Richard W. Slatta, "Chicanos in the Pacific Northwest: An Historical Overview of Oregon's Chicanos," *Aztlán* 6, no. 3 (Fall 1975): 335. Mexicans in the Columbia Basin, http://www.vancouver .wsu.edu/crbeha/ma/ma.htm (accessed November 8, 2009). "No Dogs or Mexicans Allowed," *Big Apple*, http://www.barrypopik.com/index.php/new_york_city/entry/no_dogs_ or_mexicans_allowed_no_mexicans_or_dogs_allowed/ (accessed November 8, 2009).

3. Walter Lippmann, "Functions of Civil Rights Commission," *Los Angeles Times*, November 8, 1957, B4. "FEP, Fee Bills Given Approval," *Van Wert (Ohio) Times*, February 19, 1959.

4. "Rights Hearings Set in California," *Chicago Defender*, November 28, 1959, 3. "Civil Rights Board to Hold Race Quiz Here," *Los Angeles Times*, November 15, 1959, A .

5. "Parker Angrily Denies Racial Discrimination," *Los Angeles Times*, January 27, 1960, B2.

6. "Parker Asked to Explain His Attitude toward Latins," *Los Angeles Times*, January 29, 1960, B1. "Chief Parker Denies Insult to Mexicans," *Los Angeles Times*, January 30, 1960, B1. "Parker Offers Recording of Civil Rights Remarks," *Los Angeles Times*, February 2, 1960, B1. "Council Hears Parker's Recording on 'Wild Tribes,'" *Los Angeles Times*, B1. His remarks about blacks are also said to have fueled the Watts Riots of the mid-decade.

7. Fabio Rojas, *From Black Power to Black Studies: How a Radical Social Movement Became an Academic Discipline* (Baltimore: Johns Hopkins University Press, 2007), 4, 22, 24.

8. Paul Sheldon, "Mexican American Formal Organizations," in *Mexican-Americans in the United States: A Reader*, ed. John H. Burma (Cambridge, MA: Schenkman, 1970), 267, 268.

9. Ruben Salazar, "Quick End to Bracero Use Urged," *Los Angeles Times*, April 7, 1963, B. "UCLA to Open Study of Mexican-Americans," *Los Angeles Times*, January 22, 1964, E7. "Mexican-Americans Assail UCLA Project," *Los Angeles Times*, May 4, 1966, 27. Most of Sheldon's studies were in mimeograph form, which at the time were readily available. Paul M. Sheldon, "Mexican Americans in School: A History of Educational Neglect, by Thomas P. Carter," *American Sociological Review* 36, no. 4 (August 1971): 763–764. The review of Carter's book criticized it for a lack of hard data. "The material on Mexican American reactions is necessarily weak. Carter apparently decided to limit his sources to the literature in education where he found accounts of mental withdrawal and dropout studies. In terminology he was caught short by the recent rise of the term 'Chicano' to refer to the active student of Mexican extraction." Dick Turpin, "Mexican-American Pupil Drop Outs Told," *Los Angeles Times*, November 11, 1959, B1. "Housing Called Key to Civil Rights Problems," *Los Angeles Times*, January 26, 1960, B2. Rudy Villasenor, "Group Formed to Keep U.S. Mexicans in School," *Los Angeles Times*, March 9, 1960, B3. This issue of dropouts was prominent at the time.

10. Grebler, Moore, Guzmán, *The Mexican-American People*.

11. Stella Leal Carrillo, "Importancia economica y social de la poblacion Mexicana en Estados Unidos de Norteamerica" (master's thesis, Universidad Nacional Autónoma de México, Escuela Nacional de Economica, Mexico City, 1963).

12. "Mexican-Americans Assail UCLA Project," *Los Angeles Times*, May 4, 1966, 27. Leo Grebler, "Neglect by the Federal Government of Mexican-Americans Deplored," *Los Angeles Times*, April 5, 1966, B4.

13. Robert C. Lowry, "Foundation Patronage toward Citizen Groups and Think Tanks: Who Get Grants?" *Journal of Politics* 61, no. 3 (August 1999): 758. Private foundations have a history of social engineering through research, education, and policy advocacy. Its directors

and even midlevel officers worked for the New Frontier and Great Society and serve on almost every Democratic Party presidential staff.

14. Bill Becher, "Minority in West Seeks Job Gains," *New York Times,* November 15, 1963, 22.

15. Ruben Salazar, "Heritage of El Pueblo," *Los Angeles Times,* February 24, 1963, G1.

16. Carey McWilliams, *North from Mexico: The Spanish-Speaking People of the Southwest,* 1948 (New York: Greenwood, 1968), 35–47.

17. Articles can also be found in Mario T. García, ed., *Border Correspondent: Selected Writings, 1955–1970* (Berkeley: University of California Press, 1995).

18. Ruben Salazar, "Heritage of El Pueblo," *Los Angeles Times,* February 25, 1963, A1.

19. Ruben Salazar, "Little Mexico," *Los Angeles Times,* February 26, 1963, A1.

20. Ruben Salazar, "Mexican-Americans Lack Political Power," *Los Angeles Times,* February 27, 1963, A1.

21. Ruben Salazar, "Mexican Americans Succeeding," *Los Angeles Times,* February 28, 1963, A1.

22. Ruben Salazar, "Mexican-Americans Have Culture Protected by 1848 U.S. Treaty," *Los Angeles Times,* March 1, 1963, A1.

23. Ruben Salazar, "Parley Airs Problems of Mexican-Americans," *Los Angeles Times,* January 18, 1963, A8.

24. Ruben Salazar, "Mexican and American Culture Merger Urged," *Los Angeles Times,* January 19, 1963, 4.

25. Ruben Salazar, "Youths Study Problems of Mexican-Americans," *Los Angeles Times,* April 10, 1963, A8.

26. Lyle C. Wilson, "Whites Resent Civil Rights, *Galveston News,* July 9, 1963.

27. Ruben Salazar, "Youth Drive May Skip Mexican-Americans," *Los Angeles Times,* February 4, 1963, 29.

28. "Mexicans Fight Problems of Integration Efforts," *Chicago Daily Defender,* July 17, 1963, A13.

29. "State Colleges Accused by Mexican-U.S. Group," *Los Angeles Times,* March 10, 1963, G20.

30. Ruben Salazar, "Problems of Latins Seen Thing Apart," *Los Angeles Times,* September 16, 1963, A1. "Latin Group Will Sponsor Workshops," *Los Angeles Times,* January 16, 1964, H2.

31. "Discussion of Children Due at Valley State," *Los Angeles Times,* April 15, 1964, G9.

32. Ruben Salazar, "What Causes Jose's Trouble in School?" *Los Angeles Times,* February 23, 1964, E1. There was considerable political activity during 1964. UCLA students Bob Aragon, Jesus Chaverria, Juan Gómez-Quiñones, Ricardo Maullin, and Arturo Madrid organized the "No on 14 campaign in East Los Angeles," which failed. Rodolfo Acuña led a Latin American Civic Association registration drive and campaign against Prop 14, which was an initiative to repeal fair legislation. MAPA also campaigned against Prop 14. Ruben Salazar, "Housing Issue Ignored by Mexican-Americans," *Los Angeles Times,* August 30, 1964, J7. "Latin Chamber Favors Repeal of Rumford Act," *Los Angeles Times,* August 13, 1964, 26.

33. *Xispas Magazine: An Online Journal of Xicano Culture, Art, and Politics,* December 1, 2006. Interview with Sal Castro by Diane Velarde-Hernández, http://www.xispas.com/opinion/sa11.htm and http://www.xispas.com/archives/castro/sa12.htm. Ruben Salazar, "New School Plan Sees Bilingualism as Asset," *Los Angeles Times,* February 25, 1964, E2. Vivian LeFont, Letter to the Editor, *Los Angeles Times,* March 1, 1964, N6. Eugene A Kreyche, "Ruben Salazar Series Held Highly Laudable," *Los Angeles Times,* February 29, 1964, B4. James Neal, "Readers Dispute Certain Points in Belmont High School Article," *Los Angeles*

Times, March 1, 1964, N6. In 1963 the Los Angeles County Commission on Human Relations began sponsoring annual Mexican-American Youth Leadership Conferences for junior and high school students. The next year it was moved to Camp Hess Kramer, where students would listen to inspirational speakers. Students were encouraged to be traditional school leaders, run for school offices, and go on to college. They also discussed their schools. The nucleus of the blowout leaders in 1968 came from alumni of these sessions.

34. Association of Mexican American Educators, "History," http://www.amae.org/index2.cfm?function=history.

35. Dr. Max Rafferty, "The Forgotten Minority Is Rising," *Los Angeles Times,* March 29, 1965, A5.

36. Richard Bergholz, "Pressure Groups Vie in School Board Race," *Los Angeles Times,* January 31, 1965, D6. My chapter of MAPA and the Latin American Civic Association that I was involved with endorsed Poblano. Consequently, I supported him. My split with Poblano and Phil Móntez came at the end of the campaign, at a closed meeting, when Ralph approached us about paying off the considerable debt his campaign had incurred. He came with a proposal from Superintendent Rafferty that, in turn for support, he would pay off the debt. Both Poblano and Móntez worked for state office of education. An argument broke out, in which I was called naive, among other things. This encounter led me to boycott the newly formed Association of Mexican American Educators. In retrospect, the Democrats and progressives were equally to blame because of their political neglect of Mexican Americans.

37. Jack Smith, "Dr. Nava Calls Self Practical Idealist," *Los Angeles Times,* June 4, 1967, F4.

38. "Institute to Stress Role of Minorities," *Los Angeles Times,* January 1, 1967, SF-B14. Charles Donaldson, "Teachers, Latin Parents Confront Language Barrier," *Los Angeles Times,* July 27, 1966, SF8. The colleges nudged by federal monies also had institutes for headstart teachers. There was talk of requiring teachers to learn Spanish. I was a resource teacher at the institute.

39. "Teamsters and PASSO Awoke 'Sleeping Giant' in Crystal City," *Brownsville (TX) Herald,* May 7, 1963. Sam Kindrick, "Racial Issue Bitterly Splits up Texas Town," *Los Angeles Times,* April 14, 1963, 12.

40. "Race Antagonism Splits Texas City," *New York Times,* April 14, 1963, 49. "Texas Rangers Hit by 'Pistol Rule' Charge," *Los Angeles Times,* May 3, 1963, 4.

41. "Teamsters and PASSO Awoke 'Sleeping Giant' in Crystal City." *Brownsville (TX) Herald,* May 7, 1963. "Ranchers Hire Prosecutor in Border Patrol Killing," *Brownsville (TX) Herald,* May 7, 1963. This was going on at the same time that a border patrol officer shot and killed an undocumented worker on the border. Tom McGowan, "Deputy's Arrest Called Frame," *San Antonio Light,* June 16, 1963. "Blasts LULAC: Cornejo Challenges," *San Antonio Light,* June 16, 1963.

42. Tom Henshaw, "The Latin Revolt in Crystal City," *Corpus Christi Caller-Times,* June 9, 1963. Preston Mc Graw, "PASO's Fuentes Says Latins Tolerated but Not Accepted," *Brownsville (TX) Herald,* August 22, 1963.

43. "Not All Crystal City Latins Support PASO," *Brownsville (TX) Herald,* August 22, 1963. Oral history interview with Albert Peña Jr., by José Angel Gutiérrez, CMAS 15, Special Collections, University of Texas at Arlington Libraries, 31–40,

44. Gladwin Hill, "Crystal City, Tex., Tests Mexican-Americans' Political Role," *New York Times,* September 21, 1963, 17. Ruben Salazar, "Latins' Tactics in Crystal City Win Praise," *Los Angeles Times,* May 19, 1963, N4. Indeed, the takeover inspired Mexicans elsewhere.

45. Charles Vale Fitzpatrick, "Latino Empowerment in South Texas: The Crystal City Revolts (1962–69) as a Case Study" (master's thesis, Baylor University, Waco, TX, 2004), 30, 38.

46. Fitzpatrick, "Latino Empowerment in South Texas," 23–24.

47. Clarence LaRouche, "Political Showdown Shaping," *San Antonio Light,* January 18, 1964. "Crystal City," *San Antonio Light,* September 4, 1964. Sam Kindrick, "Crystal City Keeps Bobbing from Situation to Situation," *San Antonio Express-News,* September 4, 1964.

48. Two opinions appeared in the *Del Rio (TX) News Herald.* Ramon Garces, "Why Crystal City Suffers Divisions," *Del Rio (TX) News Herald,* April 14, 1963. Dick Meskill, "Why Crystal City Suffers Divisions," *Del Rio (TX) News Herald,* April 14, 1963. According to Garces, "Unlike organizations like LULACS or the "G. I. Forum, the PASSO group is openly political, and leaders admit that the only aim of the group is to gain political power." It is a partisan organization. A split occurred after the unsuccessful run for governor of Price Daniel. Garces gives credit to the Teamsters for the victory. "When there is an emotional issue raised, such as the dangerous race issue, the constructive issues are forgotten." Meskill has another take. He says that there are a hundred other communities that are the replica of Crystal City. "PASSO and the Teamsters, typically and cynically, are playing a 'game of Russian roulette with the people of Crystal City. This is a game which the innocent participant cannot hope to win."

49. Gladwin Hill, "Mexicans' Plight Decried on Coast," *New York Times,* August 11, 1963, 70.

50. "Latin Employment Eyed by Senators, *Victoria Advocate,* September 12, 1963.

51. *The Invisible Minority: Report of The NEA-Tucson Survey on the Teaching of Spanish to the Spanish-Speaking* (Washington, DC: National Education Association, 1966), v, 3.

52. Ibid., 5, 9, 10.

53. Ibid., 18, 20.

54. Ibid., 28, 32. The National Defense Education Act (NDEA) passed in 1958. Title VI of NDEA was titled "Language Development." It allocated funds for "Centers and Research and Studies" and "Language Institutes." I attended one such summer institute for secondary schoolteachers at the University of Southern California in 1963. Teachers were paid a stipend. These were, however, soft monies, and the universities did little to institutionalize the programs.

55. *The Invisible Minority,* v–vi, 5–6, 10. John D. Skrentny, *The Minority Rights Revolution* (Cambridge, MA: Belknap Press, 2002), 190.

56. George Mowry and Blaine A. Brownell, *The Urban Nation 1920–1980,* rev. ed. (New York: Hill and Wang, 1981), 213–214. Julie Leininger Pycior, *LBJ and Mexican Americans: The Paradox of Power* (Austin: University of Texas Press, 1997), 148–151.

57. Pycior, *LBJ,* 149, 151.

58. Maris A. Vinovskis, *The Birth of Head Start: Preschool Education Policies in the Kennedy and Johnson Administrations* (Chicago: University of Chicago Press, 2005), 59–68.

59. "LBJ State of Union War on Poverty," http://www.youtube.com/watch?v= qfTo3Ihtlds (accessed November 8, 2009).

60. Mowry and Brownell, *Urban Nation,* 221–222. William O'Neil, *An Informal History of America in the 1960s: Coming Apart* (New York: Quadrangle, 1980), 130–131. Biliana María Ambrecht, "Politicization as a Legacy of the War on Poverty: A Study of Advisory Council Members in a Mexican American Community" (PhD diss., University of California at Los Angeles, 1973). V. Kurtz, "Politics, Ethnicity, Integration: Mexican Americans in the War on Poverty" (PhD diss., University of California at Davis, 1970). Greg Coronado, "Spanish-Speaking Organizations in Utah," in *Working Papers toward a History of the Spanish Speaking in Utah,* ed. Paul Morgan and Vince Mayer (Salt Lake City: American West Center, Mexican American Documentation Project, University of Utah, 1973), 121. Vernon M. Briggs Jr., Walter Fogel, and Fred H. Schmidt, *The Chicano Worker* (Austin: University of Texas Press, 1977), 38. *Forumeer* (March 1967) states that the forum almost dropped sponsorship of SER because LBJ was hedging on the White House conference. Pycior, *LBJ,* 152–153, 159, 161.

61. Pycior, *LBJ*, 164, 170, 178–182. Carey McWilliams, *North from Mexico* (New York: Greenwood Press, 1968), 17. *Forumeer* (October 1967). The forum supported the conference and said nothing about the demonstrations. See also John Hart Lane Jr., "Voluntary Associations among Mexican Americans in San Antonio, Texas: Organization and Leadership Characteristics" (PhD diss., University of Texas, 1968), 2. Richard Gardner, *Gritol Reies Tijerina and the New Mexico Land Grant War of 1967* (New York: Bobbs-Merrill, 1970), 231–232. Craig A. Kaplowitz, *LULAC, Mexican Americans, and National Policy* (College Station: Texas A&M University Press, 2005), 98–104.

62. Theodore William Parsons, "Ethnic Cleavage in a California School" (PhD diss., Stanford University, 1965).

63. Ibid., 226.

64. Ibid., 376–381.

65. Ibid., 40.

66. Ibid., 155.

67. Ibid., 158.

68. Ibid., 261.

69. Ibid., 188.

70. Ibid., 363.

71. Ernest Morgan, "Professor Endorses Bilingual Proposal," *Corpus Christi Times*, May 26, 1967.

72. David Nieto, "A Brief History of Bilingual Education in the United States," *Perspectives on Urban Education* (Spring 2009): 61–72.

73. Jasmine K. Williams, "Lupe Anguiano—A Tireless Warrior Woman," *New York Post*, March 12, 2007. Lupe Anguiano Archive Event, UCLA Chicano Research Center, http://www.chicano.ucla.edu/center/events/Anguiano.htm (accessed November 8, 2009).

74. Pycior, *LBJ*, 183–187. Harry Golden, "A Plea for Bilingual Education," *Los Angeles Times*, April 17, 1963, A6.

75. Ernest Morgan, "Bilingual Teaching Lauded," *San Antonio Express-News*, November 8, 1966. Joseph Stocker, "Dispute Arises over Bilingual Education," *Navajo Times (Arizona)*, December 15, 1966.

76. "Law Proposed to Aid Bilingual Education," *Los Angeles Times*, March 12, 1967, SF-C6.

77. "Hearings in L.A. Due on Bilingual Education Bills," *Los Angeles Times*, June 18, 1967, G1. Bob Rawitch, "Murphy Hits Lack of Bilingual Education at Senate Hearing," *Los Angeles Times*, June 25, 1967; M. S. Handler, "Spanish Endorsed for U.S. Schools," *New York Times*, July 22, 1967, 54. Puerto Rican educators were very active in pushing the bill.

78. Connie Midey, "Bilingual Education Bill Funds Called Inadequate by Fannin," *Arizona Republic*, May 28, 1968.

79. Ken Fanucchi, "Teachers Clash on Best Way to Help Minorities," *Los Angeles Times*, August 10, 1966, SF8. "Latin Group Opposes School Bond Issue," *Los Angeles Times*, February 9, 1966, 3. In an unprecedented move, the Mexican American Education Committee voted not to support the Los Angeles City Schools' bond drive in protest to its failure to teach Mexican American students. Ken Fanucchi, "Bilingual Need Predicted for Future Hemispheric Culture," *Los Angeles Times*, October 9, 1966, SF-B2.

80. "Lubbock Gets 'Head Start' Directive About Teachers," *Lubbock Avalanche Journal*, March 21, 1967. Robert S. Allen and Paul Scott, "Self-Examination Runs High For OEO; Congress Digging into Matter," *Lebanon (PA) Daily News*, March 13, 1967 (lists the money allocated by the OEO). William Trombley, "Deprived Students Find New Path to College," *Los Angeles Times*, July 29, 1965, 29. The OEO also provided money for Upward Bound, which encouraged colleges to recruit minority students, mostly black at this time.

226 NOTES

81. "Governor to Get Report on Migrant Workers," *Walla Walla Union-Bulletin*, May 11, 1967. "Timeline: Movimiento from 1960–1985," *Seattle Civil Rights and Labor History Project*, http://depts.washington.edu/civilr/mecha_timeline.htm.

82. Hob Voces, "Long March Converges on Capitol Steps," *Benton Harbor (MI) News-Palladium*, March 27, 1967. "Migrant Unit Gets Hearing with Romney," *Traverse City (MI) Record Eagle*, April 5, 1967. "Romney Aide Works with Migrants," *Holland (MI) Evening Sentinel*, April 5, 1967. "Migrants to Ask Romney to Intervene," *Holland (MI) Evening Sentinel*, April 13, 1967. "Saginaw to Lansing March, Michigan Minutes," in *Michigan Minutes: Stories*, http://www.michigantelevision.org/mi_minutes/ (accessed November 8, 2010).

83. James Maraniss, "Wautoma: New Season, Same Woes," *Capital Times*, July 31, 1967. *Appleton (WI) Post Crescent*, January 8, 1967. *Oshkosh Daily Northwestern*, August 15, 1966. *Appleton (WI) Post Crescent*, January 8, 1967.

84. Marc Simon Rodriguez, "A Movement Made of 'Young Mexican Americans Seeking Change': Critical Citizenship, Migration, and the Chicano Movement in Texas and Wisconsin, 1960–1975," *Western Historical Quarterly* 34, no. 3 (Autumn 2003): 274–299. The article draws the connection between Texas and the student movement in the Midwest.

85. *Adolfo Romo v. Tempe School District*, 1925, in F. Arturo Rosales, ed., *Testimonio: A Documentary History of the Mexican American Struggle for Civil Right* (Houston: Arte Público Press, 2000), 126–127.

86. Francisco A. Rosales, *Chicano! The History of the Mexican American Civil Rights Movement* (Houston: Arte Público Press, 1997), 211–213. F. Arturo Rosales, ed., *Testimonio: A Documentary History of the Mexican American Struggle for Civil Rights* (Houston: Arte Público Press 2000), 126–127. Dan Pavillard, "Minorities Like 'Taste of Honey—Huerta Says," *Tucson Daily Citizen*, October 20, 1967. Programs such as Tucson Neighborhood Youth Corps also created a climate for activism. Its director John L. Huerta told a group of mental health advisers, "Minorities are through being spoon-fed by a smug American middle class with a guilty conscience, through with inferior education, through with lack of . . . opportunities for employment, promotion and the lack of adequate housing." Maritza de la Trinidad, "Collective Outrage: Mexican American Activism and the Quest for Educational Equality and Reform," 1950–1990 (Ph.D. diss., University of Arizona 2008), 150, 162, 183. Trinidad reviews the history over the fight for bilingual education in which Tucson was a leader. She features Maria Urquides, a teacher who graduated in 1928 from Arizona State Teachers' College and who beginning in 1955 led the fight against the "no Spanish" rule. Urquides worked closely with the NEA. She campaigned for the Bilingual Education Act.

87. Mexican-American Organizations, *Handbook of Texas Online*, http://www.tshaonline.org/handbook/online/articles/MM/vzmvj.html (accessed November 17, 2010).

88. Enriqueta Vasquez, Dionne Espinoza, and Lorena Oropeza, eds., *Chicano Movement: Writings from El Grito Del Norte* (Houston: Arte Público Press, 2006).

89. Maurilio Eutimio Vigil, "Ethnic Organizations among Mexican Americans of New Mexico: A Political Perspective" (PhD diss, University of New Mexico, 1974), 78, 82, 83–84, 94, 137, 236, 241, 251, 254, 303, 305, 308, 317–320, 322. Féderico Reade and Richard Moore, "The Black Berets," *New Mexico Office of the State Historian*, http://www.newmexicohistory.org/filedetails.php?fileID=22436. Elizabeth "Betita" Martinez, "A View from New Mexico: Recollections of the Movimiento Left," *Monthly Review* (July–August 2002), http://monthlyreview.org/0702martinez.htm. William Slatkin, "Panty Raid 'Not In' on Campus," *Journal for Youth* [Albuquerque], September 25, 1967. Anti-Vietnam protests were heating up on most campuses—the University of New Mexico was no exception. Jerry Buck, "Viet Nam Protesters Represent Small Portion of College Students, Officials Say," *Santa Fe New Mexican*, October 28, 1965.

90. Teacher's Institute Will Emphasize Role of Minority Groups in History," *Los Angeles Times* January 9, 1966, SF-B6. "Institute to Stress Role of Minorities," *Los Angeles Times*, January 1, 1967, SF-B14.

91. Edwin Fenton, *Teaching the New Social Studies in Secondary Schools: An Inductive Approach* (New York: Holt, Rinehart & Winston, 1966).

92. Paulo Freire, *Pedagogy of the Oppressed* (New York: Continuum Publishing Co., 1970).

93. Rodolfo F. Acuña, *Cultures in Conflict: Case Studies of the Mexican American* (Los Angeles: Charter Books, 1970). Idem, *A Mexican American Chronicle* (New York: American Book Co., 1970). Idem, *The Story of the Mexican American* (New York: American Book Co., 1969).

94. Jack McCurdy "Rafferty Implies Schools Need Not Use 'Land of Free,'" *Los Angeles Times*, December 22, 1967, SF1.

95. Ernesto Galarza, "Minorities: The Mirror of Society," in *Ghosts in the Barrio: Issues in Bilingual-Bicultural Education,* ed. Ralph (Rafa) Poblano (San Rafael, CA: Leswing Press, 1973), 35–44. Galarza presented this paper before the Southern California Chapter of the National Council for the Social Studies circa 1967.

96. *Valley News*, April 6, 1967. Ken Fanucchi, "Reagan Hit as Stalling VSC's Minorities Plan," *Los Angeles Times*, June 13, 1968. SF1.

97. Julian Hartt, "Small College Planned within Large College," *Los Angeles Times*, July 26, 1964, F1. The college president was Leo Cain, who called for the establishment of a small college within a large college that would draw from the resources of the larger entity. "Dominguez College Will Build in 1967," *Los Angeles Times*, November 6, 1966, CS2. The construction of the site on the Palos Verde Peninsula ran into problems because of the price of the land and the Watts Riots that drew attention to the need of a college in the black community. William Trombley, "College Near Watts Moves Step Closer," *Los Angeles Times,* October 21, 1965, A1. Jim McCauley, "Delays in Dominguez College," *Long Beach (CA) Press-Telegram*, October 22, 1965. Lee Bastajian, "Dominguez-Carson Vow Fight to Keep PV College," *Los Angeles Times*, October 31, 1965, CS1.

98. Jim McCauley, "College Lonely, Costly," *Long Beach Independent*, March 16, 1967. There was a lot of criticism of having the college so close to Long Beach State, and enrollment was low. It was felt that the need was in Ventura or northern San Diego County. Ray Zeman, "State College Dream Turns into Nightmare," *Los Angeles Times*, March 20, 1967, 3. The campus was in the midst of operating oil wells. Jim McCauley, "Tiny Dominguez Campus Draws Legislators' Fire," *Long Beach Independent*, April 1, 1967. William Trombley, "College Site Is No Beauty Spot," *Los Angeles Times*, April 17, 1967.

99. Otto Santa Ana, *Brown Tide Rising: Metaphors of Latinos in Contemporary American Public Discourse* (Austin: University of Texas Press, 2002), 127, 178.

100. Dick Turpin, "Sanctions Urged in School District Refusal to Bargain with Teachers," *Los Angeles Times*, July 6, 1962, 2. Joe Rust, "Of Urban Misfits," *San Antonio Light*, July 12, 1962.

101. Ruben Salazar, "Johnson Speaks Here for Fair Employment," *Los Angeles Times*, November 15, 1963, 26.

102. Charles Sutton, "Mexican-Americans Move up Social Ladder," *Long Beach (CA) Press-Telegram*, January 6, 1964.

103. M. Ruiz Ibanez, "Rep. Gonzalez Makes Call for True Equality in U.S.," *San Antonio Express-News*, July 26, 1964.

104. Lloyd Larrabee, "S.A. Priest Gets Involved for Justice," *San Antonio Express-News*, October 3, 1965.

105. Ethel L. Payne, "Civil Rights Commission Has Woes," *Chicago Daily Defender*, May 24, 1967, 5.

CHAPTER 3 — FROM STUDENT POWER TO CHICANO STUDIES

1. Stephan Thernstrom, *Harvard Encyclopedia of American Ethnic Groups* (Cambridge, MA: Belknap Press of Harvard University Press, 1980), 699. See Dr. José Angel Gutiérrez, *Los Del Valle* 21 (Brownsville: University of Texas), http://media.utb.edu/ldv/vo121.html (accessed May 18, 2010). An excellent case study on the formation of moral outrage and the connections to activism.

2. "A Class Apart," *PBS*, http://www.pbs.org/wgbh/americanexperience/class/ (accessed May 18, 2010). Ignacio M. García, *White but Not Equal: Mexican Americans, Jury Discrimination, and the Supreme Court* (Tucson: University of Arizona Press, 2008).

3. David Montejano, *Anglos and Mexicans in the Making of Texas, 1836–1986* (Austin: University of Texas Press, 1987), 284. Charles Cotrel interview by Jose Angel Gutierrez, *Tejano Voices* [University of Texas Arlington, San Antonio], July 2, 1992, 4, 6, 9, 16, http://libraries.uta.edu/tejanovoices/interview.asp?CMASNo=020#. "Priests Active in Valley Strike," *San Antonio Express-News*, July 7, 1966.

4. Robert M. Utley, *Lone Star Lawmen: The Second Century of the Texas Rangers* (New York: Oxford University Press, 2007), 236–238. Interview with Gilbert Padilla, "Founding of the National Farm Workers Association (NFWA) 1962, Farmworker Movement Documentation Project, http://farmworkermovement.org/medias/oral-history/ also see http://farmworkermovement.org/media/oral_history/ (accessed November 17, 2010). H. Joaquin Jackson, *One Ranger Returns* (Austin: University of Texas Press, 2008), 14–19.

5. Oral history interview with María Martínez, Del Rio/Austin, Texas, October 26, 1997, by José Angel Gutiérrez, in Tejano Voices, *Center for Mexican American Studies*, no. 133, http://library.uta.edu/tejanovoices/interview.jsp?CMASNo=133 (accessed November 10, 2010). "U.S. Senate Sub-Committee Hearings," *San Antonio Express-News*, July 1, 1966. Gary Garrison, "Valley Strike Pondered," *Lubbock Avalanche Journal*, December 1, 1966. La Casita was called a complete failure. "Farm Strike Could Turn into Social Movement," *Big Spring (TX) Herald*, July 17, 1966. José Angel Gutiérrez, *The Making of a Chicano Militant: Lessons from Cristal* (Madison: University of Wisconsin, 1999), 105.

6. "Farm Strike Could Turn into Social Movement." *Big Spring (TX) Herald*, July 17, 1966.

7. "Union melon packers from California crossed picket lines. . . . The packers at first refused to cross the picket line but did so after calling El Centro, California" ("Melon Packers Did Cross Picket Line," *Brownsville (TX) Herald*, July 13, 1967).

8. Armando Navarro, *Mexican American Youth Organization: Avant-Garde of the Chicano* (Austin: University of Texas Press, 1995).

9. Armando Navarro, *La Raza Unida Party*, 26. Gutiérrez, *The Making of a Chicano Militant*, 101–103. The founders adopted the name MAYO in a deliberate attempt to avoid controversy.

10. Gutiérrez, *Making of a Militant*, 119.

11. Juan A. Sepúlveda, *Life and Times of Willie Velasquez: Su voto es su vos* (Houston: Arte Publico Press, 2005), 69–72. Doris Wright, "Lanier High Students Get Civic Leader Support," *San Antonio Express-News*, April 11, 1968.

12. "Lanier Parents, Students Air Complaints," *San Antonio Light*, April 12, 1968. "Panel Facing Difficult Task," *San Antonio Light*, April 14, 1968.

13. Fern Chick, "Miller Seeks to Calm Lanier 'Revolt,'" *San Antonio Light*, April 16, 1968. "Miller Replies to Student Demands," *San Antonio Light*, April 17, 1963. Fern Chick, "Lanier Group Plans to Press Protests," *San Antonio Light*, April 18, 1968.

14. Doris Wright, "South San Board Action Defended," *San Antonio Express-News*, April 25, 1968. "Walkout Threatened," *San Antonio Light*, April 25, 1968.

15. Elaine Ayala, "The Year Latino Students Stood Up, Walked Out," *San Antonio Express-News*, May 7, 2008, http://archives.chicagotribune.com/2008/may/07/news/chi-latino-fill-0507may07. Ron White, "3,000 Ask Reforms in Walkout," *San Antonio Light*, May 16, 1968.

16. "Threatened Walkout by Teachers," *San Antonio Light*, April 25, 1968. Doris Wright, *San Antonio Express-News*, April 25, 1968.

17. White, "3,000 Ask Reforms in Walkout." "School Chief Insists It's Classes as Usual v. Meet Demands," *San Antonio Light*, May 17, 1968.

18. Ron White, "Edgewood Rally Held, *San Antonio Light,* May 21, 1968.

19. Ibid. "Edgewood Hearing in Recess," *San Antonio Light*, May 24, 1968. Frank Trejo, "Board Promises Solution to Grievances," *San Antonio Light*, May 24, 1968. Frank Trejo, "School to Act on Grievances," *San Antonio Light*, May 28, 1968.

20. Baldemar James Barrera, "We Want Better Education! The Chicano Student Movement for Educational Reform in South Texas, 1968–1970" (PhD diss., University of New Mexico, Albuquerque, 2007), 102. Richard R. Valencia, *Chicano Students and the Courts: The Mexican American Legal Struggle for Educational Equality* (New York: New York University Press, 2008), 92–103.

21. Ayala, "The Year Latino Students Stood Up, Walked Out." On March 21, 1973, the Supreme Court in a 5–4 decision ruled against Rodríguez, stating that the system of school finance did not violate the federal constitution.

22. Baldemar, "We Want Better Education!" 113–117, 129.

23. "Five Arrested in School Boycott," *Galveston Daily News*, November 16, 1968. Arrested were Mirtala Villarreal, Homer Trevino, Freddie Sainz, Arnulfo Sustaita, and Xavier Ramirez. Nolene Hodges, "Edcouch-Elsa Students In Class Revolt," *Brownsville (TX) Herald*, November 14, 1968. Norma R. Cuellar, "The Edcouch-Elsa Walkout" (seminar paper, Mexican-American History 2363, Professor Rodolfo Rocha, June 29, 1984), 1.

24. Cuellar, "The Edcouch-Elsa Walkout," 3.

25. "Refuses Boycotting Pupils," *Spring (TX) Herald*, November 19, 1968. Gary Garrison, "Return to School Sought," *Corpus Christi Times*, November 19, 1968. "Edcouch-Elsa Board Hears Each Student," *Brownsville (TX) Herald*, November 20, 1968. "Edcouch Student Hearings Scheduled for Wednesday," *Brownsville (TX) Herald*, November 26, 1968. "Valley Students Stage Walkout," *Big Spring (TX) Herald*, November 14, 1968. Xavier Ramirez was identified as the leader of the walkout. Kenneth Clark, "VISTA Tied to Boycott," *Brownsville (TX) Herald*, November 25, 1968. Cuellar, "The Edcouch-Elsa Walkout," 6–8.

26. "8 Youths Suspended in School Ruckus," *Los Angeles Times*, March 2, 1968.

27. "Classes Boycotted by Student Groups at 2 High Schools," *Los Angeles Times*, March 6, 1968, 3.

28. Jack McCurdy, "Student Disorders Erupt at 4 High Schools; Policeman Hurt," *Los Angeles Times*, March 6, 1968, 3. Sharon Stensoos, "Mexican-Americans Angry," *Daily Sundial*, March 22, 1968. By the spring, UMAS was becoming impatient and was demanding a greater role; SFVSC UMAS member Henry López was chair of UMAS Central. This militancy was no doubt the result of the March Los Angeles school walkout. Sal Castro has said UMAS played a central role and singled out López.

29. Jack McCurdy, "1,000 Walk Out in School Boycott," *Los Angeles Times*, March 9, 1968, B1.

30. Jack McCurdy, "But Won't Remove Police," *Los Angeles Times*, March 12, 1968, 1. Marisol Moreno, "'Of the Community, for the Community': The Chicana/o Student Movement in California's Public Higher Education, 1967–1973" (PhD diss., University of California, Santa Barbara, 2009), 118–121, 124. Moreno makes the point that the walkouts caused a split in MASA, with some of the leadership criticizing the walkouts, while the more

radical wing criticized the leaderships' stance. It led to the formation of La Vida Nueva. In electing Olivia Velásquez and Willie Méndoza cochairs, the members unanimously agreed that a male and a female should head the organization. Velásquez had been at Los Angeles City College and active in the organization of El Matchete, a radical Chicano student newspaper. La Vida Nueva was more sensitive to gender issues.

31. "Venice High Youths, Police Clash," *Los Angeles Times,* March 13, 1968.

32. "Faculty Backs Students' Demands, but Not Walkouts," *Van Nuys Valley (CA) News,* Match 17, 1968.

33. Jack McCurdy, "Frivolous to Fundamental," *Los Angeles Times,* March 17, 1968, 1.

34. "L.A. Board to Meet at Lincoln High," *Pasadena Star News,* March 19, 1968, H1. "Charge Board with Failing on Discipline," *Valley News,* March 29, 1968.

35. Francisco A. Rosales, *Chicano! The History of the Mexican American Civil Rights Movement* (Houston: Arte Público Press, 1997), 223–225. Rosales makes the point that the movement differed in California from other parts of the country and that it relied more on abstract symbols. This misrepresents the California experience and did not take into account generational differences. For instance, Los Angeles differs from the northern part of the state and is much more like rural Texas in the San Joaquin and Imperial Valleys. Ron Einstoss, "Bail Reduced for 9 in Walkouts at 4 Schools," *Los Angeles Times,* June 4, 1968, 3. Jack McCurdy, "Lincoln High Pickets Protest Absence of Indicted Teacher," *Los Angeles Times,* September 17, 1968, 3.

36. Juan Gómez-Quiñones, *Mexican Students por la Raza: The Chicano Student Movement in Southern California, 1967–1977* (Santa Barbara, CA: Editorial La Causa, 1978), 20–21. Janis Russo, "Immediate Bomb Halt Requested by YDs," *Daily Sundial,* September 28, 1967. By September 1967 UMAS was in the process of chartering at San Fernando Valley State.

37. *El Grito: A Journal of Contemporary Mexican-American Thought* 1, no. 1 (Fall 1967).

38. Ibid., 4.

39. David G. Gutiérrez, *Walls and Mirrors: Mexican Americans, Mexican Immigrants, and the Politics of Ethnicity* (Berkeley: University of California Press, 1995), 182.

40. Grebler et al., *Mexican-American People,* 209. Bob Baker, "Campus Groups Join Grape Pickets," *Daily Sundial,* October 9, 1968. UMAS supported the pickets at local markets.

41. Frank D. Bean and Marta Tienda, *The Hispanic Population of the United States* (New York: Russell Sage Foundation, 1988), 81.

42. Ernesto B. Vigil, *The Crusade for Justice: Chicano Militancy and the Government's War on Dissent* (Madison: University of Wisconsin Press, 1999), 3.

43. Rodolfo "Corky" Gonzales, "I am Joaquin," *Latin American Studies,* http://www .latinamericanstudies.org/latinos/joaquin.htm (accessed May 19, 2010).

44. Chicano Coordinating Council on Higher Education (CCHE), "El Plan de Aztlán, El Plan Espiritual de Aztlán," Office of the Dean of Students, University of Texas at Austin, http://studentorgs.utexas.edu/mecha/archive/plan.html (accessed May 19, 2010).

45. Kate Doyle, "Tlatelolco Massacre: Declassified U.S. Documents on Mexico and the Events of 1968," *Mexico Documentation Project,* http://www.gwu.edu/~nsarchiv/NSAEBB/ NSAEBB10/intro.htm (accessed May 20, 2010).

46. David Jess Leon, "Racism in the University: The Case of the Educational Opportunity Program" (paper presented at the Annual Meeting of the American Sociological Association, San Francisco, September 1978), 3, 10–11. William Trombley, "Minority Student 'Recruits' at Berkeley above Average," *Los Angeles Times,* April 3, 1967, E7. At Berkeley the students were 65 percent black and 25–20 percent Mexican. Ray Ripton, "Value of High School Record Debated," *Los Angeles Times,* May 5, 1968, WS1.

47. William Trombley, "University Works for Educational Reform Free of Duress in Crisis," *Los Angeles Times,* November 7, 1965, E1. William Trombley, " 'Experimental College' Faces

Crisis at Berkeley," *Los Angeles Times*, May 3, 1966, B1. "School within a School Gets a Start at Valley State College," *Los Angeles Times*, September 3, 1967, SF-B1. "Experimental College Has Range of Classes," *Los Angeles Times*, October 2, 1967, SF8. "Students Press Drive for 'Unofficial' College," *Los Angeles Times*, December 26, 1967. Noel Greenwood, "No Credit, Faculty or Roll Call," *Los Angeles Times*, November 12, 1967, WS1. "College Built on Themes Rather Than Curriculum Tried at UCLA," *Los Angeles Times*, March 10, 1968, WS20. Larry Pett, "VSC Organization Paves Way for Minority Students," *Los Angeles Times*, August 25, 1968, SF-B1.

48. López, "Educational Opportunity Program," 43. Denny Mann, "Experimental College: Studies New Issues," *Daily Sundial*, February 16, 1968. Mike Stone, "Minorities View New Curriculum," *Daily Sundial*, May 9, 1968.

49. "Convention Studies Mexican Problem," *Daily Sundial*, January 10, 1968.

50. "Valley Stale Plans Help for Disadvantaged Student," *Van Nuys Valley (CA) News*, July 25, 1968. Darlene Lima, "Ninety Minority Students Living, Studying, Working on Campus," *Daily Sundial*, July 18, 1968.

51. John Glenn, "Mexican-American Project," *Los Angeles Times*, October 19, 1967, SG1. Dewey D. Ajioka, "Professor Urges Different Approach to Teach Mexican-American Youth," *Los Angeles Times*, September 4, 1967, A4.

52. William Tully, "Students Will Finance Courses on Minorities," *Los Angeles Times*, July 3, 1968, D7.

53. Ibid.

54. Hal Leiren, "Cal State, L.A., Launches First Departments for Minorities," *Los Angeles Times*, January 9, 1969, SG1.

55. Rojas, *From Black Power to Black Studies*, 45, 55.

56. Daryl E. Lembke, "S.F. State Caught in Studies, Fund Squeeze, Smith Says," *Los Angeles Times*, November 5, 1968, 3. Rojas, *From Black Power to Black Studies*, 79. "SF State Third World Student Strike," You Tube, http://www.youtube.com/watch?v=7ar2i-G5O-0 (accessed November 10, 2010). "Student Unrest at SF State College and S.I. Hayakawa," interview with S. I. Haykawa, aired December 3, 1968, http://www.youtube.com/watch?v=rYeCIaVGM9E&feature=related (accessed November 10, 2010).

57. "'Black Studies' at S.F. State," *Los Angeles Times*, November 18, 1968, B6.

58. John Aubrey Douglass, *The California Idea and American Higher Education: 1850 to the 1960 Master Plan* (Stanford: Stanford University Press, 2000), 316–317.

59. Ibid., 232.

60. "ELAC President Will Meet with Student Group," *Los Angeles Times*, December 19, 1968, SG1. Stanley Siegel, "ELAC Head Says Holiday Talks Out," *Los Angeles Times*, December 23, 1968, SG1. Kenneth Reich, "East L.A. College—The Lull before the Storm?" *Los Angeles Times*, January 19, 1969, B.

61. Lee Stacy, *Mexico and the United States* (Tarrytown, NY: Marshall Cavendish, 2003), 168–169. In 1969 less than a hundred Mexican Americans held doctorates.

62. Larry Pett, "Pierce Will Recruit Black, Brown Students," *Los Angeles Times*, April 30, 1969, SF8.

63. "VSC to Admit More Minority Group Students; Dr. Sillars Sees 'Different' Campus, Alerts Faculty to Confront Real Issues," *Los Angeles Times*, May 19, 1968, SF-B1. Bob Baker, "Black Enrollment Up, Yet Low," *Daily Sundial*, September 25, 1968. In reviewing documents what becomes apparent is the importance of numbers in pushing the paradigm. Before BSU started its recruitment there were fewer than thirty black students on campus. There were about 200 in fall 1968, three-quarters of whom were in the BSU. UMAS was in about the same place in the spring of 1969 as the blacks were in during the spring of 1968.

64. Kenneth J. Fanucchi, "Student and Faculty Confrontations Produce Major Changes at VSC; Students, Faculty at VSC Agree on Changes," *Los Angeles Times*, June 16, 1968, SF-B1. There had been demonstrations and protests at San Fernando Valley State throughout the 1967–1968 school year. Ralph Sanders, "220 Enroll in Minority Plan," *Daily Sundial*, September 24, 1968. This was the first critical mass of EOP students enrolled at SFVSC. The temporary director was Stanley Charnofsky, and the starting semester was funded $186,000 by a federal Educational Opportunity grant. SFVSC had difficulty in raising matching funds, most of which came from associate students. Charnofsky complained that they had no problem recruiting the students but were pressed in efforts to grant them financial aid.

65. Ron Einstoss, "Valley State Trial Told of Manhandling, Insults; Director of Athletics Cites Student Threats during Confrontation," *Los Angeles Times*, September 26, 1969, SF1. Ron Einstoss, "Valley State College Takeover Leader Denies Conspiracy," *Los Angeles Times*, November 13, 1969, E2.

66. Ron Einstoss, "Mass Acquittals Denied in Valley Students' Trial; However, Judge Drops One Count of Conspiracy, Kidnapping, Imprisonment Valley State," *Los Angeles Times*, November 4, 1969, B4, B19. "Students Indicted in Valley State Case Surrender in Court," *Los Angeles Times*, December 28, 1968, A1. Bob Baker, "Did CSUN Takeover Win? '69 Rebels Disagree; Two Black Leaders: One Joined Faculty, Is Accused by the Other of Settling for 'White Man's Crumbs,' " *Los Angeles Times*, June 24, 1979, SF-B1.

67. "Valley State Students Hold Peaceful March, Protest Mass Arrests," *Valley News*, November 10, 1968.

68. Richard Bergholz, "Bradley Backed across Board," *Los Angeles Times*, April 3, 1969, 1. Richard Bergholz, "Mayor Race Spotlights Struggle on Race Issue," Los Angeles, March 9, 1969, B.

69. Kenneth Reich, "Keep City Like We Want It, Is YORTY Theme in Valley; YORTY," *Los Angeles Times*, May 18, 1969, B.

70. *Valley News*, November 5, 1968, 1. Eric Malnic, "Yorty Claims Red Link in Valley State Bails," *Los Angeles Times*, January 23, 1969, C2.

71. Ron Chapell, "Illegal Assembly Broken Up," *Daily Sundial*, January 10, 1969. Ron Chapell, "BSU, Oviatt Slate Talks on Wednesday's Violence," *Daily Sundial*, January 9, 1969. "Chatman Discusses the Black Cause," *Daily Sundial*, January 9, 1969. Lee Dye, "500 March in New Student Protest at Valley State College," *Los Angeles Times*, January 8, 1969, AB. Lee Dye, "Turmoil Rocks Two College Campuses; Officers Rout Crowd of 1,000 at Valley State," *Los Angeles Times*, January 9, 1969, A1.

72. John Kumbula, "Valley State Agrees to Establish 2 Ethnic Studies Departments," *Los Angeles Times*, January 13, 1969, A1. Eric Malnic, "YORTY Claims Red Link in Valley State Bails," *Los Angeles Times*, January 23, 1969, C2. "Valley State Peace Pact Reached: 12-Point Agreement Will Be Announced," *Van Nuys Valley (CA) News*, January 24, 1969. "The Storm at Valley State," *YouTube*, http://www.youtube.com/watch?v=NB3s_3RDEIc (accessed May 20, 2010). Lee Dye, "Valley State College Has Growing Pains," *Valley News and Green Sheet*, February 4, 1969. State of emergency declared by Delmar T. Oviatt, January 9, 1969, Richard Abcarian Collection, CSUN Special Collections, http://digital-library.csun.edu/ cdm4/item_viewer.php?CISOROOT=/UniversityArchives&CISOPTR=71&CISOBOX=1 &REC=8 (accessed May 20, 2010).

73. San Fernando Valley State College's Chicano Demands, January 1969, Richard Abcarian Collection, CSUN Special Collections, http://digital-library.csun.edu/cdm4/ item_viewer.php?CISOROOT=/UniversityArchives&CISOPTR=409&CISOBOX=1& REC=6 (accessed May 20, 2010). Mort Auerbach to the faculty, memorandum, February 24, 1969, "Subject: Faculty Convocation, February 24, 1969," Richard Abcarian Collection,

Oviatt Library, California State University, Northridge. Ernesto Galarza spoke at a faculty convocation held to increase awareness of the problems and cultures of Afro-Americans and Mexican Americans.

74. San Fernando Valley State College Black Student Union's List of Demands, November 4, 1968, Richard Abcarian Collection, CSUN Special Collections, http://digital-library .csun.edu/cdm4/item_viewer.php?CISOROOT=/UniversityArchives&CISOPTR=408& CISOBOX=1&REC=5 (accessed May 20, 2010).

75. John Kumbula, "Valley State's 12-Point Peace Package Hailed," *Los Angeles Times*, January 25, 1969, B14. Historian Vern Bullough was the faculty president of the Senate and English professor John Stafford and political scientist Mort Auerbach played significant roles. Junior faculty such as Larry Littwin (political science) played supportive roles. Leonard Greenwood, "How Valley State Moved to 'New Kind of Education,' Understanding Resulted from Heated Clashes," *Los Angeles Times*, February 2, 1969, B1.

76. John Kumbula, "Valley State Agrees to Establish 2 Ethnic Studies Departments," *Los Angeles Times*, January 13, 1969, 1. Leonard Greenwood, "Minorities Peace Accord Reached at Valley State; Plan Provides Admission of More Black and Latin Students to Institution," *Los Angeles Times*, January 24, 1969, A1. According to community activist Carlos Montes, a similar process was occurring at East Los Angeles. "Education," *Los Angeles Times*, January 26, 1969, E5. "Groups Work on Valley State Studies Plan," *Fresno Bee*, January 11, 1969. Kumbula, "Valley State Agrees to Establish 2 Ethnic Studies Departments," A1. "YORTY Orders Valley State Campus Quiz," *Van Nuys Valley (CA) News*, January 16, 1969. "YORTY demanded a probe. Leonard Greenwood, "Blomgren Quits as Valley State Acting President Due to Health," *Los Angeles Times*, February 14, 1969, A3.

77. There is a note to Warren Furumoto in my archives at the CSUN library in November 1968. I expressed my reluctance to take the job if it opened and recommended Henry Orozco, who was finishing up his doctorate. After the ouster of political scientist Ralph Guzmán, I was doubtful that such programs could succeed. Rodolfo F. Acuña to Warren Furumoto, November 1968, Series III: Correspondence Files, A–Z, Rodolfo F. Acuña Archives, California State University, Northridge. Miguel Duran is currently producing an hour documentary on the founding of the department and student involvement titled "UNREST: Founding of the Cal State Northridge Chicana/o Studies Department." A trailer can be found at http://vimeo.com/15719142 (accessed November 10, 2010).

78. Nava was very helpful because of his institutional knowledge. He knew of my freewheeling style, which sometimes got me into trouble. I could afford to get fired since I had retreat rights to Pierce College and had contracts to publish two books at a university press. I also had two children's books and a high school/community college text ready for publication and in galleys. They allowed me to assume a tough bargaining stance with the administration and helped me in later battles, because they knew that I would walk if I did not get my way.

79. Julian is a very sincere human being. One did not have to agree with him. He pretty much stayed out of my way, not second-guessing me. He was a full professor and could have very easily made waves, but he was always supportive and helped me when I asked.

80. Chicano Coordinating Council on Higher Education, *El Plan de Santa Bárbara: A Chicano Plan for Higher Education* (Oakland, CA: La Causa, 1970). Frank del Olmo, "Chicano Studies Topic of Four-Day Conference," *Daily Sundial*, April 17, 1969. Denise Smith, "Take People out of the Lonely Crowd: Goal of Mexican-American Studies Department," *Daily Sundial*, July 9, 1969.

81. Kenneth Lubas, "Scholarship Urged as VSC Admittance Guide," *Los Angeles Times*, June 6, 1969, SF8. The Chamber of Commerce was concerned about allowing unprepared students into Valley State.

82. "Help for Minority Students," *Los Angeles Times*, January 31, 1969, B8. Larry Kaggwa, "Latin Students at Cal State Urge State Aid," *Los Angeles Times*, June 30, 1969, B3.

83. "Chicano Studies Degree 'Reviewed,'" *Hayward (CA) Daily Review*, November 19, 1969.

84. Scott Moore, "Ethnic Studies Program Unveiled at Cal State," *Los Angeles Times*, February 11, 1969, B1. "Demos Battle on Minorities," *Eureka (CA) Times Standard*, April 14, 1969, 1.

85. "Chicano Leader to Give Keynote Talk at 4-Day Latin Conference," *Los Angeles Times*, April 16, 1969, D1. John Dreyfuss, "Black, Mexican-American Study Centers Planned at Claremont," *Los Angeles Times*, May 9, 1969, 3.

86. Paul A. Elsner, "Northern California Community Colleges in an Era of Dissent," in *Encouraging Civility as a Community College Leader*, ed. Paul A. Elsner and George R. Boggs (American Association of Community Colleges, 2005), 14, 19. Rojas, *From Black Power to Black Studies*, 35. "Merritt Faculty 'to Go Along,'" *Oakland Tribune*, April 24, 1969. "Merritt Approves Teacher's Contract," *Oakland Tribune*, May 6, 1969.

87. "Chicano Studies Conference Slated at Moorpark College," *Press-Courier*, November 17, 1969. Kenneth Lubas, "Educator Apologizes for Grapes on Menu," *Los Angeles Times*, November 22, 1969, SF10. I was torn. The grapes should not have been there, but I could also empathize with the students. They were very young, and I stayed behind and told them that they should have been more careful, but it was not their fault. Some of the students transferred to SFVSC.

88. Lyndell Cheeves, "Mexican-American Studies: Guidelines for a Junior College Program" (seminar paper submitted to B. Lamar Johnson, August 1969, University of California, Los Angeles), 10–15, 19. SFVSC moved quickly to give transfer credit to junior college Chicano Studies classes, which was an incentive to take them. Carl G. Winter, "History of the Junior College Movement in California," Bureau of Junior College Education Release No. 20, revised December 21, 1964, ED346902. "Valley College Elects Department Chairmen," *Los Angeles Times*, September 7, 1969, SF-B7. "Special Experimental Courses, Including Seminars in Engineering, Mythology, Mexican Civilization Planned," *Van Nuys Valley (CA) News*, May 5, 1969.

89. Gutiérrez, *The Making of a Chicano Militant*, 129–132. "Education Agency Plans Social Studies Overhaul," *Abilene Reporter-New*, March 5, 1969. "Chicanos Parade in Crystal City," *Abilene Reporter-News*, December 15, 1969. "Mexican-American Studies Institute to Open Today," *San Antonio Express-News*, November 19, 1970.

90. "Ethnic Studies May Take Fire Out of Campus Protest," *Lubbock (TX) Avalanche Journal*, March 19, 1970. Frank Denton, "Social Studies in Texas," *Victoria Advocate*, March 6, 1969. Changes were being driven by political events. For the contrasting views on Chicano Studies, see "Educator Seeks Blending of Southwest Histories," *El Paso Herald-Post*, July 16, 1970.

91. "Mexican American Studies Aimed at Culture, History," *Prospector* (University of Texas, El Paso), November 4, 1969. Wayne McClintock, "Race Study Courses Approved," *El Paso Herald-Post*, December 16, 1969.

92. "THS to Consider Demands of Mexican-Americans," *Tucson Daily Citizen*, February 15, 1969. "Dist. 1 Suspends 200 Youths after Student Demonstration," *Tucson Daily Citizen*, March 20, 1969. Greg Robertson, "Dist. 1 Suspends 200 Youths after Student Demonstration," *Tucson Daily Citizen*, March 20, 1969.

93. "200 Students Suspended in Tucson for Walkout," *Arizona Republic*, March 21, 1969.

94. Ken Burton, "Students Win Partial Support for Demands," *Tucson Daily Citizen*, September 18, 1969. "Bilingual Conference Seeks Training Funds," *Tucson Daily Citizen*, November 17, 1969.

95. "People's Coalition Takes Plea for El Rio Park to Tourists," *Tucson Daily Citizen*, October 12, 1970.

96. "Chicanos Planning New Party," *Tucson Daily Citizen*, February 23, 1973. Adolfo Quezada, "Mexican-American Vote May Be Split," *Tucson Daily Citizen*, September 7, 1971. Sarah Tully Tapia, "Mexican-American Studies Urged at TUSD [Tucson Unified School District]," *Arizona Daily Star*, November 13, 1996, 1B. Salomón Baldenegro, "That '60s Story: Chicanos and the Citizen," *Tucson Citizen*, March 8, 2009.

97. Oscar Rosales Castan, "The Chicano Movement in Washington State, 1967–2006, Part 1–Political Activism," *Seattle Civil Rights and Labor History Project*, http://depts .washington.edu/civilr/Chicanomovement_part1.htm (accessed May 20, 2010). Jeremy Simer, "La Raza Comes to Campus: The New Chicano Contingent and the Grape Boycott at the University of Washington, 1968–69," *Seattle Civil Rights and Labor History Project*, http:// depts.washington.edu/civilr/la_raza2.htm (accessed May 20, 2010). Tomás A. Villanueva, interviewed by Anne O'Neill, April 11, 2003, and Sharon Walker, June 7, 2004, Toppenish, WA. Guadalupe Gamboa, interviewed by Anne O'Neill, April 9, 2004, Olympia, WA.

98. José Alamillo, "Chicano/a History Archive," presentation, Washington State University, Chicano History, http://www.josealamillo.com/wsuchicanohistory.html (accessed May 20, 2010). "Chicano Movement in Washington: Political Activism in the Puget Sound and Yakima Valley Regions, 1960s–1980s," *HistoryLink.org*, essay 7922, http://www.historylink .org/index.cfm?DisplayPage=output.cfm&file_id=7922 (accessed May 20, 2010).

99. Department of Chicano Studies, "Chicanos Issue 72-Hour Ultimatum," University of Minnesota, http://chicano.umn.edu/resources/culture.html and http://chicano.umn.edu/ about/ (accessed May 20, 2010).

100. "Colleges Outline Ethnic Studies Programs and Plans," *Los Angeles Times*, April 25, 1969, A28. I taught a political science class at the University of Southern California in the spring of 1969.

101. Rojas, *Black Power to Black Studies*, 167–168.

CHAPTER 4 — IN THE TRENCHES OF ACADEME

1. Robert Wuhl's award-winning HBO special, *Assume the Position* (2006), posits that "the key to history is who tells the story." Wuhl shows a scene from the 1962 Jimmy Stewart movie *The Man Who Shot Liberty Valance*, in which Ransome Stoddard explodes the legend that he challenged and killed Liberty Valance. The newspaper editor interviewing Stoddard gets up to leave, and when questioned if he is going to print the story, he replies, "When the legend becomes fact, print the legend."

2. Javier Rangel, "The Educational Legacy of *El Plan de Santa Bárbara*: An Interview with Reynaldo Macías," *Journal of Latinos and Education* 6, no. 2 (2007): 192.

3. Ruben Salazar, "Chicanos Set Their Goals in Education," *Los Angeles Times*, May 4, 1969, G8.

4. Ibid.

5. Chicano Coordinating Council on Higher Education (CCHE), *El Plan de Santa Bárbara: A Chicano Plan for Higher Education* (Oakland, CA: La Causa Publications, 1969), 104–115, 122–128, http://www.sscnet.ucla.edu/00W/chicano101-1/SBplan.pdf (accessed November 11, 2010).

6. Frank del Olmo, "Chicano Studies Topic of Four-Day Conference," *Daily Sundial*, April 17, 1969. Denise Smith, "Take People out of the Lonely Crowd: Goal of Mexican-American Studies Department," *Daily Sundial*, July 9, 1969. Because of my experience in education, my expectations of Mexican American Studies differed from many of the participants at Santa Barbara.

7. Michael Soldatenko, *Chicano Studies: The Genesis of a Discipline* (Tucson: University of Arizona Press, 2009).

8. Chicano Coordinating Council on Higher Education (CCHE), *El Plan De Santa Bárbara*, 9.

9. Historically, northern and southern California have had sometimes deep divisions.

10. The notion of the internal colony is evident in the expressions of the participants. The United States invaded Mexico and colonized the Southwest. Their status was that of a conquered people. Many were influenced by Frantz Fanon, *A Dying Colonialism* (New York: Grove, 1965).

11. Chicano Coordinating Council on Higher Education (CCHE), *El Plan De Santa Bárbara*, 9.

12. Ibid.

13. Ibid., 14.

14. Ibid., 15.

15. Rubén G. Rumbaut, "The Making of a People," in *Hispanics and the Future of America*, ed. Marta Tienda and Faith Mitchell (Washington, DC: National Academic Press, 2003), 24n8, http://books.nap.edu/openbook.php?record_id=11539&page=24.

16. Carlos Muñoz, *Youth, Identity, Power: The Chicano Movement* (London: Verso, 1989), 90.

17. Marita Hernandez, "Generation in Search of Its Legacy," *Los Angeles Times*, August 14, 1983, A1. Reed Johnson, "The Many Masks of *Aztlan*," *Los Angeles Times*, June 3, 2001, E1. Roberto Rodriquez, "Utal Said to Be Historical Location of the Mythical Aztlan," Archives, http://www.networkaztlan.com/history/origins_of_aztlan.html (accessed November 21, 2010).

18. Martin D. Rosen and James Fisher, "Chicano Park and the Chicano Park Murals: Barrio Logan, City of San Diego, California," *Public Historian* 23, no. 4 (Autumn 2001): 101. Dylan A. T. Miner, "With Our Hearts in Our Hands and Our Hands in the Soil: Aztlán As Utopic Space in Chicana/o Art and Visual Culture" (Albuquerque: PhD diss., University of New Mexico, 2007).

19. Richard A. Garcia, "The Origins of Chicano Cultural Thought: Visions and Paradigms: Romano's Culturalism, Alurista's Aesthetics, and Acuña's Communalism," *California History* 74, no. 3 (Fall 1995): 290.

20. Tom Peckham, "Minority Curricula Ready," *Daily Sundial*, April 23, 1969. Tom Peckham, "Minority Studies Developed," *Daily Sundial*, April 24, 1969. Another trend that was evident was that the resistance to Chicano Studies grew as the student population increased, because students became more valuable as commodities. While many faculty members were racist, they still wanted a stake in that population for enrollment purposes. The Spanish department was more acutely aware of this and therefore was resistant.

21. The UCLA Chicano Studies Center did valuable early bibliographic work. Juan Gómez-Quiñones and Albert Camarillo, *Selected Bibliography for Chicano Studies* 3d ed. (Los Angeles: Chicano Studies Center, 1975). Roberto Cabello-Argandoña, Pat Herrera Duran, and Juan Gómez-Quiñones, *The Chicana: A Comprehensive Bibliographic Study* (Los Angeles: Chicano Research Library, Chicano Studies Center, University of California, 1975). Also important was Leo Grebler, Joan W. Moore, Ralph C. Guzman, and others, *The Mexican-American People: The Nation's Second Largest Minority* (New York, Free Press, 1970).

22. Rosa Martínez and Carlos Arce did a herculean job of compiling and microfilming journal articles on Chicanos prior to 1970. Rosa was a student, and Carlos was a professor of Chicano Studies at SFVSC. The microfilm is in Rodolfo F. Acuña Archives, California State University Library, Northridge.

23. As mentioned, SFVSC hired a consulting firm to develop course proposals for Pan-African Studies (PAS). In accepting this, PAS gave up autonomy.

24. Hans Kuijper, "Area Studies versus Disciplines towards an Interdisciplinary, Systemic Country Approach," http://www.asvj91.dsl.pipex.com/Hans_KUIJPER/AREA_STUDIES_Vs_DISCIPLINES_Hans_KUIJPER.pdf (accessed May 21, 2010).

25. Thomas Ehrlich, "Reinventing John Dewey's 'Pedagogy as a University Discipline' (John Dewey: The Chicago Years)," *Elementary School Journal* 98, no. 5 (May 1998): 489–509.

26. Even to this day I get phone calls or emails from new PhD students who have just gotten their first jobs and are expected to teach a section on Chicano history, etc. They have no background other than the color of their skin. They want a historiography and lessons on how to teach.

27. "Ethnic Classes Faculty Hired," *Los Angeles Times*, September 7, 1969, SF-A4.

28. Much of the success of a program depends on hustle. I was a supply sergeant in the army and also considered myself a Sergeant Bilko. Mode and level was a way of squeezing out more than the norm, such as with high school students who graduate with 4.5 GPAs.

29. Although liberal, Richfield hobnobbed with the most conservative cliques on campus, with people such as English professor Harry Stone and German professor Myra Reid. Ironically, although Richfield considered himself a scholar, he did not have a publishing record or trajectory.

30. Another example of Jerry's arbitrary behavior was that in the early 1980s the Grant's committee turned me down for a research grant. It did not amount to much, buying out my time for one class for a semester. I learned that one of the committee members had called Chicano Studies research "shit" research. Naturally, I raised a fuss, and Richfield backed the department. The resolution was that a portion of what the committee handed out would go back to the College of Humanities. We interpreted that to mean that it would go for Chicano Studies research. However, Richfield had other plans; he took the money and distributed it to his friends in English, philosophy, and foreign languages. We protested, but many of the faculty members did not want to jam Richfield because he was a liberal.

31. John Kumbula, "Minority Pair Head Program at Valley State," *Los Angeles Times*, January 21, 1969, E1. EOP was split in Chicano and black units in later January; this gave each group total control over recruitment and retention. The Chicano EOP gave the department a tremendous boost.

32. The original structure of EOP has been weakened. The university has split it into two, with a portion in the academic sector and a larger portion in student services. It seems reasonable, but it isn't—political and student service is always maneuvering to gobble up EOP. What is wrong with this? Simply, student services is consumed by outreach, and its mission has become to recruit the most "qualified" students—unlike EOP, who wants to bring in the students with the high potential and takes into account the poor educational background of minority students. It then works to give them the necessary skills to succeed. Being housed in the academic sector, aside from the cache, gives EOP independence, and Chicano Studies is better able to defend the interests of EOP and vice versa. Thomas Lewis, "EOP Merger Ordered," *Daily Sundial*, November 21, 1972. The Department of Health, Education and Welfare had investigated San Jose State and accused it of violating the Civil Rights Act of 1964. It was found that three other campuses had separate Chicano and black EOP, which at SFVSC was part of the twelve-point agreement. Along with San Jose, Northridge and Pomona were ordered to consolidate the units.

33. Jack Meacham, "Who Should Teach General Education Courses?" *Peer Review* 5, no. 1 (Fall 2002): 11.

34. This is disingenuous. How can classes produce well-rounded students without respecting other people or cultures? This is especially true when those peoples have such large populations and are essential to the economy.

35. The University of California is a research institution. It offers various professional degrees, as well as masters and doctorate degrees. Some romanticize this role and say that the mission of the research institution is to produce knowledge. Faculty members are normally responsible for research, training graduate students, and teaching two to three courses a semester. The California State University System is a teaching institution and offers bachelor of arts and master of arts and science degrees. It has limited professional schools, such as engineering, health science, and business. Its mission is teaching, not research, and professors are supposed to be concerned with pedagogy. At one time, the mission of many of the teaching institutions was the training of teachers. A problem is that faculty at teaching institutions should not be under the illusion that they are tier-one schools.

CHAPTER 5 — THE BUILDING OF CHICANO STUDIES

1. Harry Bernstein, "Jobless Rate at 6.5%, Expected to Grow Worse," *Los Angeles Times,* December 7, 1974, 1. "Rise in Jobless Rate Largest in 14 Years," *Los Angeles Times,* December 7, 1974, 22. Howard Seelye, "Unemployment in County Hit 8.1% in January," *Los Angeles Times,* February 8, 1975, 12A. William Trombley, "Reagan Plans to Trim Raises for Professors," *Los Angeles Times,* June 17, 1972, C1. Don Speich, "Brown Defends Budget Cuts for State Colleges," *Los Angeles Times,* January 30, 1975, 8A. Don Speech, "State Adult Education Cuts Urged," *Los Angeles Times,* March 4, 1976, 1.

2. Noel Greenwood, "School Enrollments Decreasing in Many Sections of California," *Los Angeles Times,* March 5, 1972, 1. Jack McCurdy, "Minority Students Rise in Segregated Schools," *Los Angeles Times,* September 15, 1972, C1. This decline in enrollment caused budget crises, which affected the recruitment of minority students and also Ethnic Studies programs. There was a 1–2 percent drop system wide. Two years later the situation worsened, with faculty complaining that a greater proportion of their staffs were comprised of part-timers. Tenure itself came under attack as a budget-cutting device. Ultimately, there was a trend of hiring more administrators and firing faculty. Sharon Vickers, "No Large Enrollment Drop Seen," *Daily Sundial,* May 1, 1973; Steve Fesuk, "Professors Criticize the CSUC System," *Daily Sundial,* November 12, 1975. "Lay Off Administrators, Not Faculty, Dymally Says," *Daily Sundial,* May 2, 1975.

3. Oscar Lewis, *Five Families: Mexican Case Studies in the Culture of Poverty* (New York: Basic Books, 1959). Oscar Lewis, *The Children of Sánchez: Autobiography of a Mexican Family* (New York: Vintage Books, 1961). Robert R Kirsch, "Some Social Nightmares in the Land of the Siesta," *Los Angeles Times,* May 17, 1964, Y15.

4. Bernard A. Kaplan, "Issues in Educating the Culturally Disadvantaged," *Phi Delta Kappan* 45, no. 2 (November 1963): 70. "Educators Offer Way to Reduce 'Dropouts,'" *Los Angeles Times,* February 15, 1963, 20. Richard F. Shepard, "Street Audience Enjoys Moliere," *New York Times,* July 8, 1964, 37. The *New York Times* ran full-page photos of 500 black and Puerto Rican children in the Bedford-Stuyvesant sector of Brooklyn, New York, watching a live performance of the seventeenth-century French playwright Molière. Ruben Salazar, "Mexican-Americans Have Culture Protected by 1848 U.S. Treaty," *Los Angeles Times,* March 1, 1963, A1. This discourse got so ridiculous that Ruben Salazar wrote, "Presumably they want to save these poor people from this terrible void by giving them culture. . . . What they don't seem to realize is that Mexican-Americans have a culture."

5. Harry Kitano and Dorothy Miller, *An Assessment of Education Opportunity Programs in California Higher Education* (Sacramento: California Coordinating Council for Higher Education, 1970), 2.

6. Marisol Moreno, "Of the Community, for the Community: The Chicana/o Student Movement in California's Public Higher Education, 1967–1973" (PhD diss., University of California, Santa Barbara, 2009), 4n5.

7. Beverly Hendrix Wright, "Social Class and Achievement Motivation: The Educational Opportunity Program At S.U.N.Y. at Buffalo: A Case Study," *Afro-Americans in New York Life and History* 8, no. 2 (July 31, 1984): 79.

8. Kitano and Miller, *An Assessment of Education Opportunity Programs,* 38–39.

9. "UC's 9 Campuses Double Number of Minorities," *Oakland Post,* November 25, 1968, 3. "U.C. Student Demands," *San Francisco Sun Reporter,* January 25, 1969, 10.

10. "Students Launch Drive to Assist Poor at UC," *Los Angeles Times,* November 2, 1969, F2.

11. Richard Vasquez, "Chicano Course Holds Mirror to Others, Too," *Los Angeles Times,* June 17, 1970, 1. "Sandoval Appointed Cal's *EOP* Associate Director," *Oakland Post,* September 24, 1970, 10. "The *EOP* Program: UCD Expects 400 *EOP* Students This Fall," *Sacramento Observer,* May 15, 1969, B-17.

12. "*EOP* Students at Sac State," *Sacramento Observer,* October 30, 1969, 7. "Valley State Students Face New Troubles," *San Francisco Sun Reporter,* December 13, 1969, 10. "Economic Opportunity Program," *Sacramento Observer,* April 16, 1970, 38. This was a constant struggle at the California state colleges. "Doubts Voiced over Proposals to Increase Minority Freshmen," *Daily Sundial,* April 30, 1968. The 4 percent rule was under constant attack, which merely allowed the colleges to recruit 4 percent of the incoming freshman that were deemed high risks because of not meeting the academic requirements of the institution. By legislative mandate the students received support services.

13. Kitano and Miller, *An Assessment of Education Opportunity Programs,* 29.

14. Ibid., 5.

15. Deroy Murdock, "Obama Admin. Stifles Favorable DC Voucher Study," *Real Clear Politics,* April 10, 2009, http://www.realclearpolitics.com/articles/2009/04/obama_admin_ stifles_favorable.html (accessed May 21, 2010).

16. Kitano and Miller, *An Assessment of Education Opportunity Programs,* 48.

17. Moreno, "Of the Community, for the Community," 3.

18. Gilbert G. González and Raul Fernández, "Chicano History: Transcending Cultural Models," *Pacific Historical Review* 63, no. 4 (November 1994): 469–497.

19. "Ralph C. Guzman; Latino Educator, Carter Aide," *Los Angeles Times,* October 13, 1985, C14. "Ralph C. Guzman," *San Francisco Chronicle,* October 12, 1985, 12. Frank del Olmo, "Two Men Who Were More Than Hyphens in a Hyphenated Melting Pot," *Los Angeles Times,* November 7, 1985, 7. David Sweet, "Ralph Guzmán, Politics; Community Studies: Santa Cruz," *Calisphere,* http://content.cdlib.org/view?docId=hb967nb5k3&doc.view=frames &chunk.id=div00025&toc.depth=1&toc.id=&brand=calisphere (accessed May 22, 2010).

20. Carlos Muñoz has stated that Los Angeles State College was the first department of Mexican American Studies established in 1968. This is not entirely correct. It was the first program, but its momentum was broken with a student coup that led to Guzmán's resignation. Ralph Guzmán, "The Gentle Revolutionaries Brown Power," *Los Angeles Times West Magazine,* January 26, 1969, http://www.sscnet.ucla.edu/YPC/1960_data/docs/lat_west_ mag_the_gentle_revolutionaries_brown_power.html (accessed May 22, 2010). The anti-Guzman students used this article against him. Carlos Muñoz Jr., *Youth, Identity, Power: The Chicano Movement,* rev. ed. (London: Verso, 2007), 132. "Mexican-American College Students to Be Discussed," *Arcadia Tribune,* June 1, 1969. "Minorities Studies Open on Limited Basis," *Los Angeles Times,* February 9, 1969, 19.

21. "Minorities Studies Open on Limited Basis," *Los Angeles Times,* February 9, 1969, 19. The certification of a department is a college-wide process vetted by the disparate

departments, the school, the college curriculum committee, the college president and then the chancellor's office. Not only is the course of study vetted, but each individual course and proposal must be approved.

22. "Mexican-Americans to Train as Teachers," *Los Angeles Times*, June 2, 1969, SG9. Dorothy Townsend, "Students Charge Colleges Have 'Minority Quota,'" *Los Angeles Times*, May 26, 1968, EB.

23. "Mexican-American Seminar Arranged," *Los Angeles Times*, May 8, 1966, SG-B6." Cal State Plans Offices to Cater to Minorities," *Los Angeles Times*, March 4, 1968, SG8. Evelyn DeWolfe, "Program Sowing Seeds of Chicano Pride," *Los Angeles Times*, September 9, 1970, H1.

24. "Minorities Studies Open on Limited Basis."

25. Kitano and Miller, *An Assessment of Education Opportunity Programs*, 30. Kitano and Miller put the 1969–1970 number of EOP students at 238.

26. Rene Nuñez, "A Proposal of Guidelines for Reordering Educational Processes of Recruitment and Admissions," in *Proceedings of the Conference on Increasing Opportunities for Mexican American Students in Higher Education*, ed. Franklin Mayer et al. (Los Angeles: Harbor College, 1969), ED031321. Rene told the author that relations with San Diego State College President Malcolm A. Love were excellent, and he had given them everything they wanted, as Love should have. The Centro was making the college rich in terms of in-kind contributions, which often ran between 20 to 40 percent of the grant.

27. "History of the Department," Chicana/o Studies Department, San Diego State University, 3.

28. Timothy McKernan, "The Viejo Turns 30: California's First Chicana/Chicano Studies Department Comes of Age," San Diego State Marketing and Communications, February 25, 2000. Roberto Rodríguez, "The Origins and History of the Chicano Movement" (Occasional Paper No. 7, April 1996, Julian Samora Research Institute), http://www.jsri .msu.edu/RandS/research/ops/oc07.html.

29. Carlos G. Vélez-Ibañez, *Border Visions: Mexican Cultures of the Southwest United States* (Tucson: University of Arizona Press, 1996), 134–135.

30. William Trombley, "At Long Beach," *Los Angeles Times*, June 16, 1969, OC2.

31. Tom Willman, "Mexican-American Festival," *Long Beach (CA) Independent Press-Telegram*, April 29, 1971.

32. Mayer et al., "Proceedings."

33. Sándoval up to this point had good activist credentials. "Chicano Leader Faces Disturbance Charge," *Long Beach (CA) Independent Press-Telegram*, May 3, 1969. He was one of the thirteen charged with disturbing a speech by Governor Ronald Reagan at the Biltmore Hotel on April 25. Rene Nuñez, director of the Educational Clearing House for Central Los Angeles, was also charged. "La Raza Nueva Holds Celebration at CSLB," *Long Beach (CA) Independent Press-Telegram*, October 13, 1968.

34. Armando Rodríguez with Lionel Van Deerlin, *From the Barrio to Washington: An Educator's Journey* (Albuquerque: University of New Mexico Press, 2007), 90. He later became president of ELAC. Mike Castro, "Mexican-American at ELAC," *Los Angeles Times*, June 9, 1973, SG10.

35. "3-Day Chicano Study Seminar Ends Today," *Los Angeles Times*, August 2, 1970, B2.

36. Walt Murray, "Ex-Student Body President Not Optimistic," *Long Beach (CA) Independent Press-Telegram*, September 21,1969. Walt Murray, "Mexican-American Studies: Recapturing Lost Aslan [*sic*] Heritage at CSLB," *Long Beach (CA) Independent Press-Telegram*, March 21, 1970.

37. Office of Education (DHEW), *Chicano Mobile Institutes* (Washington, DC: Office of Education, 1973–1974, archived at the Education Resource Information Center), ED113117.

Julio A. Martínez, *Chicano Scholars and Writers: A Bio-Bibliographical Directory* (Lanham, MD: Scarecrow Press, 1979). "Guide to the Tomás Ybarra-Frausto Papers 1943–1988," University of Washington, https://www.lib.washington.edu/specialcoll/findaids/docs/uarchives/UA19_25_4339Ybarra-FraustoTomas.xml (accessed May 22, 2010). "Baca-Barragán, Polly: 1941– : Politician, Media Relations Specialist," *Free Encyclopedias*, http://biography.jrank.org/pages/3791/Baca-Barrag-n-Polly-1941-Politician-Media-Relations-Specialist.html (accessed November 11, 2010).

38. Tom Willman, "In Campus Trailer: Chicano Institute Running Smoothly," *Long Beach (CA) Independent Press-Telegram*, May 1, 1971.

39. "Chicanos to Fete Independence Day," *Long Beach (CA) Independent Press-Telegram*, September 16, 1971.

40. Lara Santiago Renta, "Frank Sanchez: If You've Ever Passed through the Golden Arches in Southern California, Chances Are Frank Sanchez Had Something to Do with It," *Latino Leaders: The National Magazine of the Successful American Latino*, August–September 2005, http://findarticles.com/p/articles/mi_moPCH/is_4_6/ai_n15340564/.

41. "Series Slated on Mexican Culture," *Los Angeles Times*, March 8, 1971, F18.

42. Hal Leiren, "Students Told to Bring About Peaceful Change," *Los Angeles Times*, April 21, 1969, SG8. Relations between San Fernando Valley State College and Long Beach State College were strained. In April 1969 white SFVSC professors participated in a conference that was sponsored by the Los Angeles Probation Department for 200 high school and college students at Occidental College. Two Valley State political scientists, Jane Bayes and Jack O'Neil, spoke along with United Mexican American Students from Long Beach State College, headed by Frank Sándoval. No professors or students from Valley State were invited.

43. Joe Segura, "Chicano Enrollment Losing Ground," *Long Beach (CA) Independent Press-Telegram*, September 1, 1975.

44. "Frank Cruz," *Long Beach (CA) Independent Press-Telegram*, November 4, 1975.

45. Ray Steele Jr., "Professor's View Pride: A Crutch of Mexican American," *Fresno (CA) Bee*, December 2, 1967.

46. "Firing Upheld for Teacher at Fresno State," *Los Angeles Times*, June 8, 1968, A12.

47. John Dreyfuss, "Muslim Defies Orders, Teaches College Class," *Los Angeles Times*, October 26, 1969, AA. "The Incredible Case of Marvin X," *Los Angeles Times*, October 29, 1969, B6. "Marvin X Job Offer at Fresno State Denied," *Los Angeles Times*, October 30, 1969, 33. "Fresno State Senate Backs Class Boycott," *Los Angeles Times*, February 20, 1970, D20.

48. Art Dove, "Violence Brings Emergency at Fresno State," *Los Angeles Times*, May 21, 1970, 3.

49. "Fresno State Drops La Raza Studies Classes," *Long Beach (CA) Independent Press-Telegram*, September 9, 1970. For the administration's account, see W. Donald Albright Papers, 1961–1974, 2001, University Archives, Henry Madden Library, California State University, Fresno (bulk 1967–1970), which are 1.5 linear feet. Also in the archives is the Campus Unrest Collection, 1965–1979, 1.75 linear feet.

50. "Fresno State Turns Down Chicano List," *Los Angeles Times*, September 12, 1970, B10.

51. "Fresno State Classes Open at Troubled College," *Hayward (CA) Daily Review*, September 14, 1970. "Southland," *Los Angeles Times*, December 15, 1970, 2.

52. "Dr. Smiley Explains 'Gap' between Town and Gown," *El Paso Herald-Post*, October 16, 1969. "Race Issue at UTEP Told," *El Paso Herald Post*, October 25, 1969.

53. Bob Ybarra, "Awakening Chicano Is Examined," *El Paso Herald-Post*, December 27, 1971.

54. Bob Ybarra, "JD Group Trains Leaders, Sets Protests," *El Paso Herald-Post*, December 31, 1971.

55. Ibid.

56. Abelardo Delgado, "Leader Tells How Maya, Machos Are Formed," *El Paso Herald-Post*, December 30, 1971,

57. "Dr. Smiley Explains 'Gap' between Town and Gown." "Mexican American Studies Aimed at Culture, History," *Prospector*, November 4, 1969. "30 Arrested Attempting to Seize UTEP Building," *El Paso Herald-Post*, December, 3, 1971. Bob Ybarra, "Many Aims of Conference, Aztlán Plan Similar," *El Paso Herald-Post*, January 13, 1972. Wayne McClintock, "Race Study Courses Approved," *El Paso Herald-Post*, December 16, 1969.

58. Bob Ybarra, "H-P Examines Awakening of Chicanos in Southwest," *El Paso Herald-Post*, December 17, 1971. Bob Ybarra, "Awareness Grows of Indian Identity," *El Paso Herald-Post*, December 28, 1971. Bob Ybarra, "Claim Schools Fail Mexican-American," *El Paso Herald-Post*, January 10, 1972.

59. Pat Ellis, "Outlook," *El Paso Prospector*, February 10, 1970. Frank Macias, "Chicano Studies Program to Be Recommended by MEChA Group," *El Paso Prospector*, August 7, 1970. "Noted Scholar, Author to Speak at Meeting," *El Paso Herald-Post*, Friday, August 14, 1970. Arturo Franco, "Chicano Program Long Overdue," *El Paso Prospector*, August 14, 1970. Dr. Philip D. Ortego, "A Case for Chicano Affairs Programs," *El Paso Prospector*, October 16, 1970.

60. "Chicano Studies Discussed," *El Paso Herald-Post*, April 15, 1971. "Smiley Answers Chicano Queries," *El Paso Herald-Post*, April 16, 1971. "Chicano Group Gives Demands to UTEP Head," *El Paso Herald-Post*, November 30, 1971.

61. "30 Arrested Attempting to Seize UTEP Building," *El Paso Herald-Post*, December 3, 1971.

62. "UTEP Tuition Hike in Effect," *El Paso Herald-Post*, August 28, 1972. Bob Ybarra, "Brown Berets Tell Reasons for Actions," *El Paso Herald-Post*, January 3, 1972.

63. "Chicano Studies Major Hoped for By Director," *El Paso Prospector*, October 26, 1972. Alfredo Vasquez, "Chicano Studies Hits Snag," *El Paso Prospector*, May 13, 1975 (originally published November 22, 1974).

64. "G.I. Forum Honors Fort Worth Woman," *El Paso Herald Post*, January 31, 1976.

65. "Chicano Studies Director Asked to Resign," *El Paso Prospector*, June 24, 1976.

66. Edna Gundersen, "Vacant Position Creates Turmoil," *El Paso Prospector*, September 14, 1976.

67. "Wrong Concept," *El Paso Herald-Post*, January 31, 1977.

68. "VSC Minorities Plan Still Short of Promise," *Los Angeles Times*, October 5, 1969, SF1. Phil Missimore, "Directors of Ethnic Studies Predict Department Growth," *Daily Sundial*, October 7, 1969. Approximately 450–500 students enrolled in Chicano Studies the first semester. Pan-African Studies with a large base had about 1,000 students enrolled. Chicano Studies had six full-time and seven part-time instructors. There were 385 black students (268 new and 117 continuing), 296 Chicanos (2 new and 45 continuing), and 13 other students, all new.

69. Ron Einstoss, "Charges in Valley State Trial Called Distorted," *Los Angeles Times*, September 30, 1969, I7. "Policeman Describes Threats to Hostages," *Daily Sundial*, October 21, 1969. "Prosecution Wrap-Up Insists on Conspiracy," *Daily Sundial*, November 14, 1969.

70. Dr. Frank Meza interview, *In Search of Aztlán*, August 25, 2000, http://www.insearchofaztlan.com/meza.html (accessed May 22, 2010).

71. "Plan Speakers for Rally after Moratorium March," *Valley News and Green Sheet*, July 14, 1970.

72. David Rosenzweig, "Student Senate Refuses to Pay 8 VSC Chicanos," *Los Angeles Times*, November 14, 1971, SF1.

73. Kenneth J. Fanucchi, "Students Move into Coed Dorm," *Los Angeles Times*, October 6, 1969, SF9.

74. Richard T. Cooper, "How Shooting Erupted at Kent State Campus," *Los Angeles Times*, May 5, 1970, 6. Harold Klopper and Tom Marx, "Students Call for Shutdown," *Daily Sundial*, May 6, 1970. 1,500 students at protest. "Valley College Officials Forestall Campus Clash by Lowering Flag," *Los Angeles Times*, May 7, 1970, SF1. "State Colleges Ordered Closed in Wake of Protests," *Van Nuys Valley (CA) News*, May 7, 1970. Roger Scott, "Strikers Plan to Continue, but Disagree on Tactics," *Daily Sundial*, May 11, 1970. Stu Simmons, "MEChA Loses Campus Home," *Daily Sundial*, May 11, 1970.

75. "Mexican American Dept. to Stay at Valley State," *Van Nuys Valley (CA) News*, May 8, 1970. "Valley State Chicano Unit Plans Orientation Meeting," *Van Nuys Valley (CA) News*, May 12, 1970. Kenneth J. Fanucchi, "VSC Quiet, Busy as Strike Argued," *Los Angeles Times*, May 8, 1970, SF5.

76. Kenneth Lubas, "Cleary Says He Knows of No Revolutionaries," *Los Angeles Times*, May 16, 1970, SF10. Kenneth J. Fanucchi, "Dumke Probe Sought in VSC Voting," *Los Angeles Times*, May 13, 1970, SF6. "VSC Poverty Officials Cleared in Vote Hassle," *Los Angeles Times*, May 29, 1970, SF6.

77. "$400,000 VSC Student Body Budget Attacked," *Los Angeles Times*, May 29, 1970, SF6.

78. Offie Charry Wortham, "A Project Demonstrating Excellence on Interracial Education at Antioch College: Analysis of Efforts of Antioch College to Increase Cultural Pluralism 1964–1973" (PhD diss., Union Graduate School, Schenectady, New York, 1974), 9, 13, 16, 21, 23, 29, 40. Constance Cappel, "Utopian Colleges: A Study of Five Experiment American Educational Institutions" (PhD diss., Union Graduate Institute, Schenectady, NY, 1991), 54.

79. Wortham, "A Project Demonstrating Excellence," 89, 122, 140. Milton Schwebel, "Pluralism and Diversity in American Higher Education," *Annals of the American Academy of Political and Social Science* 404 (November 1972): 91.

80. "Dropouts: New Unique Program for Degree Seekers," *Oakland Post*, February 3, 1974, 3.

81. José Angel Gutiérrez, *The Making of a Chicano Militant: Lessons from Cristal* (Madison: University of Wisconsin Press, 1999), 180.

82. Daniel Ordaz, "Once upon a Chicano College Hispanics United to Create the First School of Its Kind in the U.S.," *Valley Morning Star*, October 4, 2005.

83. Hoyt Hager, "Chicano College Bid Upsets Weslaco School Board," *Corpus Christi Caller-Times*, October 2, 1971.

84. "'Hate' Is Taught at Chicano College," *El Paso Herald-Post*, August 20, 1973. "Vows to Fire Police Chief If Rumors True," *Big Spring (TX) Herald*, January 9, 1974.

85. Oregon State University Library, "Guide to the Colegio César Chávez Collection, 1978–2005," *OSU Library Archives*, http://osulibrary.oregonstate.edu/archives/archive/mss/documents/OREcolegio.pdf (accessed May 22, 2010). "Cherish Your Heritage: The Harvest Is Great, Colegio César Chavez," *Silverton-Appeal Tribune/Mt. Angel News*, September 11, 1980, 2. Thanks to Dorinda Moreno of the Bay Area. "College Named for César Chavez," *Oxnard (CA) Press-Courier*, December 13, 1973.

86. "Students Face Eviction," *Walla Walla Union Bulletin*, January 13, 1977. "$550,000 Offered for College Site," *Walla Walla Union Bulletin*, March 10, 1977. Steve Graham, "Tiny Hispanic College Struggles to Survive," *Fredrick (MD) News*, November 12, 1981.

87. "Indian-Chicano University May Open Next February," *Oakland Tribune*, December 16, 1970. Brendan Riley, "Indians See Culture Revived by University," *Long Beach (CA) Independent Press-Telegram*, April 1, 1971. "DQU Preserve Indian Culture," *Albuquerque Journal*, October 16, 1977.

CHAPTER 6 — GROWING A PROGRAM

1. "Want College Education? California Makes It Easy," *Los Angeles Times*, September 11, 1955, A12.

2. "Non-Resident Tuition Increase Needed," *Los Angeles Times*, June 1, 1965, A4.

3. Ray Zeman, "$60 Million Cut in Brown Budget, UC Tuition Fee Urged," *Los Angeles Times*, April 26, 1966, 3.

4. William Trombley, "UC and Colleges Severely Jolted by Budget News," *Los Angeles Times*, January 8, 1967, B1. "College Reaction to Economy Plans Shocking, Reagan Says," *Los Angeles Times*, January 10, 1967, 3. Ray Zeman, "Reagan: Tuition, but No Cuts," *Los Angeles Times*, January 11, 1967, 1. William Trombley, "Entrance Freeze," *Los Angeles Times*, January 12, 1967, 1.

5. "The State," *Los Angeles Times*, February 12, 1967, F5. Maurice B Goudzwaard, R. Bruce Ricks, and Erwin M. Keithley, "Opposition to Tuition," *Los Angeles Times*, August 26, 1967, B4. "Tuition—Myth and Reality," *Los Angeles Times*, August 30, 1967, A4.

6. Tom Goff, "Unruh Group Votes to Oppose Tuition or Large Fee Hike," *Los Angeles Times*, February 9, 1968, 3. Mary Barber, "Colleges See New Trend," *Los Angeles Times*, April 14, 1968, SG-B8.

7. William Trombley, "Dumke, Hitch Sharply Criticize Measure on Deferred Tuition," *Los Angeles Times*, July 25, 1969, 3. William Trombley, "Tuition Next Year Almost Certainty," *Los Angeles Times*, November 9, 1969, 1. William Trombley, "Threat to UC, State Colleges' Enrollment Told," *Los Angeles Times*, December 14, 1969, C1. "Tuition OK for State Colleges," *Los Angeles Times*, March 29, 1970, F5. Anthony Barcellos, "The Rodda Project: Paying for a University Education, Tuition at the University of California (1970)," *Back Bench*, August 16, 2007, http://thebackbench.blogspot.com/2007/08/tuition-at-university-of-california.html (accessed May 24, 2010).

8. See Gloria Anzaldúa, *La frontera / Borderlands*, 2d ed. (San Francisco: Aunt Lute Books, 1999).

9. ChicanoArt.org, http://www.chicanoart.org/ (accessed May 24, 2010). Chicano culture, art, and politics, http://www.xispas.com/ (accessed May 24, 2010).

10. Jessica López, "Chicano: Traveling Exhibit Pays Homage to the Chicano Experience," *Lowrider Arte*, http://www.lowriderarte.com/featuredartists/02031ra_chicano_art_cheech_marin/index.html (accessed May 24, 2010). *Cheech and Chicano Art*, http://www.cheechmarinonline.com/ chicano.html (accessed May 24, 2010).

11. René Yañez, "Chicano Visions: American Painters on the Verge," Chicano Art Life, http://www.chicano-art-life.com/index2.html (accessed May 24, 2010). Shifra M. Goldman, *Dimensions of the Americas: Art and Social Change in Latin America and the United States* (Chicago: University of Chicago Press, 1995). "A Brief History of Chicano Murals," *Sparc Murals*, http://www.sparcmurals.org/present/cmt/cmt.html (accessed May 24, 2010). María Cardalliaguet Gómez-Málaga, "The Mexican and Chicano Mural Movements," *Yale-New Haven Teachers Institute* http://www.yale.edu/ynhti/curriculum/ units/2006/2/06.02.01.x .html (accessed May 24, 2010).

12. Malaquias Montoya, "Biography," http://www.malaquiasmontoya.com/bio.php (accessed May 24, 2010). *Royal Chicano Air Force*, http://www.chilipie.com/rcaf/ (May 24, 2010). Royal Chicano Air Force, "Archives," *Online Archive of California*, http://www . oac.cdlib.org/findaid/ark:/13030/kt9d5nd53d (accessed May 24, 2010).

13. *Chicano Art Magazine*, http://www.chicanoartmagazine.com/ (access May 24, 2010). Armando Vázquez, "Reflection on the Chicano Art Movimiento a Primer," Judith Hernández Work on Paper, http://jhnartestudio.com/Documents/primer_armando_vazquez.htm (accessed May 24, 2010). Nora Benavidez, "Harry Gamboa, Jr.: L.A. Urban

Exile," *Harry Gamboa Jr.*, http://www.harrygamboajr.com/text/panorama/nora.html (accessed May 24, 2010).

14. Alma López, http://www.almalopez.net/. Alma López, "The Artist of 'Our Lady,'" *Las Tres Culturas*, http://www.lasculturas.com/aa/aa040201b.htm (accessed May 24, 2010). *Just Another Poster*, http://www.art-for-a-change.com/Chicano/chicano.htm (accessed May 24, 2010). The Chicano Collection, http://www.thechicanocollection.net/artists.html (accessed May 24, 2010). Chicano Art Networks, *Handbook of Texas Online*, http://www.tshaonline .org/handbook/online/articles/CC/kjc4.html (accessed May 24, 2010).

15. Lalo Delgado (2004–2005), Denver, Colorado, http://www.denvergov.org/Poems/ tabid/389851/Default.aspx (accessed May 24, 2010).

16. Stephan Thernstrom, *Harvard Encyclopedia of American Ethnic Groups* (Cambridge, MA: Belknap Press of Harvard University Press, 1980), 697–699.

17. Numbers and Geographic Distribution, Center for Immigrant Studies, http:// www.cis.org/articles/2001/mexico/numbers.html (accessed May 26, 2010).

18. Peter Kornbluh, "Chile and the United States: Declassified Documents Relating to the Military Coup," *National Security Archive Electronic Briefing Book No.* 8, September 11, 1973, National Security Archive, George Washington University, http://www.gwu.edu/~nsarchiv/ NSAEBB/index.html.

19. Ron Einstoss, "Hotel Fire Indictments Reveal Heroism of Rookie Policeman," *Los Angeles Times*, June 7, 1969,1A. "4 Activists Surrender in Biltmore Fire Case," *Los Angeles Times*, June 10, 1969, 28, 1A. Ruben Salazar, "Brown Berets Hail 'La Raza' and Scorn the Establishment," *Los Angeles Times*, June 16, 1969, 3. "Police Agent Tells Work in Brown Berets," *Los Angeles Times*, August 10, 1971, B2. Ernesto Chávez, "*¡Mi Raza Primero!*" *(My People First!)*: Nationalism, Identity, and Insurgency in the Chicano Movement in Los Angeles, 1966–1978* (Berkeley: University of California Press, 2002), 52.

20. Richard Knee, "Professors' Union Considers Filling Suit over Bugging at CSUN," *Valley News*, November 30, 1972. John Rogers, "Police Accused of Bugging," *Daily Sundial*, November 21, 1972. "UPC President John Stafford charged that Yelverton was discovered hiding behind a vending machine while dressed in plain clothes with his service revolver sitting at his side on a nearby table." The administration denied he used the tape recorder. Yelverton was present, according to the administration, because it was standard to have a policeman present in case of trouble.

21. The case was called *Committee Against Police Abuse (CAPA) v. PDID*.

22. Victor Merina, "Reiner Defends PDID," *Los Angeles Times*, January 20, 1983, C1. Joel Sappell, "New LAPD Unit for Intelligence Asked," *Los Angeles Times*, March 4, 1983, D1. In one case, a Public Disorder and Intelligence Division (PDID) officer lived with a white female plaintiff for seven years. They had a daughter, and he spied on her friends.

23. Michael Seiler, "LAPD Accused of Spying at University," *Los Angeles Times*, June 11, 1982, D5. Editorial, "Curtain Drops Too Soon on Police Spying Case," *Daily Sundial*, February 29, 1984. "For students and several Chicano Studies professors, the denouement of this high drama came too soon. The finale, they say, left its audience hanging, with plots unresolved and facts to reveal." The plaintiffs were granted $1.8 million, the largest settlement to date. The spying began in 1970 and lasted throughout the seventies. They admitted that at least two officers spied on Chicano Studies classes between 1972 and 1979, enrolling in classes. The Anti-Terrorism Division of the LAPD took over from the PDID. Julie Parnell, "PDID Settlement Raises Security vs. Privacy Debate," *Daily Sundial*, February 29, 1984. The police were supported by Councilman Hal Bernson, who opposed the Freedom of Information Act, without which we could have never gotten the information. The article was critical of Bernson. Michael Collins and Loren Eisler, "CSUN Plaintiffs Lukewarm toward Police Spy Case Settlement," *Daily Sundial*, February 23, 1984.

24. I do not mention the individual's name because it would serve no purpose. He is a good friend who has made substantial contributions to the community. It is the police who had the duty to protect me.

25. On August 29, 1970, journalist Ruben Salazar was assassinated by LA County sheriff deputies.

26. Donnella Collison, "CSUN MEChA Members Claim Harassment by Undercover LAPD Officers," *Northridge (CA) Daily Sundial*, October 2, 2009.

27. Ibid. Pam Tapper, "Hate and the Internet," *Daily Sundial*, October 13, 2009. Hector Villagra to Assistant Chief Michel R. Moore, February 2010. Vanessa Rojas, "Cal State U. Students Have Begun 48-Hour Vigil Protest to Speak Out about the Deep Crisis in Public Higher Education," press release, July 20, 2009.

28. "UW students, Mostly Chicano, Go on Rampage after Minority Teacher Not Hired," *Centralia (WA) Daily Chronicle*, May 14, 1974. "UW Students Put on Notice That No More Sit-ins Will Be Tolerated," *Centralia (WA) Daily Chronicle*, May 14, 1974. Brian Haughton, "Dean Beckman's Office Trashed during Sitin," *Seattle Civil Rights and Labor History Project*, http://depts.washington.edu/civilr/display.cgi?image=mecha/news/1974/14-May-74%20Daily%201%20crop.jpg (accessed November 11, 2010). "Munoz Case Engulfed in the Morass of the System," *Seattle Civil Rights and Labor History Project*, http://depts.washington.edu/civilr/display.cgi?image=mecha/news/1974/27-Jun-74%20Daily%209%20crop.jpg (accessed November 11, 2010). Carlos Muñoz Jr., *Youth, Identity, Power: The Chicano Movement* (London: Verso, 1989). Carlos Muñoz Jr., *Youth, Identity, Power: The Chicano Movement Revised* (London: Verso, 2007).

29. David Hodges, "Chavarria Files Federal Charges Over Tenure," *Daily Nexus*, April 13, 1976.

30. In each of the struggles against the administration there was a pattern of a Chicano supporting change and subverting it. In my case against UCSB, it was Francisco Lomeli and Ray Huerta, with each benefiting materially from Chicano Studies. Because of a lack of historical memory, these people become serial offenders. The following is part of the student demands in 1975:

DEMAND: THE RESIGNATION OF AFFIRMATIVE ACTION COORDINATOR RAYMOND HUERTA.

In regards to his administrative position in the general University level;

a) Raymond Huerta, Affirmative Action Coordinator, agrees that there is discrimination against Chicanos in the University and yet, he is a defendant in our present lawsuit against the University and will not become a plaintiff. (As he stated at El Congreso's meeting on November 5, 1974.)

b) He allows "Spanish-American" data to destroy Chicano faculty and staff and student figures in relation to affirmative action objects. He also uses foreign student data to inflate UCSB ethnic minority enrollment figures. This is in Violation of Executive Order 11246.

c) He will not initiate a HEW compliance review as required by his duties as Affirmative Action Coordinator.

d) Presently there is no HEW approved affirmative action plan at UCSB. Huerta has made no effort in initiating a program on this campus. He has merely relied on results from Berkeley, the model campus for affirmative action.

e) He has made no effort in maintaining the position of Assistant to the Chancellor on Minority Affairs—claiming it to be a decision for management. Consequently, this position has been eliminated.

In regards to his support of Chicano programs:

a) Huerta says that he supports Chicano studies but he has failed to show any public support by not endorsing the Chicano Statement which was issued in the Spring Quarter of 1974.

b) He has not acted on the fact that the positions, Chairman of Chicano Studies, are currently held by two Anglos who do not have time, interest or the competence to deal effectively with Chicano programs.

c) He failed to issue a public statement of support, as requested by El Congreso on November 5, 1974 and later by concerned Chicano students, in regards to Chicano Studies and the lawsuit.

In regards to his political tactics on campus and in the community, Mr. Ray Huerta;

a) Tried to intimidate the community into not becoming plaintiffs in the law suit.

b) Advised Chancellor Cheadle not to go to the Concilio de la Raza meeting because it was a set up.

c) Tried to initiate behind-the-scenes meetings between Chancellor Cheadle and President of Concilio de la Raza President, Abelino Bailon.

d) Tried to intimidate Chicano students by stating that if they continued his "character assassination," they were going to be subject to a law suit by him. (Arnulfo Casillas, Students for Collective Action, "What Are the Issues?" May 1975, 5–6)

Pablo Cinesanam, "Cesa huelga de hambre en Santa Barbara: La Universidad acepta puntos de huelguistas Latinos," *La Opinion* 68, no. 234 (May 7, 1994): 1A.

31. Hermine Lees, "St. Euphrasia Church: A History," *Los Angeles Tidings,* http://www.the-tidings.com/2007/080307/euphrasiaside.htm.

32. Organizational secretary, CPUSA, Southern California District. Mandel was a very honest man; he never lied to me and always kept his word. The right should not complain about left groups on campus. David Horwitz, a heavily funded right wing nut, has informants on various campuses in the Los Angeles area.

33. Patricia Hynds, "The Ideological Struggle within the Catholic Church in Nicaragua," *No 3 Envio Digital* (August 1981), http://www.envio.org.ni/articulo/3097. Michael Dodson, "The Changing Spectrum of Religious Activism in Latin America," *Latin American Perspectives* 20 (1993): 61–74.

34. Charles Cotrell, *Tejano Voices,* http://libraries.uta.edu/tejanovoices/interview.asp?CMASNo=020 (accessed May 26, 2010).

35. Olga Rodríguez, "Chicano Liberation Report to the 1976 SWP Convention," *Marxists,* http://www.marxists.org/history/etol/document/swp-us/chicanlib5.htm (accessed November 11, 2010). An excellent summary of issues.

36. Robin D. G. Kelley and Betsy Esch, "Black Like Mao: Red China and Black Revolution," in Fred Weihan Ho and Bill Mullen, *Afro Asia: Revolutionary Political and Cultural Connections between African Americans and Asian Americans* (Durham, NC: Duke University Press, 2008), 130. Ron Hale, "Arraignment Set Today for Arrested SDS Members," November 10, 1966. Darlene Lime, "Two More Charged at Hearing," *Daily Sundial,* July 12, 1967.

37. Elizabeth "Betita" Martínez, "A View from New Mexico: Recollections of the Movimiento Left," *Monthly Review* 54, no. 3 (2002), http://monthlyreview.org/0702martinez.htm.

38. Unión del Barrio, http://uniondelbarrio.org/laverdad/ (accessed May 25, 2010). Unión del Barrio Political Program, http://www.aguilaycondor.org/pgs/polprogram/program_eng12_2009.pdf (accessed May 25, 2010).

39. Association of Raza Educators, http://www.razaeducators.org/ (accessed May 25, 2010). Teaching for Change, http://www.teachingforchange.org/node/435, (accessed May 25, 2010).

40. "First Draft Program Review, Chicano Studies, California State University at Northridge, 1975," found in Rodolfo F. Acuña Archives at Library, California State University, Northridge.

41. Departments are like states that protect their turf. The major battles are in committees that govern which discipline is represented in general education and liberal studies. These committees give the different disciplines franchises; students must take these courses or select from them. It runs like a monopoly board. Intense training goes on. Promotions and retentions are also controlled through committees.

42. The reader or readers underlined this portion and vigorously reacted to this point during the consultation periods.

43. "First Draft Program Review," 5, 7.

44. Ibid., 8.

45. Kenneth Seib, *The Slow Death of Fresno State: A California Campus under Reagan and Brown* (Palo Alto: Ramparts Press, 1979), 98–99. William Scranton, *President's Commission on Campus Unrest: The Report of the President's Commission on Campus Unrest* (Washington, DC: U.S. Government Printing Office, 1970), 21 (ED 083899). Scranton puts the Kent State shootings into context. Of Berkeley, he writes, "The Berkeley revolt did not explode in a vacuum. It was preceded by a chain of developments during the late 1950s and early 1960s which helped to revive campus activism."

46. "Students March to Capitol," *Madison (WI) Capital Times*, February 14, 1969. John Patrick Hunter, "Guard to Stay on Campus Just as Long as Needed," *Madison (WI) Capital Times*, February 14, 1969. "Police Charge 1,500 State St. Paraders," *Madison (WI) Capital Times*, February 15, 1969.

47. California is important because prior to the Reagan years it was among the most progressive states in the union and it set the standard.

48. Proposition 209 (1998).

49. Louie Gonzalez, "Court Hit on U C Admissions," *Oakland Tribune*, January 16, 1977. See Rodolfo F. Acuña, *Sometimes There Is No Other Side: The Myth of Equality* (Notre Dame: Notre Dame University Press, 1998).

50. "UC Handling of Racial Case Hit," *Los Angeles Times*, March 4, 1977, C2. "It's Up to the People to Stop Bakke," *San Francisco Sun Reporter*, June 9, 1977, 7. William Raspberry, "Minorities Have No Access," *Los Angeles Times*, July 24, 1977, I5.

51. Ralph R. Smith, "What Is the Truth About the Bakke Case?" *Oakland Post*, August 17, 1977, 1.

52. Jaime Veve, "WW in 1978: 35,000 March to 'Beat Back Bakke!" *Workers World*, April 21, 1978; reprinted as part of a special archival series.

53. "Bakke Demos Set," *San Francisco Sun Reporter*, September 22, 1977, 3. Phillip Hager, "Bakke Reverse Bias Case Dominates Court Calendar," *Los Angeles Times*, October 2, 1977, A1. Phil Kerby, "Southland Observations," *Los Angeles Times*, October 6, 1977, C1. "750 Protest State Court Decision in Bakke Case," *Los Angeles Times*, October 9, 1977, A29. John S. Holley, "Bakke Case and Affirmative Action," *Los Angeles Times*, December 2, 1977, F6.

54. "Excerpts of Marshall's and Others' Opinions," *Los Angeles Times*, June 29, 1978, B23.

55. Austin Scott, "Prop. 13, Bakke Decision Pose Serious Problems for Blacks, NAACP Believes," *Los Angeles Times*, July 5, 1978, B8. Dorothy Townsend, "50 UCLA Law Students Begin Hunger Strike, Sit-In," *Los Angeles Times*, November 29, 1978, SD10.

56. Girardeau A. Spann, *The Law of Affirmative Action: Twenty Five Years of Supreme Court Decisions on Race and Remedies* (New York: New York University Press, 2000), 15–18.

57. Gall Berkley, Bernice Cherry, Ann E. Fields, "Community Reactions to Bakke Decision Vary," *Oakland Post*, July 2, 1978, 1. Max Elbaum, *Revolution in the Air: Sixties Radicals turn to Lenin, Mao and Che* (London: Verso, 2002), 244.

58. Seib, *Fresno State*, 138.

59. Ronald L. Soble, "Minorities' Leaders Expect Setback If Prop. 13 Wins," *Los Angeles Times* June 5, 1978, A9.

60. Kenneth Reich, "Prop. 13 Tide Not Making Waves in Texas," *Los Angeles Times*, September 27, 1978, J1.

61. Jack McCurdy, "Partial Restoration of Summer School Proposed," *Los Angeles Times*, February 14, 1979, B29.

62. Thomas A. Downes, "The Implications of the Serrano Decision and Proposition 13 for Local Public Office" (PhD diss., Stanford University, 1988), 2. Soble, "Minorities' Leaders Expect Setback."

63. Don F. Speich, "State Talking Seriously About Tuition," *Los Angeles Times*, May 12, 1980, B1. Christopher W. Hoene, "Frozen Inequities: Municipal Finance after Proposition 13 in California" (PhD diss., Claremont Graduate University, Claremont, CA, 2000), 7. "13 Firms to Get $431 Million Tax Cut Under Jarvis," *Los Angeles Times*, May 10, 1978, B3. Pacific Telephone, Pacific Gas & Electric, and Southern California Edison would get over half of this amount.

64. Richard Bergholz, "PROP. 13 Landslide Younger to Oppose Brown," *Los Angeles Times*, June 7, 1978, 1.

65. The deterioration of the schools also had the effect of encouraging white middle schools to flee to private schools.

66. "Renters Considered Slighted," *Los Angeles Times*, March 12, 1978, I21. Bud Lembke, "Says Jarvis Must Be Defeated," *Los Angeles Times*, March 18, 1978, OC32. "California Farm Bureau Endorses Jarvis Initiative," *Los Angeles Times*, March 30, 1978, B26. Erwin Baker, "16 Library Closures under Prop. 13 OKd," *Los Angeles Times*, May 2, 1978, C1. Kenneth Reich, "Prop. 13 Tide Not Making Waves in Texas," *Los Angeles Times*, September 27, 1978, J1.

67. "Education Week Quality Counts 2009," *EdWeek*, http://www.edweek.org/ew/index.html.

68. Stephen J. Carroll, Cathy Krop, Jeremy Arkes, Peter A. Morrison, Ann Flanagan, "California's K–12 Public Schools: How Are They Doing?" *Rand Corp*, 2005, xxiii, http://www.rand.org/pubs/monographs/2004/RAND_MG186.sum.pdf (accessed May 26, 2010).

69. Tracy M. Gordon, Jaime Calleja Alderete, Patrick J. Murphy, Jon Sonstelie, and Ping Zhang, *Fiscal Realities: Budget Tradeoffs in California Government* (San Francisco: Public Policy Institute of California, January 2007), 39.

70. "Dropouts in California," *Latino Issues Forum: A Public Policy and Advocacy Institute*, June 2006, 1, http://www.lif.org/download/newdropout%5B1%5D.pdf (accessed May 26, 2010).

CHAPTER 7 — THE MAINSTREAMING OF CHICANO STUDIES

1. Fabio Rojas, *From Black Power to Black Studies: How a Radical Social Movement Became an Academic Discipline* (Baltimore: Johns Hopkins University Press, 2007), 130.

2. Leslie I. Hill, "The Ford Foundation Program on Mainstreaming Minority Women's Studies," *Women's Studies Quarterly* 18, no. 1/2 (Spring/Summer 1990): 24, 25. Kimberly Schuld, "How the Ford Foundation Created Women's Studies," *Front Page Magazine*, February 20, 2004, http://97.74.65.51/readArticle.aspx?ARTID=14085 (accessed May 26, 2010).

3. Robert C. Lowry, "Foundation Patronage toward Citizen Groups and Think Tanks: Who Get Grants?" *Journal of Politics* 61, no. 3 (August 1999): 760.

4. Gregory K. Raynor, "Engineering Social Reform: The Rise of the Ford Foundation and Cold War Liberalism, 1908–1959" (PhD diss., New York University, 2000), 5, 68, 160, 233, 252, 268. The Russell Sage Foundation (1907), the Carnegie Foundation (1911), and the Rockefeller Foundation (1913) preceded Ford. The Ford Foundation was founded in 1936 as a vehicle to circumvent President Franklin Delano Roosevelt's new inheritance tax. Ford came into its own in the 1950s during the cold war. An early director, Paul Hoffman was involved with the Marshall Plan that influences Ford's philosophy and geopolitics. Kathleen D. McCarthy, "From Cold War to Cultural Development: The International Cultural Activities of the Ford Foundation, 1950–1980," *Daedalus: Journal of the American Academy of Arts and Sciences* 116, no. 1 (Winter 1987): 93.

5. McCarthy, "From Cold War to Cultural Development," 102.

6. "Ford Foundation Awards $175,000 to Morgan State," *Chicago Defender*, April 27, 1963, 7. "Ford's Grant to CORE," *Chicago Daily Defender*, July 18, 1967, 13. Kathleen Teltsch, "Ford Fund May Help Police to Recruit Minority Members," *New York Times*, February 22, 1968, 28. James Petras, "The Ford Foundation and the CIA: A Documented Case of Philanthropic Collaboration with the Secret Police," *Rebelión*, December 15, 2001, http://educate-your-self.org/cn/fordfoundationandcia15dec01.shtml (accessed May 26, 2010).

7. Kathleen Teltsch, "Grant Aids Latins in the Southwest," *New York Times*, May 2, 1968, 38.

8. "Archives," *Ford Foundation*, http://www.fordfound.org/archives/searchresults? chicano&page=1 (accessed May 26, 2010). This site lists the grants to Latinos 1970–1990. Very few were awarded for undergraduate education.

9. "Strengthening Our Place in the Academy: A Summit for Women Administrators and Faculty of Color," American Council on Education, Office of Minorities in Higher Education, in partnership with the University of California Office of the President and University of California, Berkeley, February 27–March 1, 2003.

10. Hill, "Mainstreaming Minority Women's Studies," 27.

11. Ibid., 33.

12. Ward was late a senior consultant to the board of the John D. and Catherine T. MacArthur Foundation and played a role in how the "genius awards" were selected. "Ford Foundation Aide Named Vice President," *New York Times*, October 2, 1966, 67. Homer Bigart, "A New Mexican-American Militancy," *New York Times*, April 20, 1969, 1. Ward quotation in "Black Studies Programs," *Chicago Daily Defender*, July 26, 1969, 8. Donna J. Gough, "Ideas Have Consequences: Conservative Philanthropy, Black Studies and the Evolution and Enduring Legacy of the Academic Culture Wars, 1945–2005" (PhD diss., Ohio State University, 2007), 3: "Black studies programs notwithstanding, the discipline has been able to maintain 450 active departments nationwide and not only grown but thrived at elite universities such as Wisconsin, Northwestern, Harvard and Yale."

13. "Ford Foundation to Help Minority Groups Get PhD's," *New York Times*, October 14, 1969, 92. "$225,000 Fund Given to Chavez Centers," *New York Times*, December 14, 1970, 28.

14. Gough, "Ideas Have Consequences," 146. Ford was committed to its antiracist campaign, but in its own way. It wanted to integrate institutions and did so by throwing money at them. Kathleen Teltsch, "Ford Fund May Help Police to Recruit Minority Members," *New York Times*, February 22, 1968, 28. Fred M. Hechinger, "Ford Fund Pledges Drive Against Racial Prejudice," *New York Times*, February 18, 1968, 1. José Angel Gutiérrez, *The Making of a Chicano Militant: Lessons from Cristal* (Madison: University of Wisconsin Press, 1999), 118–119.

15. Armando Navarro, *La Raza Unida Party: A Chicano Challenge to the U.S. Two-Party Dictatorship* (Philadelphia: Temple University Press, 2000), 26–27. Chon A. Noriega, *Shot in*

America: Television, the State, and the Rise of Chicano Cinema (University of Minnesota, 2000), 90. According to Noriega, Ford micromanaged the Southwest Council from 1968 to 1975; it was Ford's principal benefactor. The point of this argument is whether foundations should engineer who the leadership should be in a particular community or what its ideology should be. How different is this from the current Supreme Court decision that allows financial institutions to buy elections? Ford founded the Southwest Council of La Raza in 1968, which later became the National Council of La Raza. The foundation hired Herman Gallegos, Julian Samora, and Ernesto Galarza to consult with other leaders on ways to improve conditions for Mexican American communities. The council was formed with grants from the United Auto Workers, the Council of Churches, and Ford. Gallegos was its first executive director. Ford Foundation controlled Southwest Council through funding and mainstreamed the organization. Reportedly, Ford gave the council its initial grant of $630,000, and it micromanaged its operation until 1975.

16. "A Closer Look," *Odessa American*, May 17, 1969.

17. *Congressional Record*, 91st Cong., 1st sess., April 22, 1969.

18. Hugh Davis Graham, *Collision Course: The Strange Convergence of Affirmative Action and Immigration Policy in America* (New York: Oxford University Press, 2003), 115. "The Cock Pit," *San Antonio Express-News*, April 13, 1969. The *San Antonio Express-News* reported on Ford Foundation grants to Mexican American organizations. Ford had earmarked for "Minority Leadership," $630,001 for the Southwest Council of La Raza. Of that, La Raza furnished $110,000 to the Mexican-American Unity Council. "MAYO and Ford Foundation Confirm Tax Free Funds Improper," *San Antonio Express-News*, June 19, 1969. Jim Price, "Pena Unsure About La Raza Post," *San Antonio Light*, July 18, 1969. "Gonzalez Most Effective Adversary," *San Antonio Express-News*, November 9, 1969.

19. "A Challenge to Build a New Society," *New York Times*, April 20, 1969, 55.

20. Ford Foundation, *Four Minorities and the PhD: Ford Foundation Graduate Fellowships for Blacks, Chicanos, Puerto Ricans, and American Indians* (New York: Ford Foundation, October 1973), 3, 5.

21. Estevan Flores, "Master Teacher Fought for Equity," *New Mexican*, April 9, 1985.

22. At the time, *Ramparts* was a left of center magazine. David Horowitz in this other life was a leftist. David Horowitz and David Kolodney, "The Foundations [Charity Begins at Home]," *Ramparts* 7, no. 11 (April 1969): 38–48, http://peoplesgeography.com/2008/12/11/from-the-vaults-i-the-foundations-part/ (accessed May 26, 2010). The article delves into Ford's social engineering of the civil rights movement. David Horowitz, "Sinews of Empire," *Ramparts* (October 1969): 32–42, http://www.cia-on-campus.org/internat/sinews.html (accessed May 26, 2010). Michael Barker, "The Ford Foundation and the Co-option of Dissent," *Swans Commentary*, January 25, 2010, http://www.swans.com/library/art16/barker41.html (accessed May 26, 2010).

23. The Southwestern Region and David Grant, *Ford Foundation*, http://www.fordfound.org/archives/item/0302/text/20 (accessed May 26, 2010). "Small School Study Project Program Outlined at Meeting," *Reno Evening Gazette*, April 4, 1962. "Education Dept. Not Against Smaller Schools," *Santa Fe New Mexican*, May 1, 1963. "Ford Program Assurance," *Bennington Banner*, October 6, 1965. "Huge Ford Grant for State Lost," *Las Cruces (NM) Sun News*, August 24, 1970. "Loan Planned for Ranchers in Southwest," *Los Angeles Times*, June 12, 1969, C2. James T. Wooten, "Ford Foundation to Aid Ranchers," *New York Times*, June 15, 1969, 42. "Ford Calls Magazine Article on 'Poor' Grant 'Nonsense,'" *Clovis–New Journal*, August 25, 1970.

24. Gordon H. Hanson and Craig McIntosh, "The Demography of Mexican Migration to the US," University of California San Diego, December 2008, 2, http://pwp-irps.ucsd.edu/sites/1/assets/027/9471.pdf. Ford Foundation, *Four Minorities and the PhD*, 9, 17–18. The

pamphlet ran a vignette on my career, probably because there were not that many PhDs to draw from.

25. Ford Foundation, *Four Minorities and the PhD*, 3.

26. S.R.G., preface, "American Indians, Blacks, Chicanos, and Puerto Ricans," *Daedalus: Journal of the American Academy of Arts and Sciences* 110, no. 2 (Spring 1981): v–xiii. Listed on the advisory board were Rodolfo Acuña, Bernard E. Anderson, Carlos H. Arce, John Attinasi, Houston Baker, J. Herman Blake, Frank Bonilla, Haywood Burns, Ricardo Campos, Jean Carew, Robert Coles, Phoebe H. Cottingham, Carl Degler, Vine Deloria Jr., R. Harcourt Dodds, Michael A. Dorris, Leobardo F. Estrada, Juan Flores, John Hope Franklin, George Frederickson, F. Chris Garcia, Juan Gómez-Quiñones, Nancy Grant, Edward K. Hamilton, Robert B. Hill, Barbara Jones, Faustine C. Jones, Franklin Knight, Gardner Lindzey, Reynaldo Flores Macias, Lionel Maldonado, Scott Momaday, Joan W. Moore, Carlos Muñoz, Benjamin F. Payton, Pedro Pedraza Jr., Thomas F. Pettigrew, Feliciano Rivera, Joel Williamson, and Michael R. Winston. I was included, although I specifically asked not to be. I guess the fact that I was fed and given lodging gave them license. S. R. G., "American Indians, Blacks, Chicanos, and Puerto Ricans," *Daedalus: Journal of the American Academy of Arts and Sciences* 110, no. 2 (Spring 1981): ix (I am listed on the advisory group without my permission).

27. Graduate Degrees: Doctorates, National Science Foundation, Division of Science Resources Statistics, Women, Minorities, and Persons with Disabilities in Science and Engineering, 2002 Arlington, VA (NSF 03–312) (September 2003), http://www.nsf.gov/statistics/nsf03312/c5/c5s1.htm (accessed May 26, 2010).

28. "Survey of Earned Doctorates. Fact Sheet," *National Science Foundation*, July 1, 2006, to June 30, 2007, http://www.norc.org/NR/rdonlyres/B40E56EC-9A4F-4892-B871-E330BB689CD9/0/SEDFactSheet.pdf (accessed May 26, 2010). "Vanishing Minority Historians," *PhD in History*, April 28, 2008, http://phdinhistory.blogspot.com/2008/04/vanishing-minority-historians.html (accessed November 11, 2010). "Citizenship Status, Race/Ethnicity, and Sex of PhDs, by Field of Doctorate: 1975–99 Total and 5-Year Cohorts from 1975," *National Science Foundation*, http://www.nsf.gov/statistics/nsf06319/pdf/taba2.pdf (accessed May 26, 2010).

29. In Rodolfo F. Acuña, *Sometimes There Is No Other Side: The Myth of Equality* (Notre Dame: Notre Dame University Press, 1998), I critique my case against the University of California at Santa Barbara, which we would not have been won without piercing the veil of confidentiality. The filings in the case can be found in *University of Pennsylvania v. EEOC*, 493 U.S. 182 (1990), 493 U.S. 182, Rodolfo F. Acuña Archives, California State University Library, Northridge.

30. Peter Novick, *That Noble Dream: The "Objectivity Question" and the American Historical Profession* (Cambridge: Cambridge University Press, 1988), 172–173.

31. Rodolfo F. Acuña, *Anything but Mexican: Chicanos in Contemporary Los Angeles* (London: Verso Press, 1996), 8, 9.

32. Rodolfo F. Acuña, *Corridors of Migration: The Odyssey of Mexican Laborers, 1600–1933* (Tucson: University of Arizona Press, 2007).

33. Acuña, *Sometimes There Is No Other Side*, 125, 126, 160, 163, 223. The University of California system spent $5 million on the case.

34. Art Kuhn, "Trustee May Take Children Out of School," *Oxnard (CA) Press-Courier*, September 8, 1971. "Restrictive Teacher Hiring Held Illegal," *Oxnard (CA) Press-Courier*, February 2, 1972.

35. "28 Teaching Jobs, Internship Plan Set,' *Oxnard Press-Courier*, February 16, 1972.

36. The pressure came from the growth in the Mexican American student population. Norma Aguila, Alejandro Aldana, Patricia Alfaro, Veronica del Toro, Rahiley Gómez,

Akamie Robinson, "The Struggle for Educational Justice, 1954–2004," *Teaching to Change Los Angeles,* http://tcla.gseis.ucla.edu/equalterms/history/1984/paper/paper.html (accessed May 26, 2010).

37. This breakthrough came about the time the first students were graduating. It sent the message that one could get a job with a Chicano Studies degree and that teaching was an option. Many did not have career aspirations.

38. California Department of Education, "Standards and Frameworks," http://www.cde .ca.gov/be/st/ and http://www.cde.ca.gov/be/st/ss/index.asp (accessed May 26, 2010).

39. Robinson was president of the Russell Sage Foundation, one of the nation's oldest private philanthropies, from 1979 to 1986. Sage focuses on research in the social sciences, supporting and publishing research on economic inequality. Daniel E. Contreras, "Chicano Teacher Project Adds to School System," *Daily Sundial,* February 21, 1975. The program was funded by Ford in June 1973. Twenty-three percent of the students in the Los Angeles Unified School District were Mexican American; 3 percent of the teachers had Spanish-surnames. Criticisms and problems have developed around OCT's functions and goals. The fact that the project is situated in a "conservative area" such as the West Valley builds up resistance to its aims. Critics often view and compare OCT with the Chicano Studies department as being "radical and activist."

40. Depending, these administrative costs could go as high as 30–40 percent of the grant. During this period, the department also supported other programs. Virginia Ahumada, "Chicanos for Creative Medicine," *Daily Sundial,* April 16, 1975. This club was pushed by student Frank Mesa, who later became a medical doctor. It began with ten students and expanded to thirty by 1975. It had over 500 undergraduates in Los Angeles. They offered each other support and volunteered in the community. They had close ties with MEChA and met in the Chicano Studies area.

41. Robert Fairbanks, "Reagan Signs Major Reform Bill to Improve California's Schools," *Los Angeles Times,* July 31, 1970, 3. Leo C. Wolinsky, "Education Degree Blocks Job as Teacher," *Los Angeles Times,* January 15, 1978, CS1. The good thing was that it downgraded the Department of Education led by ultra conservative Max Rafferty shifting credentialing to a fifteen-member commission. Eventually, however, this would lessen the power of the Latino community to influence the credentialing process that is today in the hands of white elites.

42. Cece Espinoza, "Operation Chicano Teacher," *Daily Sundial,* February 15, 1974. George Wanamaker, "College Advisement Stresses Unity," *Daily Sundial,* April 30, 1974. Virginia Ahumada, "OCT Stresses Chicano Awareness," *Daily Sundial,* October 18, 1974. Daniel E. Contreras, "Chicano Teacher Project Adds to School System," *Daily Sundial,* February 21, 1975. "OCT Grads Begin Job Search," *Daily Sundial,* October 24, 1975.

43. See Acuña memo and Otriz letter, Operation Chicano Teacher Proposal, in Acuña Collection, CSUN Urban Archives.

44. They also have fewer black and brown students.

45. See Tony Ortiz, Jorge García, and Rodolfo F. Acuña, "El Nuevo Maestro Proposal," Rodolfo F. Acuña Archives, California State University Library, Northridge.

46. Outside English, the humanities and social sciences we were able to identify allies who spent additional time with the students. For example, Warren Furumoto in biology taught special classes for us to get the students through on time. Ortiz, "Operation Chicano Teacher," 19–24. The documents can be found in Rodolfo F. Acuña Archives, California State University Library, Northridge.

47. Ortiz, García, and Acuña, "Nuevo Maestro," 12.

48. Ibid., 14.

49. Ibid., 15.

CHAPTER 8 — GETTING IT RIGHT

1. Jerry A. Jacobs, "Gender Inequality and Higher Education," *Annual Review of Sociology* 22 (1996): 155–158, 159–160.

2. Linda Isabel Vargas-Lew, "The Chicana Scholar: An Examination of Maternal Influences Impacting the Higher Education Attainment of Mexican American Women" (EdD diss., Baylor University, 2003), 2, 3, 9, 13, 17.

3. Leo Grebler, Joan W. Moore, and Ralph C. Guzmán, *The Mexican-American People: The Nation's Second Largest Minority* (New York: Free Press, 1970), 145, 147, 154. Maxine Baca Zinn, "Gender and Ethnic Identity among Chicanos," *Frontiers: A Journal of Women Studies* 5, no. 2 (Summer 1980): 22. Anita Tijerina-Revilla, "Are All Raza Womyn Queer? An Exploration of Sexual Identity in a Chicana/Latina Student Organization," *NWSA Journal* 21, no. 3 (Fall 2009): 47.

4. *Voces: A Profile of Today's Latino College Students* (Washington, DC: Excelencia in Education, 2007), 4, 5, http://www.diversityweb.org/diversity_innovations/student_ development/recruitment_retention_mentoring/documents/VOCESAProfileofTodays LatinoCollegeStudents_000.pdf (accessed May 27, 2010).

5. Jeanett Castellanos, "The Relationship between Chicana/Latina Value System at Higher Education," paper presented at the Annual Conference of the American Educational Studies Association, Montreal, Quebec, Canada, November 6–10, 1996, 2, 6, 7. Jacobs, "Gender Inequality and Higher Education," 155.

6. Glenn R. Hawkes and Minna Taylor, "Power Structure in Mexican and Mexican-American Farm Labor Families," *Journal of Marriage and Family* 37, no. 4 (November 1975): 807, 808. Jacobs, "Gender Inequality and Higher Education," 154.

7. Tim Hodgdon, "Fem: A Window onto the Cultural Coalescence of a Mexican Feminist Politics of Sexuality," *Mexican Studies / Estudios Mexicanos* 16, no. 1 (Winter 2000): 80.

8. Hodgdon, "Fem," 79–80, 82, 90–94.

9. Some Chicanas have individually had continual contact with Latin American nations such as Cuba and Central America. Within the Chicana/o movement as a whole there has been limited exchange of ideas. Renato Rosaldo, "Notes toward a Critique of Patriarchy from a Male Position," *Anthropological Quarterly* 66, no. 2 (April 1993): 85.

10. Joan Acker, "Inequality Regimes Gender, Class, and Race in Organizations," *Gender and Society* 20, no. 4 (August 2006): 441, 443, 445.

11. Acker, "Inequality Regimes," 445.

12. Cristian Berco, "Producing Patriarchy: Male Sodomy and Gender in Early Modern Spain," *Journal of the History of Sexuality* 17, no. 3 (September 2008): 353–355. Steve J. Stern, "Paradigms of Conquest: History, Historiography, and Politics," *Journal of Latin American Studies* 24 (1992): 32.

13. Edward Behrend-Martínez, "Manhood and the Neutered Body in Early Modern Spain," *Journal of Social History* (Summer 2005): 1079. Steve J. Stern, "Paradigms of Conquest: History, Historiography, and Politics," *Journal of Latin American Studies* 24 (1992): 9.

14. Noble David Cook, *Born to Die: Disease and New World Conquest* (New York: Cambridge University Press, 1998), 206. David Henige, *Numbers from Nowhere: The American Indian Contact Population Debate* (Norman: University of Oklahoma Press, 1998).

15. Miranda K. Stockett, "On the Importance of Difference: Re-Envisioning Sex and Gender in Ancient Mesoamerica," *World Archaeology* 37, no. 4 (December 2005): 567, 569. Randall Collins, Janet Saltzman Chafetz, Rae Lesser Blumberg, Scott Coltrane, and Jonathan H. Turner, "Toward an Integrated Theory of Gender Stratification," *Sociological Perspectives* 36, no. 3 (Autumn 1993): 186, 191, 207. Laurie Wermuth and Miriam Ma'at-ka-re Monges,

"Gender Stratification: A Structural Model for Examining Case Examples of Women in Less-Developed Countries," *Frontiers* 23, no. 1 (2002): 1.

16. Susan Kellogg, "Hegemony out of Conquest: The First Two Centuries of Spanish Rule in Central Mexico," *Radical History Review* 53 (Spring 1992): 27. Steve J. Stern, "Review: The Changing Face of Gender Complementarity: New Research on Indian Women in Colonial Mexico," *Ethnohistory* 46, no. 3 (Summer 1999): 619.

17. David Carey Jr., "Mayan Women and Expanding Gender Identities in Twentieth-Century Guatemala," *Journal of Women's History* 20, no. 1 (2008): 115.

18. John J. Swetnam, "Women and Markets: A Problem in the Assessment of Sexual Inequality," *Ethnology* 27, no. 4 (October 1988): 327, 328. Irene Silverblatt, "Lessons of Gender and Ethnohistory in Mesoamerica," *Ethnohistory* 42, no. 4 (Fall 1995): 640. Robert M. Carmack, Janine Gasco, and Gary H. Gossen, *The Legacy of Mesoamerica: History and Culture of a Native American Civilization* (Upper Saddle River, NJ: Prentice Hall, 1996): 183–184. Marie Elaine Danforth, Keith P. Jacobi, and Mark Nathan Cohen, "Gender and Health among the Colonial Mayan of Tipu, Belize," *Ancient Mesoamerica* 8, no. 1 (Spring 1997): 14.

19. Danforth, Jacobi, and Cohen, "Gender and Health among the Colonial Mayan of Tipu, Belize," 14–15.

20. Carmack et al., *The Legacy,* 181–183.

21. Caulfield, "The History of Gender," 452.

22. Supreme Council of the Mexican American Movement Papers, *Latino Cultural Heritage Digital Archives,* http://digital-library.csun.edu/LatArch/ (accessed November 16, 2010).

23. Correspondence with José Angel Gutiérrez, May 28, 2010. He is writing a book on the topic.

24. *Census of Population: Persons of Spanish Origin, Bureau of Census. U.S. Department of Commerce* (Washington, DC: U.S. Government Printing Office, 1973), 2, 9. Reneé E. Spraggins, *"We the People: Women and Men in the United States Census 2000 Special Reports"* (Washington, DC: U.S. Department of Commerce Economics and Statistics Administration, January 2005), 9. Ronald W. López, Arturo Madrid-Barela, Reynaldo Flores Macias, *Chicanos in Higher Education: Status and Issue* (Los Angeles: UCLA Chicano Studies Center, For the Nation Chicano Commission on Higher Education, 1976), 8, 20, 32, 38. Jaime Taronji Jr., *Counting the Forgotten: The 1970 Census Count of Persons of Spanish Speaking Background in the United States, A Report of the U.S. Commission on Civil Rights* (Washington, DC: U.S. Census Bureau, 1974), http://www.law.umaryland.edu/marshall/usccr/documents/ cr12sp22970 .pdf (accessed May 27, 2010). This report did not mention gender as a category. It also pointed to a dramatic undercount of the Spanish-speaking population.

25. David López Lee, Raúl Rodríguez, Joel Nossoff, Consuelo Moore, Michael Miranda, and Manuel Ruiz, *The Cal-State, L.A., Chicano Student: A Study of Academic Performance of EOP Chicanos, Non-EOP Chicanos, and Anglos, and the Relationship of Attitudes to Academic Performance* (Los Angeles: Equal Opportunity Program, California State College, 1971), 11, 12, 24. Kenneth Hepburn and Stephen Mark Sachs, *East Los Angeles College Community Demographics: Look in 1980* (Los Angeles: East Los Angeles College, August 1980), 13–14. Ronald W. López and Darryl D. Enos, *Chicanos and Public Higher Education in California* (Sacramento: California State Legislature, Joint Committee on the Master Plan for Higher Education, 1972), 44.

26. Stephen Mark Sachs, *East Los Angeles College Student Profiles: Spring and Fall, 1979,* Research Report BO-3 (Los Angeles: East Los Angeles College, 1980), 6.

27. Ibid., 3, 18.

28. Kenneth Hepburn and Stephen Mark Sachs, *East Los Angeles College Community Demographics: Look in 1980* (Los Angeles: East Los Angeles College, 1980), 36.

29. Judy Salinas, "The Chicana Image" (paper presented at the Fifth Annual National Convention Popular Culture Association, St. Louis, March 20–22, 1975). This paper provides a literary analysis of how Chicanas were portrayed.

30. Emilio A. Parrado, Chenoa A. Flippen, Chris McQuiston, "Migration and Relationship Power among Mexican Women, *Demography* 42, no. 2 (May 2005): 349. Gloria González-López, in "Fathering Latina Sexualities: Mexican Men and the Virginity of Their Daughters," *Journal of Marriage and Family* 66, no. 5 (December 2004): 1118–1130, cautions about stereotyping the *typical* Mexican father, who is also not static.

31. "María Eugenia Echenique: The Emancipation of Women (1876)," in *Reading About the World*, vol. 2, ed. Paul Brians, Mary Gallwey, Azfar Hussain, and Richard Law (Fort Worth: Harcourt Brace Custom Books, 1999), http://www.wsu.edu/~wldciv/world_civ_reader/world_civ_reader_2/echenique.html (accessed May 28, 2010).

32. Jean Libman Block, "Who Says American Women Are 'Trapped'?" *Los Angeles Times*, October 6, 1963, C10. Ellen Shulte, "Women's Big Crisis: 'Loss of Identity,'" *Los Angeles Times*, March 13, 1964, C1. "Suffragettes Won Fight 50 Years Ago," *Los Angeles Times*, June 6, 1969, C8. Lynn Langway, "Male Chauvinism in SDS Irks Coeds in Group's Ranks," *Los Angeles Times*, June 24, 1969, C2. Jack Smith, "A Liberation Generation of Women," *Los Angeles Times*, April 13, 1970, E1. Betty Friedan, *The Feminine Mystique* (Kingston, MA: R. S. Means Co., 1963).

33. Diane Monk, "Defining the New Feminists," *Los Angeles Times*, January 4, 1970, H17. Nancy L. Ross Women's Putdown Blows Up," *Los Angeles Times*, July 30, 1970, E2. A. D. Coleman, "Photography: A Mostly Male View of Females," *New York Times*, September 13, 1970, D33. Joan Cook, "'Sexism' in a Child's Books?" *New York Times*, October 16, 1970, 63. Ellen Willis, "Women, Revolution, Sexism, Etc., Etc.," *New York Times*, March 2, 1969, SM6. "Carswell Called Foe of Women's Rights," *New York Times*, January 30, 1970, 20. Jean Stafford, "Topics: Women as Chattels, Men as Chumps," *New York Times*, May 9, 1970, 24.

34. Manuel Díaz Ramírez, *Apuntes sobre el movimiento obrero campesino de México* (México, DF: Ediciones de Cultura Popular, 1974), 66, 67–68, 70, 83; John Mason Hart, *Anarchism and the Mexican Working Class* (Austin: University of Texas Press, 1978), 32–41. *Los obreros en México, 1875–1925*, http://www.monografias.com/trabajos10/obre/obre.shtml (accessed October 21, 2009).

35. Julia Tuñón Pablos, *Women in Mexico: A Past Unveiled* (Austin: University of Texas Press, 1999), 80–81. Francesca Miller, *Latin American Women and the Search for Social Justice* (Lebanon, NH: University Press of New England, 1991), 71–72. Asunción Lavrin, *Latin American Women Historical Perspectives* (Westport, CT: Greenwood Press, 1978), 291–292. Marysa Navarro, Virginia Sánchez Korrol, and Kecia Ali, *Women in Latin America and the Caribbean: Restoring Women to History* (Indianapolis: University of Indiana, 1999), 87, 91. Mtra. Ma. de Lourdes Alvarado with Elizabeth Becerril Guzmán, *Mujeres y educación superior en el México del siglo XIX*, Centro de la Educación Superior–Universidad Nacional Autónoma de México, http://biblioweb.dgsca.unam.mx/diccionario/htm/articulos/sec_10.htm (accessed October 21, 2009). Shirlene Soto, *Emergence of the Modern Mexican Woman: Her Participation in Revolution and Struggle for Equality, 1910–1940* (Denver: Arden Press, 1990), 11–12, 15, 21–23. Emma M. Pérez, "'A La Mujer': A Critique of the Parido Liberal Mexicano's Gender Ideology on Women," in *Between Borders: Essays on Mexicana/Chicana History*, ed. Adelaida R. del Castillo (Los Angeles: Floricanto Press, 1990), 459–482, 459, 461. Carolyn Asbaugh, *Lucy Parsons: American Revolutionary* (Chicago: Herr, 1976), 267–268. Anna Macías, *Contra viento y marea: El movimiento feminista en México hasta 1940* (México, DF: Universidad Nacional Autónomo, 2002), 80–83.

36. Ross, "Introduction to Feminist Theory," 4, 7, 25, 31.

37. "Chicanas Demand Changes at Mills," *Oakland Tribune*, April 30, 1972.

38. Ofelia Rodriguez, "Coeds Explain 'Chicana' Image," *El Paso Prospector*, November 4, 1969.

39. "Chicanas' Role to Be Discussed," *Los Angeles Times*, November 9, 1972, SE. Mary Barber, "At Whittier Conference," *Los Angeles Times*, November 26, 1972, SE1.

40. Mary Ellen Perry, "Minority Women Differ on 'Movement,'" *Oakland Post*, October 5, 1972, 8.

41. "First Chicana Graduate from UNM Law School," *Deming (NM) Headlight*, January 11, W3-7.

42. "CSUN Will Place Focus on Chicanas," *Los Angeles Times*, April 20, 1973, SF6. Nancy Baltad, "Chicanas Need 'Clout' to Get Ahead, Aide Tells Students," *Los Angeles Times*, May 3, 1973, SF4. Roxanne Arnold, "Chicanas: Breaking out Is Hard," *Los Angeles Times*, October 8, 1978, SE-A1.

43. Cynthia Orozco, "Mujeres por la Raza," *Handbook of Texas Online*, http://www.tshaonline.org/handbook/online/articles/MM/vimgh.html.

44. Connie Koenenn, "Arizona Chicanas Form Their Own Rights Group," *Arizona Republic*, April 3, 1972. "Arizona Chicanas Form Own Rights Commission," *Tucson Daily Citizen*, April 5, 1972.

45. Ray López, "Nuevo Aztlán," *Las Cruces (NM) Sun-News*, December 11, 1974.

46. "Chicana Meet Slated," *Greeley Tribune*, April 9, 1975. "Spanish Women Plan September Conference," *Ogden (UT) Standard-Examiner*, August 22, 1975. "2-Day Conference Scheduled for Spanish Speaking Women," *Ogden (UT) Standard Examiner*, September 16, 1975.

47. Karen B. Tancill, "Chicano Studies Program Sought by Racine Woman," *Racine (WI) Journal Times*, August 31, 1975.

48. "IWY Delegates Foresee Issues," *Albuquerque Journal*, November 16, 1977.

49. "Fact Sheet Lists Chicanas' Profile," *Los Angeles Times*, June 23, 1980, F1. "L.A. Unified Schools Principally Latino," *Los Angeles Times*, April 13, 1980, B5. Lynn Simross, "450% Growth in Two Years," *Los Angeles Times*, June 8, 1980, G1.

50. "75 Occupy Bruin Offices to Protest 'Racism,'" *Westwood (CA) Daily Bruin*, March 2, 1979, reprinted in *Los Angeles Times*, June 8, 1979, 3. At the beginning of 1970, Latinos were 22 percent of the Los Angeles public schools. A shift began during the decade, and by 1979 Latinos accounted for 41.9 percent of the total of 545,871 students. Two years later, almost 48 percent were Latinos. The white portion had fallen to 36.9 percent; blacks, 23.8 percent; and Asians, 6.9 percent. They were 50 percent of the kindergarten students. Additionally, Latinos were a majority of the K–8 parochial school students in Los Angeles, Ventura, and Santa Barbara counties—42.5 percent (32,075) vs. 41.8 percent (31,647). There was a similar trend in outlying school districts such as the Long Beach system. John Dart, "Latino Catholic School Students Outnumber Anglos," *Los Angeles Times*, November 30, 1979, B3. Mary Barber, "Anglos Outnumbered at Elementary Level," *Los Angeles Times*, December 11, 1980, SE4. Rebecca Trounson, "Minority Students Now Majority in Long Beach," *Los Angeles Times*, November 19, 1981, SE-A1. David G. Savage, "L.A. Schools' White Student Loss Continues," *Los Angeles Times*, November 24, 1981, B1.

51. "Valley State Offering Poor Chance to Continue School," *Van Nuys Valley (CA) Green Sheet*, July 24, 1969.

52. Orozco went on to Sacramento State and earned a master of arts in counseling. She later directed a teacher program at California State University, Northridge, and was a teacher in Oxnard. She died of cancer. The accomplishments of Chicanas were made despite Chicano Studies. Many suffered discrimination and physical abuse that was at the time unknown to many professors. One of the problems was that, although we had numerous professors, the workload fell on a couple of professors. In the case of CSUN, a debt is owed to Jorge García, who carried more than his share of the academic workload.

53. In May 1972 at a Chicano Studies/MEChA conference SFVSC offered a resolution that every Chicano Studies program have a *mujeres* course.

54. Interview with Carlos Ortega, UTEP, telephone and private conversations, August 2009.

55. E-mail correspondence with Norma Solis, September 10, 2009.

56. "NOW to Discuss 'Attacks on Minority Women's Rights,'" *Los Angeles Times*, February 19, 1978, I22. Antonia Hernandez, "Chicanas and the Issue of Involuntary Sterilization: Reforms Needed to Protect Informed Consent," *Chicano Law Review* 3 (1976): 3–37.

57. E-mail correspondence with Norma Solis, September 10, 2009. In addition to numerous conversations with Norma.

58. Michael Connelly, "Police Try Getting to Root of Problem Law Enforcement: A New Emphasis on Community Relations Encourages Residents to Act in Tandem with Officers. The Results Are Mixed," *Los Angeles Times*, October 18, 1992, 1. Kurt Pitzer, "Canoga Park Cutbacks Hurt Agency's Fight against Graffiti," *Los Angeles Times*, July 3, 1993, 3. Carla Rivera, "Supervisors OK Plan to Clean Up Vandalism Crime: Key Features Include 'Graffiti-Free Zones,' Diversion Programs, a Citizens Complaint Process and Restitution," *Los Angeles Times*, September 29, 1993, 8.

59. Anna came out of a different tradition. At Long Beach State, the students ran Chicano Studies affairs; however, unlike most MEChAs, many of their student leaders had paid jobs as consultants for private and public agencies. Many of her criticisms of Chicano Studies were valid and still are; it is not the point of the narrative to dispute them.

60. Dean Richfield pushed the candidacy of Fermín Herrera after Fermín gave a faculty-wide discourse on why Nahuatl should be a classical language. Fermín gave the lecture in Nahuatl, English, Latin, and Greek, comparing the different languages. He is also an accomplished harpist and an internationally known scholar of Jarocho music. Richfield evaluated him as an artist, which has different criteria than social science. At least four other persons spoke to Anna and encouraged her to go to graduate school.

61. While publicly defending our right to hire BAs, by this time I was convinced that not having a majority of faculty members with terminal degrees was hurting the students and the programs. As romantic as it sounds, there is not a doctorate from the University of the Barrio. In academe scholars are not respected if they do not have a union card. They are looked upon as unqualified, and others do not take their degrees seriously. Other institutions look at the recommender's qualifications and evaluate the author as much as the candidate. The hiring of instructors with bachelor degrees was never meant to be a final solution. To continue to grow, we had to have Chicanas/os on university committees, which are elected and appointed and generally require a terminal degree.

62. Gerald paid a heavy price for not getting a doctorate. He certainly would have become a dean and possibly a university president. He was well liked and respected by the faculty at large.

63. Fermín Herrera teaches a class at the University of California, Los Angeles, and has appeared on many campuses nationally and internationally. Everto Ruiz began one of the first student mariachis, and he has cloned groups throughout the San Fernando Valley, where over a dozen groups perform regularly. Mariachi classes are taught by former students in middle and high schools. We struggle continuously with the administration, which does not fund the art and music classes in Chicana/o Studies departments at the same level as it funds those in the art and music departments. Each department receives support for its offerings in terms of class size and resources to support them.

64. The late Lorenzo Flores, a popular professor, was denied promotion and retention, although he had a master of arts degree. He was forced to get a master of fine arts, whereupon he was rehired as a tenure track professor. He died of cancer before completing his six-year probationary period and was never granted tenure. The late Roberto Sifuentes was an ABD

(all but dissertation) in Spanish literature from UCLA. We approached the administration and asked what the possibility was that he could be considered for a tenure track appointment; this request was rejected at the dean and provost levels.

65. This was a tactical error on Anna's part because it forced students to come to my defense.

66. The administration knew students voted on personnel matters we made no secret about it. However, the administration had a policy of ignoring student involvement until someone complained. For example, during this time the department marked all of the faculty ballots. It traded them for votes on committees. This was stopped after faculty members complained.

67. "LAPD Claudia Luther, Accused of Political Spying," *Los Angeles Times*, June 9, 1978, D4. David Johnston and Teresa Watanabe, "Police Had Agents in Council Meetings," *Los Angeles Times*, May 8, 1980, D1. Michael Seiler, "LAPD Accused of Spying at University," *Los Angeles Times*, June 11, 1982, D5.

68. Carlos Muñoz Jr., *Youth, Identity, Power: The Chicano Movement*, rev. ed. (London: Verso, 2007), 190–191. Muñoz makes outlandish statements about the case. He never interviewed anyone, and he fails to mention his own denial of tenure and his part in denying tenure to Julia Curry-Rodríguez at Berkeley. Lisa Justine Hernández, "Chicana Feminist Voices: In Search of Chicana Lesbian Voices from Aztlán to Cyberspace" (PhD diss., University of Texas, Austin, 2001), 106–107. In making sweeping statements about Anna's scholarship, Hernández cites the following: Anna Nieto-Gómez, "Chicana Feminism: Pláctica de Anna Nieto Gómez," *Caracol: La Revista de la Raza* 2, no. 5 (1976): 3–5. Anna Nieto-Gómez, "Chicanas Identify," *Regeneración* 1, no. 10 (1971): 9. Anna Nieto-Gómez, "La Femenista," *Encuentro femenil* 1, no. 2 (1974): 34–47. Anna Nieto-Gómez, ed., *New Directions in Education: Estudios Femeniles de la Chicana* (San Fernando, CA: Montal Educational Associates, 1974). Gustavo Licón, "¡La Unión Hace La Fuerza!" (Unity Creates Strength!) M.E.Ch.A. and Chicana/o Student Activism in California, 1967–1999" (PhD diss., University of Southern California, 2009). The author Licón distorts events and did not interview anyone connected with the department.

69. Something that is not talked about is why more Chicanos do not elect to teach at teaching colleges and work with low income and poorly prepared students. It has not been until this century that California State University, Northridge, has had a sufficient pool of Chicana applicants. Teaching four classes a semester and teaching unprepared students is low on the priority of Chicana and Chicano scholars.

70. Marita Hernandez, "Stirrings of Independence among Latin Women," *Los Angeles Times*, September 23, 1981, B3. Diane Araujo, "Chicanas/Latinas in Higher Education" (EdD diss., University of California, Los Angeles, 2009), 63. Araujo delves into the conscience building that took place at California State College, Los Angeles, and traces the Chicana movement through the testimonies of friendships of participants.

71. Jaime Taronji Jr., *Counting the Forgotten: The 1970 Census Count of Persons of Spanish Speaking Background in the United States, A Report of the U.S. Commission on Civil Rights* (Washington, DC: U.S. Census Bureau, 1974), http://www.law.umaryland.edu/marshall/usccr/documents/cr12sp22970.pdf (accessed May 27, 2010). The 1970 census did not have detailed information on Spanish-speaking women. Harvey M. Choldin, "Statistics and Politics: The 'Hispanic Issue' in the 1980 Census," *Demography* 23, no. 3 (August 1986): 407.

72. Deluvina Hernández, "Raza Satellite System," *Aztlán* 1, no. 1 (Spring 1970): 13–36. Mildred Monteverde, "Contemporary Chicano Art," *Aztlán* 2, no. 2 (Fall 1971): 51–61. Loretta Ayala de Sifuentes, "Conspiracy and the Right to Dissent," *Aztlán* 1, no. 1 (Spring 1970): 79–100. Teresa McKenna, "Three Novels: An Analysis," *Aztlán* 1, no. 2 (Fall 1970): 47–56.

C. Cota-Robles de Suárez, "Skin Color as a Factor of Racial Identification and Preference of Young Chicano Children," *Aztlán* 2, no. 1 (Spring 1971): 107–150. Loretta Ayala de Sifuentes, "Trade Secret Protection of Pesticide Reports," *Aztlán* 3, no. 2 (Fall 1972), 283–306. Laura E. Arroyo, "Industrial and Occupational Distribution of Chicana Workers," *Aztlán* 4, no. 2 (Fall 1973): 343–382. Adaljiza Sosa Riddell, "Chicanas and el Movimiento," *Aztlán*, vol. 5, no. 1 (Spring 1974): 155–165. Maxine Baca Zinn, "Political Familism: Toward Sex Role Equality in Chicano Families," *Aztlán* 6, no. 1 (Spring 1975): 13–26. "Symposium on Linguistics and the Chicano," *Aztlán* 7, no. 1 (Spring 1976): 1–5. Rosaura Sánchez, "Presupposition: A Pragmatic Notion," *Aztlán* 7, no. 1 (Spring 1976): 19–26. Rosaura Sánchez, "Gramatica transformacional y el estudio del español chicano," *Aztlán* 7, no. 1 (Spring 1976): 7–12. Janie Louise Aragón, "People of Santa Fe in the 1790s," *Aztlán*, 7, no. 3 (Fall 1976): 391–417. Miriam J. Wells, "Emigrants from the Migrant Stream: Environment and Incentives in Relocation," *Aztlán* 7, no. 2 (Summer 1976): 267–290. Sylvia Lizarraga, "Cambio: Intento principal de . . . Y no se lo trago la tierra," *Aztlán* 7, no. 3 (Fall 1976): 419–426. Flora Ida Ortiz, "Bilingual Education Program Practices and Their Effect upon Students' Performance and Self-Identity," *Aztlán* 8, no. 1/2 (Spring/Fall 1977): 157–174. Adaljiza Sosa Riddell, "Case of Chicano Politics: Parlier, California," *Aztlán* 9, no. 1 (1978): 1–22. Janie Louise Aragón, "Cofradias of New Mexico: A Proposal and a Periodization," *Aztlán* 9, no. 1 (1978): 101–117. Patricia Pullenza de Ortiz, "Chicano Children and Intelligence," *Aztlán* 10, no. 1/2 (Spring/Fall 1979): 69–83.

73. L. M. Apodoca, "The Chicana Woman: An Historical Materialist Perspective," 1971, in F. H. Vásquez and Rodolfo D. Torres, eds., *Latina/o Thought Culture, Politics, and Society* (Lanham, MD: Rowan & Littlefield, 2002), 27–29.

74. Perlita R. Dicochea, "Chicana Critical Rhetoric Recrafting: La Causa in Chicana Movement Discourse, 1970–1979," *Frontiers: A Journal of Women Studies* 25, no. 1 (2004): 77–84.

75. The contrast must be made between the exponential growth of Chicana-related classes in Chicana/o Studies and the individual disciplines.

76. Erlinda Gonzales Berry, "La Mujer Chicana," *Women's Studies Newsletter* 2, no. 1 (Winter 1974): 3. Maxine Baca Zinn, "Political Familism: Toward Sex Role Equality in Chicano Families," *Aztlán: International Journal of Chicano Studies Research* 6 (Spring 1975): 13–26, esp. 13; Maxine Baca Zinn, "Chicanas: Power and Control in the Domestic Sphere," *De Colores* 2 (Fall 1976): 19–31; Maxine Baca Zinn, "Marital Roles and Ethnicity: Conceptual Revisions and New Research Directions," in *Hispanic Report on Families and Youth* (Washington, DC: National Coalition of Hispanic Mental Health and Human Services Organizations, 1980), 31–35.

77. Interview with Martha Cotera, October 27, 2005, http://www.umich.edu/~ac213/student_projects05/cf/interview.html. Martha Cotera Papers, 1964–, University of Texas, Austin, http://www.lib.utexas.edu/taro/utlac/00228/lac-00228.html. Martha Cotera, *Diosa y Hembra: The History and Heritage of Chicanas in the U.S.* (Austin: Information Systems Development, 1976).

78. Teresa Córdova, "Agency, Commitment and Connection: Embracing the Roots of Chicano and Chicana Studies," *International Journal of Qualitative Studies in Education* 18, no. 2 (March–April 2005): 227.

79. Rosa Martínez Cruz and Rosaura Sánchez, eds., *Essays of La Mujer* (Los Angeles: Chicano Studies Research Center, 1977). Magdalena Mora and Adelaida R. Del Castillo, eds., *Mexican Women in the United States: Struggles Past and Present* (Los Angeles: Chicano Studies Research Center, 1980). Margarita Melville, *Twice a Minority: Mexican-American Women: A History of Mexican Americans* (St. Louis: Mosby, 1980). An instructive article was

Margarita Cota-Cardenas, "The Chicana in the City as Seen in Her Literature," *Frontiers: A Journal of Women Studies* 6, no. 1/2 (Spring/Summer 1981): 13–18.

80. National Association for Chicana/o Studies Conference Archives, http://www .naccs.org/naccs/Conference_Archives_EN.asp (accessed May 28, 2010).

81. Irene Campos Carr, "A Survey of Selected Literature on La Chicana," *NWSA Journal* 1, no. 2 (Winter 1988–1989): 253–273.

82. Paula M. L. Moya, "Chicana Feminism and Postmodernist Theory," *Signs* 26, no. 2 (Winter 2001): 441, 449. Moya challenges the assumption that all Chicana feminists were or are postmodernist—drawing heavily on the field of epistemology. She heavily critiques feminist theorists Norma Alarcón and Chela Sándoval.

83. Emma Pérez, "Gloria Anzaldúa: *La Gran Nueva Mestiza* Theorist, Writer, Activist-Scholar," *NWSA Journal* 17, no. 2 (Summer 2005): 2. Emma Pérez, *The Decolonial Imaginary: Writing Chicanas into History* (Indianapolis: Indiana University Press, 1999). Deena J. González, "Gender on the Borderlands: Re-Textualizing the Classics," *Frontiers: A Journal of Women Studies* 24, no. 2/3 (2003): 15–29.

84. Cherie Moraga and Gloria Anzaldúa, eds., *This Bridge Called My Back: Writings by Radical Women of Color,* 2d ed. (New York: Kitchen Table / Women of Color Press, 1984). Moya, "Chicana Feminism and Postmodernist Theory," 449–450. Cherrie Moraga, "Queer Aztlan," in Cherrie Moraga, *The Last Generation* (Boston: South End, 1993), 147. Sandra K. Soto, "Cherríe Moraga's Going Brown 'Reading Like a Queer,'" *GLQ* 1 (2005): 243–244, 251.

85. Carol W. Pfaff, "Constraints on Language Mixing: Intrasentential Code-Switching and Borrowing in Spanish/English," *Language* 55, no. 2 (June 1979): 291–318. Gloria Anzaldúa, "*La conciencia de la mestiza:* Towards a New Consciousness," in Gloria Anzaldúa, *Borderlands / La Frontera: The New Mestiza* (San Francisco: Aunt Lute Books, 1987), 100. Anzaldúa's embracing spirituality at first knocked me off balance; however, like Catholicism (although I am no longer a Catholic), spirituality is deeply rooted in Chicano culture. Rather than create more confusion, it is better to work with the present state of the oppressed. Elva Fabiola Orozco-Méndoza, "Borderlands Theory: Producing Border Epistemologies with Gloria Anzaldúa" (master's thesis, Virginia Polytechnic Institute and State University, 2008).

86. Survey of Earned Doctorates, Fact Sheet, National Science Foundation, 2007, http:// www.norc.org/NR/rdonlyres/B40E56EC-9A4F-4892-B871-E330BB689CD9/0/ SEDFactSheet.pdf. The 2007 survey includes data on U.S. doctorate recipients who graduated between July 1, 2006, and June 30, 2007. "Vanishing Minority Historians," *PhD in History,* http://phdinhistory.blogspot.com/2008/04/vanishing-minority-historians.html. Lindsay Pérez Huber, Ofelia María C. Malagón, Gloria Sánchez, and Daniel G. Solórzano, *Falling through the Cracks: Critical Transitions in the Latina/o Educational Pipeline: 2006 Latina/o Education Summit Report* (Los Angeles: University of California Chicano Studies Research Center, 2006), 3.

87. Daniel G. Solórzano, Martha A. Rivas, and Veronica N. Vélez, "Community College As a Pathway to Chicana/o Doctorate Production," *Latino Policy and Issues Brief,* no. 11 (June 2005): 1, 3.

CHAPTER 9 — RESISTING MAINSTREAMING

1. Fabio Rojas, *From Black Power to Black Studies How a Radical Social Movement Became an Academic Discipline* (Baltimore: Johns Hopkins University Press, 2007), 94, 115, 137, 225. Donna J. Gough, "Ideas Have Consequences: Conservative Philanthropy, Black Studies and the Evolution and Enduring Legacy of the Academic Culture Wars, 1945–2005" (PhD diss.,

Ohio State University, 2007), iii, 9, 84, 146, 149–150. Bob Wing, "'Educate to Liberate!' Multiculturalism and the Struggle for Ethnic Studies," *Colorlines News for Action*, May 15 1999, http://www.colorlines.com/archives/1999/05/educate_to_liberate_multiculturalism_ and_the_struggle_for_ethnic_studies.html (accessed November 26, 2010).

2. The impression should not be formed that the mass of black students are at research institutions. They have suffered from a squeezing out at many institutions. The wiping out of affirmative action, for example, has seen a plummeting of black student enrollment at the University of California system, where they are struggling to stay above 1 percent. At the California State University system they have maintained a parity with their numbers in the community. For example, at Northridge they are at about 8 percent, which is approximately their percentage in Los Angeles.

3. Shawn A. Ginwright, *Black in School: Afrocentric Reform, Urban Youth and the Promise of Hip-Hop Culture* (New York: Teachers College Press, 2004), 16.

4. Marita Hernandez, "Chicano Studies Find Favor on Campus University Classes Fill Up, New Research Centers Sought as Latino Population Booms," *Los Angeles Times*, April 10, 1989, 3.

5. "Chicano Studies Conference Scheduled," *Los Angeles Times*, May 8, 1986, SD-A8.

6. Andrew L. Yarrow, "After Latino Boom, the Long Pull Ahead," *New York Times*, April 15, 1984, A24.

7. William Trombley, "Ohio State's Ann Reynolds to Head Cal State System," *Los Angeles Times*, June 4, 1982, B1.

8. David Lepage, "Chicano Studies Gain New Direction at Conference," *Los Angeles Times*, March 26, 1978, SF7.

9. Bert Mann, "Picketing Assails Denial of Tenure to Cal State Prof," *Los Angeles Times*, August 9, 1979, SG1. Richard Santillán, *La Raza Unida* (Los Angeles: Tlaquilo Publications, 1973). Santillán was considered the expert on district reapportionment.

10. Kenneth Reich and Henry Méndoza, "Latinos Push for Political Power," *Los Angeles Times*, August 17, 1981, B3.

11. Claire Spiege, "Academic Friction Leads to Arson," *Los Angeles Times*, May 24, 1982, OC1.

12. Claire Spiegel, "Feud among Professors May Not Be Just Academic," *Los Angeles Times*, May 24, 1982, C1.

13. Even after this point there was frequent contact with Corona. "Politics of Immigration," *Daily Sundial*, November 27, 1973. "MECHA Presents Guest Speaker," *Daily Sundial*, November 28, 1973. John Cardenas, "Chicano Labor Force Tied to Major Capitalist Elements," *Daily Sundial*, February 14, 1975. "Bert Corona to Discuss Illegal Aliens," *Daily Sundial*, February 11, 1975.

14. Rudy Holguin had been appointed chair of the department in the early 1970s. California State University, Los Angeles, did not grant him tenure because he did not have a terminal degree. He did, however, stabilize the department, hiring many of the full-time instructors.

15. Claire Spiegel, "School Cancels Chicano Summer Classes," *Los Angeles Times*, June 17, 1982, F1. The Southland: "Settles' Kin Ask New Probe," *Los Angeles Times*, June 29, 1982, OC2

16. Myrna Oliver, "3 Chicano Studies Teachers Win Back Pay but Not Jobs," *Los Angeles Times*, May 7, 1983, A30. *Los Angeles Times*, July 9, 1985, 2. Corona and a former graduate student sued the *Los Angeles Times* for libel. The case was not heard.

17. William Trombley, "New Cal State Chief Called 'a Real Doer' " *Los Angeles Times*, June 5, 1982, OC-A1.

18. William Trombley, "Loss of Students in College Fund Cutbacks Told," *Los Angeles Times*, April 5, 1983, B1. "Trustees Ratify Historic Faculty Pact at Cal State," *Los Angeles Times*, August 17, 1983, OC26. "Teachers Facing Furloughs," *Van Nuys Valley (CA) Independent*, March 21,

1983. Evelyn Dorman, "Schools Open to Steady Enrollment," *Chicago Sunday Herald*, September 16, 1984.

19. Anne C. Roark, "Cal State Trustees Urge Reynolds to Change Her Ways," *Los Angeles Times*, June 2, 1987, 3.

20. Rodolfo F. Acuña, letter to the editor, *Los Angeles Times*, January 25, 1985.

21. This is a problem that we have to this day. It seems as if the California State University trustees never come to the campuses. In my forty-three years in the system, I have never seen a trustee on campus.

22. Rodolfo F. Acuña, "Cal State Admission Plan Makes Naive Assumption," *Los Angeles Times*, January 12, 1985, 2.

23. Bernard Goldstein James Highsmith, Hal Charnofsky, Carol Barnes, Nicholas P. Hardeman, "Letters," *Los Angeles Times*, February 7, 1985, 4. Karin Furuta, "CSUN Students Join in Protest Outside Meeting, *Daily Sundial*, November 13, 1985. Alex Henderson, "Proposed Admission Requirements Stir Controversy," *Daily Sundial*, August 26, 1985.

24. Frank Del Olmo, "Bad Teachers: Putting the University on the Spot, Too," *Los Angeles Times*, February 14, 1985, 5.

25. Bobbie Rodriguez, "Cal State System to Address Need for Teachers," *Los Angeles Times*, April 27, 1985, OC-A6. "The Region," *Los Angeles Times*, July 11, 1985, OC2.

26. Larry Gordon, "Reynolds May Go from Cal State to Top Job at CUNY," *Los Angeles Times*, June 1, 1990, A3.

27. Fred M. Hechinger, "About Education: Liberation of Women Scholars in 50's," *New York Times*, July 30, 1985, C9. Linda Lloyd, "Colleges Naming Female Presidents at Record Pace, But More Gains Sought," *Philadelphia Inquirer*, November 24, 1985.

28. William Trombley, "Trustees Plan Further Evaluation of Reynolds," *Los Angeles Times*, May 18, 1987, 3. K. L. Billingsley, "State Education Funds Went for Cars, Bel-Air Mansion," *San Diego Union*," April 1, 1990, C3. "Abdication of the Queen," *Santa Ana (CA) Orange County Register*, April 23, 1990, B10.

29. "Cal State Ex-Chancellor Named to Head CUNY," *Houston Chronicle*, June 2, 1990, 6.

30. "Ex-CSU Chief Quits N.Y. Post," *Sacramento Bee*, July 18, 1997, A16. Karen W. Arenson, "Alabama University May Fire President, Ex-CUNY Official," *New York Times*, August 30, 2001, A14.

31. Laura Chang, "UW President Approves Ethnic Studies Consolidation Plan," *Seattle International Examiner*, March 21, 1984, 6. Laura Chang, "UW Students Criticize Proposal to Consolidate Ethnic Studies Programs," *Seattle International Examiner*, February 1, 1984, 2.

32. Francisco J. Samaniego, Assistant Vice Chancellor, Academic Affairs, University of California, Davis, to Rodolfo F. Acuña, Chicano Studies Department, California State University, Northridge, January 5, 1987, in Rodolfo F. Acuña Archives, California State University Library, Northridge.

33. Report of the Ethnic Studies Planning Subworkgroup of the Undergraduate Education Work Groups, [University of California, Davis], June 22, 1987, in Rodolfo F. Acuña Archives, California State University Library, Northridge. A copy of the task force report is included in this report, which does not have page numbers.

34. Rodolfo Acuña, "Minority Report of the Advisory Panel on Ethnic Studies at the University of California–Davis, May 13, 1987," California State University, Northridge, Urban Archives. The report is in rough form.

35. Jack McCurdy, "Nava Won't Run for Reelection to School Board," *Los Angeles Times*, November 1, 1978, E1.

36. Jack McCurdy and George Ramos, "Nava in Eye of Storm Over Vacant School Post," *Los Angeles Times*, January 11, 1979, C1. Nava had been called a traitor by some black politicians for not supporting a black candidate for his vacated school board seat.

37. "Chicanos Protest Selection of Black to Head L.A. State," *Los Angeles Times,* May 27, 1979, B5. Kenneth J. Fanucchi, "Latin Educators Hit Appointment of Cal State Chief," *Los Angeles Times,* June 7, 1979, SG2. Richard West, "Nava Chosen as Envoy to Mexico," *Los Angeles Times,* January 8, 1980, B1. In January 1980 Nava was appointed ambassador to Mexico by President Jimmy Carter.

38. Rodolfo F. Acuña, "Creating Another White-Male Institution," *Los Angeles Herald Examiner,* October 6, 1989.

39. Ann Levin, "CSU Hispanic Enrollment Still Lags," *Tribune San Diego,* September 12, 1988, A.1.1.2. Anthony Flint, "Still Too Few Minorities at Harvard?" *Boston Globe,* February 18, 1990, A21. The Ford Foundation announced $1.6 million in grants for programs that improve race relations on campus. Much of the money went to Ivy League schools who reported they had too few minorities.

40. Edward B. Fiske, "Colleges Are Seeking to Remedy Lag in Their Hispanic Enrollment," *New York Times,* March 20, 1988, A1. Edward B. Fiske, "Tough Road for Hispanic College Students," *San Francisco Chronicle,* June 26, 1988, 19Z2. The article breaks down enrollment into ten or more universities.

41. Hernandez, "Chicano Studies Find Favor on Campus." Hernandez, "Chicano Studies Makes Comeback on Campuses." Anne Dudley, "Chicano Program Defies Naysayers," *Fresno Bee,* August 7, 1989.

42. "Racism Still Plagues Campus Life," *Los Angeles Times,* April 10, 1989, 4.

43. Kristina Lindgren, "Sonoma State Executive to Head CSUF," *Los Angeles Times,* May 16, 1990, 1.

44. "Dinuba Suit Focuses on Minority Rights," *Ukiah (CA) Daily Journal,* January 19, 1992.

45. Sharon L. Jones, "CSU Trustees Act to Improve Ethnic Balance," *San Diego Tribune,* March 13, 1991, A3.

46. Laura Myers, "San Jose State with List of Finalists Limited to Women, Minorities," *Orange County Register,* March 12, 1992, A3.

47. Rodolfo F. Acuña, "Keep Mahony's AIDS Decision in Perspective," *Herald Examiner,* December 19, 1986. Rodolfo F. Acuña, "Archbishop Mahony's Bad Example," *Los Angeles Herald Examiner,* November 20, 1988.

48. Kimberly Y. Wong, "Faculty Senate Votes Today on Future of ROTC," *Daily Sundial,* March 22, 1990. "Students and Faculty United for Equal Rights," *Daily Sundial,* April 18, 1990. Gays and lesbians in the ROTC was an issue throughout 1990.

49. Carol Watson, "Gay-Rights Group Finds Itself at Center of Stormy Campus Debate Activism: Attitudes toward Homosexuals Are Examined at Cal State Northridge," *Los Angeles Times,* November 4, 1991. Carol Watson, "Gay-Bashing' Flyer Distribution Probed as Hate Crime," *Los Angeles Times,* October 22, 1991, 3. Carol Watson, "Gay Rights Activists Protest Flyers at CSUN," *Los Angeles Times,* October 24, 1991, 3. Sean M. Daly, "At CSUN Homosexual Students Feel Unaccepted," *Daily Sundial,* May 17, 1989. Mat had been active in a southern university. At CSUN, he started the Lesbian and Gay Alliance (LAGA) and put up a display in Sierra South to celebrate gay pride. Rodieck was not the first gay leader to have close ties with MEChA. Zeke Zeidler, who was openly gay, was a former CSUN student who served as Associated Students president during the 1985–1986 school year. He ran on a slate with Chicana/o students. Caroline Miranda, "Protesters Low on Support Are 'Rebels without a Cause'," *Daily Sundial,* April 24, 1990.

50. Greg Braxton, "Flyers Attack Gays Again: Activists Urge Caution by Students Cal State Northridge," *Los Angeles Times,* October 26, 1991, 3: "It is the second time in a week handbills calling for violence have been found. This time, they mention a group blamed for assaults." The cofounder of the group was Desiree Dreeuws. Carol Watson, "Gay-Rights Group Finds Itself at Center of Stormy Campus Debate Activism: Attitudes Toward Homosexuals

Are Examined at Cal State Northridge," *Los Angeles Times*, November 4, 1991, 3. Watson, "Gay Rights Activists Protest Flyers at CSUN," *Daily Sundial*, April 24, 1970. Kenneth Ng, "ROTC Exclusion Attacks Free Speech," *Daily Sundial*, February 21, 1970.

51. Juan Arellano and Gabriel Meza Buelna, "Homophobia: Prejudice among Us," *El Popo* 21, no. 2 (Spring 1992): 3.

52. John Chandler, "Governor's Wife Takes CSUN Tour," *Los Angeles Times*, September 20, 1995, 1: "Education: Gayle Wilson observes teacher-training program. About 75 stage a protest over her husband's policies." Susan Byrnes, "Northridge Group Holds 'Kiss-In' to Fight Homophobia," *Los Angeles Times*, October 13, 1993, 2.

53. Enrique Castrejon, "Chicana/o Queers, Come Out: Take Over," *El Popo*, no. 2 (Fall 1996): 2.

54. Rodolfo F. Acuña, "The Less Redevelopment on the East Side, the Better," *Los Angeles Herald Examiner*, July 10, 1987.

55. Rodolfo F. Acuña, "Olvera Street Faces Wholesale Changes," *Los Angeles Herald Examiner*, August 7, 1987. These articles were also published in *La Opinión* in Spanish.

56. Rodolfo F. Acuña, "Power Grabbers Threaten Dream of Latino Museum," *Los Angeles Herald Examiner*, January 29, 1988. Rodolfo F. Acuña, "Shut Out by Historical Amnesia Latinos: Denied Their Past, These Original Californians Have Become Our Political Underclass," *Los Angeles Times*, February 25, 1990, 5. Gloria L. Charnes, "LA's Olvera Street Paved with History," *Orlando Sentinel*, February 19, 1989, H3.

57. Rodolfo F. Acuña, "Our 'Fantasy Heritage' Gets Royal Touch," *Los Angeles Herald Examiner*, October 9, 1987.

58. George Ramos, "*Olvera Street* Political Battle Waged Over Plan to Upgrade Tattered Tourist Spot," *Los Angeles Times*, February 3, 1989, 1.

59. Rodolfo F. Acuña, "History Is People, Not Bricks," *Los Angeles Times*," April 2, 1990, 5: "Mexicans were here long before the gringo. A multi-ethnic museum would trample that heritage."

60. George Ramos, "Olvera Street Revival Wins Approval of Commission, but Merchants Loudly Decry the Action, Saying It Could Threaten the Area's Mexican Heritage," *Los Angeles Times*, June 12, 1990, 1.

61. Gloria Ricci Lothrop, "Italians Have a Legitimate Los Angeles History, Too," *Los Angeles Times*, June 19, 1990, 7: "Given the legitimacy and limited scope of the museum proposal, the argument against it is a red herring." Len Pitt, "Olvera Street: One Person's Fantasy Becomes Los Angeles Realpolitik Restoration," *Los Angeles Times*, July 1, 1990, 5: "Proving the past can be what you perceive it, a crime-ridden, rat-infested service road was transformed into a Mexican marketplace."

62. George Ramos, "Plan to Put Eatery in Pico House Draws Fire Development," *Los Angeles Times*, October 12, 1990, 3: "Chicano activists and Olvera Street merchants say $15-million project that includes restaurant will disrupt the Mexican flavor of El Pueblo de Los Angeles park."

63. Oral history interview with Tatcho Mindiola by José Angel Gutiérrez, 1999, CMAS No. 143b, http://libraries.uta.edu/tejanovoices/interview.asp?CMASNo=143b# (accessed May 30, 2010).

64. Lydia Ramos, "Imperiled UCLA Chicano Studies Major to Be Saved," *Los Angeles Times*, July 3, 1990, 8: "Low funding and enrollment hurt the program. An infusion of money and staff is announced." Robert A. Rhoads, "Student Protest and Multicultural Reform: Making Sense of Campus Unrest in the 1990s," *Journal of Higher Education* 69, no. 6 (November–December 1998), 621–646.

65. George Ramos, "UCLA Cuts in Chicano Studies," *Los Angeles Times*, January 9, 1991, 1: "Protests have spread off campus to involve Latino leaders. School officials say there aren't

enough qualified teachers." An exchange of words occurred between Juan Gómez-Quiñones and Ralph Ochoa, who Quiñones saw as a bagman. "Campus Life: U.C.L.A.: Upgraded Status Urged for Chicano Studies," *New York Times*, February 10, 1991, A47.

66. Sam Enriquez, "CSUN Officials Suspend Zeta Beta Tau Over Protested Flyer," *Los Angeles Times*, November 10, 1992: "Some say the ruling, which puts on hold until 1994 all university relations with the fraternity including financial support, is too lenient." Al Martinez, "'Lupe' and the Guys," *Los Angeles Times*, November 12, 1992.

67. Sharon Bernstein, "Reinstating Fraternity Weighed to Avoid Suit," *Los Angeles Times*, March 10, 1993, 3: "The university president gauges Chicano officials' reactions to possible settlement with a group that issued offensive flyer."

68. Leslie Berger, "CSUN Teachers Vote to Boycott Fraternity," *Los Angeles Times*, March 12, 1993, 1. Wilson later tried to punish me by denying me step increases, telling the provost that I may deserve it, having published two more books, but that I was not a good citizen, having supported the students. Sharon Bernstein, "Jewish Students Join in Protest of Fraternity's Reinstatement," *Los Angeles Times*, March 13, 1993, 3: "The groups back Chicano activists in denouncing the decision on Zeta Beta Tau. The controversy stems from a flyer." Sharon Bernstein and Carol Chastang, "CSUN Settles Suit on Controversial Fraternity Flyers Rights," *Los Angeles Times*, March 11, 1993, 3: "The school agrees to reinstate the Zeta Beta Tau chapter. The decision angers a group of Chicano students and professors."

69. Julio Moran, "UCLA Faculty Panel Split on Chicano Studies Department," *Los Angeles Times*, April 19, 1991, 3. Raymundo Paredes, "Chicano Studies at UCLA: A Controversy with National Implications," *Hispanic Outlook in Higher Education* 2, no. 3 (November 30, 1991): 10. George Ramos, "Plan Unveiled for UCLA Department of Chicano Studies Education," *Los Angeles Times*, January 29, 1992, 4: "Latino professors behind the proposal admit there is strong sentiment against it from administrators." Dan Trotta, "Chicano Studies Group Returns to Its Beginnings 20 Years Later," *San Antonio Express-News*, March 25, 1992, A1.

70. Larry Gordon, "UCLA Resists Forming Chicano Studies Department," *Los Angeles Times*, April 29, 1993, B1.

71. John L. Mitchell, "Coalition Backs Call for Chicano Studies Dept. Education: Students and Community Groups Ask for Meeting with Chancellor Young to Discuss Future of UCLA Program," *Los Angeles Times*, February 7, 1991, 3.

72. Larry Gordon and Marina Dundjerski, "Protesters Attack UCLA Faculty Center Education," *Los Angeles Times*, May 12, 1993, 1: "Up to $50,000 in vandalism follows the university's refusal to elevate Chicano studies program to departmental status. Police arrest 90." Larry Gordon and Marina Dundjerski, "UCLA Has 2nd Day of Protest over Program," *Los Angeles Times*, May 13, 1993, B1. "UCLA Students Demand Chicano Studies Department," *San Francisco Chronicle*, May 13, 1993, A7. "Reassessment, Please, in UCLA Controversy Rethinking Chicano Studies Issue in Wake of Protest," *Los Angeles Times*, May 13, 1993, 6.

73. George Ramos, "Echoes of '60s Ring through UCLA Protests," *Los Angeles Times*, May 17, 1993, 3. Andrea L. Rich, "Perspectives on UCLA's Ethnic Studies Decision," *Los Angeles Times*, May 18, 1993, 7.

74. "Chicano Studies Activists Begin Hunger Strike at UCLA," *Los Angeles Times*, May 26, 1993, 4. Larry Gordon and Bernice Hirabayashi, "Hunger Strikers, UCLA Still Stalemated," June 2, 1993, 1. Interview with Marcos Aguilar and Minnie Fergusson, August 12, 2009.

75. Larry Gordon and Bernice Hirabayashi, "Hunger Strikers, UCLA Still Stalemated Education," June 2, 1993, 1: "Parents of protesters appeal to chancellor, but he stands firmly against demand for a Chicano studies department." "Six Fasting to Press for a Chicano Studies Department at U.C.L.A.," *New York Times*, June 2, 1993, B7.

76. Saul Sarabia, "Campus Correspondence Chicano Studies Fight Involves a Bigger Issue," *Los Angeles Times*, May 30, 1993, 3.

77. Mary Anne Perez, "A Hunger for Change Protest," *Los Angeles Times*, June 6, 1993, 3: "Students from the central city join the fight for Chicano studies department. The fact those classes aren't offered 'sets the tone' for racism, says one." "Parents Side with Students in Hunger Strike," *Pacific Stars and Stripes*, June 5, 1993.

78. Larry Gordon and Sonia Nazario, "Fasters, UCLA Officials Meet to Defuse Protest," *Los Angeles Times*, June 6, 1993, 1: "1,000 march to back hunger strikers' bid for Chicano studies department. Talks resume today."

79. I firmly believe that Young would have allowed the students to starve to death before making it a department.

80. Robert Dalleck, "A Political Assault on Academic Values," *Los Angeles Times*, June 9, 1993, 7: "The demand for a Chicano studies department was an unnecessary distortion of the university's purpose." For a response, see Jorge R. Mancillas, "At UCLA, the Power of the Individual," *Los Angeles Times*, June 11, 1993, 7: "The hunger strike was a morally justifiable, politically reasonable use of the tactic." Tom Hayden, "The Mission of UCLA's Hunger Strike," *Los Angeles Daily News*, June 14, 1993.

81. "Chavez Center: UCLA's Apt Compromise," *Los Angeles Times*, June 8, 1993, 6. "UCLA Hunger Strikers End 14-Day Protest: Partial Victory on Chicano Studies Program," *San Francisco Chronicle*, June 8, 1993, A9. Carla Hall, "Power and Politics of Fasting," *Los Angeles Times*, June 10, 1993, 1: "Hunger strikes sometimes get results. At the least, they draw publicity. The dramatic and visceral threat of self-starvation can force both sides into a test of who blinks first." Matthew Heller, "Back from the Front: Young Hunger Striker Returns to San Fernando High School," *Los Angeles Times*, June 15, 1993, 1. Norma returned to her high school classes.

82. "Westwood UCLA Drops Charges against Student Protesters," *Los Angeles Times*, May 6, 1994, 2. "UCLA Drags Feet on Promise, Group Charges," *Las Vegas Review Journal*, September 27, 1993, 1F.

83. Semillas Community Schools, Winter 2008, http://www.dignidad.org/emailNow/ pdfs/DIGNIDAD_1208.pdf (accessed May 30, 2010).

84. Ralph Frammolino, "UCLA Picks Interim Head for Chicano Studies Education: Some Activists Criticize Appointment of Administrator Who Helped Negotiate End to Hunger Strike," *Los Angeles Times*, January 28, 1994, 3. Ralph Frammolino, "A New Generation of Rebels: Latinos Are Demanding Colleges Be More Responsive," *Los Angeles Times*, November 20, 1993, 1.

85. "Latino Hunger Strike Continues at UCSB," *Los Angeles Times*, May 5, 1994, 25. "Agreement Ends UC Santa Barbara Students' Hunger Strike," *Los Angeles Times*, May 7, 1994, A27. Tanya Schevitz, "UC Santa Barbara Pioneers Chicano Doctoral Program," *San Francisco Chronicle*, August 6, 2003, A15: "Department to be first in U.S., results from decade-old student, faculty demands, strike." Stacey Baca, "Hunger Strike Continues: Chicano Needs at CU Stressed," *Denver Post*, April 23, 1994. "Chicano Students on Hunger Strike at St. Cloud," *Minneapolis–St. Paul Star Tribune*, May 7, 1995, 7B.

86. Rosanna Ruiz, "Gutierrez Temporarily Reinstated," *Fort Worth Star–Telegram*, September 20, 1996, 1. Tracey-Lynn Clough, "Gutierrez Reinstatement Is a Victor for Hispanics," *Dallas Morning News*, October 24, 1996, 5A. Renee C. Lee, "Ex-UTA Center Director Claims Settlement Breach in Suit," *Fort Worth Star–Telegram*, February 8, 1997, 4. Eric Garcia, "UTA President's Deposition Delayed; State Officials Requested Time in Suit by Gutierrez," *Dallas Morning News*, June 26, 1997, 3A. Mindy Warren, "Settlement Cost UTA More Than $100,000," *Dallas Morning News*, August 12, 1997, 1A.

87. Rodolfo F. Acuña, *Sometimes There Is No Other Side: Chicanos and the Myth of Equality* (Notre Dame: Notre Dame University Press, 1998). Court records are in the Rodolfo F. Acuña Collection, Urban Archives, California State University, Northridge.

EPILOGUE

1. Rob Kuznia, "The Supplier Diversity Squeeze: How the Downturn Affects Minority Contracts," *Hispanic Business* (March 2010): 14, 18, 20.

2. *Militant*, April 22, September 2, 1996.

3. Ved Dookhun, "We Want to Sign Up Young Workers," *Militant*, April 29, 1996.

4. Emily Fitzsimmons, "'No to INS Raids!' Says Garza at Packinghouse," *Militant*, July 1, 1996.

5. Carole Lesnick and Gale Shangold, "Demonstrations in California Defend Affirmative Action, Immigrant Rights," *Militant*, August 5, 1996.

6. Alejandra Rincón and Carlos Alvarado, "Chicano Youth Discuss Fights in Houston, *Militant*, December 16, 1996.

7. Chessie Molano, "Fight for Bilingual Education Heats up in Arizona," *Militant*, December 11, 2000.

8. Deborah Liatos, "Oakland Marchers Defend Immigrant Rights," *Militant*, February 26, 2001.

9. Interview with Joel Britton, Socialist Workers Party candidate for California governor, *Militant* 67, no. 32 (September 2003), http://www.themilitant.com/2003/6732/673258. html (accessed November 14, 2010).

10. Michelle Malkin, "Reconquista Is Real," May 2, 2006, http://vdare.com/malkin/060502_reconquista.htm (accessed May 30, 2010). "Mexican "Mexican Reconquista Raul Grijalva in the U.S. Congress," http://www.americanpatrol. com/REFERENCE/Grijalva-Raul.html (accessed May 30, 2010). Rob van Kranenburg, "Whose Gramsci? Right-wing Gramscism," *International Gramsci Society Newsletter*, no. 9 (March 1999): 14–18, http://www.internationalgramscisociety.org/igsn/articles/a09_5.shtml (accessed May 30, 2010).

11. "An act to amend the Immigration and Nationality Act to revise and reform the immigration laws, and for other purposes, it was enacted by the Senate and House of Representatives," on November 6, 1986. Legal Services Corporation Office of Inspector General, https://www.oig.lsc.gov/legis/irca86.htm (accessed May 30, 2010). David Simcox, "Measuring the Fallout: The Cost of the IRCA Amnesty after 10 Years," *Center for Immigration Studies* (May 1997), http://www.cis.org/articles/1997/back197.htm (accessed May 30, 2010). Nancy Rytina, "IRCA Legalization Effects: Lawful Permanent Residence and Naturalization through 2001" (paper presented at the Effects of Immigrant Legalization Programs on the United States: Scientific Evidence on Immigrant Adaptation and Impacts on U.S. Economy and Society, The Cloister, Mary Woodward Lasker Center, NIH Main Campus, October 25, 2002), http://www.dhs.gov/xlibrary/assets/statistics/publications/irca0114int.pdf (accessed May 30, 2010).

12. California Postsecondary Education Commission, "Out of the Shadows: The IRCA/SLIAG Opportunity. A Needs Assessment of Educational Services for Eligible Legalized Aliens in California under the State Legalization Impact Assistance Grants Program of the Immigration Reform and Control Act of 1986," *Commission Report 89-10: California Postsecondary Education Commission*, ERIC ED318805.

13. Rick Fry and Felisa Gonzales, "One-in-Five and Growing Fast: A Profile of Hispanic Public School Students," *Pew Hispanic Center*, August 26, 2008, http://pewhispanic.org/reports/report.php?ReportID=92 (accessed May 30, 2010). "Latinos Make Up More Than Half of California's Students; Should This Milestone Bring Changes?" *Los Angeles Times*, November 13, 2010, A1. "Latinos now account for 50.4% of students, an increase of 1.4% over last year."

14. Rodolfo F. Acuña, *Occupied America: A History of Chicanos*, 7th ed. (New York: Longman, 2010), 393–406.

15. Adam Howard, "Pro-Immigrant Marches Surging Nationwide," *Nation* (April 10, 2006), http://www.thenation.com/blog/pro-immigrant-marches-surging-nationwide (accessed May 30, 2010). Jennifer Ludden, "Hundreds of Thousands March for Immigrant Rights," *National Public Radio*, http://www.npr.org/templates/story/story.php?storyId=5333768 (accessed May 30, 2010).

16. "Growing Activism: Undocumented Students/DREAM Act," *University of California Television*, http://www.uctv.tv/searchdetails.aspx?showID=12488 (accessed May 30, 2010)

17. Carlos B. Cordova, *The Salvadoran Americans* (Westport, CT: Greenwood Press, 2005), 72. Megan Davy, "The Central American Foreign Born in the United States," *Migration Policy Institute*, April 1, 2006, http://www.migrationinformation.org/Usfocus/ print.cfm?ID =385, (accessed May 30, 2010). Megan Davy, "The Central American Foreign Born in the United States," *Migration Policy Institute*, April 1, 2006, http://www.migrationinformation .org/Usfocus/print.cfm?ID=385#3 (accessed May 30, 2010).

18. Aaron Terrazas, "Salvadoran Immigrants in the United States," *Migration Policy Institute*, January 2010, http://www.migrationinformation.org/usfocus/display.cfm?ID= 765 (accessed May 30, 2010). Fact Sheet, "Hispanics of Salvadoran Origin in the United States, 2007," *Pew Hispanic Center*, September 16, 2009, http://pewhispanic.org/files/ factsheets/51.pdf (accessed November 14, 2010).

19. Roberto Rodriguez, "Academic Turf War at East Los Angeles," *Black Issues in Higher Education* 14, no. 24 (January 22, 1998): 12–14. Rita Vega-Acevedo, "Newest Trustee Gets Involved," *Pasadena Faculty Association*, http://www.profaculty.com/press/archives/ sep5_courier.html (accessed May 30, 2010). Aaron Terrazas, "Salvadoran Immigrants in the United States," *Migration Policy Institute*, January 2010, http://www.migrationinformation .org/Usfocus/display.cfm?ID=765 (accessed May 30, 2010).

20. Siris Barrios, interview, March 1, 2010, Los Angeles. Roberto Lovato, interview, March 1, 2010, Los Angeles.

21. Gregory gave tirelessly to the polishing up of proposals and overcoming the bureaucracy.

22. Rossana Pérez, ed., *Flight to Freedom: The Story of Central American Refugees in California* (Houston: Arte Público, 2007), 151.

23. Jorge had also contacted Gloria Melara, a Salvadoran computer science professor. Although supportive, she was having problems with her department.

24. Robert Monroe, Roberto Lovato, and Carlos Alsaro, "New College Minor: CSUN Offers First Central American Studies Program," *Van Nuys Valley (CA) Daily News*, May 8, 2000, N4. Solomon Moore, "CSUN Focuses on Central America," *Los Angeles Times*, May 9, 2000, 5: "A new minor offered at the school—the first of its kind in the nation—will allow students to study effects of globalization on the region." Beatriz had a dynamite case for political discrimination. In transferring her to Chicano Studies, the university ameliorated damages. The good was that this chip was used to buy support and continuance of the program.

25. Lovato has become a national voice successfully leading the campaign to dump Lou Dobbs at CNN. Roberto Lovato, "As Movement Demanding CNN Dump Him Grows, Dobbs Plays Victim," *Huffington Post*, September 21, 2009, http://www.huffingtonpost .com/roberto-lovato/as-movement-demanding-cnn_b_293566.html (accessed May 30, 2010).

26. Pedro A. Cabán, "Moving from the Margins to Where? Three Decades of Latino/a Studies," *Latino Studies* 1 (2003): 5–35; quotation on p. 6.

27. Based on the erroneous assumption of Chicano scholars, Cabán concluded that "Chicano Studies did not abruptly appear on the academic scene in the late 1960s." He does not differentiate between the corpus of knowledge and the evolution of a course of study, as well as works analyzing that production, such as in the case of Octavio Romano's *El Grito*.

28. Cabán, "Moving from the Margins," 7, 23. See responses to his paper: Deena J. González, "Enclaves y transgresiones: Historical and Contemporary Considerations in Pedro Cabán's 'Three Decades,'" *Latino Studies* 1 (2003): 36–42. Felix Masud-Piloto, "Response to Pedro A. Cabán Latino Studies: Moving Forward While Looking Back," *Latino Studies* 1 (2003): 43–46.

29. UCLA César E. Chávez Department of Chicana/o Studies, http://www.chavez .ucla.edu/ (accessed May 31, 2010). Arizona State University, Transborder Chicana/o and Latina/o Studies, http://transborder.clas.asu.edu/ (accessed May 31, 2010). University of Arizona Mexican American and Raza Studies Students, http://masrc.arizona.edu/ (accessed May 31, 2010).

30. Cabán, "Moving from the Margins," 10. Inés Pinto Alicea, "Ivy League Schools and Latino Students," *Hispanic Outlook in Higher Education* 20, no. 7 (January 4, 2010), 52–54. Masud-Piloto, "Moving Forward While Looking Back," 43. Melissa Campbell, "New Trends in Latino Studies," *Hispanic Outlook in Higher Education* 15, no. 7 (December 27, 2004): 29.

31. Mari Carmen Sarracent, "Few Latinos in Ivy League," *Hispanic Outlook in Higher Education* 11, no. 1 (October 9, 2000): 23.

32. Elise Morales, "Top 25 Colleges for Hispanics," *Hispanic Outlook in Higher Education* 22, no. 2 (February/March 2009): 52–58.

33. HACU Member Hispanic-Serving Institutions (HSIs), http://www.hacu.net/hacu/ Default_EN.asp (accessed May 31, 2010).

34. Resurrecting an old idea: In 1969, when I drew up the Chicano Studies curriculum, I called one class "Mexican Thought" and the other "Mexican American Ideas." I did not feel that Mexican Americans had a sufficient mass to categorize the corpus of knowledge as thought.

35. For many of us, it was reminiscent of dissidents issuing revolutionary plans during the Mexican national period.

36. Eliu Carranza, *Pensamientos on Los Chicanos: A Cultural Revolution* (Berkeley: California Book Co., 1969), 4.

37. Soldatenko, *Chicano Studies*, 7.

38. Ibid., 8.

39. Ibid., 40.

40. Kathy Matheson, "Prestigious Colleges using Spanish to Attract Latinos," *Associated Press*, February 8, 2010.

41. Emilio Zamora to Rudy Acuña, e-mail, September 23, 2009.

42. Roberto Alonzo, Texas Legislature, http://www.house.state.tx.us/members/memberpage/? district=104 (accessed November 14, 2010).

43. Texas Higher Education Coordinating Board, *Strategic Plan for Texas Public Community Colleges 2009–2013* (April 2008), 25.

44. Paul Abowd, "Financial Crisis Socks California," *Labor Notes*, October 23, 2008, http://www.labornotes.org/node/1949. Joyce Luhrs, "Case Studies: Success Stories at Four Universities," *Hispanic Outlook in Higher Education* 5, no. 16 (April 15, 1995): 20. Rose Carbo, "Curriculum: Ethnic Studies on the Rise," *Hispanic Outlook in Higher Education* 6, no. 8 (December 8, 1995): 11.

45. Valerie Godiness and Marla Jo Fisher, "Major Move: Chicano Studies," *Orange County Register*, June 19, 2001, A3: "As demographics shift, such programs are growing increasingly popular in high schools and colleges."

46. Dave Curtin, "Ethnic-Studies Divisions across U.S. Working to Defend Their Discipline," *Denver Post*, February 20, 2005, C4. Garry Boulard, "An Ethnic Studies Evolution," *Diverse Issues in Higher Education* 23, no. 21 (November 30, 2006): 30–32.

Shirley V. Svorny, "Make College Cost More," *Los Angeles Times*, November 22, 2010, http://www.latimes.com/news/opinion/commentary/la-oe-svorny-college-funding-20101122,0,6554772.story (accessed November 26, 2010).

47. Paul Basken, "Pell Grant Increase Could Be Cut as Talks Intensify on Student-Aid Bill," *Chronicle of Higher Education*, March 12, 2010, http://chronicle.com/article/Pell-Grant-Increase-Could-Be/64666/ (accessed May 31, 2010). Robert B. Reich, "The College Cut-Off: A College Degree Has Never Been More Important—or More Expensive," *American Prospect*, April 28, 2004, http://www.prospect.org/cs/articles?article=the_college_cutoff (accessed May 31, 2010).

48. Gale Holland, "Schwarzenegger Proposes Major Cal Grant Cuts: California's Main Financial Aid Program for College Students May Stop Covering Rises in Tuition," *Los Angeles Times*, January 13, 2009. "Cal Grants and the California State Budget," *CFA News Info Sheet*, January 27, 2009, http://www.calfac.org/allpdf/newsreleas/2009_pressrel/PR_012709_factsheetV7.pdf (accessed May 31, 2010).

49. "Teachers and Students Protest across Europe," *BlogWatch, World Focus*, November 13, 2008, http://worldfocus.org/blog/2008/11/13/teachers-and-students-protest-across-europe/2620/ (accessed May 31, 2010). Gwladys Fouché, "Teachers in France Are Angry—Sarkozy Treats Them with Scorn," *Guardian,* October 31, 2008, http://www.guardian.co.uk/education/2008/oct/31/france-baccalaureate-sarkozy-strike (accessed May 31, 2010). Parwini Zora, "Germany: Students Protest Planned Education Cuts," *World Socialist Web Site*, June 25, 2008, http://www.wsws.org/articles/2008/jun2008/ruhr-j25.shtml (accessed May 31, 2010).

50. Ian Mundell, "Student Protests May Mar Bologna Ministerial Meeting," *European Voice*, February 4, 2009, http://www.europeanvoice.com/article/imported/student-protests-may-mar-bologna-ministerial-meeting/64514.aspx (accessed May 31, 2010).

51. Candice Novak, "Students Shut Classes in Tuition Protests: Germans Take to Streets to Demand Tuition Decreases," *Global Post*, December 16, 2009, http://www.globalpost.com/dispatch/study-abroad/091124/german-students-protest-tuition-hikes (accessed May 31, 2010). "Students Protest in Belgrade," *Demotix*, November 27, 2009, http://www.demotix.com/news/189454/students-protest-belgrade (accessed May 31, 2010): "Belgrade students have been protesting on the streets of the Serbian capital for the last 3 days, demanding assistance from the government with tuition and enrollment fees."

52. Kevin O'Leary, "Tuition Hikes: Protests in California and Elsewhere," *Time Magazine*, November 21, 2009, http://www.time.com/time/nation/article/0,8599,1942041,00.html (accessed May 31, 2010). "New York Students Protest Governor's Tuition Hike Plan," *U.S. News and World Report*, March 6, 2009, http://www.usnews.com/education/blogs/paper-trail/2009/03/06/new-york-students-protest-governors-tuition-hike-plan (accessed May 31, 2010).

53. Jonathan Evans, "Students Protest Budget Cuts, Tuition Hikes across Nation," *Daily Princetonian*, March 5, 2010, http://www.dailyprincetonian.com/2010/03/05/25454/ (accessed May 31, 2010). Wes Duplantier, "Teachers, Students Protest Tuition Hikes, Funding Cuts," *Maneater*, March 9, 2010, http://www.themaneater.com/stories/2010/3/9/teachers-students-protest-tuition-hikes-funding-cu/ (accessed May 31, 2010). Jeannie Kever, "UH Committee Approves Tuition Hike," *Houston Chronicle*, February 10, 2010, http://www.chron.com/disp/story.mpl/metropolitan/6860649.html (accessed May 31, 2010).

54. Tonyo Cruz, "Students Protest 2,000-Percent Tuition Fee Hike in Philippines' Biggest State University," *Bullet Points*, March 19, 2010, http://us.asiancorrespondent.com/tonyo-cruz-blog/students-protest-2-000-percent-tuition-fee-hike-in-philippines-biggest-state-university (accessed May 31, 2010). Evans, "Students Protest Budget Cuts." Jenny Yuen, "Massive Rally Rips Tuitions: 5,000 Students March on Queen's Par," *Toronto Sun*, November 6, 2008.

55. Jessie McKinley, "Thousands in California Protest Cuts in Education," *New York Times*, March 5, 2010, A13. Terence Chea, "Angry US Students Protest Cuts to Higher Education," *Associated Press*, March 5, 2010, http://www.breitbart.com/ article.php?id= D9E8KToG1&show_article=1 (accessed May 31, 2010).

56. Alan Duke, "California University Students Protest Tuition Hikes," *CNN*, November 18, 2009, http://www.cnn.com/2009/US/11/18/california.tuition.protest/index.html. "Students Protest Tuition Increases," *New York Times*, November 20, 2009, http://www.nytimes .com/2009/11/21/us/21tuition.html?_r=1. Since 1978, politicos in California have lived in dread of taxpayer groups and the passage of Proposition 13.

57. Victoria Hernandez, "CSUN's Protest and Walkouts from Thursday Recapped," *Daily Sundial*, March 5, 2010, http://sundial.csun.edu/2010/03/csuns-protest-and-walkouts-from-thursday-recapped/ (accessed May 31, 2010). Yazmin Cruz, "Student Protesters Speak out against Police Force and Media Misrepresentation," *Daily Sundial*, March 5, 2010, http://sundial.csun.edu/2010/03/student-protestors-speak-out-against-police-force-and-media-misrepresentation/ (accessed May 31, 2010). Juana Esquivel, "Students, Faculty React to Campus Protests," *Daily Sundial*, March 5, 2010, http://sundial.csun.edu/2010/03/ students-faculty-react-to-campus-protests/. Yazmin Cruz, "Professor Injured during the March 4 Protest Speaks," *Daily Sundial*, March 9, 2010, http://sundial.csun.edu/2010/03/ professor-injured-during-the-march-4-protest-speaks/ (accessed May 31, 2010).

58. National Education Association, *The Invisible Minority: Report of The NEA-Tucson Survey on the Teaching of Spanish to the Spanish-Speaking* (Washington, DC: National Education Association, 1966), v, 3.

Appendix

Academic Institutions with Programs in Chicano/a Studies and Related Areas
*To Locate the Web Page for the Following, Simply Type the Name of the Program
and the Name of the Institution into Your Web Browser.*

ARIZONA

Arizona State University
Name: Transborder Chicana/o and Latina/o Studies
Location: Tempe, Arizona
Description: The Hispanic Research Center (HRC) promotes research on Chicanos
and Latinos. Transborder Chicana/o and Latina/o Studies Department formed in
1997. It has thirteen professors within the autonomous unit. Offers a BA through
the Center.

Northern Arizona University
Name: Ethnic Studies
Location: Flagstaff, Arizona
Description: Minors in Ethnic Studies and Latin American Studies introduce
students to theoretical and critical analyses of race and ethnicity. Excellent faculty
drawn from the disparate disciplines.

University of Arizona
Name: Mexican American Studies & Research Center
Location: Tucson, Arizona
Description: In 1981 the Mexican American Studies & Research Center was estab-
lished; and in 2009 it was formally recognized as a department. Offers a BA in
Mexican American Studies.

CALIFORNIA

California State Polytechnic University Pomona
Name: Ethnic and Women's Studies Department
Location: Pomona, California
Description: Offers a BA. Option Chicano/Latino Studies minor.

California State University at Bakersfield
Name: Interdisciplinary Concentration In Chicano Studies
Location: Bakersfield, California
Description: Offers a minor in Chicano Studies. Does not have a department and draws courses from other departments.

California State University Channel Island
Name: Chicana/o Studies
Location: Camarillo, California
Description: Chicana/o Studies program an interdisciplinary degree. It has a fulltime chair. It offers between five and six courses and a BA in Chicana/o Studies.

California State University Chico
Name: BA in Multicultural and Gender Studies
Location: Chico, California
Description: Interdisciplinary program drawn from disparate disciplines. Offers a minor in Chicano Studies.

California State University Dominguez Hills
Name: Chicano/Chicana Studies Department
Location: Carson, California
Description: Courses offered within an autonomous department. Granted departmental status to Chicana/o Studies in 1994. Offers a BA in Chicano/Chicana Studies.

California State University East Bay
Name: Department of Ethnic Studies
Location: Hayward, California
Description: Interdisciplinary department drawing from other units. Offers a BA in Ethnic Studies and undergraduate minors in Ethnic Studies and Latino/a Studies.

California State University Fresno
Name: Chicano and Latin American Studies Department
Location: Fresno, California
Description: Autonomous department, one of the oldest program in California. Offers a BA in Chicano Studies.

California State University Fullerton
Name: Chicana/o Studies Department
Location: Fullerton, California
Description: The department emphasizes a teaching credential with a Chicano studies concentration. Offers a BA in Ethnic Studies.

California State University Humboldt
Name: Ethnic Studies
Location: Humboldt, California
Description: Offered a minor in Latin American and Latino Studies. The program was discontinued after years on hold.

California State University Long Beach
Name: Department of Chicano & Latino Studies
Location: Long Beach, California
Description: One of the oldest interdisciplinary departments in the state system. Offers a BA in Chicano and Latino Studies.

California State University Los Angeles
Name: Department of Chicano Studies
Location: Los Angeles, California
Description: one of the oldest departments in the state university system, has seven full time faculty. Offers a BA and MA in Chicano Studies.

California State University Northridge
Name: Department of Chicana/o Studies
Location: Northridge, California
Description: Has twenty-seven tenure tract professors—offers 166 sections per semester and offers online classes. Two-thirds of the faculty members are women. A separate Central American Studies Department has four tenure track professors. Offers a BA and MA in Chicana/o Studies.

California State University Sacramento
Name: Chicano Studies Program
Location: Sacramento, Caifornia
Description: The Chicano Studies program is a component of the Ethnic Studies Department. Offers a minor in Chicano Studies.

California State University San Bernadino
Name: Program of Ethnic Studies
Location: San Bernardino, California
Description: Offers a minor in Ethnic Studies. Does not have a separate Chicano or Latino category.

California State University Sonoma
Name: Department of Chicano and Latino Studies
Location: Rohnert Park, California
Description: Launched in 1969, became a department in 1974. It has four full time faculty. Offers a BA in Chicano and Latino Studies.

California State University Stanislaus
Name: Department of Ethnic and Gender Studies
Location: Turlock, California
Description: Offers program minors in Chicano Studies and Ethnic Studies/ Chicano Studies. Ethnic Studies is an interdisciplinary program that enhances student understanding of the experiences and perspectives of American racial and ethnic groups. Limited classes in Chicano Studies.

Canyon College
Name: BA Online School of Chicano Studies
Location: Carmichael, California
Description: A distance learning program. Offers a BA in Chicano Studies.

Claremont Colleges
Name: Chicana/o~Latina/o Studies Department
Location: Claremont, California
Description: Chicano/Latino Studies major is part of an intercollegiate, interdisciplinary program for students of Scripps, Claremont McKenna, Harvey Mudd, Pitzer, and Pomona Colleges.

Loyola Marymount University
Name: Department of Chicana and Chicano Studies
Location: Westchester, California
Description: 'La Chicana' was taught in the 1970s, as was "Introduction to Chicano Studies," which fulfilled a social science requirement. Before the unit achieved departmental status, many of southern California's leaders in Chicano studies taught at LMU. In 2001, Professor Deena J. González was hired to chair the department. A fifth of Loyola's students are Latinas/os. It has a major and minor in Chicana/o Studies.

Mills College
Name: Ethnic Studies
Location: Oakland, California
Description: Ethnic studies began in 1969; courses also available through The Latin American Studies Program. Offers a BA.

San Diego State University
Name: Department of Chicana and Chicano Studies
Location: San Diego, California

Description: It was one of the first programs in California and at one time the largest. Offers a BA in Chicana/o Studies. Also offers a master's program in Chicana/o transnational studies with specializations in Gender and Borderland Studies.

San Francisco State University
Name: Department of Raza Studies
Location: San Francisco, California
Description: Fall 1969 became the Department of La Raza Studies, part of the College of Ethnic Studies at SFSU. Offers a BA in La Raza Studies.

San Jose State University
Name: Mexican American Studies Department
Location: San Jose, California
Description: It has three faculty members. Offers a minor and MA in Mexican American Studies.

Santa Clara University
Name: Ethnic Studies
Location: Santa Clara, California
Description: Chicano studies courses within the BA in Ethnic Studies.

Stanford University
Name: Stanford Center for Chicano Research
Location: Stanford, California
Description: Center for Comparative Studies of Race and Ethnicity, was established in 1997, Latinos are approximately 13 percent of the undergraduate population. Offers an interdisciplinary major in Chicana and Chicano Studies.

University of California Berkeley
Name: Chicano/Latino Studies Program In The Department of Ethnic Studies
Location: Berkeley, California
Description: The Chicano Studies Library collection is one of the best in the United States, founded in 1969 by José Arce. The Chicano Studies program evolved Ethnic Studies. Offers a BA and PhD in Ethnic Studies Chicano Studies Program, and a degree in Ethnic Studies.

University of California Davis
Name: Department of Chicana/o Studies
Location: Davis, California
Description: Ada Sosa Ridell laid the foundation for the department in the 1970s. Malaquias Montoya is an emeriti member of the faculty. Offers a BA through Cultural Studies and Social/Policy Studies from the College of Letters and Science.

University of California Irvine
Name: Department Chicano/Latino Studies
Location: Irvine, California
Description: A core faculty of ten professors. An interdisciplinary department. Offers a BA, a minor, a certificate program, and a graduate emphasis in Chicano/Latino Studies.

University of California Los Angeles
Name: César E. Chavez Department of Chicana and Chicano Studies
Location: Los Angeles, California
Description: Became a Department of Chicana and Chicano Studies in the 2004–05. It was established in 1993 as a result of the student Hunger Strike of that year that was the result of the vision of Marcos Aguilar, Minnie Fergusson and Professor Juan Gómez-Quiñonez. Offers a BA in Chicana/o Studies.

University of California Los Angeles
Name: Chicano Studies Research Center
Location: Los Angeles, California
Description: The UCLA Chicano Studies Research Center (CSRC) was founded in 1969. It publishes *Aztlán: A Journal of Chicano Studies*. CSRC holds six "institutional FTE" or faculty positions that are placed on loan to departments. It does not offer a degree.

University of California Riverside
Name: It is an area within Ethnic Studies
Location: Riverside, California
Description: It has five faculty members. Offers a BA in Ethnic Studies and Chicano Studies. A PhD can be earned through Ethnic Studies with an emphasis in Chicano Studies.

University of California San Diego
Name: Department of Ethnic Studies
Location: La Jolla, California
Description: UCSD had a small Chicano Studies program from 1973–1989. In 1989 consolidated into Ethnic Studies. Offers a minor in Chicana/o and Latina/o Studies, and a BA, MA, and PhD in Ethnic Studies.

University of California Santa Barbara
Name: Chicana and Chicano Studies Department
Location: Goleta, California
Description: It has ten faulty and it is an autonomous unit. Offers BA, MA, and PhD programs.

University of California Santa Cruz
Name: Latin American and Latino Studies Department
Location: Santa Cruz, California

Description: Combined B.A. majors available in LALS/global economics, LALS/ literature, LALS/politics, and LALS/sociology. Also offers an undergraduate minor.

University of Redlands
Name: Race and Ethnic Studies
Location: Redlands, California
Description: Small faculty of three professors. No Spanish surname instructors. Offers a BA in Race and Ethnic Studies.

University of San Francisco
Name: Chicano/a Studies
Location: San Francisco, California
Description: USF is a Jesuit college. Offers a Chicano/a Studies minor and a Latin American Studies minor.

University of Southern California
Name: Department of American Studies and Ethnicity
Location: Los Angeles, California
Description: Interdisciplinary; under the direction of George Sánchez. Offers a BA in American Studies and Ethnicity (Chicano/Latino Studies).

CALIFORNIA: COMMUNITY COLLEGES

Bakersfield College
Name: Associate in Arts Degree Chicano Studies
Location: Bakersfield, California
Description: An interdisciplinary program. Offers an AA in Chicano(a)/Latino(a) Studies.

Cerritos Community College
Name: Chicano Studies Program
Location: Norwalk, California
Description: Program pulled together with courses from disparate disciplines. Offers an AA.

City College of San Francisco
Name: Latin American & Latino/a Studies Department
Location: San Francisco, California
Description: The Department of Latin American and Latino Studies offers courses in two distinct fields: the study of Latin America and La Raza. Offers an AA.

College of San Mateo
Name: Ethnic Studies
Location: San Mateo, California

Description: multicultural emphasis; there are ten faculty members, three of whom are Spanish surname. Offers an AA in Ethnic Studies.

Contra Costa College
Name: La Raza Studies
Location: San Pablo, California
Description: In the bay Area, the program has been heavily influenced by San Francisco State and the historic Latino population of the area which is a mixture of Chicanos and other Latinos. Offers an AA in La Raza Studies.

De Anza College
Name: Intercultural/International Studies Division
Location: Cupertino, California
Description: Chicana/o studies is an area within Intercultural/International Studies. Offers an AA in Chicana/o and Intercultural Studies.

East Los Angeles Community College
Name: Chicana/o Studies Department
Location: Monterey Park, California
Description: Teach several Chicana studies courses each semester. Has a Southgate campus. Offers approximately 50–52 courses in the fall and spring and 10 in winter and summer. Offers an AA in Chicano Studies.

El Camino Community College
Name: Ethnic Studies Program
Location: Torrance, California
Description: Chicano Studies option within Ethnic Studies. Offers an AA.

Fresno City College
Name: Chicano-Latino Studies
Location: Fresno, California
Description: Focus on Mexican-American history, heritage, and culture. Offers an AA in Chicano-Latino Studies.

Glendale Community College
Name: Chicano Studies interdisciplinary major; Ethnic Studies Department
Location: Glendale, California
Description: Transfer agreements with state universities to accept credits. Offers an AA.

Hartnell College
Name: Chicano Studies in the Fine Arts, Language Arts and Social Sciences Department
Location: Salinas, California
Description: Hartnell is in the middle of one of California's largest agricultural belts. Offers an AA in Chicana/o Studies.

Laney College

Name: Ethnic Studies Department

Location: Oakland, California

Description: Geared to general education. Ethnic Studies Department established in 1969, student activists including members of the Black Panther Party demanded courses that reflected the diverse communities in Oakland, CA. Offers an AA in Mexican/Latin-American Studies (track within Ethnic Studies).

Los Angeles City College

Name: American Cultures: Associate of Arts: Chicano Studies

Location: Los Angeles, California

Description: Transfer agreements. Offers an AA in Chicano Studies within Social Sciences.

Los Angeles Mission College

Name: Chicano Studies and Foreign Languages

Location: Sylmar, California

Description: Taught since the 1980s. In 1998 there were only five sections of Chicano studies being taught by part-timers. Today there are approximately twenty-five to thirty courses. Offers an AA in Chicano Studies.

Los Angeles Valley College

Name: Chicano Studies Classes

Location: Van Nuys, California

Description: Once a thriving program led by Art Avila and Lydia Baines, the program is down to five classes. Offers an AA in Ethnic Studies.

Monterey Peninsula College

Name: Ethnic Studies Department

Location: Monterey, California

Description: Introductory courses in general education. Offers an AA in Ethnic Studies.

Moorpark College

Name: Multicultural – Chicano Studies

Location: Moorpark, California

Description: It has two professors and program geared to general education. Offers an AA in Chicano Studies.

Ohlone College

Name: Chicano Studies Department

Location: Fremont, California

Description: The Chicano Studies program is an interdisciplinary field of study. Courses count in a variety of Associate of Arts degrees.

Orange Coast Community College
Name: Ethnic Studies
Location: Costa Mesa, California
Description: Offers three courses in Ethnic Studies, none of which appear to have Chicano or Latino content.

Oxnard College
Name: Ethnic / Chicano Studies
Location: Oxnard, California
Description: Survived despite issues of white faculty and administrators. Large Mexican American and Latino population. Offers an AA in Chicano Studies.

Palomar College
Name: Multicultural Studies Department
Location: San Marcos, California
Description: The department is dominated by Latinos; the Movimiento Estudiantil Chicanos de Aztlan plays a role in the department. Offers an AA.

Rio Hondo Community College
Name: Department Chicana/o Studies
Location: Whittier, California
Description: The Program is comprised of students of Mexican origin. Offers an AA in Chicana/o Studies.

Sacramento City College
Name: Ethnic Studies, Mexican-American Emphasis
Location: Sacramento, California
Description: A once a thriving but struggling program. Currently there are two courses taught in Mexican American Studies. Offers an AA.

San Diego Community College
Name: Department of Chicano Studies
Location: San Diego, California
Description: The program offers courses in anthropology, bilingual studies, Chicano culture, history of Mexico and the United States, language and literature, psychology and sociology from a Chicano perspective. Offers an AA.

San Diego Mesa College
Name: Chicano Studies program
Location: San Diego, California

Description: One of the older Chicano Studies programs; identified with projects as Chicano Park and the rich artist movement in the area. Offers an AA. One of the San Diego Community Colleges.

Santa Ana College
Name: Chicano Studies Degree
Location: Santa Ana, California
Description: Huge Mexican and Latino population with a growing awakening of their power. Offers an AA in Chicano Studies.

Santa Barbara City College
Name: American Ethnic Studies
Location: Santa Barbara, California
Description: Developed ten courses in Chicano studies that are transferable to state and University of California campuses. Offers an AA in Chicano Studies and an AA in Ethnic Studies.

Solano Community College
Name: Ethnic Studies
Location: Fairfield, California
Description: Offers an AA in Latino Studies within Ethnic Studies.

Southwestern College
Name: Mexican American Studies Interdisciplinary Program
Location: Chula Vista, California
Description: Offers fourteen to seventeen courses per semester; three full time faculty members. Offers an AA.

Yuba Community College District (Woodland Community College & Clear Lake Campus)
Name: La Raza Studies Program
Location: Marysville, California
Description: Two courses in La Raza Studies. Offers an AA in Ethnic Studies.

California has one-hundred and six Public Community Colleges in seventy-one Community College districts. Disappointing is that the following Los Angeles Community Colleges do not have Chicano or Ethnic Studies Programs. They all have heavy Chicano and Latino populations surrounding the colleges.

Los Angeles Harbor Community College
Los Angeles Pierce College
Los Angeles Trade Tech
West Los Angeles College

COLORADO

Colorado State University—Fort Collins
Name: Ethnic Studies Department
Location: Fort Collins, Colorado
Description: The Center for Applied Studies in American Ethnicity (CASAE) established in 1990. In 2004 it changed its name to Ethnic Studies Interdisciplinary Studies Program. Offers a BA.

Colorado State University-Pueblo
Name: Chicana(o)/Latina(o) Studies
Location: Pueblo, Colorado
Description: Offers a minor in Chicano/a Studies. Draws from different disciplines. It complements programs such as social work.

Metropolitan State College, Denver
Name: Chicano Studies Department
Location: Denver, Colorado
Description: Six full time professors and half dozen professors from other departments. It serves the Denver area. Offers a BA.

University of Colorado at Boulder
Name: Department of Ethnic Studies
Location: Boulder, Colorado
Description: Ethnic studies program thirteen years old at the University of Colorado at Boulder. It was born out of struggle to counter the racism in sociology and other departments. Offers a BA.

University of Northern Colorado-Greeley
Name: Hispanic Studies
Location: Greeley, Colorado
Description: Offers a BA in Mexican American Studies: Liberal Arts Emphasis or secondary education. Also offers a minor in Mexican American Studies.

NEW MEXICO

Eastern New Mexico University
Name: Greater Southwest Studies
Location: Portales, New Mexico
Description: An Interdisciplinary program within the College of Liberal Arts and Sciences. Offers a minor and an AA.

New Mexico State University
Name: Chicano Program
Location: Las Cruces, New Mexico
Description: Serves as a center for various Chicano organizations. Offers a supplementary major in Chicano Studies.

University of New Mexico
Name: Chicano Hispano Mexicano Studies
Location: Albuquerque, New Mexico
Description: The UNM has various centers and programs running parallel to Chicano Studies. El Centro de la Raza was founded in 1969. The program developed an interdisciplinary minor in 1996.

Western New Mexico University
Name: Department of Chicana/Chicano and Hemispheric Studies (CCHS)
Location: Silver City, New Mexico
Description: Félipe de Ortego was the founding faculty member of the department. Offers a BA in Chicano Hemispheric Studies.

TEXAS

FOUR YEAR UNIVERSITIES

Austin College
Name: Center for Southwestern and Mexican Studies
Location: Sherman, Texas
Description: Mexican American courses within American Studies and interdisciplinary major. Latino/Latin American Studies center, known as El Centro, was established in the summer of 1995. Offers a minor and a BA.

Our Lady of the Lake
Name: Mexican American Studies Department
Location: San Antonio, Texas
Description: Center for Mexican American Studies and Research has an Old Spanish Missions Historical Research Collection and the Mexican American Collection. Offers a BA.

Southern Methodist University
Name: Ethnic Studies and Latin American Studies
Location: Dallas, Texas
Description: Offers a BA in Latin American Studies and a BA in Ethnic Studies, with concentrations in Mexican American Studies.

Sul Ross State University
Name: Mexican-American Studies
Location: Alpine, Texas
Description: No Spanish surname faculty. Offers a BA.

Texas A&M Corpus Christi
Name: Mexican American Studies
Location: Corpus Christi, Texas
Description: Although the program has fantastic potential it is still in the planning stage. It has a minor under development.

Texas Lutheran University
Name: Center for Mexican American Studies
Location: Seguin, Texas
Description: The Center for Mexican American Studies (CMAS) was established in 1971. Offers a Mexican American Studies minor. The CMAS collaborates with other academic departments to provide a variety of courses.

University of Houston
Name: Center for Mexican American Studies
Location: Houston. Texas
Description: Established in 1972 as an interdisciplinary academic program encompassing the liberal arts, education, and social sciences focusing on the Mexican American and broader Latino experience. The premier center in the nation. Offers a minor.

University of North Texas
Name: Mexican American Studies
Location: Denton, Texas
Description: Interdisciplinary Minor in Mexican American Studies proposed by the UNT History Department and authorized by the University during the 2000–2001 academic year. The Mexican American Studies Minor was formally approved in May 2001.

University of Texas Arlington
Name: Center for Mexican American Studies (CMAS)
Location: Arlington, Texas
Description: An interdisciplinary ethnic studies center with focus on the experiences of Mexican-origin people in the United States. Founded through legislative mandate in 1993. Founding Director, Professor José Angel Gutiérrez. Has the premier oral history collection on the oral history of Tejano activism created and compiled by José Angel Gutiérrez. Offers a minor.

University of Texas Austin
Name: Mexican American Studies Center
Location: Austin, Texas
Description: Established in 1970, coordinated offerings in Mexican American Studies. Offers an MA.

University of Texas El Paso
Name: Chicano Studies
Location: El Paso, Texas
Description: Established in 1970, the Chicana/o Studies Research Program offers an academic program with a BA and four minor areas of specialization.

University of Texas Pan American
Name: Mexican-American Studies
Location: Edinburg, Texas
Description: Mexican American studies major/minor online. In the center of one of the largest concentrations of Mexican Americans in the United States. Offers a BA.

University of Texas San Antonio
Name: Mexican American Studies (MAS)
Location: San Antonio, Texas
Description: Offers a BA. Also has a department of bilingual bicultural studies.

TWO YEAR COLLEGES

Alamo Colleges
Name: Mexican-American Studies
Location: San Antonio, Texas
Description: Offers an AA. See Palo Alto College.

Brazo Sport College
Name: Mexican American Studies
Location: Lake Jackson, Texas
Description: An interdisciplinary academic program in Mexican-American field of study. Offers an AA.

Collin Community College
Name: The Mexican-American Field of Study
Location: McKinney, Texas
Description: Collin County Community College District has seven centers. "Due to a legislative mandate that a Mexican-American field of study be formed in each public higher education institution, a task force was created in fall of 2005." Classes tend to be very small and ethnically mixed. Offers an AA.

El Paso Community College
Name: Chicano Studies Program
Location: El Paso, Texas
Description: One of the premier community college programs. Founded about 2004. Offers an AA.

Lone Star College System
Name: Curriculum for Mexican-American Studies
Location: Woodlands, Texas
Description: Offers an AA in Mexican-American Studies, interdisciplinary, draws from various departments.

Palo Alto College
Name: Mexican American Studies
Location: San Antonio, Texas

Description: Palo Alto College is one of five colleges that are part of Alamo Colleges. Offers an AA.

Richland College, Dallas
Name: Center for Mexican-American Studies
Location: Dallas, Texas
Description: Degree program administered through center. Began in 2004 and offers a Field of Studies degree in Mexican-American Studies.

San Jacinto College
Name: Mexican-American Program
Location: Pasadena, Texas
Description: Geographically, San Jacinto College is located in a region with a high-concentration of Latino residency and employment, making the Mexican American Studies program of utmost importance to our community. A feeder school to the University of Houston. Offers transfer courses.

South Texas College
Name: Mexican-American Studies Program
Location: McAllen, Texas
Description: Started in 2006–2007 by Gilberto Reyes Jr. It had problems in striking an articulation agreement with our neighboring university, the University of Texas-Pan American. It offers an AA and between seventeen to twenty classes. The program had hosted the Tejas Foco of the National Association for Chicana/o Studies.

PACIFIC NORTHWEST

Boise State University
Name: Mexican American Studies
Location: Boise, Idaho
Description: Small but growing number of Mexican American Studies classes. Offers a minor.

Central Washington University
Name: Latino and Latin American Studies Program
Ethnic Studies Course Program
Location: Ellensburg, WA
Description: Central Washington University has the largest group of Latino students in comparison with other regional universities in the state of Washington. Minorities make up 20 percent. There is around three to four hundred Latinas/os on campus. Offers minors.

Eastern Washington University
Name: Chicano Education Program
Location: Cheney, Washington

Description: The Chicano Education Program originated in the spring of 1977 when a group of Chicano and Chicana students proposed the formation of a program. In the 2000 decade, a minor was approved and several courses added. It is a very well developed programs. Eastern Washington has been criticized for its failure to commit tenure track positions.

Oregon State University
Name: Department of Ethnic Studies; Centro Cultural César Chávez
Location: Corvallis, Oregon
Description: Ethnic Studies established in 1995. Centro Cultural César Chávez was established to provide a location and facility for programming various, academic, cultural, recreational and social events related to the Chicano/Latino. The Centro Cultural César Chávez was originally called the Chicano Cultural Center, established in 1972. Offers a BS and a BA.

Portland Community College
Name: Chicano/Latino Studies
Location: Portland, Oregon
Description: Offers three courses. Track in Chicano/Latino Studies, Ethnic Studies, or American Studies.

Portland State University
Name: Chicano/Latino Studies Program
Location: Portland, Oregon
Description: Interdisciplinary study of social, cultural, political, economic, and historic forces that have shaped the development of the people of Mexico and other Latin American countries in the United States. Emphasis on the experience of the Chicano and other Latinos as residents and citizens in the United States and not in their countries of origin or descent. Offers a certificate.

University of Oregon
Name: Department of Ethnic Studies
Location: Eugene, Oregon
Description: A track within Ethnic Studies. In 1997 a major in Ethnic Studies was added to the minor that already existed. The department was granted full departmental status in 2008. Offers a BA.

University of Washington
Name: American Ethnic Studies
Location: Seattle, Washington
Description: One of the most student active campuses in the nation. Many of the early Chicano students arrived there from the Yakima Valley where their parents had come as migrants. Offers a minor.

Washington State University
Name: Comparative Ethnic Studies
Location: Pullman, Washington
Description: Offers a BA. Chicana/o & Latina/o sequence within Ethnic Studies. Has one of the most active MEChA organizations nationally.

Western Washington University
Name: American Cultural Studies program
Location: Bellingham, Washington
Description: Offers a BA. Category within Major in American Cultural Studies.

UTAH

University Of Utah
Name: Ethnic Studies
Location: Salt Lake City, Utah
Description: Chicano studies an option within Ethnic Studies. Offers a minor.

MIDWEST

Bowling Green State University
Name: Ethnic Studies
Location: Bowling Green, Ohio
Description: The Latino/a Studies minor is an interdisciplinary academic program with ethnic studies. Also offers a BA.

DePaul University
Name: Latin American and Latino Studies
Location: Chicago, Illinois
Description: At one time, it had a heavy Puerto Rican. Members of the Young Lords spearheaded the movement for Latino studies. Offers a BA and a minor.

Emporia State University
Name: Ethnic and Gender Studies
Location: Emoria, Kansas
Description: The courses are not specific to one ethnic group. Offers a minor.

Fort Hays State University
Name: Ethnic Studies
Location: Fort Hays, Kansas
Description: Has a Center for Interdisciplinary Studies. Based on faculty surnames there is a faint presence of Latino faculty members. Offers a certificate.

Indiana State University
Name: Latin American—Latino Studies Minor
Location: Terre Haute, Indiana

Description: Offers a minor. Courses selected from a variety of departments and programs.

Indiana University Bloomington
Name: Latino Studies Program
Location: Bloomington, Indiana
Description: In 1973 Indiana University created the Office of Latino Affairs offering services and programs to the Latino community, and served as an advocate for Latina and Latino students and faculty. Offers a minor and a PhD minor.

Indiana University Northwest
Name: Department of Minority Studies
Location: Gary, Indiana
Description: An Ethnic studies program. Four full time professors, one of whom is a Chicano. It has a large Mexican and Latino community surrounding the campus. Offers a minor in Latino Studies.

Iowa State University
Name: U.S. Latino/a Studies Program
Location: Ames, Iowa
Description: Study of Mexican Americans, Puerto Rican Americans, Cuban Americans, Dominican Americans, and Central and South Americans. A cross-disciplinary program drawing from anthropology, sociology, political science, economics, history and other social science and professional fields. Offers a BA within Interdisciplinary Studies.

Kansas State University
Name: American Ethnic Studies
Location: Manhattan, Kansas
Description: Does not have a large presence of Chicano or Latino Studies, although it was one of the first universities to explore the possibility. Offers a BS and a BA.

Michigan State University
Name: Chicano/Latino Studies Programs
Location: East Lansing, Michigan
Description: Also the home of the Julian Samora Research Institute http://www .jsri.msu.edu/latinospec/ http://www.jsri.msu.edu/ — a major research center. Offers a BA and PhD.

Minnesota State University Mankato
Name: Ethnic Studies
Location: Mankato, Minnesota
Description: No Latino faculty in Ethnic studies; one course in Latino/Hispanic Studies. Offers a BS and MS in Ethnic Studies and Multi-Cultural Studies Program.

Montana State University

Name: The Latin American and Latino Studies (LALS)

Location: Bozeman, Montana

Description: Housed in the Department of Modern Languages. Offers a non-teaching minor.

North Park Chicago

Name: Center for Latino Studies

Location: Chicago, Illinois

Description: A small program with study abroad programs. Offers a minor.

Northeastern Illinois University

Name: Latino and Latin American Studies Program

Location: Chicago, Illinois

Description: Mexican and Caribbean Studies Program draws from various disciplines. Only has one core appointment. Offers a minor.

Northwestern University

Name: Latina and Latino Studies Program

Location: Evanston, Illinois

Description: Faculty taken from across the campus. In March of 2009 the faculty of Weinberg voted to approve the Latina and Latino Studies major and minor, which welcomes students from all schools to declare.

Notre Dame University

Name: Institute for Latino Studies

Location: Notre Dame, Indiana

Description: The Institute for Latino Studies at University of Notre Dame was founded in 1999. Institute Director, Dr. Gilberto Cardenas, a Professor of Sociology, Good source for data on Latinos and Chicanos. Offers a supplementary major or a minor in Latino Studies.

Ohio State University

Name: Latino/a Studies

Location: Columbus, Ohio

Description: The program has a critical mass of Latino/a professors from disparate fields. It is a young faculty. Offers a minor.

Purdue University

Name: Latin American and Latino studies program

Location: West Lafayette, Indiana

Description: Interdisciplinary and interdepartmental Minor degree in Latin American and Latino Studies. Has twenty faculty members across seven programs.

University Of Illinois at Chicago Circle
Name: Department. Of Latin America and Latino Studies
Location: Chicago, Illinois
Description: Latin American Studies created in 1972. A heavy Puerto Rican and Mexican American presence with a growing population of Central Americans. Offers a BA.

University of Illinois at Urbana-Champaign
Name: Latina/Latino Studies Program
Location: Champaign, Illinois
Description: Expected approval date is Spring 2011. Program has been in existence since 1996. The program maintains its interdisciplinary and comparative focus. Offers a BA.

University of Michigan
Name: Latina/o Studies Program
Location: Ann Arbor, Michigan
Description: Housed within the American Culture Program. Currently offers a minor.

University of Minnesota
Name: Chicano studies Department
Location: Minneapolis, Minnesota
Description: Excellent web presentation. "In 1970, Chicana/o students in Minnesota organized a week-long summer institute to explore the feasibility of establishing a Chicano Studies Department in the Midwest. See http://chicano.umn.edu/about/ Offers a BA.

University of Nebraska Lincoln
Name: Latino and Latin American Studies program (LLAS)
Location: Lincoln, Nebraska
Description: Formed in 1993 when two previously separate programs merged. Chicano Studies focuses on U.S. Latinos, particularly Mexican-Americans, the largest Latino group in the United States. Offers a minor.

University of Wisconsin Madison
Name: Chicana/o & Latina/o Studies Program
Location: Madison, Wisconsin
Description: In the mid-seventies Chicana/o students began to agitate for a Chicano studies. Among the first were Francisco "Panchillo" Rodríguez and Carlos Reyes. Many of the first students were Tejanos. Offers a graduate minor.

University of Wisconsin Milwaukee
Name: Roberto Hernández Center
Location: Milwaukee, Wisconsin
Description: A bilingual staff assists students and guides them through the university. Offers a Latino Studies Certificate Program.

University Of Wisconsin – Whitewater
Name: Chicano Studies Race & Ethnic Cultures program
Location: Whitewater, Wisconsin
Description: Chicano studies also falls into the Race and Ethnic Culture Graduate component. Dates from the mid-seventies when agitation for a Chicano studies department began. Offers a minor in Race and Ethnic Cultures.

University of Wyoming
Name: Chicano Studies Program
Location: Laramie, Wyoming
Description: Serves a primarily Mexican American community. Publishes a department newsletter called El Clamor de Chicano Studies. It does not have faculty lines. Considering the small Chicano/Latino population the program has been virulent. Offers a minor.

Wayne State University
Name: Center for Chicano-Boricua Studies
Location: Detroit, Michigan
Description: Founded in 1972 as the *Latino en Marcha* Leadership Training Program. Founding members were community activists and labor organizers who teamed with progressive WSU faculty to bring the program to the University. Wayne State University is about 75 percent Mexican or Chicano, 24 percent Puerto Rican/Boricua and the rest is made up of Central/Antillean and South Americans. Offers a minor.

EAST COAST

Borough of Manhattan Community College
Name: Center for Ethnic Studies
Location: New York, New York
Description: Center for Ethnic Studies offers courses in Latino studies. Offers an AA.

Brandeis University
Name Latin American and Latino Studies Program
Location: Waltham, Massachusetts
Description: An interdepartmental program in Latin American and Latino Studies Program, founded in 1963. It has a major and minor for undergraduates. It facilitates communication between faculty members in eight participating departments in the social sciences and humanities.

Brooklyn College CUNY
Name: The Puerto Rican and Latino Studies Department
Location: Brooklyn, New York
Description: Founded in 1969 as the Institute for Puerto Rican Studies it evolved into a department and research Center. Offers a BA.

Brown University
Name: The Center for the Study of Ethnicity and Race in America
Location: Providence, Rhode Islanad
Description: The Center for the Study of Race and Ethnicity at Brown University is an interdisciplinary research center established in 1996. Offers a BA.

City College of New York
Name: CUNY Dominican Studies Institute
Location: New York, New York
Description: Formed to advance research and teaching at the City University of New York, focusing on the Dominican population in the United States. Offers a BA in Dominican Studies.

City University of New York
Name: Center for Latin American, Caribbean, & Latino Studies
Location: New York, New York
Description: Offers an MA. The Center for Latin American, Caribbean and Latino Studies Graduate Center provides opportunities for Latino students at the Ph.D. level.

College of the Holy Cross
Name: Latin American and Latino Studies Program
Location: Worcester, Massachusetts
Description: Heavy emphasis on Spanish language; interdisciplinary concentration. Offers a BA.

Columbia University
Name: Latino Studies Program
Location: New York, New York
Description: Center for the Study of Ethnicity and Race is housed at Columbia. Latino/a experience is placed in the context of United States, Caribbean, and Latin American history. Offers a BA.

Cornell University
Name: Latin American Studies Latino Studies Program
Location: Ithaca, New York
Description: The initial thrust in the 1970s was for a Puerto Rican Studies Program. The struggle continued through the eighties. With it came a new emphasis on all Latinos. The Hispanic American Studies Program (HASP) was formed in 1987 and became part of the College of Arts and Sciences in 1995. The name was changed to Latino Studies Program (LSP). Offers a minor.

Davidson College
Name: Ethnic Studies
Location: Charlotte, North Carolina
Description: Offers a minor. Includes a Latina American track.

Duke University
Name: Latino/a Studies
Location: Durham, North Carolina
Description: In the Fall of 1997 the Concilo Latino/Hispano, Americano was formed. In 1990–2000 students requested new course offerings leading to a certificate in Latino/a Studies in the Global South. The courses are interdisciplinary.

Florida International University
Name: Latin American and Caribbean Center
Location: Miami, Florida
Description: Founded in 1979, it is a federally funded under Title VI. It includes language studies in partnership with the University of Florida's Center for Latin American Studies. Emphasis on Cuban Studies. Offers a MA.

Fordham University
Name: Latin American and Latino Studies Institute (LALSI)
Location: New York, New York
Description: Founded as the Puerto Rican Studies Institute, the program expanded in the early 1990s and changed its name. Offers a BA and MA.

Millersville University, Pennsylvania
Name: Latino/a Studies Minor
Location: Millersville, Pennsylvania
Description: Minor began in 2003 founded. The eighteen credit minor offers three required courses. Composed of a variety of disciplines including Spanish, Education, History, Anthropology, and Sociology. The dominant group is Puerto Rican.

New York University
Name: Latino Studies Program
Location: New York, New York
Description: Dedicated to the study of the study of the historical, social and cultural experience of Latinos. Its core faculty includes distinguished specialists in all the major strands of US Latino history: Chicano (Saldana, Rosaldo), Puerto Rican (Dávila, Flores) and Cuban (Dopico, Muñoz)." It also houses the Center for Latin American and Caribbean Studies (CLACS). Offers a minor.

Princeton University
Name: Program in Latino Studies
Location: Princeton, New Jersey
Description: New program with affiliate faculty from other departments. Offers a certificate.

Queens College State University of New York at Buffalo
Name Latin American & Latino Studies
Location: Flushing, New York

Description: Offers a BA and a Puerto Rican and Latino Studies minor. Listed as one of the ten top public colleges.

Rutgers, The State University of New Jersey
Name: Department of Latino and Hispanic Caribbean Studies
Location: New Brunswick, New Jersey
Description: Emphasis on Puerto Rican Studies. Offers a BA.

Saint Peter's College (New Jersey)
Name: Latin American & Latino Studies Program
Location: Englewood Cliffs, New Jersey
Description: Came about around 2003. The Latino population is mainly Cuban, Puerto Rican and Dominican. All courses except for the introductory course are cross-listings. Offers a BA.

Smith College
Name: Department of Latin American and Latino/a Studies
Location: Northampton, Massachusetts
Description: An exclusive liberal arts women's college. Offers a BA in Latin American and Latino/a Studies and a minor in Latino/a Studies.

State University of New York at Albany
Name: Department of Latin American, Caribbean, and US Latino Studies (LACS
Location: Albany, New York
Description: Offers a BA and a PhD concentration. Also has a five year concentration a BA/MBA Five-Year Latin American and Caribbean Studies/Business Administration Degree Program and an option of concentrating in Puerto Rican Studies. The department has twenty-one professors affiliated with other departments.

State University of New York at Buffalo
Name Department of American Studies
Location: Buffalo, New York
Description: Department of American Studies is an interdisciplinary department. Lists as strength "Chicana/o, Latina/o, Caribbean, and Latin American studies." Offers a BA, an MA, and a PhD.

State University of New York, Fredonia
Name: Latino Studies
Location: Fredonia, New York
Description: Composed of faculty in disparate disciplines. Offers a minor.

Syracuse University
Name: Latino-Latin American Studies
Location: Syracuse, New York
Description: Solid online offerings. Most of faculty non-Latinos. Offers a BA.

University of Central Florida
Name: Latin American, Caribbean and Latino Studies (LACLS) Program
Location: Orlando, Florida
Description: The Latin American, Caribbean and Latino Studies (LACLS) Program was re-launched in the fall of 2004. Strong emphasis on community education and involvement. Offers an interdisciplinary minor.

The University of Connecticut
Name: The Institute of Puerto Rican and Latino Studies
Location: Storrs, Connecticut
Description: The Institute of Puerto Rican and Latino Studies (PRLS) has operated since the Fall of 1994. Supports multipurpose interdisciplinary research and teaching program with a comparative focus on the Puerto Rican, Mexican, and other Latin American origin populations. Offers a minor in Latino Studies.

University of Massachusetts Amherst
Name: Center For Latin American, Caribbean And Latino Studies
Location: Amherst, Massachusetts
Description: Interdisciplinary courses. Offers a minor.

University of Pennsylvania
Name: Latin American and Latino Studies
Location: Philadelphia, Pennsylvania
Description: Emphasis on Latin America. Offers a BA.

Index

Abcarian, Richard, 49
abortion, 151–152
Absorption period, 200, 201
academe, 75, 109, 124, 141
academic standards, 52, 91
accessibility: of Chicano Studies offices at SFVSC, 93, 97; of higher education, 146, 206; of UCLA Chicana/o Studies, 182
ACSSP (American Council of Spanish-Speaking People), 12
activism, 21, 76, 148, 208, 226n86. *See also* El Movimiento Estudiantil Chicanos de Aztlán (MEChA); protests; student activism
Acuña, Rodolfo, 33, 48, 222n32, 223n36, 266n68; Chicano Studies administration by, 99; Communist Party and, 113; CSU San Marcos and, 174; Ethnic Studies at UC Davis and, 172–173; Ford Foundation and, 128, 135; general education policies at SFVSC and, 65; LEAA and, 142; MACC and, 109; Montes and, 86; Nava and, 50, 51, 233n78; Nieto-Gómez and, 155, 157; Paredes, Raymund and, 185–186; El Plan de Santa Barbara and, 59, 64; protests and, 96, 98; Reynolds' admission standards and, 170–171; Robinson and, 135–137; student governance and, 93–94; surveillance of, 107–108; UCSB lawsuit of, 131–132, 189, 197, 259n29; at UTEP, 89–90
administration, 70, 208, 238n2
admissions, 50, 118–121, 169–171. *See also* affirmative action
Adult Degree Completion Program, 99–100
adult education, 102
affirmative action, 118–121, 130, 192–195, 246n30, 262n2

African Americans, 12, 34, 124, 176, 217n31; black/brown tensions and, 19–20, 21, 173–175; civil rights and, 15, 19; median education of, 10; PhDs and, 128; population of, 22, 173; Revolutionary Communist League and, 114; Reynolds and, 171
African American students, xxiv, 262n2; activism of, 21; admission standards for, 170; *Bakke* case and, 119–121; demands of, 41–42; enrollment of, 165; EOP and, 72–73, 78; Ethnic Studies and, 66; experimental colleges and, 46; grades of, 71; at SFVSC, 48, 52, 65, 97, 231n63; at UTEP, 89. *See also* affirmative action
African American Studies. *See* Black Studies
Afrocentrism, 124, 125
Aguilar, Elida, 38
Aguilar, Marcos, 179–180, 182–183, 184, 186–187
Aguirre, Lidia, 90
Aguirre, Yvonne, 98
AIDS, 177
Alarcón, Evelyn, 52
Alarcón, Richard, 96
Alatorre, Richard, 84, 171, 179–180
Alemán, Narciso, 100
Allee, A. Y., 22
Allende, Salvador, 105
Alonzo, Sally, 19
Alurista (Alberto Baltazar Urista Heredia), 44, 63, 82, 84
Alvárez, Rudy, 131
Amaya, Abel, 136–137
American Baptist Churches (ABC) v. Thornburgh (1991), 195–196

About the Author

RODOLFO F. ACUÑA received his PhD in Latin American Studies from the University of Southern California in 1968. A teacher in the Los Angeles City Schools from 1958 to 1965, he transferred to the community colleges, where he taught for three years before becoming an assistant professor at Dominquez Hills State College. In 1969 Acuña was the founding chair of Chicano Studies at San Fernando Valley State. The academic journal *Black Issues in Higher Education* selected Acuña as one of the "100 Most Influential Educators of the Twentieth Century," and three of his works have received the Gustavus Myers Award for an Outstanding Book on Race Relations in North America. He has also received the Distinguished Scholar Award from the National Association for Chicano Studies, as well as numerous academic and community service awards. Among his best-known books are *Latino Voices*; *Corridors of Migration: The Odyssey of Mexican Laborers, 1600–1933*; *U.S. Latinos: An Inquiry*; *Occupied America: A History of Chicanos*; *Sometimes There Is No Other Side: Essays on Truth and Objectivity*; *A Community under Siege*; and *Anything but Mexican: Chicanos in Contemporary Los Angeles*. He has also written more than 200 popular and academic articles, over 150 book reviews, and three children's books.